THE ENCYCLOPEDIA OF
FORMULA ONE

Tim Hill and Gareth Thomas
Edited by Kate Santon and Sarah Rickayzen

Bath · New York · Singapore · Hong Kong · Cologne · Delhi · Melbourne

This edition published by Parragon in 2009

Parragon
Queen Street House, 4 Queen Street, Bath, BA1 1HE, UK

Produced by Atlantic Publishing

Photographs courtesy of LAT
Text © Parragon Books Ltd 2006

ISBN 978-1-4075-6679-5

Printed in China

CONTENTS

When the internal combustion engine was developed in the late nineteenth century, there were those who viewed it purely in utilitarian terms, as simply another means of getting from A to B. And there were those who wanted to test their vehicles – and themselves – to the absolute limit; to get from A to B quicker than anyone else.

More than a century has passed since the days of the spectacular inter-city races which launched a new field of sporting endeavour. But the raw appeal remains the same: man and machine operating as one in high-risk, high-reward gladiatorial combat.

The chase for the victors' laurels gained fresh momentum in 1950, when the Federation Internationale de l'Automobile launched the world championship. The 30 men who have held the coveted title to date include legendary names who would feature in any list of all-time greats: Fangio, Brabham, Clark, Stewart, Senna, Prost, Schumacher. Others came agonisingly close to gaining a seat at the top table. Stirling Moss missed out narrowly on several occasions, Wolfgang von Trips was killed when the 1961 title lay within his grasp, while team orders robbed the mercurial Gilles Villeneuve of the crown in 1979.

The Encyclopedia of Formula One chronicles the history of the world championship, from Giuseppe Farina's victory for Alfa Romeo at Silverstone on 13 May 1950 to the present day. All the top drivers are profiled, and there is a wealth of information on the major marques and championship venues, while the comprehensive statistics section will settle many an argument. It is a story of ingenuity and endeavour, rivalry and camaraderie, triumph and tragedy, in pursuit of the greatest prize in motor sport.

INTRODUCTION

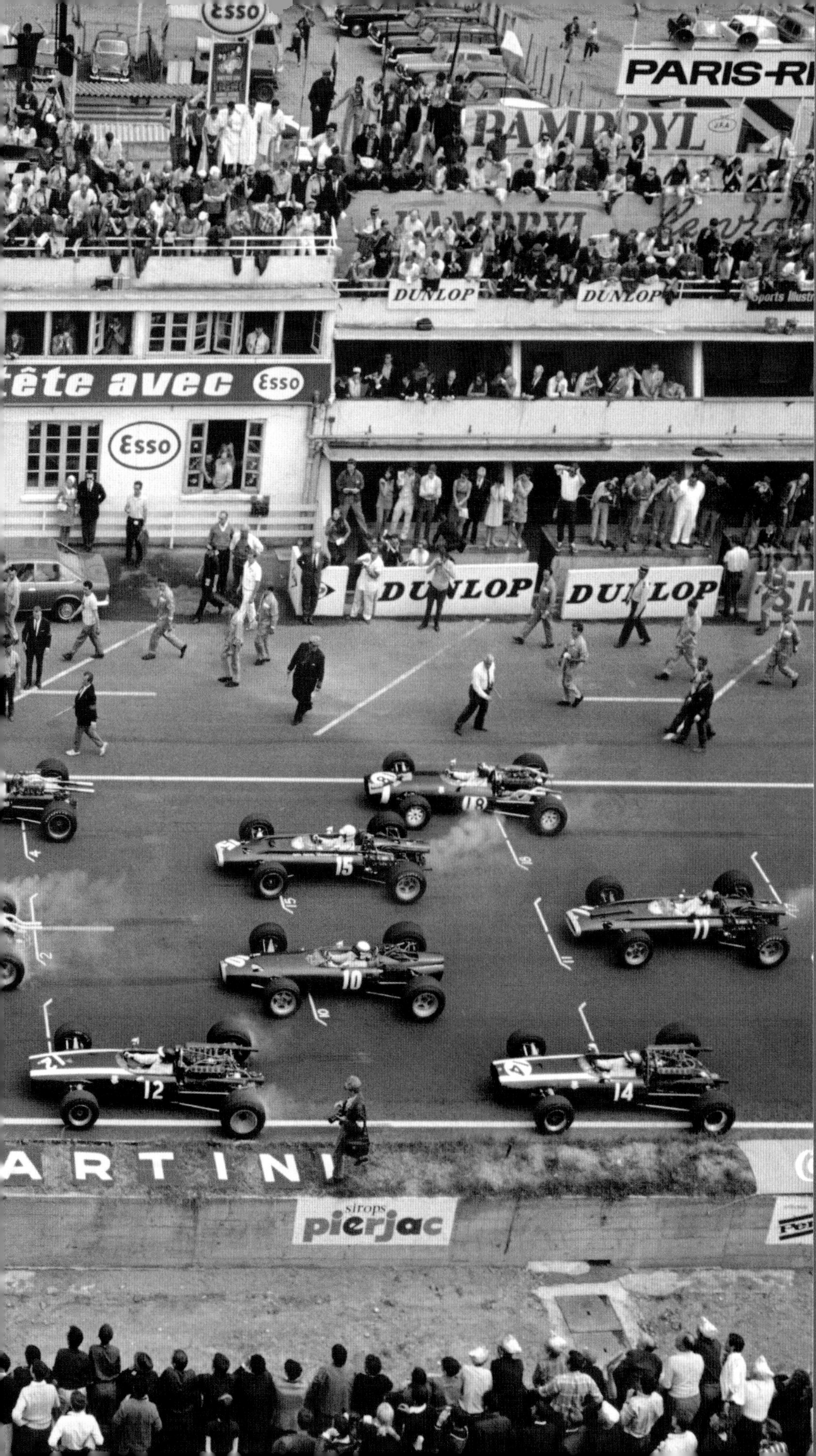

THE WORLD CHAMPIONSHIPS

1950

THE FIRST WORLD CHAMPIONSHIP

1950 DRIVERS' CHAMPIONSHIP

1.	NINO FARINA	30
2.	JUAN MANUEL FANGIO	27
3.	LUIGI FAGIOLI	24

(Constructors' title not introduced until 1958)

The first world championship in motor racing was inaugurated in February 1950. The sport's governing body, the Fédération Internationale de l'Automobile, linked six Grands Prix in one competition. Points were to be awarded based on the results of these six, and the driver with the most would become the 'World Champion'.

Fagiola, Farina and Fangio

This new competition tempted Alfa Romeo to return to the sport – it had been out of racing for a year – and the year was dominated by three star Alfa drivers: Luigi Fagioli, Giuseppe Farina and Juan Manuel Fangio. Alberto Ascari, who drove for Ferrari, was their most notable contender; Ferrari was trying to get its new car up and running, a 4500cc V-12, but it came too late for the 1950 season.

Seven-race championship

Initially the new championship technically involved seven races: six in Europe and the Indianapolis 500. However, the latter was never really fully integrated and though it continued to provide championship points until 1960, only one Formula One driver competed in this US classic.

The first race was on 13 May at Silverstone. Farina won, with Fagioli coming second. Though Fangio had retired eight laps from the end, it was still a triumph for Alfa: third place went to their works driver Reg Parnell.

Monte Carlo pile-up

The next race was at Monte Carlo a week later. A multiple pile-up on the initial lap involved Farina, who had been lying second, and blocked the road. Fangio, who was in the lead and unaware of the incident, managed to weave through the wrecked cars when he

came round again; he went on to win. Ascari came second, but a lap behind. This was followed by the Swiss Grand Prix, won by Farina with Fagioli second; Fangio had retired earlier. All three Ferraris had blown up and a Talbot, driven by Louis Rosier, came in third. Spa hosted the Belgian Grand Prix, and this time Fangio headed Fagioli home, followed again by Rosier. The French Grand Prix was won easily by Fangio, again with Fagioli second. Fangio had 26 points; Fagioli, 24, overhauling Farina.

Farina – first world champion

The last race of the year was at Monza, and Alfa added two more cars, driven by Piero Taruffi and Consalvo Sanesi. On the 24th lap Fangio's gearbox failed and he was able to take over Taruffi's car; unfortunately it then dropped a valve. His chance of the title was gone. Ascari, now driving the full 4500cc Ferrari, was lying second in the early part of the race, hoping to steal the lead from the Alfas which needed two refuelling stops; his Ferrari needed only one. He did manage to take the lead, but his car then failed. He too switched cars, taking over from Dorino Serafini, and managed to get back to second, ahead of Fagioli. He was still a minute behind Farina, whose win put him up to 30 points, ahead of Fangio, making him the first world champion.

1950 clearly belonged to Alfa Romeo. Alfa had won all six European races, and its 'big three' occupied the top places in the Drivers' championship. But there were encouraging signs for Ferrari.

ABOVE: *Alberto Ascari at the wheel of Jose Froilan Gonzalez's Ferrari 375, on his way to second position at the 1951 French Grand Prix, Reims-Gueux.*

OPPOSITE: *1950 British Grand Prix, Silverstone, England. Giuseppe Farina leads Luigi Fagioli (both Alfa Romeo 158). They finished in first and second positions respectively in the first ever GP.*

THE RISE OF FERRARI

1951

1951 DRIVERS' CHAMPIONSHIP

1. JUAN MANUEL FANGIO   31
2. ALBERTO ASCARI   25
3. JOSE FROILAN GONZALEZ   24

(Constructors' title not introduced until 1958)

Despite the excellent 1950 season, there were already signs that Alfa would not have the same hold in 1951. Ferrari's Ascari had only 12 points in the inaugural year, coming a distant fourth to the three Alfa drivers, but there had been signs that this would change at Monza.

Fangio sets the pace

Switzerland saw the opening round of the 1951 championship, and Fangio won. Ascari finished in sixth place; he had a badly burnt arm, an injury from a Formula Two race. In eighth position was an Englishman driving an HWM – Stirling Moss.

Farina took the honours in the Belgian Grand Prix but Fangio, his Alfa team-mate, had a jammed wheel during a routine pit stop which took nearly 15 minutes to fix, and finished ninth – he did pick up a point for setting the fastest lap, though. Ascari and Villoresi's Ferraris were well adrift of Farina, who led them by 3 minutes.

The next round was on the fast circuit at Reims. Ascari was chasing Fangio when his gearbox failed; a

Fangio was forced out with mechanical trouble, and Ascari and González finished first and second.

Fangio by 6 points

The last round of the season was at Barcelona. The Ferraris had enough fuel for the entire distance but had changed to smaller-diameter rear wheels than usual, and the rough Pedralbes circuit tore their tyres apart; they needed changing every few laps. Fangio won, giving him the championship by 6 points, and Ascari's chance was gone.

By the end of the season Alfa Romeo knew that the ageing 158 model, dating back to 1938, needed to be replaced. This needed government money, but it was not forthcoming, leaving Alfa with no alternative but to withdraw from Grand Prix racing. This would have resulted in an uncompetitive championship, dominated by Ferrari, and the FIA announced that the 1952 Grand Prix series would be held to 2-litre, Formula Two rules.

new Ferrari driver, José Froilán González, was called into the pits and Ascari, as senior driver, returned to the race in his car. Fangio, too, needed to switch cars, taking over Fagioli's Alfa early in the race. Fangio crossed the line first, a minute ahead of Ascari, with Villoresi again third. The Ferraris were getting closer to defeating Alfa.

Italian rivals

This finally happened in the next race at Silverstone. Ascari retired with gearbox trouble and when González came in for a routine stop, Ascari realised that his team-mate was in excellent form, so didn't pull rank. Fangio had tried to establish a healthy lead, knowing that his Alfa required two refuelling stops to the Ferraris' one, but he couldn't shake González off. González pulled clear, coming home nearly a minute ahead. There was some British success: Reg Parnell and Peter Walker's BRMs both completed the 90-lap race, finishing fifth and seventh respectively.

Recognising the threat posed by Ferrari, Alfa Romeo rushed to make last-minute repairs and adjustments to the cars during practice for the German Grand Prix. Fangio realised his car's shortcomings and drove at a fast, regular pace; he led for a time, but fell back to second after his extra stop for fuel. He maintained that position to the end and Ascari won. Fangio beat the other Ferrari drivers, González, Villoresi and Taruffi, who finished in that order after him. His second place, together with the fastest lap, meant that he left Germany with 7 more points. A new, faster version of the Alfetta was introduced at Monza, but

ASCARI'S SUCCESS

1952

1952 DRIVERS' CHAMPIONSHIP

1.	ALBERTO ASCARI	36
2.	NINO FARINA	24
3.	PIERO TARUFFI	22

(Constructors' title not introduced until 1958)

Staging the 1952 championship under Formula Two rules had the desired effect in that it attracted a lot of entries, but it failed to stop Ferrari. The new car, the 4-cylinder Tipo 500, and Ascari's undoubted skill, were irresistible.

Global appeal

The Indianapolis 500 was the eighth round of the championship and clashed with the first European event, the Swiss Grand Prix. Ferrari and Ascari decided to compete at Indianapolis, but it wasn't a good experience: Ascari was 12th when he was forced to retire. The 500 had originally been included to give the world championship global appeal, attracting American fans, but this was the only time that a driver competing in the European series tried the famous circuit.

Taruffi had a comfortable win in Berne in Ascari's absence, coming home almost 3 minutes ahead of Rudi Fischer, who was driving a privately entered Ferrari. The number of marques competing had increased which was reflected in the minor placings: Jean Behra in a Gordini was third; fourth and fifth places went to Britons Ken Wharton and Alec Brown, driving a Frazer-Nash and Cooper-Bristol respectively. Connaught, HWM and ERA also featured. Stirling Moss pinned his hopes on a new Bristol-engined ERA but crashed out on the first lap when it finally made its debut at Spa in Belgium.

Fangio out for the season

Following Alfa Romeo's withdrawal, Fangio joined Officine Maserati and his former team-mate Farina went to Ferrari. There was a new 6-cylinder car in the pipeline for Fangio at Maserati, where he was the senior driver. He had been competing in Ireland when he received word from Maserati that they wanted him to put the new car through its paces in a non-championship race at Monza. The exhausted Fangio took to the wheel after a frustrating journey and made a mistake at a corner. His neck was broken as he was flung out of the car but he survived.

Ascari was unstoppable in the six remaining European races; in both France and Belgium he led Farina home. British fans had a new name to cheer in Belgium: Mike Hawthorn, driving a Cooper-Bristol, gave the more powerful Ferraris a run for their money. He was lying third when his petrol tank sprang a leak, and finished fourth. At Silverstone Ascari led from start to finish, followed by Taruffi a full lap adrift. Hawthorn came in third; his performance in Belgium had not been a one-off. He was fast becoming the golden boy of British sport.

Ferrari clean sweep

The German Grand Prix was a walkover for Ferrari, with Farina, Fischer and Taruffi coming in behind the usual leader. It was much the same story at Zandvoort, a new championship venue. Farina and Villoresi took the minor placings in yet another clean sweep for Ferrari.

By the final race at Monza the world title was already settled, but Ascari was finally provided with some serious opposition. González had the new Maserati at last and roared into an early lead, but an overlong refuelling stop lost him the race; Ascari came through for his sixth victory in a row. González was almost a minute behind, but beat the Ferraris of Villoresi and Farina. He also shared the fastest lap with Ascari. But 1952 was Ascari's moment of glory. His 36-point maximum haul was something that not even Fangio would quite match in any of his five title successes.

The new season was keenly anticipated. Ascari had won six times, while his Ferrari team-mate Taruffi had won the remaining European event. But Fangio would be back, fully fit, and in the new Maserati. He was expected to challenge Ascari's supremacy.

BELOW: *Jose Froilan Gonzalez (Maserati A6GCM), gained second position at the 1952 Italian Grand Prix, Monza, giving Ascari some competition at last.*

OPPOSITE: *1952 German Grand Prix Nurburgring. Alberto Ascari (Ferrari, left) on the podium with Giuseppe Farina (Ferrari) after they finished in first and second positions respectively.*

MASERATI VERSUS FERRARI

1953

1953 DRIVERS' CHAMPIONSHIP

1. ALBERTO ASCARI	34·5
2. JUAN MANUEL FANGIO	28
3. NINO FARINA	12

(Constructors' title not introduced until 1958)

As anticipated, the 1953 championship was a battle between Ferrari and Maserati. Fangio made a full recovery and led the Maserati team, supported by González and the man he regarded as his protégé, Onofre Marimon. At Ferrari Ascari, Farina and Villoresi were joined by Hawthorn, who had impressed Enzo Ferrari the previous year. He took his place as the circus moved to Buenos Aires for Argentina's first championship race. As in 1952, the series was a Formula Two competition.

Ascari and Fangio battle it out

The Argentine Grand Prix made it a nine-event championship – eight, if the Indianapolis 500 was discounted – with the best four finishes counting. A new Maserati was in the pipeline but not quite ready, so Fangio drove the 1952 model. He was chasing Ascari when his engine blew up, leaving Ascari with an easy win ahead of his team-mate Villoresi. Hawthorn came in fourth, and it was only Marimon's Maserati in third which stopped another Ferrari clean sweep. The race was marred by tragedy; Farina swerved, trying to avoid a boy who ran in front of him and careered into the crowd, killing ten spectators.

In the Dutch Grand Prix Ascari was also a comfortable winner, while Fangio failed to finish again, this time because of an axle problem. Farina made it another one-two for Ferrari, but González's third place was the highlight. When his Maserati's rear axle broke, he took over team-mate Felice Bonetto's car and chased the Ferraris hard.

Superb Hawthorn

Initially it looked as though Spa might see a change. González and Fangio, finally in their new Maseratis, stormed away – then both hit trouble. Gonzalez's

BELOW: *The start of the 1953 German Grand Prix.*

OPPOSITE: *1953 French Grand Prix, Reims, France. Mike Hawthorn (number 16, Ferrari 500) and Juan Manuel Fangio (Maserati A6GCM) during their battle for the lead. They finished in first and second positions respectively, in what was Hawthorn's maiden Grand Prix victory.*

accelerator pedal broke and Fangio's engine died, but he continued in the car of one of Maserati's junior drivers. He skidded on a patch of oil and crashed out of the race, escaping with minor injuries. Ascari had yet another success – his ninth win in a row – but he was outpaced at Reims, where he came in fourth. The race turned into a duel between Fangio and Hawthorn, who raced wheel to wheel. Hawthorn squeaked home by a car's length.

At Silverstone things returned to normal; Ascari led the whole way and Fangio had to be content with second. It was becoming clear that the Maseratis' extra power was decisive on faster tracks; on slower ones, like Silverstone, the superior handling of the Ferraris gave them the advantage.

Farina's last victory

Ascari drove one of his finest races at the German Grand Prix. He started well but lost a wheel and made it to the pits on three wheels and a brake drum. He took over Villoresi's car and gave chase, setting a Formula Two record for the Nürburgring circuit; however, this car expired in a pall of smoke. Farina won, keeping up Ferrari's record. It was his final victory.

Ascari and Fangio were vying for the lead in the Swiss Grand Prix at Bremgarten when both were forced into the pits. Fangio took over Bonetto's Maserati and drove the car so hard that it expired in a cloud of heavy smoke. Ascari had only needed a change of plugs and rejoined in fourth place; he eventually took the lead from team-mates Farina and Hawthorn.

Champion Ascari in a spin

Maserati and Fangio got it right in the final race, at Monza. Fangio battled for the lead with Ascari and Farina, and it was still anybody's race going into the last lap. Then Ascari finally made a mistake, spinning his Ferrari after 313 miles of close slipstreaming. Farina mounted the grass to avoid a collision, but Fangio coolly avoided trouble, winning his only race of the season. He finished runner-up, on 28 points; the championship went to Ascari, with 34.5.

FANGIO CROWNED

1954

1954 DRIVERS' CHAMPIONSHIP

1.	JUAN MANUEL FANGIO	42
2.	STIRLING MOSS	25.14
3.	EUGENIO CASTELLOTTI	24.64

(Constructors' title not introduced until 1958)

1954 saw the end of the Formula Two era and the introduction of a 2.5-litre limit on engine size. It was already known that Mercedes-Benz would return to Grand Prix. The renowned marque signed Fangio, and it was obvious they would pose a serious threat. Ascari responded, deciding that he needed a stronger team behind him in spite of having spent five successful years with Ferrari; Lancia was also developing a new car,

and Ascari put his faith in that. Neither the Mercedes nor the Lancia was ready for the season opener.

Fangio's home soil victory

This was in Argentina. It was initially dry, and González and Farina's Ferraris dominated. When it began raining Fangio took control and went on to win. After the race, the Ferrari team lodged a protest, claiming more than the permitted three mechanics had worked on Fangio's car during a pit stop. This was thrown out.

The new Mercedes was not quite ready and Fangio had needed to borrow a Maserati to compete in Argentina; he had to do likewise in Belgium. He won there, too, despite having to drive in the latter part with a collapsed suspension. Ferrari's Maurice Trintignant came second and Stirling Moss was third. He had begun the new season with no competitive British car available. The patriotic Moss had resisted moving to a foreign team, though he had seen Hawthorn rise by joining Ferrari. The situation became urgent, and Moss bought a Maserati 250F.

Mercedes are back

The Mercedes made its appearance in the next race at Reims. It was a dazzling beginning for the streamlined W196: Fangio and his team-mate, Karl Kling, ran away with it, finishing a lap ahead of Ferrari's Robert Manzon. The third Mercedes driver, Hans Herrmann, returned the fastest lap.

The jubilant German camp came down to earth at Silverstone, however, where flaws in the car's roadholding were exposed. The streamlined bodywork concealed the front wheels and the drivers, Fangio included, found cornering difficult. Fangio's Mercedes was battered by the finish, but he did hold on to fourth place. González and Hawthorn came home first and second, making it an enjoyable day for Ferrari at last.

Tragedy at Nürburgring

For the German Grand Prix at the Nürburgring the Mercedes team produced an unstreamlined version of the W196. Fangio won, despite being deeply upset by the death of Marimon in practice. González, also a close friend of Marimon, was so distraught that he handed over his car to Hawthorn, who finished second.

Fangio was a convincing winner again in the Swiss Grand Prix at Bremgarten. He reverted to the streamlined car at Monza, and even on the fast Italian track the cornering proved suspect. Both González and Ascari, who was driving a Ferrari, vied with Fangio for the lead, but Moss stole the show. He had been so impressive in his Maserati that he was given a works car to drive, and was leading the race with nine laps to go when his oil-tank ruptured. He restarted, but his engine gave out short of the line – and he pushed the car to the finish. It earned him only tenth place; Fangio won, but later declared it a moral victory for Moss.

Title for Fangio

The final race of the season was at Barcelona, where the Lancia V-8 made its appearance. Both Villoresi and Ascari lasted only a few laps, although Ascari did record the fastest one. Fangio also had trouble after paper was sucked into the Mercedes' air intake. Hawthorn went on to his second Grand Prix victory, and edged out his Ferrari team-mate González for the second spot in the Drivers' championship, but the crown was Fangio's.

TRAGEDY AND CHANGE

1955

1955 DRIVERS' CHAMPIONSHIP

1.	JUAN MANUEL FANGIO	40
2.	STIRLING MOSS	23
3.	EUGENIO CASTELLOTTI	12

(Constructors' title not introduced until 1958)

Moss joined Fangio at Mercedes for the 1955 season, and the problems that had dogged the W196 the previous year were resolved. Both the improved car and driver line-up made Mercedes look like the team to beat.

Only two go the distance

The first race, in Argentina, was in such extreme heat that only two drivers, Fangio and Roberto Mieres, were able to finish without having to hand over to others. Fangio won, and Mieres was fifth in his Maserati, but other than that point allocation was a nightmare. The second-placed Ferrari had been driven by González, Farina and Trintignant; the latter two had also done a turn in the third-placed Ferrari, along with Umberto Maglioli. The Mercedes which came in fourth had been shared by Moss, Kling and Herrmann. Fangio's 9 points were his alone; he had also set the fastest lap. Both Ascari and his team-mate Villoresi failed to finish.

Monaco saw the next round. Ascari was leading when his Lancia hit straw bales and headed into the harbour, but he was uninjured. Fangio led for 50 laps, then retired; Moss took over, but also failed to finish. Ferrari's Trintignant moved through the ranks steadily and won.

Ascari killed in practice

Ascari was invited to give his team-mate Eugenio Castellotti's Ferrari a practice run at a deserted Monza a few days later, but took a bend full-speed and went straight on. He was killed. Lancia then withdrew from racing, leaving the potential of the D 50 unfulfilled, though Castellotti entered one privately in the next round in Belgium. He was going well but his engine failed on the 16th lap, and the race was a comfortable one-two for Fangio and Moss. Mike Hawthorn's time at Ferrari had made him the most successful British driver,

ABOVE: *Race winner Stirling Moss (Mercedes-Benz W196), on the podium at the British Grand Prix, Aintree, England in 1955.*

OPPOSITE: *Jean Behra (Maserati 250F) driving to third place in the 1956 French Grand Prix, Reims.*

eclipsing Moss, but he had decided to join Vanwall for 1955. Following mechanical problems culminating in an early departure from the Belgian race, Hawthorn returned to Ferrari for the rest of the season.

83 people die in Le Mans tragedy

The next race was at Zandvoort, but before that many drivers competed at Le Mans. Here, on Saturday, 11 June, tragedy struck – on a massive scale. Two and a half hours into the race, Pierre Levegh's Mercedes hit Lance Macklin's Austin Healey and spun over the safety barrier, exploding into the crowd. Eighty-three people, including Levegh, died. The French, Spanish, German and Swiss Grands Prix were cancelled.

Aintree Grand Prix

There were three more rounds. Fangio and Moss led the rest home again at Zandvoort. Despite his return to

Ferrari, Hawthorn suffered gearbox trouble; he did manage to finish, but seventh. Mercedes was outstanding at Aintree, which hosted the British race for the first time. Moss edged Fangio out by a matter of inches, and there was speculation that Fangio had allowed him a home victory. Kling and Taruffi occupied third and fourth places for Mercedes. The race also marked the debut of Jack Brabham, driving a Cooper.

The last round was at Monza, on the high-speed banked circuit. Moss set the fastest lap of more than 134mph but failed to finish; Taruffi followed Fangio home in another one-two for Mercedes. Castellotti finished less than a minute behind Taruffi in third, and that was where he came in the final table. His tally was just 12 points; Moss finished on 25, but Fangio had reached the 40-point mark for a second successive season, giving him his third world title.

Champions to quit

At the end of 1955 Mercedes announced that it was withdrawing from racing, so Fangio and Moss were seeking new teams. Fangio was looking for a car that would keep him at the top, Moss for one that would help him depose Fangio.

FANGIO THE UNSTOPPABLE

1956

1956 DRIVERS' CHAMPIONSHIP

1.	JUAN MANUEL FANGIO	30
2.	STIRLING MOSS	27
3.	PETER COLLINS	25

(Constructors' title not introduced until 1958)

Fangio and Moss went their separate ways in their search for new teams. Fangio joined Ferrari, though the cars fielded by it in 1956 were modified Lancias. Fangio was always suspicious about the standard of preparation his cars received, and left Ferrari when the season ended. Moss had enjoyed success with Mercedes, but was keen to go for a British car. In the end he settled on Maserati, feeling that would give him the best chance of unseating Fangio.

The rival Italian camps would dominate the 1956 championship. Alongside Fangio, Ferrari had Luigi Musso, Eugenio Castellotti and the young Englishman Peter Collins. Jean Behra and Cesare Perdisa provided strong support to Moss at Maserati.

Fangio sets the pace

The opening round was in Argentina. Fangio's car failed early on, and he took over his team-mate Musso's to win from Behra. Moss had had a spell in front, but his engine also gave out. When Fangio had a problem, he took over the cars of well-placed team-mates; when Moss got into trouble he struggled for points. Monaco was another case in point. Moss gained his second Grand Prix win, while Fangio took over Collins' car to finish second. Fangio had spun his Lancia-Ferrari, then repeatedly hit barriers and kerbs. The car was a mess when he came into the pits, but he still came away from Monte Carlo with 3 useful points for a shared second place. Behra brought his Maserati home third, while Castellotti had to take over Fangio's battered machine, finishing fourth.

Peter Collins leads the pack

Collins gained back-to-back wins in Belgium and France. Moss and Fangio both had spells in front at Spa, but hit trouble. Fangio's transmission problem was terminal, but Moss did reappear; he took over Perdisa's car and finished third. Collins got home ahead of local favourite Paul Frere, driving a Ferrari. The Ferraris of Fangio, Collins and Castellotti set the pace at Reims. Fangio was delayed by a lengthy pit stop and Collins took the honours, inches ahead of Castellotti. Behra was third, Fangio fourth, and Moss, who again had to take over Perdisa's car, settled for a shared fifth.

Championship all to play for

The works BRMs of Hawthorn and Tony Brooks made an impact early in the British Grand Prix at Silverstone. They led for the first ten laps, but both then had

1957

FANGIO'S GREATEST RACE

1957 DRIVERS' CHAMPIONSHIP

1.	JUAN MANUEL FANGIO	40
2.	STIRLING MOSS	25
3.	LUIGI MUSSO	16

(Constructors' title not introduced until 1958)

Once again, Fangio and Moss were moving. Fangio rejoined Maserati; Moss had now been impressed by the Vanwall, and another season of development and refinement made that car a serious prospect for the championship.

Two Ferrari drivers killed

Fangio's team-mate Behra and the Ferraris of Castellotti and Collins all had spells in front in Argentina, but Fangio crossed the line ahead of Behra, who was the only other driver to complete the race. It was an excellent day for Maserati: Carlos Menditeguy came third; Harry Schell, who had left Vanwall in 1956, was fourth. A Maserati even took the fastest lap, thanks to Moss driving a borrowed car – Vanwall hadn't travelled to the race. His chances of winning were ended by gearbox trouble, but he came eighth. Ferrari had a terrible time: Collins, Hawthorn and Musso retired while Castellotti lost a wheel. He had a lucky escape then, but was killed a few weeks later testing a Ferrari at Modena. Ferrari soon lost another driver: Alfonso de Portago was killed in the Mille Miglia.

problems. Moss subsequently led in his Maserati; he succumbed to axle trouble. Fangio came through to win; Collins grabbed second, but after he had taken over Alfonso de Portago's Ferrari. The championship was wide open. Collins led on 22 points, but Fangio was close on 21, and Behra was on 18.

Fangio won the German Grand Prix emphatically, with Moss second. Behra was again in the points in third. Collins ran out of luck, lying second when his fuel tank fractured. He took over de Portago's car again, but crashed out of the race. He wasn't hurt, but he was now 8 points adrift of Fangio.

Collins' magnanimous gesture

Though Collins and Behra still had a chance of overhauling Fangio, they each needed to win in Italy, and set the fastest lap, in order to do so. Fangio was forced out of the race with steering trouble. Then came an extremely generous gesture. Collins, lying second and with an excellent chance of taking the title himself, pulled into the pits and offered Fangio his car. Fangio accepted, and tore after the leaders Moss and Musso. He couldn't catch Moss, whose victory meant that he finished runner-up for the second year, but a shared second place was enough to secure Fangio's fourth world crown. It was a title that he always acknowledged owed a lot to the magnanimity of Peter Collins.

Brabham pushes it for sixth place

Moss hit the barricade at the chicane on the fourth lap at Monaco after taking an early lead. The track became scattered with poles, ending the race for Collins and Hawthorn's Ferraris. Tony Brooks, driving the second Vanwall, was also caught up but managed to escape and went on to finish 20 seconds behind Fangio, who won. Jack Brabham took his 2-litre Cooper-Climax into third, but his fuel pump failed five laps from the end. He pushed the car half a mile, finishing sixth. There was no race in Holland or Belgium because of financial constraints, so France came next. Moss was ill, missing the race, and Fangio came home 50 seconds ahead of Musso's Ferrari.

Despite early-season setbacks, Vanwall and Moss's star was rising. Moss was leading the home Grand Prix at Aintree, on 20 July, when he swapped his ailing car for Brooks', putting him down to sixth place: he made his way back into the lead. This was the first victory by a British car in a major Grand Prix since 1923.

Lap record falls ten times

Fangio was not at Aintree, but he was back at the Nürburgring on 4 August. He began the race with a half-full tank, hoping to build up a sizeable lead to compensate for the extra refuelling stop. When he came into the pits he was 28 seconds ahead, but when he left he was more than 60 seconds down on Hawthorn and Collins. He set about catching them, breaking and rebreaking the lap record ten times. He passed both on the penultimate lap, and crossed the line 3.6 seconds ahead of Hawthorn. It was his final Grand Prix success, and his greatest.

Fangio's world crown once again

The Vanwalls were never in the picture in Germany due to suspension problems, but it was different in the last two rounds, both in Italy; Pescara was added to the

ABOVE: *Jack Brabham (Cooper T43 Climax), pictured in action during the 1957 Pescara Grand Prix, Italy. (He finished seventh.)*

OPPOSITE: *Peter Collins (Ferrari) seen prior to the 1956 Monaco Grand Prix, Monte Carlo.*

series to compensate for the absent Belgium and Holland. The 16-mile road circuit was tricky and Enzo Ferrari is said to have banned his cars from participating in Italian road races, so Hawthorn and Collins were left without a drive. Musso still entertained hopes of winning the title, borrowed a car for the race and led in the early stages. Moss soon passed him, and when he retired on the tenth lap, it brought Fangio up to second. At Monza, Moss and Fangio fought an epic battle; Moss won. That gave Moss a final tally of 25 points – for the third year running he was runner-up to Fangio in the Drivers' championship.

Apart from Mercedes in 1954–55, the championship had been dominated by Italian marques. Now Maserati announced its withdrawal from racing and Ferrari was struggling. Maybe a British car could finally win the title.

THE BRITISH CHALLENGE

1958

1958 DRIVERS' CHAMPIONSHIP

1.	MIKE HAWTHORN	42
2.	STIRLING MOSS	41
3.	TONY BROOKS	24

CONSTRUCTORS' TITLE

1.	VANWALL	48
2.	FERRARI	40
3.	COOPER-CLIMAX	31

Fangio made some appearances during 1958, but had effectively retired. This opened up the field for other contenders, notably Moss. He remained with Vanwall: its line-up remained unchanged, Tony Brooks and Stuart Lewis-Evans filling the supporting roles.

There were new regulations about fuel; 130-octane aviation fuel became mandatory. The Vanwall team was carrying out adjustments when the season began in Argentina and Moss entered the race in a Rob Walker 2-litre Cooper-Climax. He won, despite the best efforts of Ferrari's Musso. The Vanwalls were ready in time for Monaco, but all three failed to finish. The little

Cooper did it again in Monte Carlo, this time with Maurice Trintignant. Faster cars fell by the wayside and Trintignant, driving steadily, emerged the winner; Ferrari's Musso and Collins followed him home. Zandvoort was dominated by British cars. Brooks and Lewis-Evans failed to finish, but Moss won, leading the BRMs of Harry Schell and Jean Behra. Roy Salvadori's Cooper-Climax was fourth, and Cliff Allison finished sixth in the new Lotus. Hawthorn took fifth in his Ferrari.

Another setback for Moss

Moss suffered a setback at Spa; he missed a gear, the revs shot up and the engine blew. It was still a great day for Vanwall, as Brooks and Lewis-Evans came first and third respectively. Teresa de Filippis became the first woman to compete in a world championship race, driving a Maserati, and finished tenth.

Fangio finished the Reims Grand Prix in fourth; his final bow. This marked a turning point for Ferrari

BELOW: *Action from the first ever Moroccan Grand Prix, Ain Diab, Casablanca, 1958. Stuart Lewis-Evans (Vanwall VW4), before the crash that was to kill him.*

OPPOSITE: *1959 United States Grand Prix, Sebring, Florida. Jack Brabham collapsed after pushing his Cooper T51-Climax across the line to finish fourth and clinch the world championship.*

and Hawthorn; he won but any delight was muted by the death of Musso who crashed at Muizon while challenging Hawthorn for the lead. Moss and Hawthorn were tied on 23 points as the circus moved to Silverstone, but Moss's race was over after 24 laps. Hawthorn finished second to his team-mate Collins.

Peter Collins killed at Nürburgring

Magneto trouble put Moss out of the race at the Nürburgring a fortnight later, after only four laps. The Ferraris of Collins and Hawthorn looked like prevailing, but Brooks passed them in his Vanwall. Tragedy then struck. On the 11th lap Peter Collins' Ferrari went off the track at 100mph; he died in the resulting crash. Hawthorn, seeing this, retired almost immediately, devastated by the loss of a team-mate and close friend. Though one big name was lost, another was making an appearance: Bruce McLaren, driving a Cooper, finished first in the Formula 2 class, and fifth overall.

At the first Portuguese Grand Prix at Oporto Moss won comfortably, having been on pole. Hawthorn finished second again, maintaining his challenge for the title. At Monza Moss succumbed to gearbox failure; Hawthorn led the race in the latter stages, but a clutch problem allowed Brooks to come through and win. Hawthorn was second, and now had 40 points from six races, the best six finishes counting for championship purposes. Moss had 32, having only finished five times.

Hawthorn by the narrowest of margins

The final round was another new venue, Ain Diab in Casablanca. With an 8-point deficit, Moss had to both win and set the fastest lap. He did exactly that, and took a maximum 9 points, finishing on 41. But for Moss to win the title, Hawthorn had to finish no better than third. The Ferrari team's tactics worked beautifully. Phil Hill, in only his second Formula 1 drive, held on to second place, then eased off to allow Hawthorn through, giving him a final tally of 42. Hawthorn had won just once, compared with Moss's four, but consistency brought him the championship by a single point. There was even worse news for Vanwall. Lewis-Evans had crashed out of the race, dying before he reached hospital.

Hawthorn killed after retirement

Hawthorn had been considering retiring even before the German Grand Prix; Peter Collins' death made this a certainty. Then, on 22 January 1959, the now-retired Hawthorn was killed when his Jaguar collided with a lorry. He was 29.

SUCCESS FOR COOPER

1959

1959 DRIVERS' CHAMPIONSHIP

1.	JACK BRABHAM	31
2.	TONY BROOKS	27
3.	STIRLING MOSS	25.5

CONSTRUCTORS' TITLE

1.	COOPER-CLIMAX	40
2.	FERRARI	32
3.	BRM	18

In January 1959 Vanwall team boss Tony Vandervell withdrew from racing, shocking everyone. Brooks went to Ferrari while Moss hovered between two teams. In some races he drove a Cooper-Climax; in others he struck a deal allowing him to drive a front-engined BRM.

Success for Brabham

The championship began at Monaco; the Argentine Grand Prix was cancelled. Moss fought for the lead with Behra's Ferrari and Brabham's Cooper-Climax, but he

ABOVE: *1959 Dutch Grand Prix, Zandvoort. Jack Brabham (Cooper T51-Climax) leads Tony Brooks (Ferrari Dino 246) and Harry Schell (BRM P25). Brabham finished in second place, on his way to the title.*

OPPOSITE: *Willy Mairesse (Ferrari D246) takes a pit stop on the way to third position in the 1960 Italian Grand Prix at Monza.*

and Behra both had to retire, leaving Brabham to score his and Cooper's first victory. Brooks came second, with Brabham's team-mate Trintignant third. This Cooper was a much better car than the one in which Moss had won the Argentine Grand Prix the year before. 1958, Cooper's first full season, saw some encouraging results, but 1959 was to be the breakthrough for the impressive rear-engined car, and for Brabham. Since arriving from Australia in 1955, Brabham had been with Cooper. He was the top works driver when it moved to Formula One in 1957.

First win for BRM

Another British marque scored a success at Zandvoort. BRM had been involved in Formula One since 1950, but had never won. Joakim Bonnier changed that, fighting off the Cooper challenge of Brabham, Moss and Masten Gregory. The best Ferrari achieved was Behra's fifth place, but in two of the next three races its speed proved decisive. At Reims Brooks and Hill made it a one-two for Ferrari, with Brabham having to settle for third. However, a Italian strike meant that Ferrari was unable to follow up this success, leaving the British teams to fight it out in the Aintree Grand Prix. Brabham led all the way; Moss chose to drive the front-engined BRM and took second, coming in just ahead of Cooper's up-and-coming McLaren.

Behra killed on 'lethal' circuit

The German Grand Prix was staged for the first time on Berlin's high-speed Avus track, and Ferrari was back.

This circuit's steeply-banked section was thought lethal by many drivers, and Behra was killed in the sports car race preceding the main event. The Grand Prix itself was split into two 30-lap heats; Brooks won both, taking overall first place. New Ferrari driver Dan Gurney was second; Hill in third made it a clean sweep.

Moss had driven the Cooper for the two laps he lasted in Germany. Hans Herrmann entered the race in the BRM but crashed out after a brakes failure, destroying the car, and Moss drove Coopers for the rest of the season. He dominated the next race, the Portuguese Grand Prix at Monsanto, where he lapped the entire field. Masten Gregory's Cooper was a distant second, ahead of Gurney's Ferrari.

The Ferraris were expected to dominate at Monza, but Moss was at his best. He sat on Hill's tail, conserving his tyres. Hill, like all the Ferrari drivers, had to stop for new rear tyres; Moss hit the front and finished the race on his original ones. Hill was second, and Brabham was third. There was only one round to go. Brabham had 31 points, Moss 25.5 and Tony Brooks 23, meaning that he, too, could overhaul Brabham by winning the final round and setting the fastest lap.

Brabham's championship at a push

The decider would be on the Sebring airfield track in Florida – the United States' first ever championship event with the exception of the Indianapolis 500 – but not until December, giving the contenders three months to prepare. Moss took pole and was out of the blocks first, but retired with transmission failure after just six laps. Brabham took over and held the lead to the last lap, running out of fuel 500 yards from the line. Again he pushed his Cooper to the finish, earning fourth place. His team-mates McLaren and Trintignant crossed the line first and second. Brooks's third place gave him four points, enough to snatch second place from Moss, but not enough to prevent Brabham gaining his first world crown.

THE END FOR FRONT-ENGINED CARS

1960

1960 DRIVERS' CHAMPIONSHIP

1.	JACK BRABHAM	43
2.	BRUCE McLAREN	34
3.	STIRLING MOSS	19

CONSTRUCTORS' TITLE

1.	COOPER-CLIMAX	48
2.	LOTUS-CLIMAX	34
3.	FERRARI	26

1960 would be the final season of the 2.5-litre Formula, and Jack Brabham retired from the opening race in Argentina with transmission trouble. His team-mate Bruce McLaren made the early championship running, winning in Argentina, helped by race leaders Stirling Moss and Jo Bonnier both hitting mechanical trouble. Moss finished third, returning to the race in Maurice Trintignant's Cooper.

Tragedy at Spa

Moss's new rear-engined Lotus 18 appeared at Monaco, and he drove brilliantly in the wet to win from McLaren; Brabham was disqualified for receiving assistance from marshals after he spun off. Moss was also on top form at Zandvoort in the Dutch Grand Prix. Challenging

Brabham for the lead, he suffered a puncture; by the time the wheel was changed he found himself in 12th place, but managed to finish in fourth. Brabham, who led from the start, was beginning a run of success; Moss was about to run out of luck in dramatic circumstances.

A series of dreadful accidents marked the Belgian Grand Prix at Spa. A wheel came off Moss's Lotus during practice and he broke both legs; there were deaths in two separate incidents in the race itself, both involving young British drivers. Alan Stacey was hit by a bird and Chris Bristow went off the road. Brabham won, with McLaren second. Jim Clark was in fifth place, gaining his first championship points. He had made an impressive debut at Zandvoort; though he succumbed to gearbox trouble, he tussled for fourth with Graham Hill.

Four in a row for Brabham

Brabham had another win on the fast Reims circuit. Phil Hill and Wolfgang von Trips, driving Ferraris, had been in contention, but both suffered from transmission failure and gave Brabham his third success. He made it

four in a row at Silverstone, although Graham Hill got most of the praise. After stalling his BRM on the line, he roared through the field and took the lead, but spun off seven laps short. Brabham received maximum points, and John Surtees, who was in his debut year, took second; the motorcycling champion was driving for Lotus. Silverstone was his best finish, but his best performance probably came in the following race, in Portugal. He built up a 10-second lead over Brabham but was forced out of the race when his radiator split. Brabham profited, and this fifth consecutive victory assured him of another world title with two races still to go. Moss was back at the wheel for the race in Oporto, and was second at one point, but was disqualified for pushing his car in the wrong direction after a spin.

Ferraris' hollow victory at Monza

The championship may have been decided by Monza, but there was still controversy. Many considered the banked sections of the circuit dangerous, and the

British teams boycotted the event in protest. Ferrari were left to sweep the board, Phil Hill winning his first championship race. Apart from that somewhat meaningless victory, it had been a wretched year for Ferrari, and the team didn't bother to contest the United States Grand Prix, staged at Riverside. Moss won, ending the series on a high note, and his victory also meant that Climax-engined cars had won every race apart from Monza. Ferrari certainly understood the implications, and their persistence with front-engined cars was about to end.

BELOW: *Jim Clark (Lotus 18 Climax) takes third position at the 1960 Portuguese Grand Prix, Porto.*

OPPOSITE: *1961 French Grand Prix, Reims-Gueux. Giancarlo Baghetti (Ferrari 156) closely followed by Dan Gurney (Porsche 718), takes the chequered flag for first position and his maiden win on his Grand Prix debut.*

FERRARI
TAKE CONTROL

1961 DRIVERS' CHAMPIONSHIP

1.	PHIL HILL	34
2.	WOLFGANG VON TRIPS	33
3.	STIRLING MOSS	21

CONSTRUCTORS' TITLE

1.	FERRARI	45
2.	LOTUS-CLIMAX	33
3.	PORSCHE	22

A 1.5-litre Formula was introduced, and Ferrari's fortunes began to change. It prepared meticulously for the new season and the introduction of the rear-engined V-6 'sharknose' paid off. British teams struggled with cars using dated 4-cylinder units which had a very modest power output.

Ferrari's assault on the championship was spearheaded by Phil Hill, Ritchie Ginther and Wolfgang von Trips, but Moss won the season opener at Monaco and the Ferraris came in second, third and fourth. Dan Gurney was next, with Porsche, a new name in Formula

One. The race was a fantastic display by Moss, who went into it with a double handicap: he had to use the old, square-shaped Lotus 18, with the outdated Climax engine under the bonnet. The new model – the 21 – was delayed because of contractual arguments. At Monaco the skill factor compensated for the fact that Moss would be outpaced on faster circuits, and he took the flag just 3.6 seconds in front of Ginther, with Hill and von Trips well behind.

Phil Hill and von Trips neck and neck

Moss was similarly impressive later in the series at the Nürburgring, but the 1961 title race was generally about the battle between Hill and von Trips. At Zandvoort von Trips got home just nine-tenths of a second ahead of his team-mate, giving Germany its first Grand Prix winner for 22 years. Jim Clark was also squeezing out all he could from his outdated Lotus. He took third, and Moss came home ahead of Ginther. This was the first time in a championship event that an entire field – 15-strong that day – completed a race without incident.

Ferrari had a clean sweep at Spa, occupying the first four places. It was Hill from von Trips this time, with Ginther third and Olivier Gendebien in fourth. Gendebien only had occasional drives during the year and the fact that Ferrari's fourth driver could get into the frame demonstrates the team's dominance. Hill, von Trips and Ginther all retired from the French Grand

Ferrari withdrew from the Watkins Glen United States Grand Prix. Moss and Brabham vied for the lead, but both retired and Innes Ireland took over and won. It was his first and only Grand Prix win. Tony Brooks gave BRM their best finish of the year, coming third, and he decided to retire. Brooks had never won the championship itself, but he had six Grand Prix wins to his name and was regarded as a highly accomplished and professional driver.

GRAHAM HILL TAKES THE CHAMPIONSHIP

1962

1962 DRIVERS' CHAMPIONSHIP

1.	GRAHAM HILL	42
2.	JIM CLARK	30
3.	BRUCE MCLAREN	27

CONSTRUCTORS' TITLE

1.	BRM	42
2.	LOTUS	36
3.	COOPER	29

Prix at Reims, but a Ferrari crossed the line first again. Giancarlo Baghetti, making his Grand Prix debut, was a narrow winner in his privately entered Ferrari, and remains the only man to win a Grand Prix on his first outing. Ferrari had another one-two-three in the British Grand Prix at Aintree: von Trips led Hill and Ginther home in torrential rain.

Black day as championship leader killed

At the Nürburgring Moss broke the Ferrari stranglehold as he had at Monaco – with superb driving and clever tactics. He knew all the intricacies of the difficult 14.2-mile circuit, but he made a gamble in tyre selection that paid off brilliantly. This time there were no objections to the combined road and banked Monza circuit. Von Trips started with 33 points, four ahead of Hill, and looked all set to clinch the title but tragedy struck on the second lap. His Ferrari collided with Clark's Lotus, and both went off at Vedano Corner. Clark emerged unscathed but von Trips was killed, as were 12 spectators. Phil Hill went on to win, taking the title in unhappy circumstances.

This was to be Graham Hill's year. He had made his Grand Prix debut in 1958, but his first two years at Lotus were bedevilled by the unreliability of the cars. Things initially looked no better when he moved to BRM, though there were signs that both team and driver were getting things right in 1960 and 1961. By 1962, BRM's new V-8 unit was ready, but it faced stiff opposition from the rival Climax V-8, which most other teams had adopted.

Moss's career ends in mystery smash

Hill's first Formula One win with BRM came at the Goodwood event, unfortunately overshadowed by a terrible crash involving Moss. Moss had been passing Hill on a fast stretch of the circuit when he left the track and his Lotus piled head-on into a bank. He sustained appalling injuries, and his career was over – though he did make a full recovery. He had done everything except win the world championship; he'd been runner-up four times in succession and had never been out of the top three in the previous seven years.

Ferrari surpassed

After another non-championship victory at Silverstone, an optimistic Hill and BRM went to the Dutch Grand Prix in Zandvoort. Hill led from early in the race and won, giving BRM their second-ever championship win. He was ahead at Monaco before engine trouble forced him out, and Bruce McLaren brought his Cooper home first, ahead of Phil Hill, who was still driving for Ferrari. The car was almost unchanged: Ferrari peaked in 1961 and stood still; the new British V-8s caught them up and overtook. Hill's second place at Monaco was his best in the year, and there was some discontent in the team. He left them at the end of the season.

Clark beset with mechanical problems

Jim Clark took the honours in Belgium. Not only did he benefit from having the new V-8 Climax unit, but he also had a new car: the Lotus 25, whose monocoque chassis was to revolutionise racing car design. Mechanical problems had ruined Clark's chances at both Zandvoort and Monaco but things came right at Spa, and he notched up the first of his 25 Grand Prix wins. Hill had to make do with second. Aintree was the scene of the British Grand Prix; Clark led from start to finish and set the fastest lap. He was also within a point of Hill in the title race, and he had finished fourth. Hill

then scored back-to-back wins at the Nürburgring and Monza. Clark suffered in both. In Germany he stalled on the line but gave chase and brought himself within striking distance of the leaders, then low fuel meant he had to ease off: he came fourth. He had to retire with engine trouble at Monza.

Four wins for Hill

Clark bounced back to win at Watkins Glen, but Hill claimed second place. Hill was now 9 points clear of his rival going into the final race at East London in South Africa. Clark needed to win to have any chance of the title, and only had a chance if Hill failed to score. Clark took pole, and was indeed leading the race, but engine failure once again put paid to his hopes, and it was Hill who came through to win. His four wins and two second places put him on 42 points, 12 ahead of Clark. The championship was his.

BELOW: *1962 Monaco Grand Prix. Monte Carlo. Race winner, Bruce McLaren (Cooper T60-Climax), on the way to gaining 9 points towards his eventual total of 27 and third position in the championship.*

OPPOSITE: *Wolfgang von Trips (Ferrari). He was killed at the Italian Grand Prix, Monza, 1961, when leading the title race.*

JIM CLARK COMES THROUGH

1963

1963 DRIVERS' CHAMPIONSHIP

1.	JIM CLARK	54
2.	GRAHM HILL	33
3.	RITCHIE GINTHER	29

CONSTRUCTORS' TITLE

1.	LOTUS	54
2.	BRM	36
3.	BRABHAM	28

The 1963 championship was a ten-race series, with the best six scores counting towards the title. Jim Clark and Lotus had been beaten into second place in both the Drivers' and the Constructors' championship in 1962, and there had been a lot of activity since. Both Porsche and Bowmaker-Yeoman decided to withdraw; Porsche's withdrawal left Dan Gurney free to drive for the Brabham team, and the end of Bowmaker-Yeoman meant that John Surtees was open to offers. He joined Ferrari.

It was a period of change for Ferrari. Engineer Carlo Chiti left at the end of the 1962 season and set up his own team, ATS, and several Ferrari people went with him, including drivers Phil Hill and Giancarlo Baghetti. It wasn't successful; the V-8 cars the team put out were poor and neither Hill nor Baghetti took a single point in the 1963 series. The new team lasted a year.

Seven wins out of ten for Clark

On the track Clark came first in seven of the ten races, and looking at the three races he failed to win shows how his domination could have been even greater. One was the opening race at Monaco, where he was leading from Graham Hill, then spun off with a seized gearbox. Hill went on to win, the first of what would be five Monaco successes in a row. On the other two occasions where Clark missed out he was similarly unlucky. He was hampered by a misfiring engine at the Nürburgring but managed to finish second, behind Surtees. Clark's misfortune helped Surtees to a breakthrough first championship victory, and gave Ferrari its first success since Monza two years earlier. At Watkins Glen Clark lost a lap and a half in the pits with battery trouble, yet still managed to finish third. Graham Hill took the race from his team-mate Ritchie Ginther.

The Flying Scot

After Monaco, Clark recorded four straight wins: Spa, Zandvoort, Reims and Silverstone. The Dutch race possibly best epitomised the level of Clark's performance. He was fastest in practice, led the race from start to finish – lapping the entire field in the process – and became the first man to lap the Zandvoort circuit at over 100mph. He secured the title with three races still to go.

Among the others, Surtees could consider himself rather unlucky. Apart from his win in Germany, he had got a fourth place at Monaco, third at Zandvoort and second at Silverstone – where he passed Hill on the last lap, the 1962 champion running out of fuel desperately close to the finish. However, Surtees failed to finish in any of the last four races, and

had to be content with fourth place in the championship, on 22 points.

Best of his era

Hill also had his share of bad luck. He finished in just six races, the two victories at Monaco and Watkins Glen, plus three third places and a fourth in Mexico. BRM introduced their own monocoque design during the season, hoping to emulate the brilliant success of the Lotus 25, but the new car handled badly and Hill was forced to revert to the old model. He ended the year on 29 points, 25 behind Clark's maximum points haul of 54. This was only the second time in the history of the event that such a feat had been achieved, and when Ascari recorded his maximum in 1952, it was the best four finishes out of eight. Clark was well on his way to his reputation as the greatest racing driver of his era.

Mike Hailwood off the mark

In three of the first four rounds of the championship Surtees had to retire; his only success was at Zandvoort, where he finished a distant second behind Clark. Earlier, in the traditional Monaco curtain-raiser, Mike Hailwood, another motorcycling ace, made his mark, finishing sixth to claim his first championship point. At Spa there were several dramatic reverses of fortune. Dan Gurney looked set to give Brabham maximum points, but ran out of fuel; Graham Hill profited from the situation, but only briefly – the BRM's fuel pump failed. Bruce McLaren now found himself in

BELOW: *John Surtees (Ferrari), pictured at the 1964 German Grand Prix, Nurburgring. This was his first win of the series in which he was ultimately triumphant by 1 point.*

OPPOSITE: *Jim Clark leads Trevor Taylor (both Lotus 25 Climax), in the final race of the 1963 season, East London, South Africa. Clark finished first but the points were not required to count for his best six results, having won six previously.*

SURTEES, WINNING ON FOUR WHEELS

1964

1964 DRIVERS' CHAMPIONSHIP

1.	JOHN SURTEES	40
2.	GRAHAM HILL	39
3.	JIM CLARK	32

CONSTRUCTORS' TITLE

1.	FERRARI	45
2.	BRM	42
3.	LOTUS	37

Ferrari had produced a new V-8 engine for the existing 1963-model chassis for the new season. It was hoped that this hardware, together with Surtees' growing skills, would prove to be a match for the British teams which had dominated the previous two years. John Surtees had won seven motorcycling world titles and, four years after making his Grand Prix debut, was in with a chance of becoming the first man to take world titles on both two and four wheels. 1964 would see the closest championship race for years. Clark and Hill were both hoping to take their second world crown, and Surtees was the third British driver vying for the title as the circus reached its final stop in Mexico.

Surtees on top

Surtees came out on top at Monza, battling with Clark and McLaren. Clark failed to finish, while Hill didn't even get out of the blocks, owing to a jammed clutch. However, Hill led the table on 39 going into the final round in Mexico; Surtees was up to 34 and Clark was still stuck on 30, but with a chance of retaining the title if he won. Third place would have been good enough for Hill, and that was the position he held until an evil-tempered battle with Bandini's Ferrari saw both cars spin off. Hill's departure improved Surtees' hopes, and these were boosted when Clark, leading the race on the penultimate lap, succumbed once again to engine trouble. Surtees moved into third, and was waved through into second by Bandini, where he finished behind Gurney. It gave Surtees the championship by a single point from Hill.

Surtees had become the first man to take world titles on both two wheels and four, a feat which remains unequalled.

front but he, too, ran out of fuel, spluttering to a halt 100 yards from the finishing line. Jim Clark won – and he too ran out of gas on the slowing-down lap.

British Grand Prix at Brands Hatch

Gurney made up for his disappointment in Belgium by winning the French Grand Prix at Rouen. Hill was second, and Gurney's team boss, Brabham himself, was third. Brabham was now trying to spend more time overseeing the team, but each time he tried to ease himself behind a desk, events conspired to keep him involved. The British Grand Prix was staged at Brands Hatch for the first time. Clark set a new lap record to win the race, chased hard by Hill. Surtees, finishing in third, was back in the points and began a run of solid performances and consistent points. He needed them: at the halfway mark Clark led with 30 points, followed by Hill on 26. Surtees had 10.

Jochen Rindt debut in Austria

He began by winning on the winding 14.2-mile Nürburgring circuit, a minute clear of Hill. All three title contenders were among the host of retirements in the next race, run on Austria's rough Zeltweg circuit, and Austria's first-ever Grand Prix went to Ferrari's no. 2 driver, Lorenzo Bandini. It also marked the debut of Jochen Rindt.

CLARK WINS AGAIN

1965

1965 DRIVERS' CHAMPIONSHIP

1.	JIM CLARK	54
2.	GRAHAM HILL	40
3.	JACKIE STEWART	33

CONSTRUCTORS' TITLE

1.	LOTUS	54
2.	BRM	45
3.	BRABHAM	27

Lack of reliability undoubtedly cost Jim Clark his second world title in 1964, but things improved radically in 1965. He managed to finish in six races – crucial, because the championship was once again decided on the best six finishes in a ten-event series. The Lotus was fitted with a new and more powerful 32-valve version of the Coventry-Climax engine, and its reliability was much improved.

Stewart the rising star

Taking place on New Year's Day, the South African Grand Prix had been held over to provide the first race

of 1965, instead of the last of 1964. Clark immediately set the tone for a series he would dominate to such an extent that races turned into a scramble for minor placings. He started on pole and also set the fastest lap; Surtees and Hill followed him home, the three protagonists who had contested the previous year's title decider. Claiming his first championship point with a sixth place on his debut was Jackie Stewart. Stewart had had offers to join Lotus and Cooper, as well as BRM.

Clark was forced to miss Monaco as the Lotus team was keen to contest the Indianapolis 500. This had not been part of the Formula One championship since 1960, and Clark had no great affection for it. He won, in record speed, having led for 190 of the 200 laps. Clark could now concentrate on his main goal: winning his second Formula One title.

Graham Hill: 'King of Monaco'
In his absence Hill had a hat-trick of wins at Monaco and was dubbed the 'King of Monte Carlo'. In the Belgian Grand Prix Clark returned to the title race with his fourth successive win at Spa; he led all the way in stormy weather, and Stewart came in second. The two drivers repeated the performance at Clermont-Ferrand, for the first time the venue for the French Grand Prix. Stewart was emerging as champion material, and another driver destined to scale the heights quietly gained his first points in this race – Denny Hulme. He was an established Formula Two driver at Brabham, and was regarded so highly that the team occasionally entered a third car for him during the 1965 series. His fourth place in France was followed by a fifth at Zandvoort.

ABOVE: *Graham Hill (BRM P261), driving to third position in the curtain-raiser to the 1965 season – the South African Grand Prix, East London.*

OPPOSITE: *Dan Gurney (Brabham BT7-Climax) winning the 1964 French Grand Prix, Rouen.*

Consecutive wins for Clark
Clark continued his devastating form with wins at Zandvoort and Silverstone. The Dutch race was comfortable, Clark winning once again from Stewart to give him three consecutive wins there. The British Grand Prix was a much closer affair; suffering a loss of oil pressure, Clark nursed his Lotus home barely three seconds ahead of Hill.

Stewart finishes third
He claimed his sixth win of the year at the Nürburgring – and this brought him his second world title, though there were still three rounds of the championship to go. It was just as well: he failed to finish at Monza, Watkins Glen and Mexico. Jackie Stewart's win in Italy was the highlight of these final rounds; it came courtesy of a mistake by Graham Hill in the penultimate lap, but was still impressive. He had 33 points in his first season, finishing third, 7 points behind Hill.

Clark's maximum points haul
But 1965, the last year of the 1.5-litre Formula, was all about one man – Clark. His maximum haul of 54 points – repeating his feat of 1963 – established him as the greatest driver of his time. Like Fangio, so dominant throughout the 50s, Clark had all the natural talents.

BRABHAM WINS — IN HIS OWN CAR

1966

1966 DRIVERS' CHAMPIONSHIP

1.	JACK BRABHAM	42
2.	JOHN SURTEES	28
3.	JOCHEN RINDT	22

CONSTRUCTORS' TITLE

1.	BRABHAM	42
2.	FERRARI	31
3.	COOPER	30

Jack Brabham planned to form his own racing company even when he was the reigning world champion. He'd won his world titles with Cooper, and his decision to go off and build his own Grand Prix car did not go down very well: the Cooper team felt that Brabham had gained a great deal of knowledge which he would now be using in direct competition. Brabham's new car made its first appearance in 1962 and Dan Gurney joined the team in 1963.

Denny Hulme joins Brabham

Gurney won two Grands Prix in 1964 but, largely because of problems with reliability, 1965 had been a bad year for Brabham. However, the start of the 1966 campaign, which brought with it the new 3-litre Formula, saw the Brabham team better prepared than most. Its cars were powered by an Australian-built V-8 Repco engine that proved to be a model of reliability. Gurney also had thoughts of setting up his own outfit and left Brabham after three years to head up the Eagle team. His place was filled by Denny Hulme.

However, Brabham didn't set the world of racing alight at the start of the season. He had gearbox trouble at Monaco, in a race with a high casualty count. Another early victim was Bruce McLaren, who had decided to branch out on his own like Gurney, and Monaco was the first time he had run a car under his own name. Jackie Stewart won the race, one of only four classified finishers, giving BRM its fourth Monaco success in a row.

Surtees and Rindt battle at Spa

The very wet conditions at Spa reduced the 15-strong field to seven after a series of first-lap incidents. Surtees and Rindt battled it out and finished in that order, with Brabham in the points, but a distant fourth. At Reims Brabham set a record, averaging over 136mph to win ahead of Ferrari newcomer Mike Parkes. Hulme took third that day, and the team went one better at Brands Hatch, Brabham leading all the way and crossing the line 1.6 seconds in front of his no. 2. He notched up his third win in a row at Zandvoort, taking the race from Graham Hill, while Clark just held on for third place from Stewart.

ABOVE: *Dan Gurney drives the Eagle T1G Weslake to first place in the 1967 Belgian Grand Prix at Spa-Francorchamps (the car's only success).*

OPPOSITE: *1966 United States Grand Prix, Watkins Glen, New York with Jim Clark (Lotus 43 BRM) on the grid at the start. This was the BRM 75 H16 engine's only Grand Prix win.*

Next came the Nürburgring. Brabham had never won in Germany, but he did this time, with a magnificent victory in the wet. John Surtees, now driving a Cooper-Maserati, followed him home. Surtees had begun the season with Ferrari, who had produced a very competitive new V-12 unit for the season, but friction between Surtees and the Ferrari team boss Eugenio Dragoni led him to join Cooper after his win at Spa. Surtees was to finish second in the championship, driving the rather less impressive Cooper, and might have gone one better if he had remained with Ferrari.

Three times world champion

As the circus moved on to Monza, however, it was Brabham who had the title within his grasp. He led here before retiring with an oil leak, but those who had a chance of catching him also retired. Ludovico Scarfiotti won the race for Ferrari but, more importantly, Brabham was confirmed as world champion for the third time. There was another retirement for Brabham in the penultimate race at Watkins Glen. Jim Clark won, his Lotus by now fitted with the new H16 engine, his only victory of the series in what was a frustrating year. Surtees took the final honours in Mexico, with Brabham and Hulme occupying second and third places. This left Brabham 14 points clear of Surtees in the final table, and made him the first driver to win in a car bearing his own name.

BRABHAM'S FIRST AND SECOND

1967 DRIVERS' CHAMPIONSHIP

1.	DENNY HULME	51
2.	JACK BRABHAM	46
3.	JIM CLARK	41

CONSTRUCTORS' TITLE

1.	BRABHAM	67
2.	LOTUS	50
3.	COOPER	28

Brabham and Hulme were able to capitalise on the teething trouble suffered by the new Lotus 49, the car of the future. The less sophisticated Repco-Brabham was able to prevail in 1967 because of its reliability: it was a real workhorse, much less temperamental. Unusually, both Brabhams experienced problems in the opening round, on the new Kyalami track in South Africa; however, both limped home in the points. Hulme, who had led for 60 laps, finished fourth, with Brabham sixth. Privateer John Love nearly pulled off a stunning win in an outdated Cooper-Climax but ran out of fuel late in the race and had to content himself with second. Pedro Rodriguez won, giving a flying start to the team he had recently joined, Cooper-Maserati.

Hulme had his first Grand Prix success at Monaco, coming home over a lap ahead of Graham Hill, but the result was overshadowed by a horrific crash in which Lorenzo Bandini was killed. On the 82nd lap Bandini's Ferrari struck straw bales and burst into flames; he was trapped and died shortly afterwards.

Clark wins at Zandvoort

At Zandvoort Lotus finally showed off the new Ford-powered 49 model which had tempted Graham Hill to leave BRM and join Jim Clark at Lotus. It was immediately clear that the new car was something special. Hill led early on but retired, leaving Brabham in front; Clark then came through to register a brilliant win. Unfortunately for Lotus, Hill's experience, rather than Clark's, was to set the pattern. Brabham and Hulme grabbed the minor placings at Zandvoort, establishing their own pattern of being regularly in the points.

Spa was another example of Lotus's ill-fated year. With Hill already out of the race, Clark was leading, and was forced into the pits with spark-plug trouble. Both Brabham and Hulme had also retired, and Dan Gurney gave his Eagle-Weslake car its first and only success. In the French Grand Prix, run on the Bugatti track at Le Mans, both Clark and Hill were going well until the Lotus 49s gave out again. The Brabhams dominated the race on this occasion, Brabham himself leading, with Hulme second and Jackie Stewart in third.

British Grand Prix – Clark again

Clark enjoyed a trouble-free race at Silverstone and duly won. Hulme and Brabham took second and fourth respectively, with Chris Amon coming third in his Ferrari. But Clark was out at the Nürburgring after just three laps, with a broken suspension. Hill fared even worse: his retirement was his sixth out of the seven races so far. Hulme and Brabham made it another one-two, with Amon third once again. In the Formula Two section of the race, Jacky Ickx drove his Matra brilliantly before suffering suspension trouble. Before that, he actually held overall fourth, ahead of several Formula One cars.

At the inaugural Canadian Grand Prix it was much the same story. Clark left with ignition trouble and Brabham and Hulme took the points again. Monza proved to be the most dramatic race. Clark suffered early problems as usual, but this time pulled back, breaking the lap record repeatedly. This took him into the lead but he ran short of fuel on the final lap. In an exciting final half-lap, Brabham passed Surtees to lead, but the latter retook it and won by just 0.2 seconds. Clark struggled home in third.

Hulme wins world crown with 51 points

It came right for Lotus at Watkins Glen. Clark and Hill came home first and second, though they both had problems late in the race; another solid third place for Hulme enhanced his title hopes still further. There was another win for Clark in the final round in Mexico, but there was also another third place for Hulme which was enough to give him the title with 51 points, 5 ahead of Brabham, who had finished second in the race. This was the first 'team double' since Hill and von Trips in 1961. Clark had accumulated 41 points to finish a frustrating third.

THE LOSS OF CLARK

1968

1968 DRIVERS' CHAMPIONSHIP

1.	GRAHAM HILL	48
2.	JACKIE STEWART	36
3.	DENNY HULME	33

CONSTRUCTORS' TITLE

1.	LOTUS	62
2.	McLAREN	51
3.	MATRA FORD	45

By this point in the decade, only six drivers had lost their lives; the change to rear-engined cars had brought a slight improvement in safety. However, 1968 saw two further fatalities, and Mike Spence and Ludovico Scarfiotto died in other events on the motor sport calendar.

Jim Clark won the opening round of the series, at Kyalami; this victory – his 25th in just 72 Grands Prix – took him one ahead of the great Fangio. He took part in a Formula Two race at Hockenheim on 7 April and was killed when his Lotus 48 left the track on a gentle right-hand bend and went into trees.

Sponsorship arrives

Lotus then brought in Jackie Oliver to team up with Graham Hill, who had finished second to Clark in South Africa. Kyalami was the last race in which Lotus sported its green and yellow livery; by the next, the outfit had become Gold Leaf Team Lotus, and the car was bedecked in red, white and gold. Sponsorship had arrived.

King of Monte Carlo

For the first time since 1954, Spain was back on the championship calendar. A pre-race accident put Stewart out of contention for several races, and he lost vital ground which was to prove crucial in the latter stages. Hill then scored his fourth Monaco success. After two wins and a second place, he had a run of bad luck which saw him fail to finish in the next four races. The first of these was Spa, where his main rival Stewart looked certain to give Matra their first win in Belgium – he was 25 seconds ahead of Bruce McLaren with just two laps left – but he ran out of fuel. McLaren was able

to bring home the car which bore his name for its debut victory. Although it wasn't a successful year for either Ferrari and Brabham, these two were at the forefront of experiments with rear-mounted aerofoils, a trend which would soon become the norm.

Brilliant Stewart at Zandvoort

Stewart drove brilliantly in the wet at Zandvoort. On his way to victory he lapped the entire field, except for Beltoise in the works Matra. The French Grand Prix at Rouen was also run in atrocious conditions, and brought another fatality: Jo Schlesser's Honda crashed out of the race and burst into flames. Stewart was less happy with his Dunlop wets here, and finished third. Ickx gave Ferrari their first win since Monza in 1966.

The Lotuses of Hill and Oliver both led for a time in the British Grand Prix at Brands Hatch, but neither finished. Stewart was desperate for points, but the circuit put too much strain on his injured wrist and he could do no better than sixth. Rob Walker's Lotus,

BELOW: *Jacky Ickx (Ferrari 312) takes the chequered flag at the 1968 French Grand Prix, Rouen-les-Essarts. This was the only race of the season that was won by a car not powered by a Ford engine.*

OPPOSITE: *Denny Hulme (Brabham BT24 Repco) in action during the 1967 German Grand Prix, Nurburgring. He went on to win the race in a consistent year that saw him take the title.*

driven by Jo Siffert, won the race, holding off the Ferrari challenge from Amon and Ickx. There was more torrential rain and a heavy mist for the German Grand Prix. Stewart was now happy with the special Dunlop rain tyres fitted to his car. He still had the wrist problem, but was determined to continue. His plan was to get in front so that he could have clear track ahead. It worked brilliantly, and he took the flag four minutes ahead of Hill; he was now within 4 points of Hill in the championship.

Late surge from Hulme
Stewart was forced out at Monza by engine trouble, but Hill's Lotus lost a wheel, so the balance remained unchanged. Hill then slightly extended his lead at the Canadian Grand Prix. Both drivers were hampered by suspension trouble, but Hill was fourth, while Stewart could only finish sixth. Denny Hulme scored back-to-back wins in these two races, which helped him finish third overall.

Second world crown for Hill
Mario Andretti was given a works Lotus-Ford for the race at Watkins Glen. Andretti and Bobby Unser had practised at the Italian Grand Prix, but were disqualified for taking part in an event in America within a day of Monza. At Watkins Glen Andretti made an immediate impact, setting the fastest lap in practice. He led in the early part of the race, too, but was overhauled by Stewart, who had his third success of the series. Hill finished second, meaning that he would take a 3-point lead into the final race in Mexico.

The Matra and Lotus vied for the lead in the early stages, but Stewart's engine – and his title hopes – fizzled out. He finished seventh. Hill drove impeccably to take the race, and with it his second world title.

STEWART'S YEAR

1969

1969 DRIVERS' CHAMPIONSHIP		
1.	JACKIE STEWART	63
2.	JACKY ICKX	37
3.	BRUCE McLAREN	26

CONSTRUCTORS' TITLE		
1.	MATRA	66
2.	BRABHAM	51
3.	LOTUS	47

Jackie Stewart's prospects for 1969 looked good and his disappointment at missing out on the 1968 championship soon vanished. He had been runner-up despite losing points through injury and the fuel miscalculation at Spa, and his hopes were further boosted by the fact that he would have a new Ford-powered Matra, the MS80. Matra had withdrawn its works team at the end of 1968, leaving its Formula One involvement in the hands of Ken Tyrrell. Honda, Cooper and Eagle also withdrew.

Hill and Rindt foiled
Stewart dominated the first race at Kyalami in spite of the fact that the new car wasn't ready – the previous year's car was dusted off for the race. His closest challenge came from Mario Andretti, who was

contesting the lead with Stewart before his Lotus gave out with transmission trouble. Stewart won again in Barcelona, recovering well after a poor start and clawing back lost ground. His victory was also partly down to some bad luck on the part of those ahead of him: Amon was particularly unfortunate, for he was well ahead when his Ferrari failed. Hill and Rindt's Lotuses both crashed out, with the cause put down to the aerofoils the cars were sporting. Hill was unscathed, but Rindt's injuries forced him to miss Monaco.

The 'wings' debate was one of the contentious issues of the year. Most teams had adopted aerofoils but, following Barcelona, they were banned at Monaco. Stewart again looked well set, sharing the lead with Amon; when both retired, Hill came through to score a fifth Monte Carlo success. It was his only win of the year, and one of the few moments to savour for Lotus, which was an unhappy camp this season. Monaco was also good for the independents: Piers Courage, driving a Frank Williams-entered Brabham-Ford, was second, with Jo Siffert, in a Walker-Durlacher, third.

Stewart back in command

The Belgian Grand Prix was cancelled because of a dispute about safety, and the circus moved to Zandvoort, where Rindt recovered from his injuries to take pole. He led the race until succumbing to driveshaft failure, and Stewart claimed a third win. Several cars sprouted 'wings' again, although they were smaller and less imposing than those which had attracted criticism. Stewart was in commanding form again in France. His latest triumph contrasted with the situation at BRM, whose slow and unreliable V-12 gave John Surtees and Jackie Oliver a miserable season. They didn't bother to enter at Clermont-Ferrand.

ABOVE: *Jackie Stewart (Matra MS80 Ford) on his way to his third win from the first four races, at the 1969 Dutch Grand Prix, Zandvoort.*

OPPOSITE: *1968 French Grand Prix, Rouen-les-Essarts. Graham Hill (Lotus 49 Ford) who had retired, gives his team-mate Jo Siffert (Lotus 49-Ford) his visor on the trackside.*

Stewart had a high-speed crash in practice at Silverstone and was forced to take over team-mate Jean-Pierre Beltoise's car in the race; he and Rindt were involved in a battle until Rindt was forced into the pits with a loose wing. Both Lotus and McLaren showed off their innovative four-wheel-drive cars, with mixed results. John Miles had a smooth ride and brought his Lotus home in tenth, while Derek Bell's McLaren lasted just five laps.

Civic reception for champion Stewart

Stewart was beaten into second place at the Nürburgring, hampered by gearbox trouble. Jacky Ickx gave Brabham its first win of the season; he had been signed after Rindt decided to go to Lotus the previous year. Brabham himself had an indifferent, injury-hit year but Ickx was impressive, lying second in the championship with 22 points. Stewart was almost unreachable on 51, and removed any further doubt at Monza where he headed home Rindt, Beltoise and McLaren. The title was definitely his.

Stewart's last three races saw him retire twice, and manage only fourth in Mexico. Ickx won in Canada, and Rindt finally had his first win at Watkins Glen in the United States. Graham Hill was badly injured after a tyre blew on the straight as he was heading for the pits; long convalescence looked likely, but Hill was determined to be back for the start of the 1970 season. He made it, but there were to be no more Grand Prix successes in his career.

TRAGEDY FOR RINDT

1970

1970 DRIVERS' CHAMPIONSHIP

1.	JOCHEN RINDT	45
2.	JACKY ICKX	40
3.	CLAY REGAZZONI	33

CONSTRUCTORS' TITLE

1.	LOTUS	59
2.	FERRARI	55
3.	MARCH	48

In 1970 things began to look favourable for Jochen Rindt, whose five years in the sport had been frustrating. Following his accident in 1969, Graham Hill vowed to race on, but not with Lotus, so Rindt was now their no 1. There was also a new car, the Lotus 72, with which Rindt could mount a serious challenge.

Stewart races with March

At Kyalami, in the opening round, Rindt received a bump from Brabham early in the race. He continued, but engine trouble put paid to his chances. Brabham, now in his 23rd year of racing, won in his new Brabham-Ford BT33; Graham Hill claimed a point by finishing sixth. The new Lotus made its appearance in Spain, sporting many technical advances. There were early glitches, however, and Rindt retired with ignition trouble. Stewart won; he was driving the new March 701 as the Tyrrell outfit and Matra had parted at the end of 1969.

McLaren killed while testing

There was a sensational finish at Monaco. Brabham was well ahead in the latter stages. Rindt, who had been forced to revert to the old Lotus 49, was driving increasingly quickly in an attempt to catch him. Brabham got the danger signal from the pits and responded but Rindt was on his tail going into the final lap. Brabham overshot his braking on the last bend; Rindt swept through and won.

He had to retire at Spa. This race saw BRM – now sponsored by Yardley – back on top: Pedro

BELOW: *Monaco Grand Prix Monte Carlo. Jochen Rindt (Lotus 49C Ford) powers to victory for the first of five wins in 1970.*

OPPOSITE: *Ken Tyrrell confers with Jackie Stewart in the pit lane during the 1971 season.*

Rodriguez gave it its first success since 1966. The McLarens had withdrawn from the race as a mark of respect for Bruce McLaren, who had been killed a few days earlier testing his CanAm car.

The revised Lotus 72 made a brilliant reappearance at Zandvoort; Rindt took the lead on the third lap and held it to the end. His victory was marred by the death of his friend Piers Courage, whose de Tomaso had crashed and exploded early in the race. Rindt considered retiring from the sport but decided that a mid-season withdrawal was out.

Three in a row for Rindt

He now led the championship and consolidated by winning the next three races. The first was in France, where he came through after Ickx's Ferrari and Beltoise's Matra both hit trouble. At Brands Hatch, Brabham shadowed Rindt and succeeded in passing him, but ran out of fuel on the final lap. There was more to come: a protest regarding the height of the Lotus's aerofoil was upheld, and Brabham was declared the winner. That decision was later reversed and Rindt was reinstated. This was John Surtees' first season running his own team and he showed off his new car, the TS7, at Brands Hatch; it made a promising start before succumbing to engine trouble. Another feature of that race was the performance of the young Emerson Fittipaldi. He had been given Team Lotus's old 49c car and finished eighth.

Safety issues at the Nürburgring meant that the German Grand Prix moved to Hockenheim for the first time. Rindt again came out on top, a narrow winner over Ickx. Ickx was on form again in Austria, and made it a Ferrari one-two with his team-mate Clay Regazzoni. Ickx was now a clear threat, but the Lotus camp knew that a win at Monza would give Rindt an unassailable lead. However, in final practice on 5 September, Rindt was killed when his Lotus lurched into a crash barrier. He was 28.

Rindt posthumous champion

Lotus withdrew from the race, which was won by Regazzoni in his first season in Formula One. It also scratched from the Canadian Grand Prix, the first of a trio of trans-Atlantic races ending the series. Ickx was the only driver who could top Rindt's 45 points, and only if he won all three final rounds. He succeeded in Canada, and in the final race in Mexico, but he was fourth at Watkins Glen. Rindt was the first posthumous winner of the Drivers' championship.

1971

TYRRELL ON THE MARCH

1971 DRIVERS' CHAMPIONSHIP

1.	JACKIE STEWART	62
2.	RONNIE PETERSON	33
3.	FRANCOIS CEVERT	26

CONSTRUCTORS' TITLE

1.	TYRRELL	73
2.	BRM	36
3.	MARCH	34

Early in 1970 Jackie Stewart realised that the March was inferior to his 1969 Matra. Ken Tyrrell had a new car under development, and Stewart drove it in the final three rounds of the 1970 series. It was further refined by the time the 1971 championship began, and a second was prepared for Stewart's team-mate, Francois Cevert. The ubiquitous Ford Cosworth engines should have made all the teams using them fairly even, but Stewart's Tyrrell-Ford proved to be more powerful and reliable than its rivals.

Ferrari threat

Ferrari were a threat to all the Ford-powered cars. Mario Andretti won the opener, at Kyalami. It was Andretti's first Grand Prix success – he had been a star of American racing for some time – and it marked a step on the way to fulfilling a lifelong ambition. He was champion material, but after this he came back to earth; his day was still several years away.

At the Spanish Grand Prix Stewart began to steamroll his way to the title. He took over the lead from Jacky Ickx's Ferrari on the sixth lap and stayed there, crossing the line 3.4 seconds ahead, giving the Tyrrell team its maiden success. He was on form at Monaco, dominating the race from start to finish. There were many plaudits for Ronnie Peterson, who came in second; Ickx took third after Siffert retired.

Rodriguez killed in Germany

The Tyrrell had engine problems during practice at Zandvoort, and there was no time to set it up for the wet conditions; Stewart went through the motions and trailed home 11th. Ickx, by contrast, gave a masterclass in wet-weather driving and came out on top after a battle with Pedro Rodriguez in the BRM. The French Grand Prix was at the new Paul Ricard circuit, near Marseilles. Stewart won again, and Cevert followed him

home; Emerson Fittipaldi put up a great show in third. Before the British Grand Prix Pedro Rodriguez was killed in a minor sports car event in Germany. He had won only twice in his eight-year career in Formula One, but was regularly in the points. Clay Regazzoni took pole at Silverstone, and led in the early stages. Stewart then took over and dominated from the front. Peterson gave another fine showing to finish second, half a minute behind Stewart. Fittipaldi was third again.

The Nürburgring brought another top two finishes for Tyrrell. Stewart won, but Cevert set the fastest lap. Ickx was Stewart's closest rival, but he still only had a theoretical chance of catching him, and though Stewart crashed out of the Austrian Grand Prix, Ickx also failed to finish. Jo Siffert won the race for BRM. Two Austrians made their first Formula One appearance here: one was Helmut Marko who finished 11th. The other fared worse, retiring in his rented March-Ford after 20 laps: Niki Lauda.

BELOW: *Ronnie Peterson (March 711-Alfa Romeo) pictured at the March-Alfa Romeo Formula One launch. The 1971 season saw Peterson take second position in the championship.* OPPOSITE: *Emerson Fittipaldi (Lotus Ford) pictured prior to the start of the 1972 German Grand Prix, Nurburgring.*

Thrilling duel

Stewart was also unlucky at Monza. Just 0.61 seconds covered the first five cars across the line, the tightest Grand Prix finish ever; Peter Gethin squeaked home first. He had begun the season with McLaren but had moved to BRM. Peterson, Cevert and Howden Ganley were three of the others in the shake-up, finishing second, third and fifth respectively. Stewart's season seemed to be petering out, though the title was settled. In Canada, however, he got the better of a duel with Peterson, who came second. Conditions were bad and the race was halted after 64 of the 80 laps.

Stewart had enjoyed six wins. The final race, at Watkins Glen, added icing to the cake for Tyrrell. Cevert took the lead from Stewart on the 14th lap and held on, winning from Siffert and Peterson; Tyrrell had won seven of the eleven championship rounds. Peterson and Cevert finished second and third in the final table, with 33 and 26 points respectively. Stewart's 62 points underlines just how far ahead of the field he was.

The season finished on a tragic note. Jo Siffert was killed in a specially arranged race at Brands Hatch when his BRM crashed and caught fire.

FITTIPALDI'S YEAR

1972

1972 DRIVERS' CHAMPIONSHIP

1.	EMERSON FITTIPALDI	61
2.	JACKIE STEWART	45
3.	DENNY HULME	39

CONSTRUCTORS' TITLE

1.	LOTUS	61
2.	TYRRELL	51
3.	McLAREN	47

Lotus had an unsuccessful 1971; the Lotus 72 proved no match for the Tyrrells, Ferraris and March 711. Fittipaldi had done well, despite being injured for part of the season, and having numerous mechanical troubles: he managed a second place and two thirds, finishing sixth overall. Lotus undertook a lot of work in the close season, and the car was reborn as the John Player Special in black and gold colours. It was now as quick and reliable as any other.

Jackie Stewart won the opening race in Argentina, suggesting that Tyrrell was going to sweep the board again, but his year was blighted by a stomach ulcer. He still recorded four victories, but this time that wouldn't quite be enough. Fittipaldi had retired with suspension trouble. He took second in South Africa, behind Denny Hulme. Hulme had got off to a good start in the title race, the South African win following his second behind Stewart in Argentina. This was a great change for McLaren, who hadn't won a race in three years, instead concentrating on the Indianapolis 500 and the CanAm races the previous year. Now, with Yardley's sponsorship, the focus was back on Formula One.

Appalling conditions for Monaco

The Spanish Grand Prix at Jarama was the first 1971 victory for Fittipaldi. Monaco followed, where there were many slides in appalling conditions; Jean-Pierre Beltoise won in his BRM – the marque's last success. Fittipaldi had a far from happy race, but he stayed in contention and avoided errors; his efforts were rewarded by a third place. Stewart's Tyrrell fell back with wet electrics.

The Belgian Grand Prix at the new Nivelles circuit, a race which Stewart's ulcer caused him to miss, gave Fittipaldi his next win. Stewart was back in time for the French race at Clermont-Ferrand; he won, with Fittipaldi second. They contested the British Grand Prix at Brands Hatch, but Fittipaldi came out on top: the championship was looking like a two-horse race. As they headed for the next round at the Nürburgring, Fittipaldi led with 43 points to Stewart's 27.

Jacky Ickx notches eighth victory

Fittipaldi was chasing Ickx's Ferrari in the German Grand Prix when oil leaking from his gearbox ignited. Ickx had his eighth Grand Prix victory, also his last. His team-mate Clay Regazzoni was second, giving Ferrari their first one-two since the duo had finished in that order two years before, in Canada. Stewart failed to finish and was unable to make up any ground on Fittipaldi in the championship.

In Austria Fittipaldi bounced back, taking the lead from Stewart at around the half-distance mark. He was pressed all the way to the line by Denny Hulme, not Stewart – who finished seventh and out of the points. Hulme's team-mate Peter Revson finished third, giving him his third podium finish of the year.

Fittipaldi now led Stewart by 52 points to 27. The title was nearly safe, but not quite. The next race was Monza, and Fittipaldi took up the running after the Ferraris of Ickx and Regazzoni both retired. Easing off, he crossed the line 14 seconds clear of Hailwood. His 61 points was now unassailable; Denny Hulme was his nearest challenger on 31 with just two races to go. Fittipaldi didn't add to his tally in those, in Canada and the United States; Stewart finished strongly to win both. That was enough to take second place from Hulme, but he was still 15 points below Fittipaldi. The new champion also put himself into the record books by becoming the youngest ever holder of the title – at 25 years, 8 months and 29 days.

ABOVE: *Jean-Pierre Beltoise (BRM P160B), on the way to victory at the 1972 Monaco Grand Prix, Monte Carlo, in very wet conditions.*
OPPOSITE: *1973 Italian Grand Prix, Monza. Ronnie Peterson (Lotus Ford) celebrates his win on the podium with team boss Colin Chapman.*

1973

STEWART AND TYRRELL A SECOND TIME

1973 DRIVERS' CHAMPIONSHIP

1.	JACKIE STEWART	71
2.	EMERSON FITTIPALDI	55
3.	RONNIE PETERSON	52

CONSTRUCTORS' TITLE

1.	JPS/LOTUS	92
2.	TYRRELL	82
3.	McLAREN	58

Once again, Fittipaldi and Stewart were the main features for Lotus and Tyrrell respectively; Ronnie Peterson and Francois Cevert were able supporting acts for the same teams. The season started well for Fittipaldi, he won both South American races. Cevert had led for much of the race in Argentina, but Fittipaldi took over, and Cevert and Stewart settled for the minor placings. In Brazil he led all the way, though he hadn't taken pole; Peterson had, but he failed to finish, as he had in Argentina.

South Africa gave Jackie Stewart his first win; he was already considering retiring and wanted to leave at the top. Revson pipped Fittipaldi for second. Revson's team-mate Denny Hulme gave the new McLaren M23 its first outing; he had taken pole in a machine that was to be very successful for McLaren over the next few years. He could finish only fifth, but Revson got his second in the old M19. Both would race the new machine from this point.

James Hunt debuts at Monaco

Fittipaldi got his third win out of four in Spain. Cevert came a distant second and Stewart succumbed to brake problems. Peterson also failed to finish. He had taken pole, and set the fastest lap; he led for most of the race but gearbox trouble allowed Fittipaldi to take the lead. Stewart now had back-to-back victories in Belgium and Monaco. Cevert was second at Zolder, giving Tyrrell their first one-two of the year and Fittipaldi finished a distant third. They were the only drivers to complete the full 70 laps. Stewart won narrowly from Fittipaldi at Monaco; Peterson finally had some luck and finished third, ahead of Cevert. Revson and Hulme's McLarens came fifth and sixth. In ninth was James Hunt, making his debut in a March 731 for Hesketh Racing, the team of the eccentric Lord Alexander Hesketh.

Denny Hulme won for only the second time in four years as the Formula One circus went to Sweden for the first time. A puncture allowed Hulme to win but Peterson held on to take second place from Cevert. It finally came right for Peterson at the French Grand Prix. Jody Scheckter was an occasional third driver for McLaren, and France was only his third Grand Prix outing; he crashed out, having led to the three-quarter mark, and Peterson won.

Impulsive Scheckter

Scheckter went off on the first lap and took out 13 other cars in the next race at Silverstone. Revson won after a restart, with Peterson edging out Hulme for second. Hunt was in the points for the second time, at fourth. There were no major casualties in the Silverstone pile-up, but that was not so at Zandvoort. Roger Williamson's March crashed; he was killed. Stewart and Cevert finished first and second, and repeated the feat at the Nürburgring.

Monza decides the championship

Peterson led in the opening stages in Austria, then allowed Fittipaldi through. Peterson won in spite of the ploy as a broken fuel line ended Fittipaldi's hopes a few laps from the end. Monza turned out to be the championship decider, and tactics employed there had wider implications. Again Peterson and Fittipaldi were first and second, but this time Peterson didn't allow his team-mate through. Though they finished in those positions, it wasn't enough to prevent the title going to Stewart. His fourth place put him on 71 points: his third world championship.

Revson won the penultimate round in Canada. Stewart had finished fifth, his 99th race. He then withdrew, after Francois Cevert was killed in practice, never racing again. His five wins made a total of 27, putting him two ahead of Jim Clark on the all-time list, a record that would stand for 14 years.

Peterson won the final round, and finished the season on 52 points. He had won four races, but he had taken nine poles and led in 11 of the 15 races. He finished just 3 points behind Fittipaldi in the final table.

McLaren, for the first time

1974

1974 Drivers' Championship

1.	Emerson Fittipaldi	55
2.	Clay Regazzoni	52
3.	Jody Scheckter	45

Constructors' Title

1.	McLaren	73
2.	ferrari	65
3.	Tyrrell	52

There were many changes. Fittipaldi moved to McLaren, now backed by Texaco and Marlboro. He was replaced at Lotus by Jacky Ickx; Ronnie Peterson remained. Clay Regazzoni had spent three seasons with Ferrari before joining BRM where he teamed up with Niki Lauda; between them they accumulated only 5 points. Ferrari had not done much better with Jacky Ickx and Arturo Merzario and was keen for Regazzoni to return. Lauda decided to go with him.

Denny Hulme's swansong

Hulme took the opening race in Argentina, his final win; Carlos Reutemann led virtually all the way in the Brabham BT44, but ran out of fuel two laps from the finish. Fittipaldi prevailed in Brazil, also having a stroke of luck: a mid-race tussle ended when Peterson had a puncture. In South Africa, Reutemann held the lead in both of the first two races, and claimed his maiden Grand Prix victory at Kyalami; it was overshadowed by Peter Revson's death in practice. Lauda and Regazzoni scored a one-two success for Ferrari in the Spanish Grand Prix.

Quiet start for Scheckter

Regazzoni led for the first half of the Belgian Grand Prix, having taken pole. But Fittipaldi won, marginally ahead of Lauda, with Regazzoni fourth. Jody Scheckter was third. He had made a quiet start – his third place in Belgium followed a fifth in Spain – but was to play a part in the final shake-up for the title.

Ronnie Peterson came out on top at Monaco. His victory there coincided with Lotus's decision to revert to the 72 model; the new 76 had been trialled in the previous three races, but had been disappointing. Scheckter took second, while Regazzoni came fourth.

BELOW: *1974 United States Grand Prix, Watkins Glen, New York State. Emerson Fittipaldi (McLaren M23-Ford), clinched the championship with fourth place and 3 points.*

OPPOSITE: *James Hunt (Hesketh Ford) pictured prior to the 1975 Dutch Grand Prix, Zandvoort. This was his and the team's maiden Grand Prix win. It was also Hesketh's only Grand Prix victory.*

The see-sawing continued in Sweden, as Scheckter and Depailler gave Tyrrell their first win. Neither Ferrari finished that day, but Lauda once again led Regazzoni home in the Dutch Grand Prix.

Third pole in a row for Lauda

In the French Grand Prix Lauda took pole and led in the early stages; Peterson took over on lap 17 and stayed in front for the remainder of the 80-lap race. Lauda then took his third pole in a row at Brands Hatch. He led for 69 of the 75 laps, but delayed coming into the pits for a tyre change and suffered a puncture. Scheckter profited from Lauda's miscalculation, holding off Fittipaldi for the remaining six laps. Lauda was gaining the reputation of being the quickest driver; of the 15 championship races he would take pole position no less than nine times. His rise had been relatively swift, however, and he tended to make mistakes. The next came at the Nürburgring where he failed to warm up his tyres; his race ended on the first lap in a bump involving Scheckter who went on to finish second. The winner was Regazzoni.

Regazzoni in the lead

Regazzoni led the table with 44 points to Lauda's 38, with four races to go. Lauda retired from the Austrian Grand Prix; Regazzoni finished fifth. Carlos Reutemann gave the Brabham another success at Osterreichring, dominating the race. At Monza Ferrari went into self-destruct mode. Lauda led for 30 laps, then Regazzoni for 10. Regazzoni felt that Lauda was in a position to cover him and give him the best possible chance of picking up maximum points, but both drivers went all out to win and both retired with engine trouble. Three of their chief rivals took the top honours: Peterson, Fittipaldi and Scheckter, finishing in that order.

Fittipaldi wins the title in the final race

Lauda made another mistake in Canada. He shot into the lead and held it to the three-quarter distance, but skidded out, allowing Fittipaldi to win. Regazzoni was again critical of Lauda's tactics; as a result Fittipaldi had now drawn level with him going into the final round at Watkins Glen. Scheckter also had a slender chance of taking the title which disappeared when he failed to finish: it was thus a straight fight between Fittipaldi and Regazzoni. Regazzoni experienced terrible handling problems. Reutemann won, but Fittipaldi's fourth place was enough to bring him his second championship, and McLaren their first.

LAUDA FROM FITTIPALDI

1975

1975 DRIVERS' CHAMPIONSHIP

1.	NIKI LAUDA	64.5
2.	EMERSON FITTIPALDI	45
3.	CARLOS REUTEMANN	37

CONSTRUCTORS' TITLE

1.	FERRARI	72.5
2.	BRABHAM	54
3.	MCLAREN	53

Both Lauda and Regazzoni stayed at Ferrari for 1975, though the latter was now the clear no. 2. Lauda was determined to learn from his mistakes and was focused on winning the title.

Fittipaldi made a strong start, winning in Argentina, and followed it up with a second place in Brazil. Ferrari's start was quieter. Lauda and Regazzoni squeezed into the points in both South American races, but were behind Fittipaldi. However, for the third race of the series, at Kyalami, Ferrari played its ace: the new

312T model. It didn't win in South Africa – that honour went to Scheckter – but it was the crucial turning point. Its teething problems were relatively minor and Lauda enthused over its handling.

Both Ferraris were on the front row in Spain, but Lauda's race was quickly over, following a shunt from Mario Andretti; Regazzoni got caught up in the ensuing chaos. Accidents took out many cars, and Embassy Racing's Rolf Stommelen found himself an unlikely leader. Then, on the 25th lap, his car somersaulted over a barrier, killing four spectators – practice had earlier been disrupted when the Grand Prix Drivers Association lodged a protest about the safety of the circuit, particularly the barriers. The race was halted soon afterwards and half points were awarded. Jochen Mass had been leading, from Ickx and Reutemann.

Lauda makes a charge

Lauda's challenge seriously began at Monaco. He enjoyed a 3-second win over Fittipaldi, and followed it up with more comfortable winning margins over Scheckter and Reutemann in Belgium and Sweden respectively. In the Dutch Grand Prix he had to settle for second place; James Hunt made a brave decision with his Hesketh's tyres, earning him a narrow 1-second win over the Austrian. Hesketh's triumph was short-lived; running a team without a major sponsor was impossible and Hesketh had to quit at the end of the year. Although the name carried on, it wasn't such a force.

Lauda avenged that defeat in France, edging out Hunt. There were only a couple of seconds in it at the finish, but Lauda had dominated, having taken pole and led from the start to lap 54. Silverstone was the next venue, a race which was also curtailed when a downpour caused a dozen cars to slide off. Of the top six finishers, only two were still running when the red flag was waved. Fittipaldi was ahead at the time.

Williams' team in the points

Lauda suffered a puncture in Germany, which meant only a third-place finish, well behind Reutemann and Jacques Laffite in the Williams. Laffite's second place provided a welcome boost to Frank Williams' outfit, striving to keep going at the time. There was more bad weather for the Austrian Grand Prix; Mark Donohue, of the Penske team, lost his life in the warm-up. Vittorio Brambilla won, although he too crashed over the line in his works March. Half points were again awarded for the curtailed event.

Single-minded Lauda takes the title

Regazzoni got the better of his team-mate for only the third time in the season at Monza, the penultimate race. But Lauda's third place was enough to put him out of sight as far as the championship was concerned. He capped it with another victory at Watkins Glen, putting him 19.5 points clear of Fittipaldi.

1975 ended sadly, with the death of Graham Hill and several members of his Embassy Racing team. Hill had run the team for two years, and had announced that he was retiring in order to concentrate on management. In November, he was piloting the light aircraft bringing the team home from Paul Ricard. The plane crashed in fog near Elstree airfield. Hill and several members of the crew died, including the talented young driver Tony Brise.

HUNT: BY ONE POINT

1976

1976 DRIVERS' CHAMPIONSHIP

1.	JAMES HUNT	69
2.	NIKI LAUDA	68
3.	JODY SCHECKTER	49

CONSTRUCTORS' TITLE

1.	FERRARI	83
2.	MCLAREN	74
3.	TYRRELL	71

There was drama on the track this year, and controversy off it. Lauda won in Brazil and South Africa, followed by a second behind team-mate Regazzoni in the US West Grand Prix at Long Beach. Hunt had two retirements, and ran second to Lauda at Kyalami. He was now fronting for McLaren.

The first drama came in the fourth round, at Jarama. Lauda was the early leader, despite recovering from two broken ribs. Hunt overtook him on lap 32 of the 75-lap race, and crossed the line first. He was disqualified after it was discovered that his car was 1.8cm too wide; Lauda was awarded first place, and increased his lead. McLaren appealed, but it took weeks to resolve – in favour of Hunt, whose win was reinstated.

Tyrrell's six-wheel wonder

In Belgium, Lauda and Regazzoni finished well ahead of the field. They were now driving the Ferrari 312T2, a revised version of the car in which they had enjoyed so much success. Tyrrell was giving the six-wheeled P34 its second outing at Zolder; Scheckter brought it into a respectable fourth place. Lauda beat off the challenge of both Jody Scheckter and Patrick Depailler in the six-wheelers in Mexico, but Tyrrell then took first and

ABOVE: *1976 Japanese Grand Prix, Fuji. James Hunt (McLaren M23 Ford) leads away from the front row, in atrocious weather conditions, at the start. Hunt came third to gain the points required to win the Drivers' championship.*

Opposite: Niki Lauda (Ferrari 312 T2) made a dramatic return to racing at the 1976 Italian Grand Prix, Monza, in September. This was only five weeks after his dreadful crash at the Nürburgring.

second in Sweden. However, the innovative P34 never won another race.

Lauda well ahead

Lauda was third in Sweden. Hunt picked up a point in sixth, having retired in both Belgium and Monaco; Lauda's lead stood at 47 points. The next race, in France, was the final round in the first half of the championship. Hunt won at Paul Ricard, while Lauda had his first bad luck of the year, retiring with mechanical trouble. Immediately after this came the news about the result of the Spanish Grand Prix. Lauda's lead was reduced to 27 points.

Since 1968 the championship had been split into halves, with drivers having to derive points from a stipulated number of races in each half. In 1975 Brands Hatch began the second phase, with more controversy. Regazzoni tried to get a flyer at the start, and there was a collision involving Hunt and Lauda. Hunt won the restarted race, with Lauda second. However Hunt had some repairs done to his car before the restart and another inquiry was instigated. It went against Hunt, who was disqualified; maximum points were awarded to Lauda.

Lauda badly burned

1 August 1976 was the day Lauda nearly died. On the second lap at the Nürburgring he cut a corner, ran over a kerb and tried to keep control of the Ferrari, but it went into a full spin. It hit a bank, bouncing back onto the track, where it burst into flames. It was hit by at least two more drivers with Lauda unconscious inside. Others managed to stop, helping until the ambulance arrived. Lauda was not expected to survive, but was soon off the danger list. Amazingly, he reappeared in his Ferrari just five weeks later.

Hunt won the restarted race to put himself within 14 points of Lauda. He was in the points in the two races Lauda missed, taking fourth at Osterreichring and winning at Zandvoort. Lauda returned for Monza on 12 September, his championship lead now down to just 2 points. He was still recovering, but took fourth. As Hunt had retired from the race, he increased his lead.

Hunt stripped of points

McLaren now received the news that Hunt would be stripped of the points from Brands Hatch, but he took back-to-back victories in Canada and the United States.

Lauda was out of the points at Mosport Park, and third at Watkins Glen. Going into the last race, the first Japanese Grand Prix, he led – by 3 points. Conditions were appalling and Lauda returned to the pits after two laps. If Hunt finished in the first three the championship would be his. He led for 61 of the 73 laps, but a tyre change put him back in fifth. He managed to claw his way up to third, and took the title by a single point.

LAUDA REPAYS FERRARI'S TRUST

1977

1977 DRIVERS' CHAMPIONSHIP

1.	NIKI LAUDA	72
2.	JODY SCHECKTER	55
3.	MARIO ANDRETTI	47

CONSTRUCTORS' TITLE

1.	FERRARI	95
2.	LOTUS	62
3.	MCLAREN	60

Enzo Ferrari had doubts about Lauda's future, but gave him the benefit of the doubt and confirmed him as lead driver. His partner for the new season was Carlos Reutemann, now in his sixth Formula One season, with four Grand Prix wins.

Scheckter the Wolf

After three years at Tyrrell, Jody Scheckter decided to join the new Wolf team. This concern became only the third in the event's 28-year history to win at the first outing. Watson, Hunt and Carlos Pace had all led in Argentina, but Scheckter took over five laps from home to win from Pace's Brabham. Watson and Hunt both retired, as did Lauda, and Reutemann flew the Ferrari flag in third.

Ferrari's newcomer did even better at Interlagos, having a 10-second lead over Hunt at the finish. Lauda was third, and went on to win at Kyalami, his first victory since his crash. The race was overshadowed by another tragedy: Tom Pryce crested a rise in his Shadow and hit a marshal who was crossing the track. Pryce had no time to react and both men were killed.

Mario Andretti edged out Lauda by a second at Long Beach, marking a resurgence in Lotus's fortunes. The Lotus 77 had now given way to the 78. Sidepods on either side of the cockpit channelled air under the car to create huge amounts of downforce. 'Ground effect' wasn't a new idea, but the Lotus put the theory into very successful practice.

Lauda mystery in Spain

Lauda was missing from the Spanish Grand Prix at Jarama. There were rumours of an injury, but relations between driver and team were cooling and an argument was possible. Lauda could not afford to miss many races; the Ferrari 312/T2 was no longer dominant. Andretti was on target again in Spain, taking pole and leading for the entire 75 laps. Scheckter gave Wolf its second win of the season at Monaco; Lauda was second once again.

The Lotus eclipsed the Ferrari again at Zolder, but this time it was Andretti's team-mate Gunnar Nilsson who won. Andretti took pole at the next race in Sweden, and led for 67 of the 72 laps, setting the fastest lap. Five cars overhauled him in the dying stages, and he emerged with just 1 point to show for his efforts. The French Grand Prix was one of his good days. John Watson had led virtually all the way, only to have the lead snatched from him on the 80th, final, lap.

Hunt wins at Silverstone

James Hunt had been having an awful time, but improvement began at Silverstone. He was involved in a close tussle with Watson for two-thirds of the race, until

ABOVE: *1977 Monaco Grand Prix, Monte Carlo. Jody Scheckter (Wolf WR1 Ford) powers away at the start of the race. He went on to take the chequered flag in first position.*

OPPOSITE: *Alan Jones (Shadow DN8 Ford) takes his maiden Grand Prix win and the Shadow Racing Team's last at the 1977 Austrian Grand Prix, Osterreichring, Zeltweg.*

the latter's Brabham developed a fuel injection problem. Lauda finished second to Hunt, but even a big improvement wasn't going to put Hunt in the final frame. One of those who failed to finish at Silverstone was Jean-Pierre Jabouille, driving a Renault. Renault, returning to racing after 70 years, was showing off the 1.5-litre RS01, the first turbo-charged car in a Formula One race.

Lauda won only his second race of the year at Hockenheim, then took his fifth second in Austria. That race provided the Shadow team with their only win, for Alan Jones; welcome news after the Kyalami crash. Another win followed for Lauda at Zandvoort, but success was barely masking discontent within the team. Before Monza – where he finished second yet again, this time to Andretti – he made it clear that his days at Ferrari were numbered. The next round, at Watkins Glen, gave Lauda a fourth, and an unassailable lead in the championship. Lauda walked away from Ferrari and signed for Bernie Ecclestone's Brabham team.

Jody Scheckter won the penultimate race in Canada, and Hunt won in Japan. Scheckter was runner-up to Lauda in the championship, but it was Andretti who might easily have got closer. He had scored four wins to Lauda's three, but lost valuable points through a spate of collisions and engine failures.

LOTUS ONE-TWO

1978

1978 DRIVERS' CHAMPIONSHIP

1.	MARIO ANDRETTI	64
2.	RONNIE PETERSON	51
3.	CARLOS REUTEMANN	48

CONSTRUCTORS' TITLE

1.	LOTUS	86
2.	FERRARI	58
3.	BRABHAM	53

With Lauda's move to Brabham, Carlos Reutemann was promoted to Ferrari's no. 1 driver, with Gilles Villeneuve filling the other slot. The team Ferrari had to beat was going to be Lotus. They, too, had a change: Andretti remained, while Gunnar Nilsson left to join the new Arrows team, but cancer prevented him ever contesting a race for Arrows. Ronnie Peterson took over at Lotus; he knew he would be running as second-string to Andretti in 1978, but rejoining Lotus put him back on top, where he belonged.

In Argentina, Andretti led from start to finish. Lauda followed him home, but the Brabham's Alfa Romeo engine was to be a bone of contention for the entire season. Reutemann then won the Brazilian Grand Prix for Ferrari. Back came Lotus at Kyalami, Peterson this time edging out Patrick Depailler's Tyrrell on the last lap. Battle lines were being drawn up between Lotus and Ferrari. Reutemann won from Andretti in the US West Grand Prix at Long Beach, but the next race, Monaco, was the only one in the series in which neither Ferrari nor Lotus registered a single point. Peterson and Villeneuve retired, and Reutemann and Andretti finished out of the points. Patrick Depailler eased home ahead of Lauda.

More improvements by Chapman

That was a turning point for Lotus; it was the last time that both Andretti and Peterson featured in the 78 model. In the following round, at Zolder, Andretti drove the 79, an improved version of an already impressive car. He duly won in Belgium, with Peterson following him home in the old 78 model. They followed this with another one-two in Spain, although both drivers were in 79s.

BELOW: *1978 Spanish Grand Prix, Jarama. Mario Andretti leads team-mate Ronnie Peterson (both Lotus 79 Fords). They finished first and second respectively.*

OPPOSITE: *Carlos Reutemann (Ferrari 312T3) on the way to victory in the 1978 British Grand Prix, Brands Hatch. Although winning four rounds in 1978, he could not prevent an Andretti/Peterson, one-two for Lotus.*

The last round in the first half of the championship season saw Lauda score his first win. His Brabham was fitted with a controversial rear-mounted fan in an attempt to create the kind of downforce that Lotus was working on. Lauda's victory at Anderstorp prompted immediate outcry from rival teams. The innovation was immediately banned by the FIA, although the Swedish result was allowed to stand. The 'fan car' never raced again.

High Court ban for Arrows

Andretti and Peterson had yet another one-two at Paul Ricard. Reutemann won the British Grand Prix at Brands Hatch, helped by the fact that neither Andretti nor Peterson finished. Peterson was performing in an exemplary manner as no. 2 to Andretti. Sometimes he was quicker, but respected the terms of his contract. Andretti crashed out at the start in atrocious conditions in Austria, however, and Peterson came home ahead of Depailler and Villeneuve. The race at Osterreichring was notable for the introduction of the new Arrows car, the A1. The car with which the fledgling team started the season had been banned, the High Court ruling that it was similar enough to the Shadow DN9 to constitute breaking copyright.

Ronnie Peterson dies from crash injuries

Andretti was back on form at Zandvoort, so Peterson reverted to his usual role of second-place man. As the circus moved to Monza, the title was between the two Lotus men. Peterson crashed in the warm-up and had to start the race in the old 78 model, but was then involved in a huge pile-up at the start. Andretti won from Villeneuve in the restarted race, but they were both penalised for jumping the start and Lauda inherited his second win of the year. Andretti was now confirmed as champion, but this was overshadowed: Peterson, a close friend as well as team-mate, had died. His injuries

had not been considered life-threatening, but a fatal embolism developed.

Reutemann scored his fourth win of the year at Watkins Glen on his way to third place in the title race. Villeneuve was a popular winner in the final race of the season in Canada. 1978 was all about Lotus. Peterson, the quickest driver of his time, had fulfilled his contract and finished runner-up as a result. For Andretti, meanwhile, the title was the culmination of a ten-year dream.

SCHECKTER EDGES OUT VILLENEUVE

1979

1979 DRIVERS' CHAMPIONSHIP

1.	JODY SCHECKTER	51
2.	GILLES VILLENEUVE	47
3.	ALAN JONES	40

CONSTRUCTORS' TITLE

1.	FERRARI	113
2.	WILLIAMS	75
3.	LIGIER	61

Ferrari believed that Carlos Reutemann was talented but prone to the occasional expensive mistake. He bore the consequences of failure, and was shown the door. Reutemann asserted that the Lotuses were, quite simply, better cars – and joined the team, where he teamed up with Andretti. Ferrari went into the new season with Jody Scheckter partnering the mercurial Villeneuve.

However, it had a disappointing start: Scheckter

had an accident in Argentina and was only sixth in Brazil. Villeneuve fared little better, with just 2 points for finishing ahead of his team-mate at Interlagos. The star of these opening races was Jacques Laffite and Ligier. Laffite won both, with his team-mate Patrick Depailler following him home in Brazil. Ferrari took one-two in the next two races, at Kyalami and Long Beach, Villeneuve taking the top honours. Ferrari's new car, the 312-T4, was introduced at Kyalami; it wasn't without problems, but they were ironed out as the season went on. It was powerful and reliable, and it needed to be. As the early challenge from Ligier faded, strong opposition was provided by Williams and the turbo-powered Renault.

James Hunt bows out

The Ligier came back in Spain, Depailler leading from start to finish. Lotus took first and second at Jarama, a rare good day for Reutemann and Andretti. The Lotus 80, the successor to the 79, was plagued by problems. Scheckter won the next two races, in Belgium and Monaco: significantly, for Ferrari was considering putting all the team's efforts behind Villeneuve's title bid. More significant was the debut of the Williams FW07, which took the ground-effect principle to a different level. Williams, now backed by Saudi money, was firmly on the way. Monaco also saw James Hunt decide that it was time to call it a day.

Turbo-charged Renault

At the French Grand Prix it was the other looming threat to Ferrari that took centre stage. Renault's perseverance with turbo-charged cars paid off as Jabouille crossed the line first in the RS10. His team-mate Rene Arnoux lost out to Villeneuve for second place in a ding-dong battle,

their cars often touching as they passed each other repeatedly. Villeneuve squeaked home a quarter of a second ahead.

Opposition to Ferrari became more intense. Regazzoni and Arnoux came home first and second at Silverstone. Regazzoni, now 39, brought Williams its maiden victory. His team-mate Alan Jones then built on that success; he had taken pole and led for 38 of the 68 laps in the British Grand Prix before retiring with water-pump trouble. He won four of the next five races, dominating the latter half of the season.

However, Scheckter was in the points in every one of these races: second behind Jones at Zandvoort, and fourth in Germany, Austria and Canada – vital in terms of the championship. As the championship was to be decided on the best four finishes from the first seven races, plus the best four finishes from the final eight rounds, Jones's superb run wasn't going to be enough. By Monza only Scheckter and Villeneuve could take the crown. Team orders were issued; Villeneuve followed them and protected race leader Scheckter, who won the race and with it the championship.

Comfortable first and second for Ferrari

Jones won the penultimate round in Canada. In practice there, Niki Lauda decided he'd had enough after a frustrating season at Brabham. Villeneuve rounded off his season with a win in the US East Grand Prix at Watkins Glen, putting him 4 points behind Scheckter in the final table. Ferrari had emulated Lotus's 1978 achievement, taking first and second in the drivers' championship and comfortably winning the Constructors' title (the points system for the latter changed in 1979 to include each car from a constructor that finished in the top six in any race).

A CLEAN SWEEP FOR WILLIAMS

1980

1980 DRIVERS' CHAMPIONSHIP

1.	ALAN JONES	67
2.	NELSON PIQUET	54
3.	CARLOS REUTEMANN	42

CONSTRUCTORS' TITLE

1.	WILLIAMS	120
2.	LIGIER	66
3.	BRABHAM	55

Alan Jones featured in Williams' new campaign: predictably, after his performances in 1979. Less predictable was the rise of Nelson Piquet, Brabham's second driver behind Lauda; following Lauda's departure he became Brabham's number one. 1979 had been his first full season. Brabham reverted to Ford power in the BT49, and that, together with Piquet's skill, gave Brabham its best season for a decade.

The first race was in Argentina; Jones won from Piquet and third was Keke Rosberg who had signed with Fittipaldi for 1979. In Brazil and South Africa, Rene Arnoux scored back-to-back wins in the new Renault, the RE20. Piquet scored his first win in the US West Grand Prix at Long Beach; he took pole, led from laps 1 to 80 and set the fastest lap. This race was marred by a career-ending accident for Clay Regazzoni. He had been replaced at Williams by Carlos Reutemann and had rejoined Ensign. The throttle of his car jammed open and he hit a concrete wall. He survived, but was confined to a wheelchair. Coming fifth at Long Beach was Jody Scheckter in the latest Ferrari, the 312-T5. The 2 points were to be his season total, and Villeneuve only gained 6 – a turn in Ferrari's fortunes.

Didier Pironi headed the rostrum in the Belgian Grand Prix at Zolder. He joined the Ligier team for the 1980 campaign after two successful Formula One seasons with Tyrrell. Jacques Laffite was the team leader but Pironi matched him throughout the season; 2

BELOW: *Alan Jones pictured in the cockpit of his Williams FW07B-Ford Cosworth, prior to the 1980 Canadian Grand Prix, Montreal. He clinched a win thanks to a 60-second penalty against Pironi for jumping the start.*

OPPOSITE: *1979 Austrian Grand Prix, Osterreichring, Zeltweg. Gilles Villeneuve (Ferrari 312T4) leads Alan Jones (Williams FW07 Ford) and Niki Lauda (Brabham BT48 Alfa Romeo) at the start.*

points separated them by the end, though they both finished well adrift of Jones and Piquet.

Arnoux the new French talent

Williams took the honours in the next three races. Reutemann had his first success at Monaco, after Pironi crashed. Then Jones won the French and British Grands Prix to give him three victories plus a second and third from the first eight races. The Williams team was performing well, but there was still a threat from the Ligiers, Arnoux's Renault and, particularly, Piquet in the Brabham.

Spanish Grand Prix declared void

In-fighting between FISA and FOCA (the governing body and the constructors' association) meant the Spanish Grand Prix – won by Jones – was declared void for championship purposes. Next came the German Grand Prix, and Jones suffered a puncture while leading, allowing Laffite to come through and give Ligier their second success. Reutemann took second, while Jones came third. Piquet was fourth: out of the nine races so far, he had been in the points seven times, and had retired in Brazil and Belgium. The sport's latest tragedy came in practice: Patrick Depailler was killed after a crash in his Alfa Romeo.

Piquet challenging hard for Brabham

In the Austrian Grand Prix, Jabouille in the Renault held off Williams, leading from the halfway mark and

crossing the line just ahead of Jones. Reutemann took third. With four races to go, Jones had an 11-point lead. At Zandvoort Arnoux took pole but Jones shot into a first-lap lead; he then had to pit with damaged bodywork and was out of the points. Piquet won, bringing him to within 2 points of Jones, whose slender advantage became a 1-point deficit after Monza. Piquet took up the running on lap 4 and held it to the end. Jones was second.

Piquet took pole in Montreal, with Jones in the other front row spot. Both hurtled out of the blocks and neither backed off as they approached the first corner; there was a pileup. Jones led in the restart, but was passed by Piquet on the third lap. On the 24th, Piquet's engine blew. Jones followed Pironi home, but he received a 60-second penalty for jumping the start and Jones had maximum points. Piquet couldn't overhaul him, even if he won in the final race at Watkins Glen. In fact Jones won, with team-mate Reutemann second. Williams had become the latest team to celebrate a clean sweep of the honours, following Lotus in 1978 and Ferrari in 1979.

BELOW: *Nelson Piquet (Brabham BT49C Ford), on the way to winning the 1981 German Grand Prix, Hockenheim. This was his last win of the season – therefore the points gained were vitally important to Piquet's quest for the title.*

OPPOSITE: *Nigel Mansell made the first of many podium appearances by coming third at the 1981 Monaco Grand Prix, Monte Carlo.*

BRABHAM AND PIQUET'S CHALLENGE

1981

1981 DRIVERS' CHAMPIONSHIP

1.	NELSON PIQUET	50
2.	CARLOS REUTEMANN	49
3.	ALAN JONES	46

CONSTRUCTORS' TITLE

1.	WILLIAMS	95
2.	BRABHAM	61
3.	RENAULT	54

FISA and FOCA were in dispute again, over the decision to ban side skirts for the new season. The ruling had huge implications for the 'ground effect' cars, which were predominantly British, and Lotus had to field the old 87 model as a result. Jones and Reutemann were still at Williams, and Piquet remained at Brabham. Laffite continued as Ligier's no. 1, with the team reverting to Matra power.

Reutemann in team orders row

Jones and Reutemann began the season at Long Beach the way they had finished in 1980. When Jones took the lead from his team-mate on lap 32, the race was all but over, because Reutemann's contract specified that he could only go for a win if he was 7 seconds ahead of Jones; otherwise he had to let him through. This fell apart in Brazil. Reutemann led the whole way but was signalled to let second-placed Jones pass with four laps to go; he disregarded the order and won. There was a huge row afterwards and Reutemann's race fee was withheld; the relationship between the two drivers broke down.

Mansell's first podium finish

In Argentina and San Marino Piquet scored successive victories. In Buenos Aires he had led the whole way and won by nearly half a minute from Reutemann. Villeneuve took pole and led in the early stages at Imola, but Piquet came through to win from Patrese and Reutemann. Jones went off the track at Zolder as he tried to impose himself on Reutemann; with Jones out of contention his team-mate went on to win the

rain-shortened race. Nigel Mansell was third in his Lotus, his first podium finish in his first full season in Formula One.

Jones was leading at Monaco when a fuel feed problem hampered him with just four laps to go. Villeneuve came through, giving Ferrari their first win for two years. He then crossed the line first in a tight finish in Spain. Laffite, Watson, Reutemann and de Angelis were hot on his heels: less than 1.5 seconds separated all five.

Dennis and Barnard in control at McLaren

Like Mansell, another future champion had his first taste of success in 1981. Alain Prost did even better, winning at Dijon two seconds ahead of Watson's McLaren.

Watson came out on top at Silverstone in a win for the MP4 – an early sign of the huge success that McLaren would enjoy during the 1980s. Reutemann's second place at Silverstone gave him a 17-point lead, but the man who had been trying to win the title for nine years could only score 2 points in the next three races, a fifth in Austria sandwiched between retirements at Hockenheim and Zandvoort. In Germany Piquet won his third race of the year, taking the lead from Jones, who had fuel feed problems again. Laffite became the year's seventh different winner when he won from

A TRAGIC YEAR

1982

1982 DRIVERS' CHAMPIONSHIP

1.	KEKE ROSBERG	44
2.	DIDIER PIRONI	39
	JOHN WATSON	39

CONSTRUCTORS' TITLE

1.	FERRARI	74
2.	MCLAREN	69
3.	RENAULT	62

Williams was obviously a team on the up, but both Jones and Reutemann decided to call it a day: Jones at the end of 1981 and Reutemann after the 1982 opener in South Africa. Williams signed Keke Rosberg, who had experienced a disastrous couple of years with Fittipaldi. The only potential problem at Williams was that the team was still running the normally-aspirated V-8 Cosworth engine, bucking the turbo trend.

Piquet and Rosberg disqualified

Prost recovered from a puncture to win the South African Grand Prix. Reutemann came second, in his last completed race for Williams, and Rosberg was fifth. Prost also won in Brazil: an inherited victory after Piquet and Rosberg were disqualified for running underweight cars.

After being out of the sport for two years, Niki Lauda returned to Formula One in 1982. His first win came at Long Beach, his third race. Andrea de Cesaris took pole and led until the 14th lap, when an accident put him out of the race; Lauda remained in front for the remaining 60 laps, with Rosberg second. Villeneuve crossed the line third, but his Ferrari was found to have an illegal wing and Patrese moved up from fourth to take the 4 points.

Villeneuve killed in practice

The Brazilian disqualifications led to a mass withdrawal from the San Marino race by the FOCA teams. There were only 14 starters, and just 5 finishers. The lead changed hands several times between Villeneuve and Pironi's Ferraris, and Arnoux in the Renault. He retired with engine trouble, and Pironi passed Villeneuve on the last lap to win. This infuriated Villeneuve, who vowed not to speak to him again. Tragically, this feud lasted just two weeks as Villeneuve was killed in practice

Arnoux and Piquet in Austria. Piquet was second behind Prost at Zandvoort, giving him 19 points for the three races and edging him ahead of Reutemann with three races to go.

Piquet by a single point

Prost joined Piquet with three wins by leading all the way at Monza. Jones and Reutemann finished behind him; Piquet picked up just 1 point in sixth. Laffite won in Montreal from tenth place on the grid; Piquet scored 2 points in fifth, while Reutemann was out of the top six.

Going into the final round Reutemann still led with 49 points, despite the latter half of the season. Piquet was one behind, with Laffite on 43. In Nevada, Reutemann was superb in practice and took pole; in the race itself, however, he put in a lacklustre performance and finished eighth. Laffite, sixth, scored 1 point, and was overhauled by Jones, who stormed to victory. Piquet's fifth place proved decisive: it was enough to give him his first championship by a single point from Reutemann.

for the Belgian Grand Prix at Zolder. There Rosberg had victory in his sights when he locked his brakes, and John Watson came through.

At Monaco the lead changed hands four times in the last three laps, and Riccardo Patrese claimed his first Formula One win, giving Brabham their first win of the season. Watson won a restarted race at Detroit, after which another tragedy occurred at Montreal: Riccardo Paletti was killed in a start-line accident when his Osella collided with Pironi's Ferrari. At the restart Mansell was involved in a nasty spill, his car overshooting Bruno Giacomelli's Alfa. Piquet and Patrese made it a one-two for Brabham. Their cars were differently powered: Piquet had the BMW turbo, Patrese the normally-aspirated Cosworth engine.

Pironi's career over

The Dutch Grand Prix was dominated by Pironi, who next took second at Brands Hatch behind Lauda. After a third at Paul Ricard, he led the championship on 39 points, 9 clear of his nearest rival. Hockenheim was next, and the dreadful season got worse: Pironi broke both legs in a crash during practice, ending his career. Patrick Tambay, also driving for Ferrari, won.

Lotus was now in decline. The new 91 model performed well on fast circuits, but struggled against the turbos. The Osterreichring was one of the few tracks which suited it, and Elio de Angelis won narrowly from Rosberg, but only after much of the turbo-powered opposition was out of the race. After a string of finishes in the points, Rosberg finally scored a win in the Swiss Grand Prix – held at Dijon because of Switzerland's ban on circuit racing. He passed Prost, who had gearbox trouble, on the last lap.

Only one win for champion Rosberg

At Monza, Arnoux led from start to finish and Rosberg finished out of the points, while Watson picked up 3 in fourth place. Rosberg went into the final round at Caesar's Palace with 42 points from his nine finishes. Watson, on 33, needed a win to have a chance of snatching the title but came second, behind Alboreto's Tyrrell. Rosberg finished fifth, taking the crown by 5 points. He had won only once, but his consistent run of ten finishes was the decisive factor.

BELOW: *Alain Prost leading his team-mate Rene Arnoux (both Renault RE30B), at the 1982 South African Grand Prix, Kyalami. They finished in first and third positions respectively.*

OPPOSITE: *1982 Detroit Grand Prix, Detroit, USA. Eddie Cheever (Ligier JS17B-Matra), leads Rene Arnoux (Renault RE30B) and Niki Lauda (McLaren MP4/1B-Ford Cosworth), into a hairpin, on the way to second place.*

PIQUET AND PROST HEAD-TO-HEAD

1983

1983 DRIVERS' CHAMPIONSHIP

1.	NELSON PIQUET	59
2.	ALAIN PROST	57
3.	RENE ARNOUX	49

CONSTRUCTORS' TITLE

1.	FERRARI	89
2.	RENAULT	79
3.	BRABHAM	72

Nelson Piquet remained at Brabham for 1983, with Patrese. The famous Cosworth engine, with over 150 wins to its credit, finally had to give way as one by one the teams turned to turbo power. Brabham had hedged its bets by running a turbo and normally-aspirated car side by side in 1982. They concentrated on the turbo in 1983.

Williams wait for Honda

Piquet won the opening race in Brazil. Williams had an unfortunate start: Rosberg crossed the line second but was disqualified for receiving a push start in the pits. The team had done an engine deal with Honda, but was continuing with Ford until the new unit was ready. Lauda had been third in Brazil, but came home second in a McLaren one-two at Long Beach, behind Watson. Prost won his sixth race for Renault at Paul Ricard, and followed it up with a second behind Tambay at Imola. It was the beginning of a consistent run which would put the title within his grasp.

Keke Rosberg, driving a flat-bottomed version of the FW08 to comply with the new regulations, scored a win over Piquet and Prost at Monaco. Prost had his third pole and second win of the year at Spa. The seventh round was at Detroit, and provided a landmark in sports history: Michele Alboreto's win in his Tyrrell was the 155th – and last – for the famous Cosworth engine, which had made its debut in 1967. Montreal saw Rene Arnoux score his first win for Ferrari since his move from Renault, and Eddie Cheever, his replacement, was behind him.

Mansell gets competitive

Nigel Mansell finally got his hands on the Renault-turbo car at Silverstone. After a dismal beginning to the season, he finished fourth, some 40 seconds behind race winner Prost. Arnoux kept up his title hopes by winning at Hockenheim. It had been a Ferrari front row, with Arnoux's team-mate Tambay on pole and Arnoux should have let Tambay have a clear run – he trailed Tambay by 12 points in the championship. As it was, Tambay retired with engine trouble. Despite that, the Ferraris were now enjoying a good run. Tambay was on pole again in Austria, and led for the first 21 laps. After an oil problem put him out, his team-mate took over. Arnoux held the lead until 6 laps from home, when Prost overtook. They finished in that order, with Piquet third. Ferrari then had a one-two at Zandvoort. Piquet had led up to lap 41, when an incident involving Prost

put them both out. Arnoux took over and won by 20 seconds from Tambay.

Prost's four wins had helped him to an 8-point advantage over Arnoux, with Piquet and Tambay a further 6 points behind, but Monza was disastrous for Prost. His turbo went at the halfway mark, while Piquet, Arnoux and Tambay finished first, second and fourth respectively. Prost was second in the European Grand Prix, staged at Brands Hatch. But Piquet dominated this race, too, crossing the line 7 seconds ahead.

Piquet overhauls Prost for second title

Neither Ferrari was in the points, so it was a straight fight between Prost and Piquet in the final round, Prost's lead now down to 2 points. Piquet was on the front row, with Tambay on pole. Piquet got the better start and led for the first 59 laps of the 77-lap race, but Prost could only qualify fifth and his race ended with a turbo failure on the 35th lap. He now had to hope that Piquet finished no better than fifth. Though Piquet did relinquish the lead, being passed by both Patrese and de Cesaris, his 4 points for third place were enough to give him his second title. Prost was criticised for letting the championship slip from his grasp, one of the factors leading to a parting of the ways between him and Renault.

The opening race was in Brazil. Elio de Angelis took pole in the Lotus-Renault, but Alboreto, beside him on the front row, got the better start. Lauda took over in front; when his car succumbed to an electrical fault, the race turned into a fight between Prost and Derek Warwick, who had replaced him at Renault. Warwick's suspension gave out and Prost scored the first in a succession of McLaren successes.

First points for Senna

At Kyalami, Prost and Lauda qualified in only fifth and eighth places respectively, but had a one-two success, with Lauda more than a minute clear of Prost. Warwick was third, more than a lap behind. Here, gaining his first championship point in sixth, was Ayrton Senna. He

BELOW: Ayrton Senna (Toleman Hart) finished in second position at the rain-affected 1984 Monaco Grand Prix. This was the Brazilian's first podium finish.

OPPOSITE: Action from the 1983 Brazilian Grand Prix, Rio de Janeiro. Nelson Piquet (Brabham BT52 BMW) won the opening race of the 1983 season. His next win was six months later at Monza in Italy.

1984

McLaren, with Lauda and Prost

1984 Drivers' Championship

1.	Niki Lauda	72
2.	Alain Prost	71.5
3.	Elio De Angelis	34

Constructors' Title

1.	McLaren	143.5
2.	Ferrari	57.5
3.	Lotus	47

Towards the end of 1983, when Piquet and Prost were battling for the title, McLaren drivers Watson and Lauda gave their new TAG Porsche engine a quiet start. Lauda stayed with the team and was joined by Prost. McLaren was ready: there was an impressive new turbo unit fitted to the MP4, and two top drivers.

had tested for both Williams and McLaren but decided that he was better off being a bigger fish in a smaller pond, and joined Toleman.

Mansell loses grip

Both Lauda and Prost retired at Zolder, one of just two 1984 races when neither finished in the points. Alboreto took pole and enjoyed a start-to-finish victory. Piquet had suffered three retirements in a row, and had another at Imola: he took pole, but his turbo failed 12 laps from the line when he was second. Prost won, having led for the entire distance. Lauda's engine blew in the early stages at San Marino, but he won the French Grand Prix at Dijon. Second was Patrick Tambay, who, along with Warwick, made up Renault's partnership for 1984. Nigel Mansell scored his first points of the year by finishing third; he had stayed with Lotus. Monaco was run in torrential rain. Mansell should have won; he passed Prost to take the lead, but lost grip on the painted white lines and slid into the Armco; frustratingly, the race was stopped shortly after. Prost was ahead again by then and was declared the winner. Senna drove brilliantly: ninth on the opening lap, he was within 8 seconds of Prost when the race was halted.

Piquet finally had some luck in Montreal, relegating the McLarens to the minor placings. He repeated this at Detroit, in a race that was restarted after a first-lap shunt. Martin Brundle finished within a second of him, but his achievement was short-lived: he was disqualified for a weight irregularity in his Tyrrell. In Dallas, Mansell and de Angelis occupied the front row, the first time Lotus had done so for six years. Mansell led up to halfway, when Rosberg passed him in the

ABOVE: *Although winning the 1984 Portuguese Grand Prix, Estoril, Alain Prost (McLaren MP4/2 TAG Porsche) could only clinch second place in the championship. (Lauda came second in the race, which was enough to edge out his team-mate.)*

OPPOSITE: *Keke Rosberg (Williams FW10 Honda) whose pole position time at the 1985 British Grand Prix, Silverstone, was the fastest ever qualifying lap.*

Williams-Honda. Rosberg went on to win, while Mansell had transmission failure on the last lap. He fainted while he pushed his car to the line, but earned a point – he was classified sixth. Lauda won at Brands Hatch, leading after Prost hit gearbox trouble. At Hockenheim it was Prost's turn to benefit from others' misfortune: he headed Lauda home after De Angelis and Piquet both fell by the wayside.

Lauda joins the exclusive club

In Austria the entire field was made up of turbo-powered cars for the first time. Lauda crossed the line 24 seconds ahead of Piquet; Prost spun off. Zandvoort saw the third McLaren one-two of the year. Piquet was again first away, but retired on the tenth lap with an oil leak. Prost took over and won, 10 seconds ahead of Lauda.

Lauda won again at Monza, and Prost won the European Grand Prix at the new Nürburgring. Prost had retired in Italy, and Lauda took 3 points for fourth in Germany. The decider was at Estoril, and Lauda led Prost 66 to 62.5. Prost took the lead and held on to win, but Lauda moved through to finish second. Prost had won seven races to Lauda's five, but Lauda had a half-point advantage. He joined Fangio, Brabham and Stewart as one of the few three-times winners.

FIRST TITLE FOR PROST

1985

1985 DRIVERS' CHAMPIONSHIP

1.	ALAIN PROST	73
2.	MICHELE ALBORETO	53
3.	KEKE ROSBERG	40

CONSTRUCTORS' TITLE

1.	McLAREN	90
2.	FERRARI	82
3.	WILLIAMS	71

Lauda stayed with McLaren for one more season, alongside Prost. At Williams, Rosberg had a new no. 2, Nigel Mansell moving from Lotus to replace Laffite.

Prost won the opener in Brazil from sixth on the grid. Alboreto and Rosberg had occupied the front row; both had spells in the lead but Alboreto finished in second place, while Rosberg went out early with a failed turbo. Mansell also retired in Brazil, but he was in the points at Estoril. He had to start in the pit lane because of a bump on the warm-up lap, but recovered and finished fifth. Ayrton Senna won; he had joined Lotus to replace Mansell. Senna took the first pole of his career and led all the way in terrible conditions, finishing more than a minute clear of Alboreto.

It ought to have been two in a row for Senna at Imola, where he took pole and led for most of the 60-lap race, but he ran out of fuel. Prost crossed the line first, only to be disqualified after his McLaren was found to be underweight. Elio de Angelis profited, gaining only his second win in six years of Formula One. Senna was quickest in Monaco, and led until his engine failed on lap 13. Prost then traded the lead with Alboreto for 20 laps, before establishing an advantage that he held to the line.

Rosberg sets 160mph record

Alboreto ended a barren spell for Ferrari at Montreal; Stefan Johansson followed him home, giving Ferrari their first one-two since Zandvoort two years earlier. Both drivers were on the podium in Detroit, though well adrift of winner Keke Rosberg. Both he and Mansell had experienced handling problems with the Williams-Honda, but things improved with the arrival of the new Honda engine. It looked good for Williams at Paul Ricard, too. Mansell was out after a 200mph spill in practice, but Rosberg took pole. He led early on, and set the fastest lap. He had to settle for six points; Piquet passed him on the 11th lap and kept the lead to the end. Rosberg was on pole again at Silverstone, becoming the first man to lap at more than 160mph in a Grand Prix. Both he and Mansell, who hadn't really recovered from his crash, had to retire; they needed more reliability. Senna led for 57 of the 65 laps, when he ran out of fuel. Prost took over and won, a lap ahead of Alboreto and Laffite.

Alboreto qualified eighth at the Nürburgring, but led for the last 20 laps, winning from Prost after Rosberg and Senna retired. He now headed the championship on 46 points, 5 ahead of Prost, who brought the two drivers level by winning in Austria, with Alboreto third. Lauda led in the middle part of the race,

then had his eighth retirement in ten races; he was about to retire for good. He had the 25th and final win of his illustrious career at Zandvoort.

Prost, second in Holland, went one better at Monza; Alboreto's season dried up. The Williams-Honda was now more reliable and Mansell and Rosberg were second and fourth at Spa. Senna won his second Grand Prix there, giving him five podium finishes in the five races he'd completed. Prost was third, racking up the points.

First win in 72 outings for Mansell

The European Grand Prix was at Brands Hatch. It was Nigel Mansell's 72nd Grand Prix and he finally won; Rosberg gave Williams further cause for optimism by coming third. He recovered from a spat with the fiercely competitive Senna on lap 7, the two cars touching; Senna finished second. Prost picked up 3 points for fourth place. He now had 72 points from the required 11 finishes, becoming the first Frenchman to win the title.

Williams dominated the last two rounds. Mansell had another success after taking pole at Kyalami; Rosberg, second that day, won in Adelaide. The Williams-Honda was obviously a car with a future, and Senna could be a threat in the right machine. There would be no comfortable 20-point margin for Prost and McLaren the next season.

THE LAST OF THE ALL-POWERFUL TURBOS

1986

1986 DRIVERS' CHAMPIONSHIP

1.	ALAIN PROST	72
2.	NIGEL MANSELL	70
3.	NELSON PIQUET	69

CONSTRUCTORS' TITLE

1.	WILLIAMS	141
2.	MCLAREN	96
3.	JPS/LOTUS	48

1986 was the last full year in which the unfettered turbo engines were allowed to dominate Formula One. Prost, Mansell and Senna remained with their teams from 1985. Piquet had been with Bernie Ecclestone's Brabham team since 1978, but teamed up with Mansell at Williams, the team with the car of the year.

Senna on pole eight times

Senna took pole in Brazil, and he, Piquet and Prost all

enjoyed time in front. Piquet took over and held on to win; Prost retired, and an accident meant that Mansell's race was over before it started. Senna was on pole again in Spain and won by a whisker from Mansell, his third Grand Prix victory. At Imola he took his third successive pole, an honour he would hold in eight of the sixteen races though he won only twice. His Lotus-Renault was up against the formidable Williams and McLaren cars, but he showed his worth.

He retired at Imola, and Prost scored his first win of the year. Piquet, the only other man to complete the distance, came in second. Prost also won at Monaco; his McLaren team-mate Rosberg followed him home. Rosberg soon discovered that he had left Williams just as they were coming up with a superb car.

Mansell dominates

Mansell won four of the next five races, in Belgium, Canada, France and Britain; Piquet got within six seconds of him at Brands Hatch. In the middle of this winning streak, Senna came out on top in Detroit, a race where the lead changed several times. The next two races saw a return to Hockenheim for the German Grand Prix and a new venue, Hungary's Hungaroring, providing Williams with their sixth and seventh wins of the season, but this time it was Piquet who crossed the line first. Senna was second both times. The inaugural race in Hungary was the first time Formula One had gone beyond the Iron Curtain. Piquet and Senna traded the lead, surprisingly – overtaking opportunities were limited on the winding circuit, later voted Course of the Year.

Senna, Mansell and Piquet all retired in Austria. Prost didn't, and won. Some of the other drivers had a chance to get in the frame: the Ferraris of Alboreto and Johansson, together with the Lolas of Jones and Tambay, followed Prost home, though none got to within a lap of him. Teo Fabi took pole at Monza, as he had in Austria. His BMW-engined Benetton had awesome power in short bursts, but he regularly failed to finish. This was another one-two for Williams, Piquet taking the flag 10 seconds ahead of Mansell, who hit back at Estoril: his fifth win of the season.

Mansell's tyre agony

The penultimate round saw a return to Mexico. Gerhard Berger got his first Grand Prix success as the Benetton lasted the full distance. Benetton had taken over the Toleman team only this year; the change from being sponsors to running a team had thus brought an early reward.

ABOVE: *The inaugural Hungarian Grand Prix was staged at the Hungaroring, Budapest in 1986. It was won by Nelson Piquet (Williams FW11 Honda), seen here during the race.*

OPPOSITE: *1986 German Grand Prix, Hockenheim. Alain Prost (McLaren MP4/2C TAG Porsche) ran out of fuel on the last lap and dropped from third to sixth position, as he pushed his car across the finish line.*

Mansell was in the box seat going into the final race at Adelaide. Third place would be enough to give him the title, whatever happened, but a tyre on his Williams blew on lap 63 and his race ended. Piquet lost ground, making a precautionary pit stop, and Prost came through to take the race and the title, the first to win successive championships since Brabham in 1959–60. Piquet and Mansell had been scoring off each other all season, splitting points, making Williams victims of their own success; the car had won nine of the sixteen races and took the constructors' title by a mile. But Prost had won four races and been consistent; he added to his reputation for being the most complete driver of his time.

1986 also had its share of tragedy. Elio de Angelis was killed testing his Brabham at Paul Ricard; a crash at Brands Hatch ended Jacques Laffite's career. Off the track Frank Williams was involved in a car crash which confined him to a wheelchair.

MANSELL EDGED OUT BY PIQUET

1987 DRIVERS' CHAMPIONSHIP

1.	NELSON PIQUET	73
2.	NIGEL MANSELL	61
3.	AYRTON SENNA	57

CONSTRUCTORS' TITLE

1.	WILLIAMS	137
2.	McLAREN	76
3.	LOTUS	64

ABOVE: *Alain Prost (McLaren MP4/3 TAG Porsche) leads Nelson Piquet and Nigel Mansell (both Williams FW11B Hondas) into Copse at the start of the 1987 British Grand Prix, Silverstone.*

OPPOSITE: *Ayrton Senna (McLaren Honda) celebrates on the podium after winning the 1988 Japanese Grand Prix, Suzuka. The result also delivered him the championship.*

The 1987 season was almost a rerun of the year before. Prost, Senna, Piquet and Mansell were the main focus.

Prost, in an all-new car, got off to a good start, winning two of the first three races and surprising everybody; Piquet and Mansell were still using the tried and tested Williams-Honda. They were quickest in practice in Brazil, but Prost won from Piquet. It was a Williams front row in Belgium, too. Early on there was a huge shunt involving both Tyrrells, and Senna and Mansell's cars touched in the restart; both went off. Piquet profited briefly, but he, too, failed to finish and

Prost went on to win. This was his 27th win, equalling Jackie Stewart's record.

Japan's Nakajima and Honda join Lotus

Between these Prost victories Mansell won at Imola. Prost's alternator failed, while Piquet had been involved in a crash in practice. Senna took pole and led early on, but Mansell took over, winning easily. Senna won the next two, Monaco and Detroit. It was his third year at Lotus and he saw it as a make-or-break season. Lotus had switched to Honda power; Renault had withdrawn from Formula One and Lotus clinched the Honda deal by taking on Satoru Nakajima, Japan's first Formula One driver. Senna's wins in Monte Carlo and the United States were not without some good fortune. At Monaco he inherited the lead from Mansell, who retired on lap 29. Mansell had pit-lane trouble while leading in Detroit, and Senna took advantage. Mansell had scored just 2 points from three races, all of which he might have won.

Mansell's heroics at Stowe

In France Mansell was on pole again and eased home 8 seconds ahead of team-mate Piquet. It was another one-two for Williams at Silverstone. Mansell won, passing Piquet on the 63rd lap out of 65 at Stowe. He'd been almost half a minute down on Piquet, following an unscheduled wheel change. He took his sixth pole of the year at Hockenheim, but a seized engine ended his hopes. The McLaren team had ironed out a technical problem that blighted the cars in the two previous races and the race looked to be going Prost's way when his alternator failed 5 laps from home. Piquet, who had seemed resigned to his sixth second place of the year, came through for his first win instead.

Senna was third at Hockenheim, though a lap down. Around this time he decided that Lotus wasn't competitive enough, and began negotiations with McLaren. He and Piquet fought for top spot in Hungary; Piquet won, taking the lead from Mansell 6 laps from the line. Mansell had led for 70 laps, then lost a wheel nut. Senna was second, Prost third. However, Mansell won from Piquet in Austria; only the Williams duo went the full distance. By this point Senna, on 43 points, was still 4 ahead of Mansell – but couldn't see his Lotus reproducing the form of Monaco and Detroit in the final races. Prost had 31; Piquet led with 54 points and extended this by winning at Monza. Senna may have been unhappy with his Lotus but drove a superb race, finishing second.

Derek Warwick's 160mph smash

Prost won for a record-breaking 28th time at Estoril, but Piquet's third place was critical. Senna and Mansell failed to score. Mansell won in Spain and Mexico, putting himself back in contention. He led all the way at Jerez, while he came out on top in Mexico on aggregate; the race was split into two halves as the result of Derek Warwick going into the tyre wall at 160mph. Neither Prost nor Senna finished, and their title hopes were over. The championship was decided in practice for Suzuka: Mansell went off and was ruled out of the race.

Piquet's honour

The honour was now Piquet's, whatever happened in the last two rounds. He failed to score – both were won by Gerhard Berger for Ferrari, and Senna crossed the line second in each, but was disqualified at Adelaide over a brake irregularity. This cost him second place in the championship, but he still had 57 points to put him third behind the Williams pair.

PROST AND SENNA

1988 DRIVERS' CHAMPIONSHIP

1.	AYRTON SENNA	90
2.	ALAIN PROST	87
3.	GERHARD BERGER	41

CONSTRUCTORS' TITLE

1.	MCLAREN	199
2.	FERRARI	65
3.	BENETTON	46

By the end of 1987, it was known that Senna was joining Prost at McLaren. Senna took pole in Brazil but gestured that he had a gear selection problem and was forced to start from the pit lane; he cut his way through to lie second behind Prost. He was disqualified for switching cars after the light had gone green.

Senna slip lets Prost in at Monaco

At Imola Senna won from Prost, though there was a problem with his car which ground to a halt just over the line. At Monaco he made an expensive mistake, hitting the Armco before the tunnel. He had been well clear of Prost, who moved into the lead, with Ferrari's Berger and Alboreto following him home. The Ferraris continued well in Mexico, Berger and Alboreto finishing third and fourth; McLaren were dominant again, however. The pair occupied the front row and Prost led the whole way. In Canada, Prost led from his team-mate until the 19th lap; Senna then took over for the remaining 50. Detroit saw Senna take his sixth successive pole, equalling a record set by Moss and Lauda. The race was another McLaren procession, although there was a gap of some 40 seconds between Senna and second-placed Prost.

Berger takes pole at Silverstone

Prost broke Senna's run by taking pole at Paul Ricard. He set the pace, then lost the lead to Senna when he came into the pits with tyre trouble, re-emerging 3 seconds behind his team-mate. He regained the lead at the three-quarter distance. At Silverstone Gerhard Berger took pole, with Alboreto's Ferrari beside him on the front row, and led for 13 laps. It was the halfway

ABOVE: *1988 Italian Grand Prix, Monza. Gerhard Berger won the race in his Ferrari F187/88C, the only driver, other than Senna or Prost, to win that year.*

OPPOSITE: *1989 Brazilian Grand Prix, Jacarepagua, Rio de Janeiro. Ayrton Senna (McLaren MP4/5 Honda) in the pits having a new front wing fitted after the original one was lost in a collision with Berger and Patrese at the start.*

mark in the championship and the first time that anyone other than Prost or Senna had led at any stage in any race. Senna passed him on lap 13 and held the lead to the end. Mansell finally had some success in his Williams-Judd by finishing second. Prost retired with handling problems, declaring the rain-soaked track a safety risk. He led Senna by 54 points to 48, and was criticised in some quarters for his withdrawal. Conditions were similar at Hockenheim but he went the distance, finishing second behind Senna, who led all the way. His lead was cut to 3 points.

Two weeks later, at the Hungaroring, the result was just the same, although this was a much closer affair, Senna edging Prost out by half a second. Senna had yet another start-to-finish win at Spa. It was his fourth in a row, and seventh of the season. This put him ahead of Prost for the first time: 75 to 72. There were five rounds to go.

Ferrari break McLaren's hold

The 12th race of the year broke McLaren's stranglehold. All looked well as Senna took a record-breaking ninth pole and led for 49 of the 51 laps. He then hit Jean-Louis Schlesser's Williams, and his race was over. Prost had retired, and the way was left clear for a Ferrari one-two, Berger heading Alboreto home. McLaren came back at Estoril. Running level with each other, Prost and Senna vied to gain the upper hand on the first lap, coming close to touching. Prost pressed on to take the advantage, and the race; Senna trailed home sixth. Prost won again in Spain. He and Senna were next to each other on the front row; Prost got his nose in front and led all the way. Senna, getting a negative reading from his fuel gauge, eased his car home in fourth.

The best 11 finishes counted towards the title, which favoured Senna. After Suzuka, Prost had another 6 points, while Senna's win enabled him to swap 9 points for the single one gained in Portugal. The title was now his. He had been left at the start, and was 14th by the time his engine caught. Prost was then leading, with clear track in front of him. Senna's charge through the field was extraordinary and he took a decisive lead on lap 27. Prost won the final, academic race in Australia, followed home by the new world champion.

ANOTHER FOR PROST

1989

1989 DRIVERS' CHAMPIONSHIP

1.	ALAIN PROST	76
2.	AYRTON SENNA	60
3.	RICCARDO PATRESE	40

CONSTRUCTORS' TITLE

1.	MCLAREN	141
2.	WILLIAMS	77
3.	FERRARI	59

The unrest between Senna and Prost turned to open hostility in 1989, the start of the new non-turbo era. Both remained with McLaren, but it became clear that they could not continue in the same team for long.

As early as the first race, Brazil, Senna was involved in controversy – this time with Gerhard Berger. He, Senna and Patrese approached the first corner abreast, and there wasn't room for three cars. Senna would never give ground in such circumstances, and he and Berger touched. Mansell won; he was now driving

time visit to Phoenix, saw Senna break the record. He was out of luck in the race, though, retiring after leading for 10 laps. Prost took over, winning his first race of the year.

Boutsen wins in the Montreal rain

Stormy conditions followed by a drying track made tyre selection difficult in Montreal. Repeated pit stops meant that the lead changed hands several times. Senna made up the time he'd lost and was ahead with 3 laps to go when his engine failed. With Prost also out of the race, victory went to Boutsen. Patrese made it a one-two for Williams.

Senna retired in both France and Britain; Prost won both races, with Mansell second each time. At Hockenheim, Prost lost top gear with three laps to go and Senna powered past to win. Mansell had his fourth podium finish that day, but the best was to come in Hungary. He started 12th on the grid, carved his way through the field, overtook Senna on lap 58 and was nearly half a minute clear at the flag. At Spa less than 2 seconds covered Senna, Prost and Mansell as they crossed the line in that order.

Race ban for ignoring black flag

Before Monza, Prost revealed that he had had enough and was moving to Ferrari the following year. In the race Senna led for 44 laps when his engine blew up; Prost stepped in to increase his lead in the championship. At Estoril Mansell overshot the pits and reversed, breaching regulations: he rejoined the race, ignoring the black flag, and collided with Senna on the 48th lap. Mansell was fined $50,000 and given a one-race ban, but that was little consolation to Senna, who believed Mansell might have cost him the title.

Senna won comfortably in Spain, ahead of Berger and Prost. He now needed to win at Suzuka and Adelaide to retain his title. He took his 12th pole of the year in Japan, but Prost got the better start. Senna made his move at the chicane on lap 47, Prost closed him off, the cars touched and both spun off. Prost headed back to the pits, and Senna rejoined the race with the help of a push start. He won but disqualification was inevitable because he'd received assistance, and Alessandro Nannini scored his debut victory for Benetton.

Prost saw no reason to risk competing on a very wet Adelaide circuit. Senna's season fizzled out with a shunt involving Martin Brundle, whose Brabham he was trying to lap. Prost joined the club of drivers who had won three world titles.

for Ferrari. He was determined to win the title, and Ferrari offered him the best chance. His victory first time out meant jubilation in the Ferrari camp.

The race at Imola was restarted after Berger had a spill early on; he escaped with minor injuries. Senna slipped past Prost on the first corner and stayed in front all the way. Prost claimed a breach of the agreement that the leading McLaren at the first corner wouldn't be challenged by the other. Senna claimed his manoeuvre began before the corner. Senna also took pole and led all the way at Monaco. There was no argument here; he was on form and finished nearly a minute ahead of Prost. He got his third start-to-finish win in Mexico, and this provided another landmark: it gave him his 33rd pole, equalling Jim Clark's record. The next race, a first-

PROST AND SENNA – WAR CONTINUES

1990

1990 DRIVERS' CHAMPIONSHIP

1.	AYRTON SENNA	78
2.	ALAIN PROST	71
3.	NELSON PIQUET	43
	GERHARD BERGER	43

CONSTRUCTORS' TITLE

1.	McLAREN	121
2.	FERRARI	110
3.	BENETTON	71

During the close season Senna was told to retract allegations he had made about FISA's handling of the Japanese incident. Senna grudgingly accepted that FISA hadn't acted unduly, McLaren paid his fine and he was welcomed back into the fold for 1990.

The first race was at Phoenix. Senna lost the lead to Jean Alesi's Tyrell, but retook it, winning by 10 seconds. He didn't win in Brazil, colliding with Nakajima while lapping him, but the fire was back. His car needed a new nosecone and he finished third, behind Prost's Ferrari and Senna's new McLaren team-mate, Gerhard Berger. Senna was on pole at Imola, but his race was over after three laps, when a stone damaged his brakes. Riccardo Patrese, in his third season with the Williams team and his fourteenth in Formula One, scored the third win of his long career.

Ferrari back on form

Senna won the next two races, at Monaco and Montreal. He led the whole way in the former, but owed his victory in Canada to a 60-second penalty given to Berger, who had jumped the start – a mistake relegating him to fourth. Piquet, now with Benetton, finished second, with Mansell's Ferrari third. Senna led for 60 of the 69 laps in Mexico, then had a puncture. Prost won, Mansell was second: a good day for Ferrari.

The lead changed hands no fewer than six times at Paul Ricard. One leader was Senna, but a 16-second pit stop for tyres spoiled his chances. Ivan Capelli held the lead for 44 laps, but was passed by Prost three laps

BELOW: *1990 Japanese Grand Prix, Suzuka. The wrecked car of Ayrton Senna (McLaren MP4/5B Honda), after the collision with Alain Prost (Ferrari 641) at the start of the race.*

OPPOSITE: *1989 Monaco Grand Prix, Monte Carlo. Andrea De Cesaris (Dallara 189 Ford) pictured at Loews Hairpin.*

from home. He had to be content with second. Prost scored his fourth win for the rejuvenated Ferrari team at Silverstone. Boutsen was a distant second; Senna, who had had a spin, came third. Mansell retired with gearbox trouble, tossed his gloves into the crowd and announced his retirement; he believed Prost was getting preferential treatment.

Senna won at Hockenheim, then became embroiled in another controversy at the Hungaroring. Boutsen led for the entire race. Behind him was a four-way fight involving Senna, Mansell, Berger and Nannini. Senna attempted to pass Nannini's Benetton at a corner on lap 64; their cars touched. Nannini's car was pitched into the air, while Senna carried on and finished second. Senna had appeared to infringe the rule stating that a driver had to draw alongside a rival to claim a corner.

Arch-rivals fight it out

Senna won from Prost in the next two outings, at Spa and Monza. With Senna now on 72 points to Prost's 56, and just four races to go, the sport's top two would be fighting for the spoils for the third year running. Senna increased his lead to 18 points at Estoril, where he came

second and Prost was third. Mansell cut across Prost at the start, which dropped Prost several places down the field. Prost all but conceded the title before the Spanish Grand Prix, then won. A damaged radiator meant that Senna failed to finish. He still led by 9 points, but if Prost could score well in the last two races he had a fifth and fourth place to discard. Senna, by contrast, had fared no worse than third in the 11 finishes he had racked up. Prost could still take the title but Senna could prevent that with a win in the penultimate round, Suzuka. He took pole, but Prost got a better start. However, both ended up in the run-off area after Senna drove into Prost by the first corner.

Tactical crash

The collision gave Senna the title. Even if Prost won at Adelaide and Senna failed to score, it wouldn't be enough. As it happened, Prost came third in Australia, behind Piquet and Mansell. Senna went off the track while holding a comfortable lead. Prost suspected foul play at Suzuka, and Ferrari waded in, complaining about 'tactical crashes'. FISA set up an inquiry, but only one man could know for sure. Later, Senna admitted that it had been deliberate.

FOUR IN A ROW FOR McLAREN

1991

1991 DRIVERS' CHAMPIONSHIP

1.	AYRTON SENNA	96
2.	NIGEL MANSELL	72
3.	RICCARDO PATRESE	53

CONSTRUCTORS' TITLE

1.	McLAREN-HONDA	139
2.	WILLIAMS RENAULT	125
3.	FERRARI	55.5

Prost took a back seat in 1991; by the end he'd failed to register a single win. Minor placings put him on 34 points: respectable, but only good enough to give him fifth place. Even before the season was out, it was announced that he and Ferrari were parting company.

Four straight wins for Senna

However, Senna and McLaren didn't have everything their own way, though it looked like it at the beginning. Senna had four straight victories. Patrese was close at Interlagos, as was Berger at Imola. There were more generous margins over Prost and Mansell, at Phoenix and Monaco respectively. Senna's haul for these efforts was 40 points – a new points structure meant 10 for a win. All 16 races now counted towards the championship, too.

Williams' success

Piquet ended Senna's run in Montreal. Mansell led all the way but suffered engine failure with victory in sight; Piquet nipped through and Mansell trailed in a disconsolate sixth. Senna had retired with alternator trouble. In Mexico he had his first defeat in a race where he went the full distance. The two Williams cars came home first and second, with Senna third. Mansell

OPPOSITE: *Michael Schumacher (Jordan 191 Ford) made his Formula One debut in the 1991 Belgian Grand Prix at the Spa-Francorchamps circuit. It ended on the first lap with clutch failure.*

RIGHT: *Nigel Mansell (Williams FW14 Renault) takes the chequered flag, for his fourth win of the season, at the 1991 Italian Grand Prix, Monza.*

finished behind his team-mate Patrese in Mexico, but at the French Grand Prix, at Magny-Cours for the first time, he won – starting a great mid-season run. He and Prost traded the lead several times, but Mansell was in front when it mattered. A start-to-finish triumph at Silverstone was a far cry from his frustrating experience of 1990; Senna was unlucky on this occasion, running out of fuel just before the finish. He dropped from second to fourth, his McLaren team-mate Berger and Prost slipping by him to finish second and third. Mansell made it three in a row at Hockenheim, and Patrese gave Williams a second one-two. Again Senna ran out of fuel on the penultimate lap, finishing out of the points in seventh. His lead was cut to just 8 points.

Jordan picking up points

It was becoming a McLaren–Williams battle. Senna got back to form in Hungary, leading all the way with Mansell 5 seconds behind him. Patrese was third, ahead of Berger. The fastest lap was set by Bertrand Gachot, driving the new Team 7-Up Jordan. It was the latest in a fine first season for the team: Gachot and team-mate de Cesaris had both finished in the points in Canada and Germany, and one of the Jordans had finished in the top six in three other rounds.

In the next race, Spa, de Cesaris's engine overheated when he was running second. His fine effort was overshadowed by the man driving the other Jordan that day – not Gachot, but a new and temporary team-mate: Mercedes sports car driver Michael Schumacher. Schumacher amazed everyone by qualifying seventh on an unfamiliar circuit. A clutch problem meant that he didn't complete one lap of the race, but he'd done more than enough to make people take notice. Senna and Berger enjoyed a McLaren one-two in the race; Mansell failed to finish. The top of the table was opening up again.

Enter Michael Schumacher
The next race was Monza. Benetton had swooped to sign Schumacher, who outscored his new team-mate Piquet, finishing fifth, one place ahead of the three-times champion. Mansell scored his fourth win, but Senna took second, so Mansell only pegged back 4 points. Senna was second again at Estoril, behind Patrese; Mansell was disqualified after a pit lane error.

Senna clinches second title for McLaren
Mansell had his fifth win in Spain, while Senna managed just 2 points back in fifth place. However, he had a lead of 16 points, and there were only two races left. He clinched the title at Suzuka, sacrificing first place on the final lap and allowing Berger to come through for his sixth career win. Senna and Mansell finished first and second in the academic final round in Adelaide. It was McLaren's year, but the team's four-year winning streak was about to end.

MANSELL BREAKS RECORDS

1992

1992 DRIVERS' CHAMPIONSHIP
1.	NIGEL MANSELL	108
2.	RICCARDO PATRESE	56
3.	MICHAEL SCHUMACHER	53

CONSTRUCTORS' TITLE
1.	WILLIAMS-RENAULT	164
2.	McLAREN-HONDA	99
3.	BENETTON-FORD	31

Senna had blown the opposition away in the early rounds of 1991; Mansell was even more dominant as 1992 began. The Williams he was driving was basically the same as the preceding year's model, but with active suspension. The team had flirted with this several years earlier but got it right in 1992.

Mansell wins the first five Grands Prix
Mansell won the first five races, starting on pole each time. In four of them – South Africa, Mexico, Spain and San Marino – he was never headed. This was a record in itself, and there was even more good news for Williams as Patrese followed Mansell home in four of the races, giving an awesome display of early-season domination. Michael Schumacher, the new sensation,

prevented a clean sweep of the first five rounds: he finished second to Mansell in Spain. Patrese fell by the wayside after an early spin.

Fifth Monaco success for Senna

Senna had just two third places at this point; even the introduction of the new MP4/7 didn't make much difference. He did end Mansell's run at Monaco, but had to put in a superhuman effort. He also needed Mansell to have an off day, and that manifested itself in a delay with a tyre problem. Mansell finished the race just 0.2 seconds behind Senna despite losing time, and Senna was shattered at the end of the race. His first win of the season enabled him to equal Graham Hill's record of five Monaco wins.

Both Williams cars missed out in Canada. Mansell spun out of the race, later blaming Senna. Gearbox trouble did for Patrese. Gerhard Berger won, a welcome boost for McLaren and the new car. It was yet another Williams one-two in France, a race that was restarted due to rain. Patrese was the early leader but Mansell passed him just after the restart. That took Mansell to Silverstone and a fervent, 200,000-strong home crowd. He didn't disappoint them, and victory that day brought another record: his 28th win, taking him past Jackie Stewart's British record of 27.

Mansell champion by August

There were rumblings of discontent behind the scenes at Williams, however: Frank Williams was sounding out Mansell on the prospect of Prost joining the team for 1993. Mansell had felt undermined by Prost's presence at Ferrari in 1990, and wanted to block the move, but it was already settled. On the track, meanwhile, the Williams bandwagon continued. Mansell beat Senna into second place at Hockenheim. Even though there were six rounds still to go, a win or second place in the next race would give him an unassailable lead.

The place was Hungary, the date: 16 August. There were no team orders, and Patrese was out of the blocks quickest; he spun off at the halfway mark and, though he rejoined the race, he was out of contention. That left Mansell tracking Senna; he only needed to hold his place to take the greater prize. A puncture forced him into the pits, putting him back to sixth, but Schumacher spun out, and Mansell passed Hakkinen, Brundle and Berger to reclaim second. He held the position to the end, and was champion at last.

Controversy to the bitter end

Mansell scored one more win, at Estoril, giving him a record-breaking nine victories for the season. Another season highlight was Michael Schumacher's debut win, in Belgium: he had finished in 12 races, scoring points in all but one and stepping onto the podium eight times.

There were dramatic events off the track. Mansell reluctantly agreed to team up with Prost for 1993, but Senna then let it be known that he would drive for Williams on almost any terms. Williams made Mansell an unfavourable offer, which he promptly refused, deciding that if Williams didn't want him – and if he couldn't defend his title in a competitive car – then he would retire. Williams relented, putting the original deal back on the table, but the damage was done. Mansell turned his back on Formula One.

Senna flying in the rain

Senna was impressive at the European Grand Prix at Donington Park. The Williams pair were quickest in practice, but were beaten in wet conditions. Senna, who had been so desperate to get inside a Williams that he had allegedly offered to drive for nothing, now had two wins and a second place in the McLaren-Ford. He was apprehensive, though: he had a race-by-race deal. He was running second at Imola when his hydraulics went. Hill led, but spun off; Prost took over, holding the lead for the last 50 laps to win from Schumacher, with Martin Brundle's Ligier third. Spain was almost a repeat: Prost took pole, but Hill was quickest away and led for the first 10 laps. This time Hill's race ended with engine failure, and Prost again took over to win from Schumacher.

At Monaco, Senna took maximum points; race leader Schumacher was forced out with hydraulics problems. Senna led the title race but Prost then had four straight wins, in Canada, France, Britain and Germany. The only driver who headed him in any of these races was his team-mate Hill. He was away first in all of them, but Prost hit the front, and stayed there, each time. Prost had seven wins from ten starts but, like Mansell, found that critics tended to put his stunning victories down to the car, while defeats were down to the driver.

Hill's run of bad luck

During Prost's run, Hill was delayed in the pits at Magny-Cours, his engine blew up at Silverstone, and he suffered a puncture while leading at Hockenheim with just two laps to go. He now reeled off three wins. He was on the front row of the grid behind Prost in Hungary, Belgium and Italy. At the Hungaroring he led all the way, Prost being relegated to the back of the grid after stalling on the parade lap. Schumacher pushed him hard all the way to the line at Spa, while at Monza he inherited the lead from Prost after his engine gave out five laps from home. The Williams pair were beaten into the minor placings by Schumacher at Estoril, his best race in a season which would see him on the podium nine times. This would have received greater attention had he not been up against the dominant Williams.

51 wins recorded by Prost

Prost's second place behind Schumacher in Portugal secured his fourth world title. He then announced that he was retiring from the sport, a decision influenced, at least partly, by the fact that Senna was to join Williams

PROST IS BACK

1993

1993 DRIVERS' CHAMPIONSHIP

1.	ALAIN PROST	99
2.	AYRTON SENNA	73
3.	DAMON HILL	69

CONSTRUCTORS' TITLE

1.	WILLIAMS-RENAULT	168
2.	McLAREN-FORD	84
3.	BENETTON-FORD	72

Alain Prost returned after a year's sabbatical, stepping into Mansell's shoes as the Williams no.1. Patrese wasn't retained, and moved to Benetton, lining up with rising star Schumacher. Senna remained with McLaren. Prost's team-mate came from within the Williams camp: Damon Hill was promoted from test driver.

The first race was in South Africa. Prost won, with only second-placed Senna on the same lap when he crossed the line. Senna faced an additional handicap in taking on the mighty Williams cars: Honda had withdrawn, and the latest MP4 was powered by an unspectacular Ford V-8 unit. However, he followed up his second place at Kyalami with a win in Brazil. Prost and Hill had occupied the front row at Interlagos; Prost spun off, Senna picked off new leader Hill, then held the advantage to the end.

in 1994. Senna won both of the remaining races, in Japan and Australia, beating Prost into second each time. In third place at Suzuka was Mika Hakkinen, whose gamble to leave Lotus and become a McLaren test driver had paid off; he'd replaced Andretti as McLaren's no. 2. There was also some off-track drama; Senna and Jordan driver Eddie Irvine came to blows because Senna felt that the lapped Irvine had blocked him.

Prost had a record of 51 wins from his 199 Grands Prix. His four championships put him second only to Fangio in the all-time rankings.

1994

SENNA KILLED

1994 DRIVERS' CHAMPIONSHIP

1.	MICHAEL SCHUMACHER	92
2.	DAMON HILL	91
3.	GERHARD BERGER	41

CONSTRUCTORS' TITLE

1.	WILLIAMS-RENAULT	118
2.	BENETTON-FORD	103
3.	FERRARI	71

Now it was Senna's turn at the wheel of the Williams. There were a few niggling problems with the FW16 – the latest Williams – in the early part of the year; it performed well in practice, but struggled in the opening two races.

Williams slow off the mark
Senna took pole in Brazil, with Schumacher beside him. He led in the early stages, but Schumacher's Benetton took over after the first pit stop and Senna spun out on lap 55. Schumacher won, with Damon Hill in the other Williams second, though a lap down. The second race was in Japan, the first of two visits. This round, called the Pacific Grand Prix, was held on the narrow TI circuit. Senna was again on pole, but a nudge from Hakkinen's McLaren ended his interest in the race on the first lap. Schumacher led all the way. Only Berger's Ferrari finished on the same lap, over a minute behind.

Horror at Imola
Next came Imola, where Senna had won three times. The weekend of 29 April–1 May was one of the worst for

the sport. Rubens Barrichello had a lucky escape after a major spill during the Friday practice session; prompt action from Formula One's renowned doctor Sid Watkins prevented him from swallowing his tongue. The following day Roland Ratzenberger lost his life when his Simtek crashed into a wall. The next day Senna was on pole again. He got away first, with Schumacher close behind. After five laps Senna's Williams went into a concrete wall at Tamburello Corner. It was a huge impact, but Senna might have survived had not part of the suspension become dislodged and struck his head.

Schumacher won the shortened, restarted race, and made it four out of four with a victory at Monaco two weeks later. With pole position, fastest lap, a start-to-finish win and Senna lost to the sport, Schumacher was suddenly looking unstoppable. Damon Hill, now Williams' no.1, won in Spain, profiting from Schumacher's gearbox problems. Schumacher still finished second, less than half a minute behind. At Montreal Schumacher won again; Hill was a distant second.

BELOW: *Ayrton Senna (Williams FW16 Renault) leads at the start of the 1994 San Marino Grand Prix, Imola, Italy. Senna was killed after the fifth lap when he left the track and crashed into a wall.*

OPPOSITE: *1993 Hungarian Grand Prix, Hungaroring, Budapest. Damon Hill (Williams FW15C Renault) holds his fist aloft as he takes the chequered flag for his maiden Grand Prix win.*

David Coulthard promoted at Williams

David Coulthard was promoted internally, becoming no.2 at Williams. He was in the points second time out, in Montreal, where he came fifth. For the next race the team brought back Nigel Mansell but transmission problems ended his race at Magny-Cours after 45 laps, when he was running third. Schumacher won and Hill followed him home.

Silverstone marked the halfway point. Hill won, and Schumacher, who crossed the line second, was dramatically disqualified; he had broken ranks on the parade lap, then ignored the black flag. He forfeited his six points, and received a two-race suspension. Neither scored at Hockenheim: Schumacher retired with engine trouble, Hill finished out of the points. A first-lap accident took ten cars out of the race, which was won by Berger, giving Ferrari their first win for four years. Schumacher won from Hill in Hungary, the fourth time they had finished in that order. Third was Schumacher's Benetton team-mate Jos Verstappen, who had had a miraculous escape in Germany when he'd been engulfed in a fireball during refuelling.

At Spa Schumacher crossed the line ahead of Hill, but he was disqualified again, for illegal skidblock wear. Hill inherited first place, and turned up the heat by winning in Italy and Portugal, the two races for which Schumacher was suspended. It was very nearly a Williams one-two in both of these rounds. Coulthard was second at Estoril, as he was when he ran out of fuel close to home at Monza.

Schumacher by one point from Hill

Hill's 30-point haul, with Schumacher failing to register, put him only one point behind. They each took a first and second in the next two races, so Schumacher carried his advantage into the final race at Adelaide. He led until lap 35, when he hit a wall and rebounded into Hill's path; Mansell won. It was an unsatisfactory ending to the championship, but Schumacher had become the first German to hold the title.

SCHUMACHER AGAIN...

1995

1995 DRIVERS' CHAMPIONSHIP

1.	MICHAEL SCHUMACHER	102
2.	DAMON HILL	69
3.	DAVID COULTHARD	49

CONSTRUCTORS' TITLE

1.	BENETTON-RENAULT	137
2.	WILLIAMS-RENAULT	112
3.	FERRARI	73

Michael Schumacher set the pace with a win at Interlagos. Damon Hill was unlucky; he took pole in Brazil and was leading when his suspension failed. He then scored back-to-back wins in Argentina and San Marino, with Alesi bringing his Ferrari home second in both. Schumacher was third in Buenos Aires, and crashed out in the early stages at Imola. The San Marino Grand Prix was also notable for Nigel Mansell's first outing in the McLaren Mercedes. An undersized cockpit caused him to miss the first two rounds; now he discovered that though the cockpit was improved the car was still unimpressive. He finished tenth at Imola, retired in the next race in Spain, and told McLaren that he had had enough.

Early exit for big two at Silverstone

Schumacher was back on form in the Spanish Grand Prix, and Johnny Herbert made it a one-two for Benetton. The team had switched from Ford engines to the same Renault unit that powered the Williams cars; with evenly matched hardware Schumacher looked unbeatable. Damon Hill was on pole at Monaco, but lost out to Schumacher: Williams opted to run a two-stop race to Benetton's one. They occupied the front row again at Montreal, but with Hill out of the race, Schumacher seemed set for yet another win. An unscheduled pit stop allowed Alesi, Barrichello, Irvine and Panis to come through, giving Alesi his first victory in his eighth year. Magny-Cours was a repeat of Monaco; Hill got the better of Schumacher in practice, with the roles reversed when it mattered. Benetton bested Williams when it came to pit-stop strategy, and that played a crucial part. The big two departed the Silverstone scene after clashing at Priory Corner on the 46th lap. The race still centred on Benetton and Williams, though; their no. 2 drivers vied for victory. Johnny Herbert came out on top for Benetton, after Coulthard, who had taken the lead, was penalised for speeding in the pit lane. Hill took his third successive pole at Hockenheim, but crashed out again, this time on the first lap. Schumacher crossed the line 6 seconds ahead of Coulthard, extending his championship lead over Hill to 23 points.

Schumacher's stunning victory

Williams enjoyed their only one-two success of the season in Hungary. Hill and Coulthard were first and second on the grid, and finished the race in that order, Hill leading the whole way while Schumacher succumbed to a fuel pump problem. Incredibly, Schumacher qualified only 16th at Spa, but drove one of the races of his life to win from Hill. Coulthard was unlucky, suffering gearbox trouble while leading on lap 13; at Monza he was again blighted while leading, also on the 13th lap, but by a wheel bearing. Hill and Schumacher collided on lap 23. Johnny Herbert came through to win his second race of the year, ahead of Hakkinen and Frentzen. After two unlucky races, it came right for Coulthard at Estoril where he dominated: he took pole, set the fastest lap, and led for 66 of the 71 laps. Schumacher held off Hill for second place.

ABOVE: *Michael Schumacher (Benetton Renault) celebrates winning the 1995 Pacific Grand Prix, Tanaka International, Aida, Japan and taking his second successive Drivers' world championship on the podium.*

OPPOSITE: *1994 Spanish Grand Prix, Barcelona. David Coulthard (Williams FW16 Renault), impressed on his Grand Prix debut. Unfortunately he had to retire after an electronics failure.*

10th pole for Williams

The European Grand Prix was at the Nürburgring. Coulthard was on pole once more, but Schumacher again produced the goods. He passed Alesi, who had dominated the race, 3 laps from home, crossing the line less than three seconds ahead. Damon Hill crashed out in Germany for the fourth time in seven races, meaning that he trailed Schumacher by 29 points with just three races to go. Schumacher won at the TI circuit. Again the Williams duo occupied the front row; again Schumacher came out on top. He eased past Coulthard on the 50th lap and finished the race 15 seconds clear. The title was in the bag.

Schumacher out on his own

Schumacher scored his ninth win at Suzuka; Hill won by two laps in the final race at Adelaide. A string of retirements took out many big names, and only eight cars were running when Hill crossed the line. Despite this, Hill finished the season 33 points behind Schumacher.

HILL'S CHANCE

1996

1996 DRIVERS' CHAMPIONSHIP

1.	DAMON HILL	97
2.	JACQUES VILLENEUVE	78
3.	MICHAEL SCHUMACHER	59

CONSTRUCTORS' TITLE

1.	WILLIAMS-RENAULT	175
2.	FERRARI	70
3.	BENETTON-RENAULT	68

When Schumacher joined Ferrari for 1996, it hadn't won the championship since 1979. Williams still looked like the team to beat. Hill won the first three races, at Melbourne, Interlagos and Buenos Aires. His main rival was his new Williams team-mate Jacques Villeneuve, replacing David Coulthard, who had moved to McLaren. Not even Schumacher could work miracles at Ferrari; after those three rounds he had registered just one third place, in Brazil, and two retirements.

Brundle's spectacular crash

Melbourne staged the Australian Grand Prix for the first time, and Villeneuve took pole in his very first outing. He clipped a kerb on lap 33, damaging an oil-line, then eased off to ensure a finish and took a creditable 6 points on his debut, coming second behind Hill. The race was memorable for a spectacular spill: Martin

Brundle's Jordan barrel-rolled through the air, landing on Johnny Herbert's Sauber before coming to rest in the sand. Brundle dusted himself off, obtained the necessary medical clearance and climbed into his spare car for the restart. Villeneuve spun off in Brazil, and was second to Hill again in Argentina. His maiden victory came in only his fourth race, the European Grand Prix, held at the new Nürburgring. From second on the grid, behind Hill, he led all the way, crossing the line less than a second ahead of Schumacher. With Coulthard and Hill half a minute back, followed by Barrichello, Brundle, Herbert, Hakkinen and Berger, Villeneuve had outgunned all the big names very early on.

Only four finish in Monaco

Schumacher hadn't taken long to squeeze the best out of the Ferrari 310 and took pole at Imola; Hill edged him into second place in the race. Gerhard Berger brought his Benetton home in third. A spate of accidents swept the field at Monaco and only four cars were running at the end of the race, which was won by Olivier Panis. He was in his third Formula One season, all with Ligier.

Ferrari on the march

The seventh race of the year saw Michael Schumacher put Ferrari back on top of the podium. Hill retired, but Schumacher relegated Alesi and Villeneuve to the minor placings. Schumacher's car didn't allow him to build on this success, failing him in each of the next three races, all won by Williams. Villeneuve followed Hill home at Montreal and Magny-Cours. Villeneuve lost out to Hill in Canada, and returned the favour by winning at

Silverstone. With six races to go, Hill's championship lead was down to 15 points. The margin went back up to 21 after Hockenheim, where Hill won and Villeneuve finished third. It was a lucky win for Hill; he inherited the lead two laps from home when Berger's car suffered a blown engine. His Benetton team-mate Jean Alesi split the Williams duo, coming second.

Williams pair battle it out

The championship was now a two-horse race. Villeneuve clawed 4 points back by crossing the line a whisker ahead of Hill at the Hungaroring. At least one issue was now settled: Williams had a record-equalling eighth Constructors' championship.

The next two races, Spa and Monza, were Schumacher's, the latter giving Ferrari its first home success since 1988. Villeneuve was second to Schumacher at Spa, while Hill could finish only fifth. Neither scored in Italy, so with two races to go Hill led Villeneuve by 13 points. Estoril was the scene of the penultimate round. The pressure was on, though Hill was still hot favourite. The heat was turned up when it was announced that Heinz-Harald Frentzen would replace Hill the following year.

The Williams pair slugged it out in fine style in Portugal. Villeneuve gained a vital edge after the third of their pit stops and pressed home to win by 20 seconds. A 9-point lead for Hill going into Suzuka meant that just one point would be enough. Villeneuve took pole, but Hill got away first. He led for the entire race, although the championship was settled even before he took the flag: Villeneuve lost a wheel and crashed out on the 37th lap.

ABOVE: *1997 German Grand Prix, Hockenheim. Gerhard Berger (Benetton B197 Renault) on the way to first place. This was his final Grand Prix win.*

OPPOSITE: *1996 Australian Grand Prix, Melbourne. Jacques Villeneuve (Williams FW18 Renault) at Marina. He went on to secure second position on his debut Grand Prix.*

VILLENEUVE'S CROWN

1997

1997 DRIVERS' CHAMPIONSHIP

1.	JACQUES VILLENEUVE	81
2.	HEINZ-HARALD FRENTZEN	42
3.	JEAN ALESI	36
	DAVID COULTHARD	36

CONSTRUCTORS' TITLE

1.	WILLIAMS-RENAULT	123
2.	FERRARI	102
3.	BENETTON-RENAULT	67

Marlboro and McLaren parted company after 23 years; the sponsor now supported Ferrari. The new car, the 310B, was unveiled in January; Schumacher and Irvine remained. Hill was now with Arrows. Villeneuve had lost to Hill in 1996; his new Williams team-mate, Heinz-Harald Frentzen, was under pressure, having displaced the reigning champion.

At Melbourne Irvine took out Villeneuve and Herbert as he tried to overtake. Frentzen and Coulthard

at Silverstone, although a pit stop nearly proved expensive: Schumacher had built up a lead, but a wheel-bearing failure ended his chances. Gerhard Berger had missed the last three races but returned at Hockenheim, putting his Benetton on pole and winning the race from Schumacher and Hakkinen. He retired at the end of the season.

In Hungary, Schumacher looked like increasing his 10-point lead. He took pole and led for the opening laps, but had to pit as the team had chosen the wrong tyres. Hill took up the running; victory was in sight when clutch problems slowed him right down. Villeneuve passed him on the last lap, denying Arrows their maiden success.

Before the race at Spa it poured; the safety car was deployed until lap 4. Schumacher had opted for intermediates – most of his rivals had wets – and stormed to victory. There was great pressure on him to win at Monza, but he qualified only ninth on the grid, his worst position of the year. He crossed the line sixth; Villeneuve finished only one place ahead. Coulthard scored his and McLaren's second win; Alesi and Frentzen occupied the minor placings.

10-second penalty setback for Schumacher
In Austria Schumacher was lying third when Irvine and Alesi were involved in an accident that brought out the yellow flag. He didn't see it, overtook Frentzen and incurred a mandatory 10-second penalty, putting him back to ninth. He got back to sixth, and a point, by the end of the race. Villeneuve won, cutting Schumacher's championship lead to a single point. Next came the Luxembourg Grand Prix. Schumacher's race ended early; he was thumped by his brother Ralf. Hakkinen and Coulthard were first and second, then both hit trouble, clearing the way for Villeneuve. At Suzuka, he was disqualified for a yellow flag infringement during practice; Schumacher won and led by one point going into the decider, the European Grand Prix at Jerez. They occupied the front row, with Villeneuve on pole. By lap 48 Schumacher held the advantage. Villeneuve dived through on the inside; Schumacher tried to shut him out, clipping the side pod of the Williams and putting himself out. Villeneuve nursed his car over the remaining 21 laps; both McLarens passed him, but third was enough for him to take the title by 3 points.

Schumacher stripped of all points
The FIA held an inquiry into the race's decisive moment; Schumacher was stripped of all the points he had gained over the season.

traded the lead, but Frentzen suffered a brake disc failure three laps from home, leaving Coulthard and McLaren to take the honours. Villeneuve then won in Brazil and Argentina. At Interlagos he crossed the line less than five seconds ahead of Gerhard Berger's Benetton. His Buenos Aires win was tighter: he staved off a Ferrari challenge by less than a second.

Stewart team make the podium
Frentzen had his first win at Imola, emerging from the final pit stop just ahead of Schumacher. They finished in that order; Irvine was third. A wet Monaco saw the race curtailed but Schumacher dominated, winning by nearly a minute from Barrichello in second, whose performance meant a podium finish for the Stewart team. Villeneuve, failing to finish at Imola and Monte Carlo, hit back in Spain. He led for 62 of the 64 laps and took the flag ahead of Prost's Olivier Panis, who drove superbly. Next, the Montreal race was stopped after an accident involving Panis, who broke both legs. Schumacher was declared the winner; Coulthard had been leading but a pit-stop delay had relegated him to seventh when the race was halted.

Berger's final victory
Schumacher came out on top at Magny-Cours, his Ferrari sporting the new 046/2 engine. Villeneuve won

HAKKINEN WINS BATTLE

1998

1998 DRIVERS' CHAMPIONSHIP

1.	MIKA HAKKINEN	100
2.	MICHAEL SCHUMACHER	86
3.	DAVID COULTHARD	56

CONSTRUCTORS' TITLE

1.	McLAREN-MERCEDES	156
2.	FERRARI	133
3.	WILLIAMS-MECACHROME	38

1998 saw the introduction of new tyre regulations to improve safety, the departure of Renault and a battle royal between Schumacher and Hakkinen for the title.

New engine deal for Williams

Jacques Villeneuve's immediate concern was trying to keep Williams on top now that Renault had departed the scene; a deal with BMW had been done, but wouldn't come into effect until 2000. The McLaren-Mercedes looked like the car to beat and dominated the opening race in Melbourne, Coulthard leading from Hakkinen with no one else in sight. Coulthard stuck to the pre-race agreement and allowed his team-mate

through to win. Another one-two for McLaren followed in Brazil, Hakkinen again crossing the line first. It was already looking ominous for the other teams but Schumacher, third that day, could not be written off. He won the very next race, Argentina; Irvine finished third, making it a good day for Ferrari. Hakkinen's second place meant that he had 26 points from three races as the circus headed for Europe.

Hakkinen was out of the race at Imola; Coulthard held off Schumacher to take what would be his only win of the year. Hakkinen was back in form at Barcelona, where he notched his fourth win; Coulthard and Schumacher took the minor placings. Monaco was even better for Hakkinen. Not only did he win, but his closest rivals failed to score. Schumacher clashed with one of Benetton's new young drivers, Alexander Wurz, and was classified tenth, then scored his second win of the year in a restarted race at Montreal, with the advantage of having no McLaren to push him. Hakkinen's car failed on the grid; Coulthard suffered his second successive retirement after holding the lead. Fisichella took 6 points.

BELOW: *Jarno Trulli (Prost AP01 Peugeot) runs away from his crashed car during the 1998 Canadian Grand Prix, Montreal, Quebec.*

OPPOSITE: *Pedro Diniz (Arrows A18 Yamaha) leads Olivier Panis (Prost JS45 Mugen Honda), in the 1997 Luxembourg Grand Prix, Nürburgring, Germany.*

Schumacher took maximum points at Magny-Cours and Silverstone. The French Grand Prix also had to be restarted; Schumacher and Irvine managed to get the Ferraris ahead, then staved off the challengers. The safety car at a waterlogged Silverstone held up Hakkinen, eating into his sizeable lead, and a spin allowed Schumacher to come through for victory. Hakkinen and Coulthard hit back with successive one-two finishes in Austria and Germany. Schumacher was in the points in both – finishing third and fifth – but he lost ground. Third place at Hockenheim went to the reigning champion. Villeneuve gave it his best shot in the FW20, and often put the car further up the field than it had any right to be. Williams' success this year came from scrambling for points; the occasional podium win was a bonus.

Hakkinen and Schumacher tied on points

Schumacher was on top form in Hungary, where the team ran a three-stop race that worked to perfection. Hakkinen gained just 1 point: Hakkinen 77 points, Schumacher 70. That position was unaltered after a dramatic race in the wet at Spa, where neither driver finished. Damon Hill seized the opportunity and brought his Jordan through, giving the team a first

victory. After Monza, Schumacher and Hakkinen were tied on 80 points. Schumacher won after Coulthard, who had been leading, retired; Hakkinen dropped back to fourth with brake problems. Hakkinen's win over Schumacher in the Luxembourg Grand Prix was probably his best performance of the year. It gave him a 4-point advantage going into the final round at Suzuka.

Hakkinen worthy winner

Schumacher stalled on the grid in Japan and, in accordance with regulations, had to start from the back of the field. A brilliant drive took him up to third, when some track debris punctured a tyre. Hakkinen went on to score his eighth win of the year, giving him a round 100 points for the season. Schumacher had excelled himself, but Hakkinen was a worthy champion. Of the 16 races he had completed 13, scoring in every one. He had nine poles, 6 fastest laps – and eleven podium finishes, including 8 victories.

1999

TWO IN A ROW FOR HAKKINEN

1999 DRIVERS' CHAMPIONSHIP

1.	MIKA HAKKINEN	76
2.	EDDIE IRVINE	74
3.	HEINZ-HARALD FRENTZEN	55

CONSTRUCTORS' TITLE

1.	FERRARI	128
2.	MCLAREN-MERCEDES	124
3.	JORDAN-MUGEN-HONDA	61

The 1999 opener was in Australia. The McLarens dominated practice, but both Hakkinen and Coulthard were out of the race by the halfway mark. Irvine held the lead to the end: his first Grand Prix victory. Frentzen pushed him hard all the way, finishing just 1 second behind in his first outing for Jordan.

Barrichello off to a flyer

Rubens Barichello was first away at Interlagos but Michael Schumacher took up the running after he pitted; Hakkinen passed him and led to the line. He had

a comfortable lead in the early stages at Imola, but crashed out; Coulthard, who had been in the front row alongside his team-mate in all three races, took over in front. After a pit stop he emerged in traffic and lost vital time; Schumacher finished 5 seconds ahead. Schumacher split the two McLarens at the front row of the grid in Monaco, and dominated the race. A mistake by Hakkinen let Irvine come through for a Ferrari one-two. Hakkinen had to settle for third, while Coulthard failed to finish.

The McLarens took first and second in Barcelona where they were followed home by the two Ferraris; the season was shaping up into a battle between the giants. Montreal saw Schumacher break Hakkinen's run of five successive poles, but his race ended after he made a mistake on lap 29 and crashed into a wall, one in a spate of accidents. Hakkinen scored his third win and edged ahead of Schumacher by 4 points in the championship.

Schumacher breaks leg at Silverstone

Difficult qualifying conditions made for an odd grid at Magny-Cours: Barrichello took pole; Hakkinen and Irvine were back in 14th and 17th. Hakkinen stormed

ABOVE: *1999 French Grand Prix, Magny-Cours. Heinz-Harald Frentzen (Jordan Mugen Honda) celebrates his first position on the podium. The result was remarkable in the fact that he had a fractured leg.*

OPPOSITE: *1998 Brazilian Grand Prix, Interlagos, Sao Paulo. Mika Hakkinen leads David Coulthard (both McLaren MP4/13 Mercedes-Benz). Hakkinen finished in first place, Coulthard retired after 22 laps with a gearbox problem.*

through to lead with 7 laps to go, but a pit stop pushed him down to second, where he finished. Frentzen scored his and Jordan's second Grand Prix victory: remarkably, as he was nursing a fractured leg from Montreal. Silverstone was both the halfway point and the turning point. Schumacher's first-lap crash resulted in a broken leg and an enforced lay-off that lasted for six races. The race changed hands several times and Coulthard came out on top.

Irvine is Ferrari's new no.1

Irvine rose to the challenge of becoming Ferrari's no.1 by winning in Austria. Coulthard was the early leader, nudging his team-mate into a spin on the opening lap. Irvine took over when he pitted, and built up enough of

Schumacher returned for the Malaysian Grand Prix. He took pole, but had to provide support for Irvine. He did so, lying second and acting as a buffer between Irvine ahead and Hakkinen behind. Irvine had a 4-point lead going into the final race at Suzuka. Hakkinen was on peerless form and won the race comfortably, with Schumacher in second. Irvine was a distant third, finishing 2 points behind Hakkinen in the final table.

FERRARI, AFTER 21 YEARS

2000

2000 DRIVERS' CHAMPIONSHIP

1.	MICHAEL SCHUMACHER	108
2.	MIKA HAKKINEN	89
3.	DAVID COULTHARD	73

CONSTRUCTORS' TITLE

1.	FERRARI	170
2.	McLAREN-MERCEDES	152
3.	WILLIAMS	36

McLaren and Ferrari once again engaged in a long struggle for supremacy in 2000. There was one driver change at the top: Barrichello moved from Stewart-Ford to Ferrari, replacing Irvine.

Ferrari was the first to succeed, despite the McLarens having the edge in qualifying. At Interlagos the McLarens ran with one heavy load, but Ferrari opted for an extra stop – and extra speed. Both Schumacher and Barrichello started from the second row and passed their McLaren rivals. Barrichello's engine blew, but Schumacher built up a sizeable lead. Jenson Button crossed the line in seventh in the Williams-BMW, gaining his first championship point.

Hakkinen and Coulthard finally got into their stride at Imola, but Schumacher relegated them to the minor placings. Then Coulthard had an excellent win at Silverstone, despite gearbox problems, and a flawless performance by Hakkinen at Barcelona saw him take the flag 16 seconds ahead of Coulthard.

Schumacher won convincingly at the Nürburgring with only Hakkinen finishing on the same lap; Coulthard was the best of the rest. At Monaco he

a lead to hold first place when he in turn made his stop. He crossed the line less than 0.1 seconds before Coulthard.

Irvine won narrowly again at Hockenheim, this time over his stand-in Ferrari team-mate Mika Salo. Hakkinen was on pole but lost his lead because of a lengthy refuelling stop; a tyre then blew, putting him out. Salo could have won, but team orders prevailed and he waved Irvine through. Irvine now led the championship by 8 points, but McLaren responded with a one-two in Hungary. The result looked as if it would mirror the grid positions: Hakkinen, Irvine, then Coulthard. A mistake by Irvine in the latter stages allowed Coulthard to swap places.

Hakkinen spun out while leading at Monza; Coulthard and Irvine could finish only fifth and sixth respectively. Frentzen's second win put him on 50 points, 10 behind joint leaders Hakkinen and Irvine. In the European Grand Prix at the Nürburgring, Frentzen went out of the race halfway with an electrical problem. Coulthard spun out a few laps later and Johnny Herbert came through, giving the Stewart team its first success. Hakkinen crossed the line in fifth, with Irvine seventh, meaning that Hakkinen had a 2-point advantage.

looked like having a fifth win of the year, but a cracked exhaust caused the rear suspension to overheat and fail. Coulthard won, with Barrichello and Fisichella following him. Eddie Irvine was fourth, bringing Jaguar their first points. At the next race, Coulthard, Schumacher's only serious challenger, received a 10-second stop-go penalty for an infringement at the start of the parade lap. Schumacher got his fifth win.

Barrichello's joy as long wait ends

Then Coulthard won again at Magny-Cours, despite Schumacher's blatant attempts to block him – a tactic prompting Coulthard to gesticulate at his rival. He eventually managed to get by, and Hakkinen made it a McLaren one-two after Schumacher's car failed to finish. In the Austrian Grand Prix, BAR-Honda driver Ricardo Zonta pitched Schumacher out at the first corner, turning the race into a walk-over for McLaren: Hakkinen won, with Coulthard second. Barrichello finally won at Hockenheim: his maiden success, after seven years and 123 races. No other Grand Prix winner had waited so long.

Schumacher was back in the points in Hungary where he started on pole, ahead of Coulthard and Hakkinen. He had to settle for splitting them and taking 6 points; Hakkinen scored his third win of the season,

and followed it up with a victory at Spa. Schumacher was now 6 points adrift of the top spot.

However, he did brilliantly in the last four rounds. At Monza, his victory over Hakkinen put him to within 2 points, and he cruised to victory at Indianapolis, swinging the balance back towards Ferrari. It was his 42nd win, taking him ahead of Senna, whose record he had equalled at Monza. After the Japanese Grand Prix his 8-point lead became an unassailable 12. The big two again slugged it out in front; Ferrari judged pit-stop strategy brilliantly, Schumacher did the rest – and delivered the prize the team had sought for 21 years. Schumacher's ninth victory followed in the final race at Kuala Lumpur, a win which also sealed the constructors' title for Ferrari. The season's statistics show the extent of McLaren and Ferrari's domination: 442 points were available in the 17-race series; they scored 332 between them.

SCHUMACHER OVERHAULS 'PROFESSOR'

2001

2001 DRIVERS' CHAMPIONSHIP

1.	MICHAEL SCHUMACHER	123
2.	DAVID COULTHARD	65
3.	RUBENS BARRICHELLO	56

CONSTRUCTORS' TITLE

1.	FERRARI	179
2.	MCLAREN-MERCEDES	102
3.	WILLIAMS	80

Michael Schumacher's 19-point margin of victory in 2000 became a 58-point chasm as he retained the crown, repeating his mid-90s achievement with Benetton. Schumacher dominated the series, edging ever closer to becoming the most successful driver in F1 history by any yardstick the sport had to offer. Victory at Spa – his eighth of the year and 52nd in total – took him past Alain Prost's all-time mark. By the end of the season he had also passed 800 points, once again relegating the Professor into second place in the record books.

Schumacher shrugged off a spill during practice at Melbourne to cruise to victory from pole, the first of 11 races in which he would head the grid. Coulthard, who qualified sixth, did well to split the Ferraris in a race that was marred by the latest F1 fatality: a marshal was killed by a flying wheel from Villeneuve's BAR-Honda after the Canadian's high-speed shunt into the back of Ralf Schumacher's Williams on lap 4.

Pit-stop debacle

Not even a pitstop debacle could prevent a Ferrari one-two at Sepang. In monsoon conditions, the safety car was out by early on. The Ferraris were parked up together, Schumacher having to wait over a minute before being attended to. They emerged 10th and 11th, though the decision to run with intermediates rather than wets proved a canny choice. The Rainmaster clinched his sixth successive victory, with Barrichello picking up 6 points.

Coulthard won at Interlagos, but Juan Pablo Montoya stole the show. The former CART star, in his

BELOW: *Mika Hakkinen (West McLaren Mercedes MP4/16), winner of the 2001 British Grand Prix, Silverstone, on a pit-stop.*

OPPOSITE: *Juan Pablo Montoya (BMW Williams FW23) leads at the start of the 2001 Italian Grand Prix, Monza, as Jenson Button (Benetton Renault B201) and Jarno Trulli (Jordan Honda EJ11) collide. Montoya went on to win, the Colombians' maiden Grand prix victory in his first F1 season.*

debut season with Williams, performed a stunning overtaking manoeuvre on the champion to take the lead but was bumped out of the race by the lapped Arrows of Jos Verstappen.

Ralf completes record family double

There was no such misfortune for Williams at Imola. Ralf Schumacher scored his maiden victory, the first in four years for the Didcot outfit. Michelin celebrated their return to F1; it was the first time since 1984 that a Michelin-shod car had won a race. Michael Schumacher suffered the first of his two retirements of the year but joined in the celebrations as he and Ralf became the first brothers to stand atop an F1 podium.

Barcelona saw the return of traction control, ending an eight-year ban. It was back to business as usual for Michael Schumacher, though he had the gremlins in Hakkinen's engine to thank, the McLaren expiring on the final lap. Montoya followed the champion home for his first podium finish.

Barrichello profited from a gladiatorial joust between Schumacher and Montoya in Austria, but was ordered to give way to the champion, who finished second to Coulthard. In fourth place was 21-year-old Kimi Raikkonen, who had signed for Sauber-Petronas with just 23 races behind him. The Finn fared better than another young tyro making his first steps in the sport. At 19 years and seven months, Minardi recruit Fernando Alonso had been the third youngest driver in history when he qualified for Melbourne.

First podium for Jaguar

It was another scarlet one-two at Monaco, with Eddie Irvine giving Jaguar its first podium. Ralf got the better of Michael in Canada, and might have done so again as they battled for the lead at the European GP. Ralf infringed regulations emerging from the pit lane, the stop-go penalty ending his chances. The champion dominated in France, while McLaren had a miserable day. Hakkinen stalled on the grid, while Coulthard's penalty for speeding in the pit lane meant that fourth place was a disappointment.

Hakkinen ended his run of cruel luck with a superb win at Silverstone, leading the Ferraris home. At Hockenheim Schumacher survived a spectacular lap-one crash involving Prost's Luciano Burti, but retired at mid-distance. Brother Ralf claimed his second win. Ferrari sealed both the Drivers' and Constructors' championships with another one-two in Hungary. It was the 11th win in each category for Maranello.

The champion added two more wins to his haul, at Spa and Suzuka, but at Monza he was clearly affected by the recent terrorist outrage in America. The Italian

GP saw Montoya become only the seventh man to win in his rookie season. At Indianapolis a fortnight later Hakkinen notched his 20th career victory, having already announced he would be taking a sabbatical from F1 in 2002. But this was Schumacher's year. Of the 15 races he completed, the German was first or second in all but one. His sights were now set on Fangio's five titles, and Senna's record 65 times on pole.

SCHUMACHER EQUALS FANGIO'S RECORD

2002

2002 DRIVERS' CHAMPIONSHIP

1.	MICHAEL SCHUMACHER	144
2.	RUBENS BARRICHELLO	77
3.	JUAN-PABLO MONTOYA	50

CONSTRUCTORS' TITLE

1.	FERRARI	221
2.	WILLIAMS	92
3.	McLAREN-MERCEDES	65

Ferrari was even more dominant in 2002, Schumacher and Barrichello's aggregate 221 points eclipsing the previous year's emphatic mark by 33. The rest of the field combined just managed to accumulate the same points total. A scarlet car crossed the line first in 15 of the 17 races, though the way in which Maranello manufactured the finishing order brought forth cries of

ABOVE: *2002 Monaco Grand Prix, Monte Carlo. A view of the Grand Hairpin with David Coulthard (McLaren MP4/17 Mercedes) on course to victory.*

OPPOSITE: *2002 British Grand Prix, Silverstone, England. Michael Schumacher (Ferrari F2002) takes the chequered flag for the 60th Grand Prix win of his career.*

'foul' from many quarters. Austria was the most blatant example, Barrichello handing victory to his team-mate at the final corner. There was no infringement of the rules, but it seemed to contravene the spirit of racing, and at the end of the year the FIA acted to bring an end to team orders.

Schumacher avoided a pile-up at the start to win the Melbourne curtain-raiser. Barrichello was among the casualties, Montoya and Raikkonen filling the minor placings. Montoya would not add to his tally of victories this campaign, but seven poles, following the three in his debut season, showed that Williams had on their books a driver of immense potential. Raikkonen, meanwhile, had wasted no time in getting on the podium with McLaren, having taken Hakkinen's berth. The Finn also claimed the fastest lap. Home fans were able to cheer a fine debut for Mark Webber, who took fifth for Minardi on his debut. Unfortunately, that was to be the high watermark of the year for Paul Stoddart's outfit.

Penalty leaves Montoya fuming

Williams enjoyed a one-two at Sepang, though the order should have been reversed. Second-placed Montoya was left fuming at the drive-through penalty imposed for his early clash with the reigning champion. Michael Schumacher recovered from 21st place to get on the podium, easing past Jenson Button's ailing Renault on the last lap.

The new Ferrari was unveiled in Brazil, which saw the first of four successive wins for Schumacher. There was another first-lap spat with Montoya, but at least the Colombian recovered to finish fifth; home favourite Barrichello had yet another Interlagos nightmare, his car failing after Schumacher allowed him to take the lead. Imola was a processional Ferrari clean sweep which left even aficionados bemoaning the lack of excitement – not that Jean Todt or the tifosi would have agreed with the doom-mongers.

Montoya took 6 points in Spain, though more than half a minute behind Schumacher and only after Barrichello suffered yet another retirement. When things did finally go well for the Brazilian, as it did in Austria, he had to contend with his bosses, who told him to let the champion through. Schumacher's first victory on the A1-Ring meant he completed the set for the championship circuits, but it left an unpleasant taste in the mouth and the crowd showed their displeasure. Schumacher turned PR man by allowing Barrichello to join him on top of the podium, but the damage was done.

David Coulthard wins in Monaco

Montoya and Coulthard occupied the front row at Monaco, but the superior launch and traction control of the McLaren saw those positions reversed by the first corner. The Colombian's engine eventually gave out, and Coulthard held off Schumacher's challenge for the last 27 laps of the street classic. Coulthard managed to split the Ferraris in Montreal, but forthwith the season turned into a Maranello juggernaut. Canada had been Ferrari's 150th Grand Prix victory; after the remaining nine rounds that figure stood at 159.

A rare Schumacher error at the European GP left him tracking Barrichello, with the spectre of another Austria looming. In the event Todt chose not ruffle any more feathers – or antagonize the FIA three days before a hearing concerning events at the A1-Ring – and the Brazilian took maximum points. Raikkonen again showed his promise with another podium for McLaren.

Records tumble

Schumacher clocked up his 60th career win at Silverstone, but Ferrari's dominance was best exemplified by Barrichello, who started from the back of the field after stalling on the formation lap, had a spin during the race, yet still carved his way through the field to finish second. It was Montoya's turn to pick up the podium scraps. Victory at Magny-Cours gave Schumacher a record-equalling fifth crown, and with three wins garnered from the last six rounds, he made it a record 11 victories for the season, beating the nine maximums that he had held jointly with Nigel Mansell. Third place in Sepang had been Schumacher's 'worst' return, making him the first man to record a podium finish in every race.

FERRARI AGAIN – BUT IT GOES TO THE WIRE

2003 DRIVERS' CHAMPIONSHIP

1.	MICHAEL SCHUMACHER	93
2.	KIMI RAIKKONEN	91
3.	JUAN-PABLO MONTOYA	82

CONSTRUCTORS' TITLE

1.	FERRARI	158
2.	WILLIAMS	144
3.	McLAREN-MERCEDES	142

The prospect of the F1 roadshow becoming increasingly predictable and sterile – and thus less attractive televisually – galvanised the sport's bosses into action in the winter of 2002. They came up with a back-to-basics package aimed at levelling the playing field and making their product a more exciting spectacle. Unsurprisingly, this was received more favourably by the teams with lesser budgets than by the Big Three. Out

ABOVE: *2003 Hungarian Grand Prix, Hungaroring, Budapest. Fernando Alonso (Renault R23) at the start. He went on to win and become the youngest ever winner of a Grand Prix.*

OPPOSITE: *2003 British Grand Prix, Silverstone, England. Race winner Rubens Barrichello, (Ferrari F2003 GA), lifts his trophy aloft, applauded by second-placed Juan-Pablo Montoya (BMW Williams FW25).*

went team orders and telemetry; in came a revised qualifying procedure, consisting of two single-lap sessions; points were now awarded to the top eight; and cars had to go into the race with the fuel load left after qualifying – no topping up the tank. The changes certainly livened things up: eight drivers topped the podium, and although Ferrari eventually came up trumps again, it was only after an absorbing battle that went to the wire.

First podium for Alonso

In Melbourne it looked like business as usual as the Ferraris scorched away. But Barrichello crashed out, and Michael Schumacher lost time after running over a kerb and damaging the F2002's bargeboards. That meant a Ferrari-free podium, David Coulthard's consistency winning the day in an error-strewn race. New Renault recruit Fernando Alonso was immediately in the points, finishing seventh, and in Malaysia the Spaniard claimed his first pole, the youngest driver to take that honour.

He converted that into a first podium, despite suffering gearbox trouble. Schumacher made another mistake, penalised for running into the back of Alonso's team-mate Jarno Trulli on lap one. Kimi Raikkonen won, finishing some 40 seconds ahead of Barrichello.

The drama was cranked up even further at rain-soaked Interlagos, where the race was red-flagged after Mark Webber totalled his Jaguar, then Alonso struck the debris. Raikkonen was awarded victory, but Jordan successfully appealed on the grounds of a timing error and Giancarlo Fisichella got the decision, receiving his trophy from the Iceman a week later.

Michael Schumacher now stood 16 points behind Raikkonen in the championship, Ferrari 23 behind McLaren in the Constructors' race. That picture changed to a more familiar one as the champion won four of the next five rounds. In San Marino, Spain and Austria, Schumacher converted poles into victories. There were muted celebrations following the win at Imola as it came within hours of the death of Schumacher's mother, a tribute to his professionalism, dedication and concentration. Spain saw the unveiling of the 2003 Ferrari, Schumacher's victory made all the sweeter as Raikkonen left Barcelona empty-handed. The German brushed aside a pit-lane fire to notch another win at the A1-Ring. Kimi took second, but his championship lead was now down to just 2 points.

Spa dropped from championship

When the stops unwound at Monaco, Montoya held off Raikkonen and Schumacher to claim his second F1 victory, less than 2 seconds covering all three cars. Montreal – the season's halfway mark following the dropping of Spa over a tobacco advertising row – saw Schumacher top the table for the first time. He nursed his ailing tyres and brakes to victory, superbly fending off the Williams duo in the process.

Ralf Schumacher led a Williams one-two at the European GP, though it surely would have been Raikkonen's race had his engine not expired. It was the same story in France, though there was no luck this time; the FW25 and new Michelins were proving a formidable package. Barrichello took the full set at Silverstone – pole, fastest lap and 10 points – in a race remembered for a kilted spectator dicing with death on the track. Montoya did likewise at Hockenheim. He was away and clear of a first-lap shunt involving Raikkonen, Barrichello and team-mate Ralf, which helped his cause, but even so, finishing the race over a minute ahead of Coulthard was impressive.

Alonso breaks McLaren's record

Fernando Alonso, aged 22 years 26 days, took over from Bruce McLaren as the youngest ever GP winner with a start-to-finish victory in Hungary. Renault's first win for 20 years came in their second season back in F1. Schumacher now led Montoya by a single point, Raikkonen just a point further back. Back-to-back wins for the champion, at Monza and Indianapolis, made the situation a lot rosier for Ferrari: Schumacher 92, Raikkonen 83, Montoya 82. Schumacher won in Italy at an average speed of 153.814 mph, setting yet another F1 record.

In order to pip Schumacher for the title, Kimi needed to win at Suzuka with the champion failing to score. In the event the Finn only managed second, and a point for eighth place was enough for Schumacher to clinch his sixth crown, beating Fangio's 46-year-old record.

SCARLET JUGGERNAUT ROLLS ON

2004

2004 DRIVERS' CHAMPIONSHIP

1.	MICHAEL SCHUMACHER	148
2.	RUBENS BARRICHELLO	114
3.	JENSON BUTTON	85

CONSTRUCTORS' TITLE

1.	FERRARI	262
2.	BAR	119
3.	RENAULT	105

Going into the 2004 season, all the signs suggested that if McLaren and Williams could manage one more heave, Ferrari could finally be toppled from their perch. What transpired was the very opposite, the prancing horse looking as frisky and uncatchable as ever in a devastatingly consistent display. Round 13, Hungary, saw Michael Schumacher notch his 12th win. With five races to go only the champion's Ferrari team-mate could catch him, a mathematical possibility that soon evaporated.

Schumacher and Barrichello rocketed into the distance in Australia. Alonso, in third, never had a prayer of catching them. The signs were already ominous as the McLarens were running 2 seconds a lap down on the scarlet cars.

The Ferraris invariably ran well in Australia, and the cool temperatures suited the Bridgestones. Perhaps, some thought, Sepang would be a different matter. It wasn't. Schumacher took pole and came home 5 seconds clear of Montoya, setting the fastest lap in the process. Jenson Button, in his second season with BAR-Honda, grinned from ear to ear as he climbed onto the podium for the first time; he would repeat the achievement on nine further occasions, the surprise winner of the 'best of the rest' category as the season unfolded.

F1 goes to Bahrain

At the inaugural Bahrain GP, the chasing pack found that even the climate was favouring the Maranello cars. Stifling heat during qualifying turned into a relative cold snap on race day, once again suiting the Bridgestones more than the Michelin-shod teams. A Ferrari one-two duly followed. Raikkonen's latest engine failure meant that the man who narrowly lost out to Schumacher six

months earlier now trailed 30-0. Coulthard had given McLaren their 4 points to date; Ferrari already had 51 on the board.

Button took his first pole in San Marino and got away well, but when he peeled off into the pits Schumacher streaked away and the result was never in doubt. Button had the consolation of a career-best second place, crossing the finish line comfortably clear of Montoya. Schumacher battled to victory in Spain despite a damaged exhaust, which could easily have halted his perfect start to the season. It seemed that everything was conspiring to Ferrari's advantage as the champion chalked up win number 75.

First retirement in 19 races

Monaco brought temporary solace to those who found Ferrari's metronomic performances uninspiring. Schumacher and Montoya tangled, and the former was out of the running for the first time in 19 races. Schumacher had been leading, having stayed out when the safety car was deployed. Ross Brawn hoped having a clear track ahead would have enabled Schumacher to put daylight between him and the field. The clash with the Colombian's Williams made that academic. At the business end of the race Jarno Trulli had Button breathing down his neck hoping for a mistake but the Italian held firm to score his maiden victory.

McLaren's nightmare continued with another brace of engine failures at the European GP. Even worse for the race, second-placed Raikkonen stayed out long enough to hold up those who might at least have made

a fight of it. Schumacher established a 17-second advantage in eight laps, and by the time the Finn pitted no one was going to reel him in.

Schumacher won for the seventh time in Montreal, setting another record for victories in an individual race. He qualified only sixth, having run with a heavy fuel load, but the two-stop strategy worked perfectly. It was a frustrating day for Williams, for whom Ralf Schumacher and Montoya finished second and fifth but had their points expunged for a technical infringement. A home victory for Renault at Magny-Cours was craftily prevented by Ferrari's clever four-stop strategy. Schumacher was stuck in second behind Alonso anyway, so Brawn calculated that it was worth a try in order to give the champion a clear track. It worked perfectly. Alonso at least had the consolation of splitting the Maranello pair and taking eight points.

Replacement engine costs Button

McLaren finally had something to cheer about as Raikkonen finished second to Schumacher at Silverstone. Button took the supporting role at Hockenheim, though it could have been 10 points had

he not fallen foul of the new rule which dropped a driver 10 places down the grid if the car needed a replacement engine. Hungary provided Ferrari with their seventh one-two of the year, and although McLaren at last made the MP4-19 a winner, at Spa, Schumacher's second place sealed his seventh title. A 13th win followed at Suzuka, meaning that Schumacher dropped just 32 points in another crushing campaign.

ALONSO BECOMES YOUNGEST CHAMPION

2005

2005 DRIVERS' CHAMPIONSHIP

1.	FERNANDO ALONSO	133
2.	KIMI RAIKKONEN	112
3.	MICHAEL SCHUMACHER	62

CONSTRUCTORS' TITLE

1.	RENAULT	191
2.	McLAREN-MERCEDES	182
3.	FERRARI	100

Following Michael Schumacher's leisurely stroll to a fifth successive crown in 2004, F1 was sorely in need of a title race that extended beyond the summer holidays in order to stave off the widespread murmurings that

the championship was becoming a predictable procession. If that was the wish, it was granted in thrilling style. The record 19-race series produced a battle royal between Fernando Alonso and Kimi Raikkonen, the Spaniard clinching the title with two rounds to spare to become the youngest champion in the event's 56-year history.

Double for Renault

Renault and McLaren dominated, between them winning every race apart from the farcical US GP, where the Michelin-shod teams withdrew on safety grounds, leaving the way clear for Schumacher to clock up victory number 84. The Constructors' title went right to the wire. When Alonso took his seventh chequered flag of the year in Shanghai, it put the icing on a marvellous year for Renault, while the Iceman and McLaren were no doubt left to ponder what might have been if the car had been less temperamental.

Renault were out of the blocks first, the much-vaunted new R25 chassis giving the team a maximum return from the first four races. Giancarlo Fisichella dominated from pole in the Melbourne curtain-raiser, but a hat-trick of wins for Alonso followed, sending an early signal to Schumacher, Raikkonen et al that this might be the breakthrough year for Spain's rising star.

Ferrari's indifferent start to the season prompted the team to hasten the introduction of the new car, at Bahrain. Schumacher's race ended in hydraulics failure, the first time in four years that a mechanical problem had caused the seven-times champion to retire.

Iceman dogged by bad luck

If Raikkonen thought his ill-luck was behind him when he scored successive wins, in Barcelona and Monaco, he was to be sadly mistaken. At the European GP, staged at the Nürburgring, the McLaren's suspension failed within sight of victory. The fact that Alonso snatched his fourth win of the year made it even harder to take. The Finn did win an error-strewn Montreal GP, but with three blown engines in the next six rounds, his luck was definitely out. Those engine changes dropped him 10 places down the grid at Magny-Cours, Silverstone and Monza, Raikkonen performing miracles to finish in the top four in each race.

Alonso's win in France gave Renault their first home victory since Alain Prost's victory at Paul Ricard in 1983. Jenson Button's fourth place was his and BAR's first points of the year. It was a welcome boost for the team which had seen Button's third place at Imola chalked off for a technical infringement, then been hit with a two-race ban.

About-turn by Button

It would be a disappointing year for BAR, after finishing second to Ferrari in 2004. Yet before the season was out, Button nailed his long-term colours firmly to the team's mast. His dramatic about-turn came at a heavy cost: Button was reported to have stumped up over £10 million to buy himself out of the contract which tied him to Williams in 2006.

Juan Pablo Montoya scored his maiden victory for McLaren at Silverstone, heading Alonso and Raikkonen. Another 10 points for Alonso at Hockenheim – after Raikkonen ground to a halt while leading – gave the Spaniard a 36-point cushion going to the Hungaroring. That was cut to 26 when the Iceman scored a maximum while Alonso failed to score for only the third time in 13 races.

Istanbul, a new venue for the F1 circus, proved a happy hunting ground for Kimi, but Alonso capitalised on a Montoya mistake to snatch second and limit the damage. Another Raikkonen – Alonso one-two at Spa meant that the Finn had only shaved 2 points off the Spaniard's lead with races running out. Alonso's third place at Interlagos made the title secure, taking the edge off a McLaren clean sweep. The Spaniard had realised his dream in the back yard of Emerson Fittipaldi, whose record as the youngest F1 champion he had broken.

Alonso dominated from pole as the curtain on the season came down at Shanghai. He had thus mounted the podium 15 times in 18 starts – discounting the US fiasco – and stood atop it on seven occasions. He was undoubtedly a worthy champion, though if Raikkonen kept away from ladders in the close season, 2006 had all the makings of another titanic battle.

SCHUMACHER CALLS TIME

2006

2006 DRIVERS' CHAMPIONSHIP

1.	FERNANDO ALONSO	134
2.	MICHAEL SCHUMACHER	121
3.	FELIPE MASSA	80

CONSTRUCTORS' TITLE

1.	RENAULT	206
2.	FERRARI	201
3.	MCLAREN-MERCEDES	110

The defining event of the 2006 season was certainly the announcement after the Italian Grand Prix that Michael Schumacher was to retire from F1.

A slow start to the season made Shumacher's chances of a final victory unlikely, but the Ferrari team returned to form as the season progressed and Schumacher celebrated three consecutive wins in America, France and Germany in July. Renault's fortunes began to change at the same time as Ferrari's, albeit in the opposite direction. Fernando Alonso had started well, winning the first race in Bahrain and securing a run of victories, beginning on his home ground at the Spanish Grand Prix in May and ending in Montreal three races later. However, several FIA rulings went against Renault and Alonso faced a dry-spell, finishing fifth in Indianapolis and Hochenheim and retiring altogether from the Hungaroring.

A two-horse race

Schumacher began to close the gap in the Drivers' Championship, which Alonso continued to dominate in spite of his bad run. The young Spaniard was beset by further difficulties, most notably he was penalized for obstructing Massa in qualifying for the Italian Grand Prix. The penalty, which saw him demoted from fifth to tenth position on the starting grid, was the subject of some controversy, but serious protest was averted when he was forced to retire with engine trouble. Schumacher won the race and was by then trailing Alonso by just two points. His victory had also allowed Ferrari to nudge ahead of Renault in the Constructors' Championship for the first time that season.

The next meeting in Shanghai three weeks later saw Alonso gain pole position with Schumacher starting back in sixth. However, Schumacher turned the race around and pushed Alonso into second place. Schumacher's victory meant the two titans were level on points, with Schumacher clinching first place owing to a greater number of wins. With just two races to go, Schumacher's last season was proving to be one of the most nail biting. At the Suzuka Circuit in Japan the following week, Schumacher's engine trouble forced him to retire and handed Alonso victory.

BELOW: *2006 Chinese Grand Prix, Shanghai. Fernando Alonso, (Renault R26), 2nd, Michael Schumacher, (Ferrari 248F1) winner, and Giancarlo Fisichella, (Renault R26), 3rd .*

Alonso seals victory

Going into the final race in Brazil with ten-points clear, Alonso would have taken some beating; Schumacher needed to win and for his rival to score no points whatsoever. In the event, neither of them won, Felipe Massa was victorious, the first native to take the Brazilian Grand Prix since Ayrton Senna in 1993. Schumacher could not even hope for second place after suffering a puncture and losing considerable ground. However, confirming his place as the world's greatest driver, he pulled back from nineteenth to finish a respectable fourth. It was not good enough to pry the Drivers' Championship from Alonso, who finished in second place. No other driver came close to challenging Alonso or Schumacher for the Drivers' Championship. Of the three other drivers to win a race during the season, only Jenson Button was not in a Ferrari or Renault. Button's victory in Hungary for the Honda Racing Team was his first ever. The other two winners were Massa in Turkey and Brazil and Fisichella in Malaysia.

Constructors' championship

If the Drivers' Championship had been all but won by Alonso before any competitors arrived in Sao Paulo, the race for the Constructors' Championship was still to play for. Ferrari was just eleven points adrift of Renault going into the race and Massa's surprise victory handed Ferrari ten points. Despite Schumacher's best efforts to storm his way around the Autodromo Carlos Pace, Renault was unbeatable once Alonso had secured second place and Fisichella's three points merely sealed the victory.

An exit for Villeneuve

The 2006 season also marked the exit of former Champion Jacques Villeneuve. The Canadian suffered from injuries after a crash in Hochenheim and BMW Sauber replaced him with the young Polish driver Robert Kubica in the next race at Hungaroring.

ABOVE: *2006 Italian Grand Prix, Monza. Kimi Räikkönen, (McLaren MP4/21-Mercedes-Benz), leads the eventual winner, Michael Schumacher (Ferrari 248F1) at the start of the race.*

Underperforming Juan Pablo Montoya also departed F1 in July 2006 and headed for NASCAR. After a lacklustre season, Montoya decided to leave McLaren, who had already snapped up Alonso for the 2007 season and had not yet settled upon a second driver. Two months later, Kimi Raikkonen also left McLaren to fill the void left by Schumacher at Ferrari. It was later announced that Lewis Hamilton, a rising British driver, would become Alonso's teammate at McLaren.

A season of change

The season heralded lots of changes in the sport. 2006 was to be the last season that Michelin would supply tyres for F1. The FIA had wanted to have just one tyre supplier in the interests of fairness and safety. However, Michelin believed the move went against the interests of competition and innovation in the tyre industry and withdrew from the sport, leaving Bridgestone as the sole supplier.

Several established teams disappeared in 2006 following a series of buy-outs. Peter Sauber sold-up to the German car giant BMW, Jordan became Spyker and BAR changed to Honda, after the Japanese colossus assumed total control of the team. Minardi was bought by Red Bull to develop rookie drivers. As well a changes to exiting teams, a new team also made its debut in 2006, albeit with strong support from Honda. Super Aguri was introduced at the last minute by Aguri Suzuki, the former F1 driver and served to give the Japanese driver, Takura Sato, a new lease of life after being left out of the Honda team in favour of Button and Barrichello.

'ICEMAN' WINS THREE-WAY SHOOT-OUT

2007

2007 DRIVERS' CHAMPIONSHIP

1.	KIMI RÄIKKÖNEN	110
2.	LEWIS HAMILTON	109
3.	FERNANDO ALONSO	109

CONSTRUCTORS' TITLE

1.	FERRARI	204
2.	BMW-SAUBER	101
3.	RENAULT	51

Formula One adjusted to life after Schumacher by hailing the arrival on the scene of a 22-year-old from Stevenage who made an even bigger impact than the German ace managed in his rookie year. Lewis Hamilton may have been off the radar for many fans, but insiders were well aware that here was a rising star who regarded F1 as his dream and his destiny, and had been working tirelessly towards fulfilling both for over a decade.

Hamilton's debut season didn't include a trip to Imola, as San Marino was dropped from the schedule after a quarter of a century on the F1 roster. There was no German Grand Prix, either, though that country maintained its representation in the circus via the European GP. Spa, meanwhile, had had a facelift and was restored to the circuit line-up, making 2007 a 17-round extravaganza.

Record rookie performance

Hamilton quickly showed he was in no mood to play the part of understudy to double world champion Fernando Alonso, recruited from Renault to spearhead McLaren's bid for honours. He followed up a third-place finish at the Melbourne curtain-raiser with eight consecutive podium finishes, a record performance by a rookie in the 58-year history of the championship. One person who remained aloof as the Hamilton bandwagon rolled on was Alonso. The frosty relationship between the two drivers never thawed.

The season turned into a virtual duopoly and a four-horse race for the title, such was the dominance of McLaren and Ferrari. If one didn't take the chequered flag, the other did. Ferrari, who had lost the services of technical wizard Ross Brawn, as well as Schumacher, recorded nine wins to McLaren's eight. It was also pretty much a two-way carve-up of the minor placings. Of the 51 podium spots up for grabs during the course of the season, Ferrari and McLaren bagged 46, and with a little more luck that figure could have been even higher.

Nick Heidfeld and Alex Wurz took the minor placings in Canada, the scene of Hamilton's maiden triumph. They were helped by the fact that Alonso was handed a 10-second penalty for pitting when the safety car was out, and Massa was disqualified for leaving the pits when the exit was closed. Wurz had been promoted to the Williams team following Mark Webber's departure to Red Bull. He didn't even see the season out, retiring from F1 before Interlagos, but he had the honour of giving the team its first podium of the new Toyota-powered era.

BELOW: *2007 Monaco Grand Prix, Monte Carlo. Fernando Alonso, (McLaren MP4-22 Mercedes), on his way to taking the chequered flag for his second win of the season.*

Heidfeld was the only driver outside the big four to claim a top-three spot in two races, bringing his BMW-Sauber home behind Hamilton and Räikkönen in Hungary. Once again, things might have been different had Alonso not been bumped back five places on the grid, to sixth, for impeding his teammate during qualifying. Even so, BMW-Sauber was the surprise package of the year, outpacing reigning champions Renault in the race for the Constructors' title.

Mark Webber took third at the European Grand Prix, after Räikkönen retired and Hamilton slid off in a downpour that claimed several victims. Hamilton finished ninth after being craned back onto the track, the last driver to be afforded that assistance before the FIA ruled against it.

Kovalainen impresses

The only other man to loosen the Ferrari-McLaren grip on the podium was another impressive rookie, Heikki Kovalainen, who had taken Alonso's seat at Renault. He finished second to Hamilton in Japan from 11th on the grid, keeping his head as a string of drivers hit trouble. The Finn held off his compatriot, 'Iceman' Räikkönen, to secure his first podium in F1.

Hamilton was joint-leader after Bahrain, and out on his own by round four, Barcelona. There were setbacks along the way, notably a disastrous Shanghai sortie, where the Briton beached his MP4-22, but he clung to his lead until the final round. Massa had fallen by the wayside by then, making it a dramatic three-way shoot-out involving Alonso and Räikkönen: the current McLaren duo battling with the man who had left the team to step into Schumacher's shoes.

And so to Brazil, with Hamilton holding a four point lead over Alonso and a seven-point advantage over Räikkönen. Pole-sitter Felipe Massa would have

ABOVE: *British Grand Prix, Silverstone. The top three drivers of 2007 occupy the podium after Kimi Raikkonen's victory. Fernando Alonso (left) second and Lewis Hamilton (right) third.*

sent his legions of fans delirious with a home victory, but after leading for much of the race, he made way for his Ferrari teammate. Alonso needed second place to pip the Finn but never looked like threatening the Ferraris and had to settle for third. Fate was against Hamilton, who recovered from an off-road excursion, only to suffer a gearbox problem and slip to 18th – 16 places down on his grid position. Many an eyebrow was raised at the three-stop strategy, which backfired badly. Hamilton battled on gamely to finish seventh, when fifth would have been enough to give him the title. McLaren's appeal over a fuel temperature irregularity involving the Williams and BMW-Sauber cars that finished ahead of their man came to nought, and Hamilton was gracious enough to say he didn't want to win by default.

Räikkönen became the third Finnish driver to don the crown, following in the footsteps of Keke Rosberg and Mika Hakkinen, and by taking the title from third place going into the final round, he emulated the achievement of Guiseppe Farina in the inaugural championship.

'Spygate'

The 'Spygate' scandal turned the Constructors' Championship from a tight, two-horse race into a stroll for Ferrari. The FIA slapped a £50 million fine on McLaren and expunged the team's points from the records when it was revealed that chief designer Mike Coughlan had been found in possession of a dossier detailing Ferrari F1 update 2007 technical data.

HAMILTON SNATCHES THE TITLE

2008

2008 DRIVERS' CHAMPIONSHIP

1.	LEWIS HAMILTON	98
2.	FELIPE MASSA	97
3.	KIMI RAIKKONEN	75

CONSTRUCTORS' TITLE

1.	FERRARI	172
2.	MCLAREN-MERCEDES	151
3.	BMW SAUBER	135

How could the 2008 season possibly match a three-way shoot-out in the deciding race and a final table that saw the top trio separated by a single point? Simple. Have the title won and lost in the last corners of the eight-month-long battle; and witness the shortest victory party on record as the team first across the line realised that the chequered flag had not delivered the championship. 2008 had an emotional wringer of a finale, one that Hollywood scriptwriters might have thought twice about serving up.

Raikkonen and Massa again spearheaded Ferrari's challenge, but the frosty relations between Hamilton and Alonso meant that something had to give at McLaren. Alonso returned to Renault, swapping places with Heikki Kovaleinen, who had impressed in his debut season. Nelson Piquet Jr was promoted from test driver to partner Alonso, which left no room for Giancarlo Fisichella. He joined Force India, the new incarnation for Spyker, which had billionaire businessman Vijay Mallya at its helm. Cash-strapped Super Aguri had no such benefactor and folded after four races. David Coulthard announced that 2008 would be his final lap, while Ralf Schumacher departed to join the DTM Touring Cars series. Schumacher's replacement at Toyota was compatriot Timo Glock, the 2007 GP2 champion who had enjoyed a brief spell in the limelight with Jordan in 2004.

New street circuits

Indianapolis lost its place on the schedule, but two new street circuits were added, Valencia and Singapore. The former took over the European Grand Prix slot, leaving the Nurburgring to alternate with Hockenheim when the circus visited Germany. The Singapore GP, staged at the Marina Bay harbourside circuit, heralded the elite division's first ever night race.

Lewis Hamilton got off to a flier in the post-traction control era, avoiding a first-lap pile-up on his way to taking maximum points from pole in Melbourne. Nick Heidfeld gave BMW Sauber second place, while Nico Rosberg brought his Williams home third to record his first podium finish. Ferrari had a forgettable day; neither car made it home and the team registered a solitary point as Raikkonen was classified seventh.

Ferrari hit back at Sepang. Pole-sitter Massa again failed to finish, but Raikkonen scored maximum points to get his title defence well under way. Robert Kubica took a career-best second, while Kovaleinen, who had outqualified Hamilton, bagged six points and his first podium. Lewis crossed the line fifth, an acceptable return for McLaren considering both drivers were demoted five grid places for qualifying misdemeanours.

Ferrari took one-two in Bahrain, but it was a black day for Hamilton, who dropped six places in a disastrous first lap, then tangled with Alonso's Renault to effectively end his interest. Kovaleinen gave McLaren a consolation fifth as he trailed home the BMW Sauber duo. Kubica and Heidfeld put their team atop the constructors' pile after three rounds, but when Raikkonen won from pole in Barcelona, and Massa matched that achievement in Istanbul, the picture assumed a more familiar hue. Hamilton picked up minor placings in those two races, then struck a major blow by winning from third on the grid behind the Ferraris in Monaco. An early puncture worked in his favour, allowing the MP4-23 to be fully fuelled so that he could stay out on a drying track. He became the first Englishman to win in Monaco since Graham Hill in 1969.

Maiden win for Kubica

There was high drama in Montreal. Hamilton got away well from pole, but when the safety car came out and the leading cars dived into the pits, he failed to spot a red light at the exit and rear-ended Raikkonen, taking them both out of the race. Kubica claimed his and BMW Sauber's maiden victory, with Heidfeld following him home. Hamilton was docked ten grid places at Magny-Cours for his indiscretion, and the Ferraris made hay with another one-two. Massa profited from Raikkonen's exhaust problem to take the flag and with it the championship lead for the first time in his career.

ABOVE: *Rival drivers Felipe Massa (l) of Brazil (Ferrari) and Lewis Hamilton (r) of Great Britain (McLaren Mercedes) pictured prior to the Brazilian Grand Prix. The race, at the Interlagos Circuit in Sao Paulo, would decide the destination of the drivers' world championship.*

Hamilton cruised home a minute ahead of the field at Silverstone, and followed it up with another 10-point haul at Hockenheim. If anyone had a bigger grin on his face than Lewis after the German GP it was second-placed Piquet Jr, who led eight laps from home after qualifying 17th. A puncture ended Hamilton's chance of making it a hat-trick in Hungary, but McLaren celebrated a maiden win for Kovaleinen, while Glock took second to give him his first experience of spraying the champagne.

Raikkonen was third at the Hungaroring, but his campaign faltered with blanks in his next four outings. Massa won two of those, Valencia and Spa, to become the Ferrari front-runner. He inherited the victory in Belgium after race winner Hamilton was penalised for cutting a chicane, enough to drop him to third. Massa pegged another point back on Hamilton at Monza in a scrap for the minor placings. Top honours went to Toro Rosso and Sebastian Vettel, who replaced Fernando Alonso in the record books as F1's youngest winner.

Alonso himself won the next two races, in Singapore and Japan, though it was somewhat late for a third championship bid. Massa had a forgettable race in Singapore, incurring a drive-through penalty for taking off down the pitlane with the fuel hose attached. He finished well down the field while Hamilton garnered six points. Both men were penalised for infringements at Fuji Speedway, but Massa recovered to take seventh, Hamilton finishing out of the points.

Hamilton stretched his lead to seven with a win in China. Raikkonen, now out of contention, ceded second place to his team-mate, while Kubica's slim hopes of taking the title disappeared. It was now a straight fight between the top two going into Massa's home race.

The Brazilian could have done no more at Interlagos. He took pole, set the fastest lap and scored maximum points, knowing that it counted only if Hamilton finished out of the top five. That looked a distinct possibility as a cloudburst made the track treacherous in the latter stages. All the front-runners dived into the pits for intermediates, except for Glock. He inherited fourth place in the shake-up, hoping to nurse his Toyota home on dry tyres. Behind him, Vettel seized upon a Hamilton mistake to take the all-important fifth spot two laps out. The Ferrari camp began celebrating, prematurely, for both Vettel and Hamilton passed Glock at the death. It was a desperately close-run thing but Hamilton had done just enough to be crowned the youngest ever champion, while Ferrari had the consolation of landing a 16th Constructors' title.

THE DRIVERS

32 PODIUMS FOR FLYING FRENCHMAN

JEAN ALESI

B. 11 JUNE 1964, AVIGNON, FRANCE

GRAND PRIX STARTS: 201

GRAND PRIX VICTORIES: 1

POINTS TOTAL: 242

One solitary victory from 201 F1 starts might seem deeply unimpressive until you realize that Jean Alesi suffered 83 retirements and made the podium on 32 occasions. Then a more accurate reflection of his ability over a 13-year career at the top is revealed.

Alesi won the French F3 championship in 1987, and in 1989 took the European Formula 3000 title for Eddie Jordan's team. In the same year Ken Tyrell gave him his F1 debut in the 1989 French GP where, from sixteenth on the grid, he finished a brilliant fourth. In just half a season's racing he finished ninth place overall.

A full season with Tyrell produced two second places, one of those being at the US GP, where he was spotted by Frank Williams. However, in the end Alesi opted to join Ferrari in 1991 and spent five years there, making the podium 16 times. When he eventually took a victory, at the 1995 Canadian GP, it still only helped him to fifth in the title race.

A move to Benetton in 1996 initially held promise as eight podiums gained Alesi a fourth in the championship, and in 1997 he peaked with third before moving to Sauber. After one false dawn there, and another with Prost, he briefly returned to Jordan in 2001 before announcing his retirement from F1.

TWO TIME WORLD CHAMPION

FERNANDO ALONSO

B. 29 JULY 1981, OVIEDO, SPAIN

GRAND PRIX STARTS: 123*

GRAND PRIX VICTORIES: 21*

POINTS TOTAL: 551*

WORLD CHAMPION : 2005, 2006

*TO END OF 2008 SEASON

In 2005, Fernando Alonso completed a hat-trick of records: the youngest ever pole-sitter (2003), race winner (2003) and now world champion, the latter breaking Fittipaldi's long-standing record of 1972.

The son of an amateur kart racer, Alonso first climbed into the cockpit at the age of three, later competing successfully in competitions, firstly in his native Spain, then internationally.

By 2000 he had graduated to F3000 earning fourth place in that year's championship. He made his F1 debut with Minardi the following year at the Australian GP, at the age of 19. No points that season,

but the Spaniard's potential was spotted and he signed as test driver for Renault for 2002.

2003 saw Alonso promoted into a race seat and the start of his determined efforts to reach the very top of the tree. His maiden victory came in Hungary, taking three more podiums that year to finish with 55 points and sixth place.

By contrast, the early part of 2004 was disappointing with team-mate Jarno Trulli out-racing him. As the season progressed Alonso's performance improved, and he finished the year in fourth place.

Teamed with Giancarlo Fisichella in 2005, Alonso's first win of the campaign came in Malaysia, followed by victories in Bahrain and at San Marino. Battling against the improving form of McLaren in the shape of Kimi Raikkonen, he clinched the world title in Brazil, finishing third that day. He added 7 wins, 15 podiums and 133 points to his score-sheet, having led the championship from the second race of the season.

Alonso moved to McLaren in 2007, ceding his crown to Ferrari's Raikkonen in a final-round thriller. He tied for the runner-up spot with rookie team-mate Lewis Hamilton. Relations were strained between the two and it was little surprise when Alonso rejoined Renault at the end of the year. He won back-to-back races in 2008, the inaugural Singapore GP and in Japan, to finish fifth in the championship.

CHRIS AMON

FOURTEEN YEARS AT THE TOP

B. 20 JULY 1943, NEW ZEALAND

GRAND PRIX STARTS: 96

GRAND PRIX VICTORIES: 0

POINTS TOTAL: 83

Chris Amon made his F1 debut aged 19 and spent 14 years racing at the top level, appearing on the podium 11 times. Having caught the eye of Reg Parnell during the 1962–63 Tasman series, he was invited to compete in the 1963 world championship. The following year he claimed his first points at Zandvoort.

After Parnell's death Amon went through a period of upheaval before moving to Ferrari in 1967, where he scored in six of the first eight races. After team-mate Lorenzo Bandini was killed at Monaco, Amon led the way for Ferrari, finishing fourth in the championship.

The next two seasons with Ferrari were generally disappointing, and in 1970 Amon teamed up with Siffert for the new March enterprise. He won the non-championship International Trophy at Silverstone, and took three podiums to finish seventh overall.

Then two seasons with Matra promised more than they delivered. Having won the non-championship Argentina GP in 1971, he then lost his visor while leading in the latter stages at Monza. At Clermont Ferrand in 1972, where he looked a clear winner, a puncture relegated him to third.

He managed just a single point in 1973, driving for Tecno, and drew a blank running his own car in the following year. His move to Ensign in 1975 saw him record one fifth place in ten outings. In late 1976 Amon turned to the fledgling Wolf team but an accident prior to the Canadian GP ended his F1 career.

AMERICA'S GREATEST WORLD CHAMPION

MARIO ANDRETTI

B. 28 FEBRUARY 1940, MONTONA, ITALY

GRAND PRIX STARTS: 128

GRAND PRIX VICTORIES: 12

POINTS TOTAL: 180

WORLD CHAMPION: 1978

Mario Andretti's record makes him America's greatest world champion. His family emigrated to the US when he was a teenager, and within a decade he had won a hat-trick of Indy Car titles. He made his F1 debut for Lotus at Watkins Glen in 1968, where he took pole. In 1969 Andretti appeared for the STP March team, with whom he scored his first points, finishing third at Jarama.

On joining Ferrari in 1971, he won first time out at Kyalami, but didn't concentrate on F1 full-time until 1975, with Parnelli. After a couple of indifferent seasons the team folded and he returned to Lotus. In the Lotus 78 Andretti drove to four victories in 1977 and third place in the championship. His performance continued to improve in 1978, winning six races; helped along the way by team-mate Ronnie Peterson, who acted as the perfect foil, following him home four times.

By the time they reached Monza, Lotus had the championship won, though either driver could have claimed the crown. Peterson was injured in a shunt and Andretti went on to win yet again. The title was his when the news came through that Peterson had died from complications.

Lotus lost its way over the next two years. Andretti's move to Alfa Romeo produced a disappointing 3 points. In 1982 he returned to Indy Cars, taking yet another title in 1984.

VICTORIES WITH RENAULT AND FERRARI

RENE ARNOUX

B. 4 JULY 1948, NEAR GRENOBLE, FRANCE

GRAND PRIX STARTS: 149

GRAND PRIX VICTORIES: 7

POINTS TOTAL: 179

Having just won the F2 championship in a works Martini, Rene Arnoux arrived in F1 in 1978 and ended the year driving for Surtees. In 1979 he moved to Renault and in the competitive RS10 he twice took pole, finishing second at both Silverstone and Watkins Glen.

Although winning two early races at Interlagos and Kyalami in 1980, Arnoux could not sustain his form and ended the year in sixth place, well adrift of Jones and Piquet. 1981 proved a thin year; he failed to convert speed into wins and a second in Austria was the highlight. Two wins in 1982 gained him sixth place in the championship, but a breach of team orders meant that it was his last season with Renault.

In 1983 he moved to Ferrari and won three GPs but failed to score in the last two rounds and finished third in the championship. His performance thereafter was disappointing and, after the opening round of the 1985 championship, he was fired. He spent the final four years of his F1 career with Ligier, gaining eighth place in the 1986 championships. The final three seasons yielded a total of just 3 points.

THE LAST ITALIAN WORLD CHAMPION

ALBERTO ASCARI

B. 13 JULY 1918, MILAN, ITALY

D. 26 MAY 1955

GRAND PRIX STARTS: 31

GRAND PRIX VICTORIES: 13

POINTS TOTAL: 140.64

WORLD CHAMPION 1952, 1953

Alberto Ascari and his father Antonio had careers which followed an eerily similar path. Ascari Snr. – one of the premier drivers of the post-WWI era – was killed at the age of 36 while competing at the 1925 French GP. Thirty years later Alberto lost his life on the track at the age of 36.

Ascari began his racing career with motorbikes before moving to four wheels with Ferrari in 1940 in the famous Mille Miglia road race, but it was not until 1947 that he made his Grand Prix debut. Having moved to Maserati, he and team-mate and mentor Luigi Villoresi started from the back of the grid at the 1948 British GP as a result of arriving late. They carved their way through the field to finish first and second. Villoresi took top honours, but Ascari was recognised as a driver with enormous potential.

By the end of the following season, with wins at the Swiss and Italian GPs, Ascari was back with Ferrari. He finished fifth in the inaugural world championship of 1950. A year later he won in Germany and Italy, but it wasn't quite enough to take the title from Fangio and Alfa Romeo. In 1952 he won at Spa and the following five Grand Prix races, assuring him the world championship for that year. Ascari's victory at Spa in June 1953 completed a run of nine successive wins in a twelve-month period and he retained his title with a win at Bremgarten.

Ascari's move to Lancia in 1954 resulted in a disappointing Championship Series that year. In 1955 he walked away unscathed from a dramatic crash into the harbour at Monaco, only to be killed four days later while testing a Ferrari sports car at Monza. He remains the last Italian to win the world championship.

RUBENS BARRICHELLO

CONTENDER FOR THE WORLD CROWN

B. 23 MAY 1972, SAO PAULO, BRAZIL

GRAND PRIX STARTS: 271*

GRAND PRIX VICTORIES: 9*

POINTS TOTAL: 530*

*TO END OF 2008 SEASON

n 2004 Rubens Barrichello completed his fifth season as foil to Michael Schumacher's perennial assault on the championship. His efforts helped Ferrari lift the Constructors' title in each of those seasons. Runner-up to Schumacher in 2002 and 2004, Barrichello has shown on numerous occasions that he has the talent to beat anyone on his day. Indeed, in Austria 2002 Barrichello led until the final lap before team orders forced him to allow Schumacher through. The bad publicity this attracted led to the banning of such practices.

Barrichello went to Europe after winning five national kart titles in his teens. He immediately won the GM Lotus Euroseries, then beat Coulthard to the 1991 British F3 title, driving for West Surrey Racing. He made his F1 debut for Jordan in 1993. In only his third race, the European GP at Donington, he was running second before retiring, while his first points came at Suzuka, where he finished fifth.

He began 1994 strongly, including a podium finish at the Pacific GP, but suffered a big spill during practice at Imola. Deeply affected by Senna's death, he showed great fortitude in taking a brilliant pole at Spa. He was sixth that year, and having failed to

improve on that in the next two seasons, left to join the Stewart team in 1997.

Finishing second to Schumacher at Monaco was that year's highlight. After a disappointing 1998, his loyalty to Stewart was rewarded with three podiums and seventh in the 1999 championship, though it was team-mate Johnny Herbert who gave the team its first victory. In 2000 he replaced Irvine as Ferrari no. 2, scoring his maiden win from 18th on the grid at a wet Hockenheim. After six years as Ferrari's No.2, 33-year-old Barrichello took up a fresh challenge with Honda. The next three seasons yielded just 41 points, though the 2008 Turkish GP, his 257th, did see him pass Riccardo Patrese's record for F1 starts. Barrichello went into the 2009 season, his 17th in F1, driving for the new Brawn GP team.

GERHARD BERGER

200 FORMULA ONE RACES IN 14 YEARS

B. 27 AUG 1959, WORGL, AUSTRIA

GRAND PRIX STARTS: 210

GRAND PRIX VICTORIES: 10

POINTS TOTAL: 386

Gerhard Berger is one of only a handful of drivers to compete in over 200 F1 races, a consistent performer in his 14-year career at the top level. He made his debut at the 1984 Austrian GP for ATS, finishing sixth in only his second race. A move to Arrows yielded 3 points in 1985, but his career then took off. He joined Benetton, which had just evolved from Toleman, scoring both his and the team's maiden victory in Mexico.

Ferrari came calling, and Berger embarked on the first of two stints at Maranello. He won the final two races to secure fifth place in 1987; only the 'big four' – Prost, Senna, Piquet and Mansell – finished ahead of him. A year later only the runaway McLarens of Senna and Prost got the better of him, and his one victory came in the best place of all for a Ferrari man, Monza. New team-mate Mansell outscored him in 1989, though in an indifferent season he enjoyed a huge slice of luck: escaping a big accident at Imola with minor injuries.

Three years at McLaren followed, a period where he was naturally in Senna's shadow. He was a regular on the podium, but scored just three wins. At Suzuka in 1991 Senna moved over on the last lap to let him taste victory. And in Montreal

a year later he inherited the lead after Senna retired with electrical trouble.

Berger returned to Ferrari in 1993, a period when Maranello was playing second fiddle to Williams and Benetton. He did win at Hockenheim in 1994 to break Ferrari's longest winless streak, a season in which he finished third yet again, a position he would never improve upon.

His final two campaigns were back at Benetton. With team bosses hinting that his days were numbered, Berger announced his retirement before Hockenheim, then won the race in brilliant style again.

THREE TIMES WORLD CHAMPION

JACK BRABHAM

B. 2 APRIL 1926, HURSTVILLE, AUSTRALIA

GRAND PRIX STARTS: 126

GRAND PRIX VICTORIES: 14

POINTS TOTAL: 261

WORLD CHAMPION: 1959, 1960, 1966

Jack Brabham moved from the dirt-track circuits of his native Australia to Britain in 1955 to test himself against the cream of Europe. He joined the Cooper Car Company team and made his F1 debut at the British GP that year. He gave the works team its first success at Monaco in 1959, going on to win the championship title ahead of Moss.

In 1960 Brabham retained his title with two rounds to spare. When he slipped down the rankings in 1961, he set up his own team, and before the 1962 season was out had become the first man to notch championship points in his own car.

The fledgling team achieved its first victory with Dan Gurney, in the 1964 French GP. Two years later Jack matched that achievement, followed by three more victories in 1966, to win his third world championship. He remains the only man to lift the crown in a car bearing his name.

Brabham competed for four more years, claiming his fourteenth and final victory at Kyalami in 1970. He retired after finishing fifth in that year's championship, and sold the team to Bernie Ecclestone the following year.

TONY BROOKS

CHAMPIONSHIP RUNNER-UP FOR FERRARI

B. 25 FEBRUARY 1932, DUKINFIELD, ENGLAND

GRAND PRIX STARTS: 38

GRAND PRIX VICTORIES: 6 (1 SHARED)

POINTS TOTAL: 75

Tony Brooks gave up a career in dentistry to concentrate on motor racing. 1955 was his breakthrough year when he moved to single-seaters, winning the non-championship Syracuse GP in a Connaught on his F1 debut. The following year Brooks contested his first world championship, with BRM, but it was to prove a false dawn as he was thrown from his car during practice at Silverstone, and spent the rest of the year competing in sports car events.

Having signed for Vanwall in 1957, he finished fifth in the championship that year. Brooks won three times in 1958 – in Belgium, Germany and Italy – but a number of retirements meant that he had to settle for third place overall, behind Hawthorn and Moss.

Vanwall withdrew at the end of the year and Brooks moved to Ferrari where he finished the season runner-up, 4 points behind the formidable Jack Brabham. In his final two seasons he slipped down the rankings, garnering a total of just 13 points. Having joined the Yeoman Credit team in 1960, Brooks moved back to BRM for his final campaign. He retired at the end of 1961 to concentrate on his garage business.

JENSON BUTTON

YOUNGEST BRITON TO ACHIEVE A CHAMPIONSHIP POINT

B. 19 JANUARY 1980, FROME, ENGLAND

GRAND PRIX STARTS: 155*

GRAND PRIX VICTORIES: 1*

POINTS TOTAL: 232*

* TO END OF 2008 SEASON

Having starred in Cadet Karts at the age of 8, Button won the British championship in 1990 and 1991, finishing runner-up in the world championship in 1995. In 1997, at the age of 17, he became the youngest winner of the European Super A championship, and was seen as one of motor sport's rising stars.

In 1998 he continued his upward surge, taking the British Formula Ford title, and a third in the F3 championship. In late 1999, Button finally signed with Williams, finishing sixth in only his second GP, Interlagos 2000, and becoming the youngest Briton to notch a championship point. He ended the year in eighth place.

Button spent the next two seasons with Benetton-Renault. In 2002 he scored in seven races and finished seventh in the final table. He moved to BAR in 2003, regularly outperforming team-mate Jacques Villeneuve, a former world champion. In 2004 only the Ferraris got the better of Button, who stood on the podium ten times and scored 85 points.

Button started 2005 poorly, with a disqualification at the San Marino GP, and hence a three-race ban. His performance improved with third places at both Hockenheim and Francorchamps, ending the season with 37 points and ninth place overall.

A number of contractual controversies during 2004 and 2005 between Button, Honda and Williams, led to speculation that he would be leaving BAR. In fact he remained with the Honda team during 2005 and went on to win his first race with them at the Hungaroring in 2006. Button notched just nine points over the next two seasons, and went into the 2009 campaign under the new Brawn GP banner following Ross Brawn's buy-out of the Honda team.

PETER COLLINS

TRAGIC END FOR GENEROUS ENGLISHMAN

B. 6 NOVEMBER 1931, KIDDERMINSTER, ENGLAND

D. 3 AUGUST 1958

GRAND PRIX STARTS: 32

GRAND PRIX VICTORIES: 3

POINTS TOTAL: 47

Peter Collins moved up to F1 at the age of 20, and made his championship debut with HWM at the 1952 Swiss GP. Over the next three years he made little impression but Ferrari recognised his potential and signed him for 1956 to play the supporting role to Fangio. This he did most notably at Monaco, where he handed his Lancia-Ferrari over after the three-times

champion's car failed. Victories at Spa and Reims demonstrated that Collins was a serious contender in his own right.

Then, at Monza, Collins made the ultimate sacrifice: both he and Jean Behra went into the race knowing they could take the title from Fangio with a victory and fastest lap, provided Fangio failed to score. With Behra and Fangio out of the race, Collins sacrificed his own championship ambitions and allowed Fangio to take over his car. Fangio duly took the title, and Collins was relegated to third in the final table behind Moss.

1957 saw Collins recording just two third places in a season dominated by Fangio and Maserati. 1958 looked set fair with Collins registering two top-six finishes and beating team-mate Mike Hawthorn into second place at Silverstone. At the Nürburgring, lying third in the championship, Collins was vying for the lead with Tony Brooks' Vanwall, when he was flung from his car and fatally injured. He was 26 and finished a posthumous fifth in that year's championship. However, he is best remembered for his spirit of generosity and self-sacrifice in helping Fangio take his fourth world title.

TRAGIC END FOR SUPREME RACER

JIM CLARK

B. 4 MARCH 1936, KILMANY, SCOTLAND

D. 7 APRIL 1968

GRAND PRIX STARTS: 72

GRAND PRIX VICTORIES: 25

POINTS TOTAL: 274

WORLD CHAMPION: 1963, 1965

Famous for his smoothness, effortless control and computer-like brain, Jim Clark inherited the mantle of supreme champion from Fangio. Having joined Lotus in 1960, he spent his whole career there, forging a formidable partnership with team boss Colin Chapman. His GP debut came at Zandvoort in 1960 picking up a respectable 8 points by the end of the season. The following year, he gained eighth place overall but the campaign was overshadowed by his involvement in the crash at Monza in which fourteen spectators were killed and Ferrari's Wolfgang von Trips lost his life.

Clark's maiden victory came at the 1962 Belgian GP and he went into the final round in South Africa with a chance at the championship. He was heading for the victory which would have snatched the crown from Graham Hill when his Lotus failed.

Brushing aside disappointment, Clark took the championship the following year, winning seven of the ten rounds. His chances of retaining his title in 1964 were lost when the Lotus failed on the penultimate lap of

the final race in Mexico. He took his second world crown in 1965 with another maximum haul from the six races where he reached the line. Victory in the Indy 500 made it a notable double.

1966 was a relatively lean season but early in 1967 the new Cosworth DFV engine arrived and Clark was immediately back in contention. Four more wins put him third in the championship behind the two powerful Brabhams.

His first victory in 1968 came at Kyalami, giving him his 25th career success, and putting him one ahead of Fangio in the all-time list. Clark was 31 and at the height of his powers when he competed in a F2 race at Hockenheim on 7 April. His car left the track and hit a tree, killing him instantly.

DAVID COULTHARD

SCOT'S RECORD RACE HAUL WITH McLAREN

B. 27 MARCH 1971, TWYNHOLM, SCOTLAND

GRAND PRIX STARTS: 247

GRAND PRIX VICTORIES: 13

POINTS TOTAL: 535

From winning a string of Scottish karting titles in the mid-1980s David Coulthard progressed through the ranks of Formula Vauxhall, F3 and F3000. He tested for Williams in 1993, but it was not until 1994, and Senna's death at San Marino, that he got his chance in the F1 team, partnering Damon Hill. From eight races he amassed 14 points, but was replaced by the returning Nigel Mansell for the final three races. Even so, Coulthard was offered the drive for the 1995 season, and earned third place with eight podiums in that year's title race.

He joined McLaren in 1996, and remained there for nine years, driving 150 races: a record for a driver with one team. Initially, Coulthard's ranking slipped to seventh in 1996, but two wins at Melbourne and Monza the following year helped him to equal third in that season's title race. Over the next two years his team-mate Mika Hakkinen dominated the championship, winning both the 1998 and 1999 titles, with Coulthard managing just third and fourth respectively.

By 2001 he had emerged from Hakkinen's shadow, but Schumacher's time had come and Coulthard finished a distant second in the championship. By 2003 Kimi Raikkonen had taken over as McLaren's front runner, and at the end of the following year Coulthard left to sign for the Red Bull Racing Team. Although not managing any podiums, he ended the season with 24 points and twelfth place overall. He continued racing with Red Bull in 2006 and achieved the team's first podium finish at Monaco, where he came in third. He ended the 2007 season in 10th place after amassing 14 points.

Coulthard announced that he would retire at the end of the 2008 season. He got into the points only twice in his swansong year, but there was a final flourish at the Canadian GP, where he made it onto the podium for the 62nd time.

GIUSEPPE FARINA

ITALIAN BECOMES FIRST FORMULA ONE CHAMPION

B. 30 OCTOBER 1906, TURIN, ITALY

D. 30 JUNE 1966

GRAND PRIX STARTS: 33

GRAND PRIX VICTORIES: 5

POINTS TOTAL: 127.33

WORLD CHAMPION: 1950

Giuseppe Farina was a protégé of Lazio Nuvolari in the 1930s, becoming Alfa Romeo's no. 1 driver when Nuvolari left to join Auto Union in 1937. He won a hat-trick of Italian championships prior to the outbreak of WWII, and afterwards drove Maseratis and Ferraris, but returned to Alfa on the eve of the new drivers' championship in 1950. Farina won the very first race, held at Silverstone on 13 May 1950, and snatched the title by 3 points.

The following year the tables were turned: Farina won just once and slipped to fourth in the title race, 12 points behind Fangio. Farina moved to Ferrari for 1952, where he was a regular runner-up to team-mate Ascari, and finished second and third in the championship for 1952 and 1953 respectively.

Ascari departed Ferrari in 1954 leaving Farina the team's no. 1 driver, but his season was blighted by injury. He sustained a broken arm in the Mille Miglia, then suffered terrible burns during a sports car race at Monza. He returned in 1955 to finish fifth in that year's championship, retiring at the end of the season. He was killed in a road accident while on his way to watch the 1966 French GP.

VETERAN ACE BECOMES FIVE TIMES WORLD CHAMPION

JUAN MANUEL FANGIO

B. 24 JUNE 1911, BALCARCE, ARGENTINA

D. 17 JULY 1995

GRAND PRIX STARTS: 51

GRAND PRIX VICTORIES: 24

POINTS TOTAL: 277.14

WORLD CHAMPION: 1951, 1954, 1955, 1956, 1957

In 1949 at the age of 37 Juan Manuel Fangio left his native Argentina to try his hand on the racetracks of Europe. He was an unknown quantity, but six wins in ten starts changed all that. Alfa Romeo quickly signed him for the inaugural world championship in 1950. With team-mates Farina and Fagioli – 'The Three Fs' – Alfa dominated the series. Having ceded the championship title to Farina that year, in 1951 Fangio went into the final round, the Spanish GP, holding the advantage and won easily to claim the first of his five world titles.

A broken neck put him out of the title race for 1952. He returned the following year with Maserati, but it was Ascari and Ferrari's year. At the beginning of the 1954 season, with two wins for Maserati, Fangio moved to Mercedes to drive the W196. He gave it a maiden victory at Reims, followed by three more wins and the world title.

1955 brought four more victories, and a third championship title, in a season truncated by the tragedy at Le Mans, where over 80 spectators were killed. Fangio's fourth world title was with Ferrari in 1956 and is best remembered for the magnanimity of team-mate Peter Collins, who twice gave him his car; the second time Collins himself had a chance of lifting the title. His generosity allowed Fangio a shared second behind Moss, giving him the championship by 3 points.

He returned to Maserati for 1957, and four wins in the first five European rounds set up his fifth world title. Fangio retired midway through the 1958 campaign, with a victories-to-starts ratio of almost 50 per cent.

EMERSON FITTIPALDI

WORLD CHAMPION AT TWENTY-FIVE

B. 12 DECEMBER 1946, SAO PAULO, BRAZIL

GRAND PRIX STARTS: 144

GRAND PRIX VICTORIES: 14

POINTS TOTAL: 281

WORLD CHAMPION: 1972, 1974

In becoming world champion at the age of 25 years and 298 days, Emerson Fittipaldi became the youngest world champion F1 had known. This record stood until 2005 when the honour passed to Fernando Alonso, world title-holder at 24 years and 59 days.

Within two years of arriving in Britain, Fittipaldi had earned a F1 place with Lotus, running with team-mate Jochen Rindt. Following Rindt's death, Fittipaldi drove to victory at the US GP, his maiden win coming in only his fourth start.

The Brazilian enhanced his reputation in 1971, gaining three podiums and sixth place in the championship. The following year, in the John Player Special, Fittipaldi swept to the championship with five victories. Former champion Jackie Stewart finished runner-up, and the following year their positions were reversed.

In 1974 Fittipaldi moved to McLaren. Stewart had retired and after three wins the Brazilian went into a final-race showdown at Watkins Glen with Ferrari's Clay Regazzoni. Taking fourth place Fittipaldi was assured his second championship.

Fittipaldi joined his brother's Copersucar team after finishing runner-up again in 1975, this time to Niki Lauda. Over the next five years he won a couple of podiums and retired in 1980 only to return and take the Indy Car title in 1989, winning the Indy 500 that year and in 1993.

SILVERSTONE SPECIALIST RUNS FANGIO CLOSE

JOSÉ FROILÁN GONZÁLEZ

B. 5 OCTOBER 1922, ARECIFES, ARGENTINA

GRAND PRIX STARTS: 26

GRAND PRIX VICTORIES: 2

POINTS TOTAL: 77.64

González earned backing from the Argentinian government to try his hand in Europe just as the inaugural world championship was gearing up. He drew a blank in 1950, but a move to Ferrari the following year brought a dramatic improvement, and he ran Fangio close for that year's world title. His victory at Silverstone in 1951 gave Ferrari their maiden success and González took five consecutive podium positions to finish the season third overall.

He spent the next two seasons at Maserati, the second of those with Fangio as his team-mate, but could manage no higher than sixth and ninth in the championships over that period. He returned to Ferrari in 1954 to yield his best return – runner-up to Fangio, albeit 17 points adrift of the title holder. He won the British GP again and retained a special affection for Silverstone.

However, he mainly restricted his appearances to the Argentinian GP, sharing second place in Buenos Aires in 1956, behind Fangio. He returned to Silverstone that year but there was to be no glorious hat-trick: a broken driveshaft meant that he didn't even complete one lap. He then retired to concentrate on his garage business.

MIKA HAKKINEN

TWO WORLD TITLES FOR FLYING FINN

B. 28 SEPTEMBER 1968,
HELSINKI, FINLAND

GRAND PRIX STARTS: 165

GRAND PRIX VICTORIES: 20

POINTS TOTAL: 420

WORLD CHAMPION: 1998,
1999

Mika Hakkinen took over from Keke Rosberg as Finland's F1 star. From winning the 1990 British F3 title he graduated to F1 with Lotus the following season. He scored in six races in 1992, finishing a creditable eighth in the championship, but showing potential for more. He signed for McLaren, and after Michael Andretti was fired he teamed up with Senna, finishing third behind Senna and Prost at Suzuka in just his second start.

Hakkinen took fourth place in the championship in 1994, having made six podiums. He sustained life-threatening head injuries at the 1995 Australian GP, but recovered to finish fifth in the next two seasons. His maiden victory came at Jerez, the final round of the 1997 championship. He was helped by Villeneuve reining in his Williams and allowing him to win; securing third was enough for Villeneuve to take the title and he could afford to be generous.

Victories then came thick and fast for Hakkinen: he took eight races in 1998 to claim the crown, then topped the podium five times in 1999 in defence of the title. There were four wins in 2000, one of them after a dazzling 200-mph battle with Schumacher at Spa, but he finished as runner-up to Schumacher in the table. The 2001 season gave him two more victories, in Britain and the US, a year in which he slipped to fifth in the title race. A sabbatical the following year turned into full-time retirement. Plans in 2004 for a F1 comeback came to nothing, and he began his new career in touring cars the following year.

LEWIS HAMILTON

RECORD BREAKING FIRST SEASON

B. 7 JANUARY 1985, STEVENAGE, ENGLAND

GRAND PRIX STARTS: 35*

GRAND PRIX VICTORIES: 9*

POINTS TOTAL: 207*

WOLRD CHAMPION: 2008

*TO END OF 2008 SEASON

After winning the British Cadet championship in 1995, 10-year-old Lewis Hamilton went to the Autosport Awards ceremony, a star-struck youngster keen to fill his autograph book. Among the luminaries of the sport he approached that evening was Ron Dennis, who added 'Call me in nine years' time' next to his signature. He was responding to Lewis's bold statement of intent that he wanted to drive in F1 for McLaren, following in the footsteps of his hero, Ayrton Senna. In fact, just three years went by before Dennis's team took the karting prodigy under its wing. It was a huge relief for the Hamilton family, who for years had scrimped and saved to fund Lewis's racing.

The honours continued to come thick and fast: European Champion and World Cup Champion in Formula A in 2000; Formula Renault UK Champion in 2003, winning 10 out of 15 races; and F3 Euroseries Champion in 2005, with 15 wins and 13 poles. For 2006 it was on to GP2 with the ART team, where he took the title after battling with Nelson Piquet Junior. That autumn, McLaren confirmed his F1 seat for 2007, alongside double world champion Fernando Alonso. Elated but not overawed, Hamilton made a blistering start to his rookie year at the top table, with nine straight podium finishes, including back-to-back wins in Canada and the USA. He headed the championship race from Round Three until the final twist at Interlagos, where Kimi Räikkönen's victory was enough to snatch the crown by a single point. Hamilton was philosophical about the defeat, which he took with great humility. At 22 he had become the youngest driver to lead the championship, breaking Bruce McLaren's record, and knew his talent and extraordinary focus would give him many more tilts at the title. Hamilton had to wait just one year to put the disappointment of 2007 behind him. It was another championship that went to the wire, a last-gasp overtaking manoeuvre at Interlagos securing him fifth place, enough to snatch the title from Ferrari's Felipe Massa by one point. At 23 years 301 days he became the youngest ever Formula One champion, taking the record from Fernando Alonso, who was 122 days older when he was crowned in 2005.

BRITAIN'S FIRST WORLD CHAMPION

MIKE HAWTHORN

B. 10 APRIL 1929, MEXBOROUGH, ENGLAND

D. 22 JANUARY 1959

GRAND PRIX STARTS: 45

GRAND PRIX VICTORIES: 3

POINTS TOTAL: 127.64

WORLD CHAMPION: 1958

Mike Hawthorn made his GP debut at Spa in 1952 for his father's team, finishing joint fourth in the championship. Ferrari snapped him up for the 1953

season. His first GP victory came at Reims that year, and again he finished fourth overall, having shown great consistency as well as courage and skill.

Despite the 1954 campaign being marred by an accident at the non-championship Syracuse GP, Hawthorn recovered to win the Spanish GP and finish third overall. He briefly joined Vanwall in 1955 before rejoining Ferrari, but the championship races proved fruitless. His win at Le Mans in a Jaguar was tainted by an accident which resulted in over 80 deaths, and Hawthorn was criticised for the manoeuvre that precipitated the tragedy.

After a forgettable 1956 season, Hawthorn returned to form, reunited once again with Ferrari. 1958 saw him pip Moss for the title by a single point. He announced his retirement almost immediately, having been deeply affected by team-mate Peter Collins' death at the Nürburgring that year. He was killed in a road accident on 22 January 1959, just three months after becoming Britain's first world champion.

DAMON HILL

EIGHT VICTORIES CLINCH TITLE

B. 17 SEPTEMBER 1960, LONDON, ENGLAND

GRAND PRIX STARTS: 116

GRAND PRIX VICTORIES: 22

POINTS TOTAL: 360

WORLD CHAMPION 1996

Despite the inevitable comparisons with his father, Damon Hill overcame media scrutiny to make his own mark. Moving from motorcycles, his first love, to four wheels was not, initially, a resounding success. Between 1986 and 1988 Hill competed in the British F3 championship, improving each year to finish third in his final campaign. Three years in F3000 followed, where he showed himself to be a genuine racer, despite mediocre hardware, and helped him secure a test-driving contract at Williams.

In 1992 Hill landed his F1 debut with Brabham but struggled to qualify. 1993 saw him move to Williams and promotion behind Prost. After a series of podium finishes Hill scored a start-to-finish victory in Hungary and followed it up with two more wins, giving him third place in the title race.

Senna replaced Prost at Williams the following year, but after Senna's death at Imola, Hill became Williams' no. 1. He rose to the challenge, battling with Michael Schumacher, and losing the championship to him in the final race of the season at Adelaide.

Hill was again runner-up in

1995, but in the following season he took the world title, scoring eight victories in the sixteen-race series, ironically parting company with Williams at the end of it. A season with Arrows followed by two years with Jordan produced just one victory, after which Hill announced his retirement.

GRAHAM HILL

BRITAIN'S BLUE RIBAND CHAMPION

B. 15 FEBRUARY 1929, HAMPSTEAD, LONDON

D. 29 NOVEMBER 1975

GRAND PRIX STARTS: 176

GRAND PRIX VICTORIES: 14

POINTS TOTAL: 289

WORLD CHAMPION: 1962, 1968

Graham Hill was an outstanding driver whose extrovert character was very different from that of his great rival, Jim Clark, although the two shared a steely resolve. As Clark signed for Lotus in 1960, Hill left for BRM, accumulating just 7 points in his first two seasons with them. By 1962 both the car and Hill's results had improved: his maiden victory in the opening race at Zandvoort was followed by wins in Germany and Italy, snatching the title from Clark in the final race that season. In the next three championship series Hill finished runner-up: to Clark in 1963 and 1965, and to Ferrari's John Surtees in 1964, losing the title by a single point that year.

In 1966 Hill had a disappointing championship, although he did win the Indy 500. In 1967 he rejoined Lotus, now with the new Cosworth DFV engine, and looked set for an assault on the 1968 championship. Team-mate Clark's death early in the season shattered the morale of the Lotus camp; Hill restored it with three victories on the way to a second world title.

He slid down the rankings in 1969, although he took his fifth Monaco victory. A crash at Watkins Glen left him with severe leg injuries and it was clear that his best days were behind him. He retired in 1975 and remains the only man to complete the blue riband treble: the world championship, the Indy 500 and Le Mans.

After retirement, Hill concentrated on establishing his own team. He and five team members were killed in November 1975 when the plane he was piloting crashed in fog near Elstree.

AMERICA'S FIRST WORLD CHAMPION

PHIL HILL

B. 20 APRIL 1927, MIAMI, USA

D. 28 AUGUST 2008

GRAND PRIX STARTS: 48

GRAND PRIX VICTORIES: 3

POINTS TOTAL: 98

WORLD CHAMPION: 1961

Having enjoyed success in sports cars and winning Le Mans, Phil Hill made his debut at the 1958 French GP, finishing seventh. He had already caught the eye of Ferrari and was soon signed; he spent the next four years with the team. His progress was steady: two second places, in France and Italy moved him to fourth in the 1959 championship; in 1960 he dropped one place though he took a victory at Monza.

Having lagged the field in 1960, Ferrari introduced the new 1.5-litre formula in 1961, and by the penultimate race, Monza, the title was up for grabs between Ferrari team-mates Hill and Wolfgang von Trips. The German clashed with Jim Clark's Lotus on the first lap and was killed, along with 12 spectators. Hill won the race and with it the title, but his achievement was overshadowed by the tragedy.

In 1962 Ferrari fell behind the British teams, and the following year Hill joined a Ferrari breakaway team which left to set up ATS. He failed to gain a single point, and a season with Cooper was scarcely better, yielding only a sixth place at Brands Hatch. After that Hill concentrated on sports car racing, and retired in 1967 due to ill health. He died in 2008.

HULME EDGES OUT BRABHAM

DENNY HULME

B. 18 MARCH 1936, NELSON, NEW ZEALAND

D. 4 OCTOBER 1992

GRAND PRIX STARTS: 112

GRAND PRIX VICTORIES: 8

POINTS TOTAL: 248

WORLD CHAMPION 1967

Denny Hulme travelled to Britain in 1960 to compete in Formula Junior, and a year later was working as a mechanic for Jack Brabham's fledgling outfit. Having driven works Brabhams in Formula Junior, the Tasman series and F2, Hulme was promoted to F1 in 1965. Replacing Dan Gurney, who was competing at Indianapolis, he made his debut at Monaco, finishing eighth. Two races later, Brabham made way for the New Zealander at Clermont-Ferrand, and he repaid his boss with fourth place.

In 1966 Gurney's departure left Hulme as official no. 2. Brabham won his third title that year, and Hulme made the podium four times to secure fourth place in the championship. A year later it was his turn. At Monaco he took the lead after the fatal crash of Ferrari's Lorenzo Bandini, and went on to score his maiden victory. Victory at the Nürburgring, and third place in the final race, the Mexican GP, was enough to give Hulme the title from Brabham.

In 1968, Hulme joined McLaren, taking two more victories to finish third in that year's championship. There were just four more wins over the next six years, 1972 being his best, with a 39-point haul giving Hulme third behind Fittipaldi and Stewart. He remained at McLaren until his retirement in 1974. Hulme died from a heart attack while competing in Australia's Bathurst touring car race in 1992.

THRILLING HUNT 'THE SHUNT' LIFTS WORLD CROWN

JAMES HUNT

B. 29 AUGUST 1947, BELMONT, ENGLAND

D. 15 JUNE 1993

GRAND PRIX STARTS: 92

GRAND PRIX VICTORIES: 10

POINTS TOTAL: 179

WORLD CHAMPION: 1976

James Hunt's early forays into motor racing began with a humble Mini, moving on to Formula Ford and F3, signing for the March F3 team in 1972. Within a year he had departed to join forces with Lord Hesketh's maverick outfit and a step-up to F2.

Having made his F1 debut in 1973, Hunt finished second behind Ronnie Peterson in the final race of the year at Watkins Glen. This gave him a highly respectable eighth place in the championship and the following season saw him match that performance, this time in the team's own car. In 1975 improvements to the car saw him finish fourth in the table, having beaten eventual champion Niki Lauda into second place at Zandvoort to score his maiden victory.

Hesketh's withdrawal from the GP circuit at the end of 1975 saw Hunt replacing Emerson Fittipaldi at McLaren. 1976 was a thrilling season, with Hunt and Ferrari's Niki Lauda battling for the crown to the finish. His first win for McLaren came in Spain, but at Silverstone his victory points were expunged following an infringement of the rules governing the car's dimensions. With Lauda out following his horrific accident at the Nürburgring, Hunt was back in contention, and he went into the final race, the Japanese GP, 3 points behind Lauda. Lauda withdrew in appalling weather conditions and Hunt went on to secure third place and the title.

Despite three more victories in 1977, McLaren was in decline, and by the following year Hunt appeared to lose motivation and enthusiasm. He quit mid-season in 1979 and went on to become a F1 TV commentator until his death from a heart attack in 1993.

JACKY ICKX

BELGIUM'S BRIGHT YOUNG TALENT

B. 1 JANUARY 1945, BRUSSELS, BELGIUM

GRAND PRIX STARTS: 116

GRAND PRIX VICTORIES: 8

POINTS TOTAL: 181

Emerging as one of motor racing's brightest young talents in the 1960s, Jacky Ickx progressed from trials riding, hill climbs to saloon cars in rapid succession. In 1965 he signed for Tyrell and was given his world championship debut in the 1966 German GP, albeit in an F2 Matra-Ford.

In 1967 he divided his time, winning the European F2 title while making the occasional F1 appearance. He qualified his F2 car at the Nürburgring, and made his way from the back of the grid through to fourth before his suspension gave out. Two races later, driving for Cooper at Monza, he finished sixth to gain his first championship point.

There followed a move to Ferrari where he finished fourth in the title race, outpacing team-mate Chris Amon and giving Ferrari their only win of the season, at Rouen. When Rindt left Brabham for Lotus, Ickx was drafted in as replacement and had a fine year, winning in Germany and Canada to finish runner-up to Stewart, and adding a Le Mans victory to his achievements.

He returned to Ferrari and remained there for the next four years, adding five more wins over the first three seasons. After 1970, the car became increasingly uncompetitive and Ickx quit midway through the 1973 series to join Lotus, scoring 15 points in two seasons. Outings for Williams, Ensign and Ligier between 1976 and 1979 were not noteworthy and from then on he concentrated on sports cars, winning Le Mans for a sixth time in 1982.

EDDIE IRVINE

DRIVING A FINE LINE

B. 10 NOVEMBER 1965,
NEWTOWNARDS,
NORTHERN IRELAND

GRAND PRIX STARTS: 146

GRAND PRIX
VICTORIES: 4

POINTS TOTAL: 191

Having performed well in F3000, Eddie Irvine made his GP debut for Jordan in 1993 at Suzuka. The race produced his first championship point, but was more noteworthy for the spat – which came to blows afterwards – with race winner Ayrton Senna, who took exception to an overtaking manoeuvre from a driver he had already lapped.

There was further controversy at the first race of 1994, Interlagos, where Irvine received a one-race ban for his part in a pile-up, which was increased to three races at appeal.

His podium debut came at the 1995 Canadian GP, but in the championship Jordan lagged the field. In 1996 Irvine signed for Ferrari, only to find himself playing a supporting role to Michael Schumacher. He picked up useful points in 1997, including a fine second in Argentina, but was always conscious of playing second fiddle. He notched 47 points to finish fourth in the 1998 title race, and the following year, with Schumacher sidelined through injury, Irvine finally got full team backing. After three victories he went into the final round two points behind Mika Hakkinen, but was unable to overtake him. Irvine left Ferrari in 2000 to lead Jaguar's assault on F1, but three seasons yielded only few noteworthy results, and after scoring just 8 points in 2002 his contract was not renewed.

ALAN JONES

FIRST CONSTRUCTORS' TITLE FOR WILLIAMS

B. 2 NOVEMBER 1946, MELBOURNE, AUSTRALIA

GRAND PRIX STARTS: 116

GRAND PRIX VICTORIES: 12

POINTS TOTAL: 206

WORLD CHAMPION: 1980

Unlike his racing driver father, Alan Jones travelled to Europe from Australia to compete on the biggest stages. Having spent five years in the junior ranks, his F1 debut came in a privately entered Hesketh in 1975. He also drove that year for Graham Hill's fledgling Embassy Racing, and gained a fifth place in Germany. The deaths of Hill and five of his team in a plane crash at the end of the year left Jones looking for a new challenge.

He then spent a year with John Surtees, notching up 7 points in his one season there. By the fourth race of the 1977 series he was driving for Shadow to replace Tom Pryce, who had been killed at Kyalami. Jones scored a stunning success in Austria, giving him and the team their first podium finish, and beating Lauda into the bargain.

In 1978 he linked up with Williams and towards the end of the 1979 season, Jones took four wins in five starts to finish third in the championship. With five more wins in 1980 he took the crown, and Williams had their first Constructors' title. Jones scored two more wins to make third in the 1981 championship, then announced his retirement. He made two comebacks but failed to do justice to his talent.

NIKI LAUDA

REMARKABLE COMEBACK FROM THE THREE TIMES CHAMPION

B. 22 FEBRUARY 1949, VIENNA, AUSTRIA

GRAND PRIX STARTS: 171

GRAND PRIX VICTORIES: 25

POINTS TOTAL: 420.5

WORLD CHAMPION: 1975, 1977, 1984

Niki Lauda's return to F1 racing just six weeks after the horrific fireball accident at the Nürburgring is one of sport's most remarkable comebacks. His self-belief and determination were evident from the start, working his way from F2 into F1 with March by 1970. A season at BRM in 1973 produced just 2 points for a fifth place at Zolder. The following year Lauda began his four-season association with Ferrari, teaming up with Clay Regazzoni. In their first season, Regazzoni out-pointed him, the duo finishing second and fourth respectively in the championship, although Regazzoni had won just once, and Lauda twice – but he had suffered a number of retirements.

But in 1975, Lauda won five races to clinch the world crown with a race to spare, and give Ferrari its first title since Surtees 11 years earlier. 1976 saw epic battles with Hunt and McLaren, and that crash at the Nürburgring, where Lauda received the last rites. Terribly scarred, he returned to the fray at Monza six weeks later. He pulled out of the final race at Suzuka owing to appalling conditions, allowing Hunt to take the title by one point.

Despite roaring back in 1977 to take a second title with Ferrari, Lauda had a difficult year with the team and quit to join Brabham in 1978. This move produced a respectable 44 points and fourth place, but 1979 proved disastrous, and the Austrian announced his retirement.

Three years later he returned, with McLaren, topping the podium in just his third race, and finishing fifth overall in the 1982 championship. 1983 was disappointing, but a year later he blew away his

competitors, taking the title from his team-mate Alain Prost by half a point, the closest championship finish ever.

Lauda is the only man to come out of retirement to reclaim the world title. He won his twenty-fifth and final GP at Zandvoort in 1985, retiring at the end of that season.

NIGEL MANSELL

FIERCE COMPETITOR FIFTH ON ALL-TIME LIST

B. 8 AUGUST 1953, UPTON-ON-SEVERN, ENGLAND

GRAND PRIX STARTS: 187

GRAND PRIX VICTORIES: 31

POINTS TOTAL: 482

WORLD CHAMPION: 1992

Mansell's championship-winning season of 1992 was the crowning glory of more than two decades in competitive motor sport. It was a year of outstanding achievement, as he took pole in all but two of the races and won nine of them to become the first man to rack up over a century of points. His nearest rival, Riccardo

Patrese, finished a staggering 52 points behind. Having made his F1 debut for Lotus in 1980, at the Austrian GP, Mansell spent four more seasons with the team. Moving to Williams in 1985 transformed his career, with two victories, at the European and South African GPs, helping him to sixth place in the championship.

In 1986 and 1987 he was runner-up; first to Prost when he blew a tyre in the final race, allowing Prost to snatch the crown. In the second, he lost out to team-mate Nelson Piquet, despite scoring six wins that year. Over the next three years Mansell was out of contention for the title. Lured back to Williams in 1991, he finished runner-up for the third time, a tally of five wins not being quite enough to outdo Senna.

After his victory in 1992 Mansell turned to Indy cars, winning the 1993 championship. He made a dramatic return to F1 and Williams following Senna's death in 1994, recording his 31st and final win at Adelaide. Hill and Coulthard were confirmed as drivers for Williams for 1995, and Mansell began the season with McLaren, but quit for permanent retirement after two races. He stands fifth in the all-time list for GP victories, behind Schumacher, Prost, Senna and Piquet.

FELIPE MASSA

FERRARI'S NEW BRAZILIAN ACE

B. 25 APRIL 1981, SAO PAULO, BRAZIL

GRAND PRIX STARTS: 105*

GRAND PRIX VICTORIES: 11*

POINTS TOTAL: 298*

*TO END OF 2008 SEASON

For a few brief moments at Interlagos on 2 November 2008 the Ferrari camp thought Felipe Massa had secured the world crown, and the passionate home fans were ready to acclaim their first champion since Ayrton Senna in 1991. Lewis Hamilton spoiled the party with his last-gasp manoeuvre that saw him pass Timo Glock to snatch fifth place, and with it the title by a single point. Massa hid his disappointment and congratulated the new champion in a display of magnanimity that was a fitting template for all sportsmen. 'I know how to lose and I know how to win,' said the Brazilian ace. He certainly showed the winning mentality in 2008, outgunning Hamilton 6–5 in terms of top-of-the-podium finishes, and he had the consolation of helping Ferrari to yet another Constructors' title. Perhaps more significantly, after three successive top-four finishes in the Drivers' Championship, the pre-eminent individual award was getting ever closer.

Sao Paulo-born Massa had seven years in karting before stepping up to Formula Chevrolet at the age of 17. He took just one season to adjust before lifting that title, after which he moved to Europe to compete in Formula Renault, following in the footsteps of such luminaries as Alain Prost and Rene Arnoux. In 2000 he won both the European and Italian Formula Renault titles, at a time when future Ferrari team-mate Kimi Raikkonen was taking the laurels in the British equivalent. The Euro F3000 series was the next port of call, and six wins out of eight brought him that championship. It also earned him an invitation from Sauber to join the F1 ranks in 2002, replacing the departing Raikkonen. That proved a steep learning curve, and he had his share of spins when pushing hard. Four points and 13th place was not the kind of return the Brazilian was used to for a season's efforts.

He spent the following year as a Ferrari test driver, and he was older and wiser when he returned to Sauber in 2004, helped by the fact that the team was using Ferrari power. He garnered 12 points, with a best-place finish of fourth in an accident-ridden race at Spa. There was a similar return in 2005, the year in which Peter Sauber sold out to BMW, after which Massa moved to Ferrari to take over Barrichello's long-held number two berth to Michael Schumacher. Schumacher and Alonso fought a ding-dong battle in 2006, but Massa was the best of the rest, albeit 41 points adrift of his team-mate. That campaign was notable for his first two victories, scored in Istanbul and in his home race. It was Schumacher's swansong year, and Massa found himself partnering Raikkonen in 2007. There were three more victories, though he eventually finished fourth in a Ferrari-McLaren duel that went to the wire. Raikkonen snatched the championship from rivals Hamilton and Alonso in the final race in Brazil, but a year later it was the Finn who was out of contention and pushing for a Massa victory. The cards didn't fall right for Felipe in 2008, but in taking the runner-up spot he had shown that he was no supporting act but a genuine contender.

BRUCE McLAREN

McLAREN FOLLOWS BRABHAM'S LEAD

B. 30 AUGUST 1937, AUCKLAND, NEW ZEALAND

D. 2 JUNE 1970

GRAND PRIX STARTS: 101

GRAND PRIX VICTORIES: 4

POINTS TOTAL: 196.5

Bruce McLaren won a scholarship in New Zealand which allowed him to travel to Europe to compete in F2, and within a year he had won his first GP. Having made his F1 debut at the Nürburgring in 1958 for Cooper, he launched a full campaign the following year.

McLaren won at Sebring to become the youngest-ever Grand Prix winner at 22 years and 104 days old. That took him to sixth place in the championship, and in 1960 he finished runner-up to his mentor, Jack Brabham. McLaren stayed with Cooper for the next five seasons, his best being 1962, when he won in Monaco and ended the year third behind Hill and Clark.

In 1966, McLaren followed Brabham's lead to set up on his own, but struggled to find a decent engine for his car. By 1968, the car had Cosworth DFV power and he had lured reigning champion Denny Hulme from Brabham. McLaren's fourth GP win, at Spa, was the first for the marque and it helped him to finish fifth in the championship. Consistent scoring put him third in the table for 1969, though there were no victories. McLaren contested three rounds of the 1970 series – finishing second at Jarama – before he was killed while testing one of his CanAm cars at Goodwood.

AUDACIOUS AND BRILLIANT COLOMBIAN

JUAN PABLO MONTOYA

B. 20 SEPTEMBER 1975, BOGOTA, COLOMBIA

GRAND PRIX STARTS: 95

GRAND PRIX VICTORIES: 7

POINTS TOTAL: 307

Juan Pablo Montoya's audacious style and brilliance throughout his four seasons with Williams has won him legions of fans, though his combative nature cost him dearly on occasions. He signed on as test driver for Williams in 1997, and fully expected to be awarded a F1 seat for 1999, after winning the F3000 title the previous season, but Williams opted for the Ralf Schumacher– Alex Zanardi pairing instead.

Montoya finally got his chance in 2001, taking three poles that year, and converting one of them, Monza, into a famous maiden victory. A year later, on the same track, he broke Keke Rosberg's 1985 record for the fastest qualifying lap, averaging 161.17 mph. His seven poles that year clearly reflected his aptitude for raw speed. In 2002, Montoya was on the podium seven times, finishing third overall behind Schumacher and Barichello. Taking two wins at Hockenheim and Monaco in 2003, he finished third again, this time behind Schumacher and Raikonnen in a tight title race. Montoya slipped to fifth in 2004, and before the season was out it was announced that he would be replacing Coulthard at McLaren.

Teaming with Raikonnen, 2005 proved to be a mixed year for Montoya: early hopes thwarted by bad luck, interspersed with brilliant moments. Overcoming the unpredictability of his new McLaren, he took three wins and five podiums to finish fourth overall in the championship. He continued to drive for McLaren in 2006, but consistent underperformance put his future with the team in jeopardy. The announcement that the reigning champion, Alonso, would join McLaren for the 2007 season made Montoya's future with the team more uncertain. Eventually he decided to call it a day and dropped out mid-season in favour of NASCAR racing.

STIRLING MOSS

GREATEST DRIVER NEVER TO WIN WORLD CROWN

B. 17 SEPTEMBER 1929, LONDON, ENGLAND

GRAND PRIX STARTS: 66

GRAND PRIX VICTORIES: 16 (1 SHARED)

POINTS TOTAL: 186.64

Despite never winning the world title, Stirling Moss was nevertheless acclaimed as one of the greatest of his generation. His competitiveness and supreme professionalism ensured him rapid progress through the junior ranks to make a F1 debut with HWM in 1951.

In 1954 he ran a privately entered Maserati, and secured a fine third at Spa. Having signed for Mercedes for 1955, Moss scored his maiden victory in the British GP, finishing runner-up to team-mate Fangio in the championship that year. He was second behind Fangio for the next two seasons, rejoining Maserati in 1956 and missing out on the title by 3 points. A year later, having signed with Vanwall, Moss scored three more victories – one of which came at the British GP – but again they weren't enough to stop Fangio.

Moss came closest to winning the world crown in 1958. In the title showdown race, the Moroccan GP, Moss crossed the line ahead of Mike Hawthorn's Ferrari, but lost the title to him by a single point.

The following year, Moss joined the Walker outfit and once again had a chance of taking the crown going into the final race, the US GP, but mechanical failure meant he had to settle for third overall. He drove the new Lotus 18 for Walker in 1960 and gave the car its maiden victory, at Monaco, but finished a distant third overall behind Brabham and McLaren when a crash during practice for Spa put him out for four rounds.

Moss won at Monaco and the Nürburgring the following year, despite Ferrari's dominance, but in 1962 he sustained horrific injuries in a non-championship race at Goodwood, which ended his career in top-level motor sport. He had, however, already established himself as one of motor racing's legendary names and received a knighthood in 2000 for his contribution to the sport.

RICCARDO PATRESE

FORMULA ONE RECORD BREAKER

B. 17 APRIL 1954, PADUA, ITALY

GRAND PRIX STARTS: 256

GRAND PRIX VICTORIES: 6

POINTS TOTAL: 281

Having won the European F3 title the previous season, Riccardo Patrese made his F1 debut for Shadow in 1977, scoring his first championship point in the final race, the Japanese GP.

He followed members of the Shadow team when they left to form Arrows in 1978. Encouraging results that season were overshadowed by the accident at Monza which resulted in Ronnie Peterson's death. Patrese was barred from the next race though later investigations exonerated him from any blame for the Monza accident.

The next three seasons yielded a total of just 19 points, and in 1982 he moved to Brabham, where he took his first win at Monaco and came tenth in the championship that year. Playing second fiddle to Piquet in 1983, he won the final race of the season in South Africa.

Following two disastrous years with Alfa Romeo, Patrese returned to a Brabham team in decline. In 1988 he moved to Williams where his career began to improve, twice finishing third and taking runner-up slot behind Mansell in 1992. His final victory came 11 years after his first, a F1 record. He retired after a season with Benetton, playing support to Michael Schumacher. Patrese's record of 256 races stood for 15 years, Rubens Barrichello overhauling his tally midway through the 2008 season.

RONNIE PETERSON

TRAGEDY FOR TWO TIMES RUNNER-UP

B. 14 FEBRUARY 1944, OREBRO, SWEDEN

D. 11 SEPTEMBER 1978

GRAND PRIX STARTS: 123

GRAND PRIX VICTORIES: 10

POINTS TOTAL: 206

Twice a world championship runner-up, Ronnie Peterson made his F1 debut in 1970, the year Jochen Rindt was killed at Monza. Many felt that he was Rindt's natural successor.

After his stunning performances in F3 and F2 Max Mosley signed Peterson for the new March outfit in 1970. He was promoted to the works team in 1971, and took four second places, one of them being Monza, which provided the closest F1 finish ever when the Swede ended the race 0.01 seconds behind Peter Gethin's BRM. He ended the year as runner-up to Stewart.

Peterson switched to Lotus in 1973, scoring his maiden victory at Paul Ricard, and winning in Austria after team-mate, Fittipaldi, retired from the race. Four victories in all gave him third in the championship that year.

Peterson stayed with Lotus for the next two seasons and scored three wins, but the car lagged behind the competition. Back with March in 1976 he took a victory at Monza; then a year with Tyrell and in 1978 saw him return to Lotus, playing support to Mario Andretti. Peterson suffered serious leg injuries in a crash at the start of the Italian GP at Monza, and died the next day from complications. He finished the year as posthumous runner-up in the championship.

NELSON PIQUET

23 VICTORIES AND A HAT-TRICK OF WORLD TITLES

BORN 17 FEBRUARY 1952, RIO DE JANEIRO, BRAZIL

GRAND PRIX STARTS: 204

GRAND PRIX VICTORIES: 23

POINTS TOTAL: 485.5

WORLD CHAMPION: 1981, 1983, 1987

Nelson Piquet is in the all-time top ten for race victories, poles and fastest laps, and in 1987 he became only the fifth man to win a hat-trick of world titles.

Piquet made his F1 debut with Ensign at Hockenheim in 1978, had three outings in a privately entered McLaren then joined Brabham for the final race of the season. 1979 was a disappointing year. When team-mate, Lauda left to join McLaren in 1980, Piquet became the team's no. 1, and finished runner-up to Alan Jones in the championship.

In 1981, Piquet went into the final round, Las Vegas, trailing Reutemann by one point, but fifth place was enough to give him the crown, as Reutemann failed to score. 1982 proved unsuccessful for Piquet, but he and Brabham roared back in 1983, clinching his second title with third place at Kyalami. Piquet won just three races over the next three seasons, switched to Williams in 1986 and took his third world title the following year. Two indifferent years at Lotus saw him move to Benetton, where he ended his F1 career winning three final GPs. His 485.5 point career haul has been bettered only by Schumacher, Prost and Senna.

DIDIER PIRONI

TYRELL CALL-UP AND A WORLD OF PROMISE

B. 26 MARCH 1952, PARIS, FRANCE

D. 23 AUGUST 1987

GRAND PRIX STARTS: 70

GRAND PRIX VICTORIES: 3

POINTS TOTAL: 101

Didier Pironi rose through the ranks in the mid-1970s to finish behind team-mate Rene Arnoux and Eddie Cheever in the 1977 F2 championship, and earning himself a F1 call-up from Ken Tyrell the following year. He finished sixth in the Brazilian GP, only his second race, and got into the points on four other occasions.

Pironi's second season with Tyrell saw him on the podium for the first time, coming third both at Zolder and the US Grand Prix at Watkins Glen to finish on 14 points and in tenth place. In 1980 Pironi moved to Ligier, scoring his maiden victory at Zolder and unluckily missing out on two more wins at Monaco and Brands Hatch.

He took Scheckter's place at Ferrari in 1981, but was overshadowed by team-mate Gilles Villeneuve. Peroni was determined to make his mark in 1982 and passed Villeneuve on the last lap at Imola to take victory against team orders. Villeneuve was killed during qualifying for the next race, leaving Pironi as the focus of Ferrari attention. He won at Zandvoort, and by Hockenheim he led by 9 points. During practice there he suffered leg injuries which ended his career, although he still finished joint runner-up with Watson, just 5 points behind Rosberg. Pironi took to racing powerboats, and was killed while competing off the Isle of Wight in 1987.

MASTER TACTICIAN WINS FOUR WORLD CROWNS

ALAIN PROST

B. 24 FEBRUARY 1955,
ST CHAMOND, FRANCE

GRAND PRIX STARTS: 199

GRAND PRIX VICTORIES: 51

POINTS TOTAL: 798.5

WORLD CHAMPION: 1985, 1986, 1989, 1993

Alain Prost became only the second man to win the world championship four times, following Fangio into the record books. Michael Schumacher has since joined them.

His smooth and calculated driving style and mastery of tactics earned him his nickname: 'The Professor'. He made his F1 debut in 1980 for McLaren, taking a poor car to sixth place on his debut in Buenos Aires, and showing his enormous potential. This was confirmed when he moved to Renault in 1981, winning three races to finish fifth, just 7 points behind champion Piquet. A third place in 1982 was improved to that of runner-up behind Piquet the following year.

On returning to McLaren in 1984 Prost won a remarkable seven races, but he again had to settle for the runner-up spot, half a point behind team-mate Niki Lauda.

Prost took the 1985 championship with two races to spare and retained the title after getting the better of the Williams pair Mansell and Piquet in a three-way showdown in Australia in 1986. Mansell's tyre blew and Piquet was brought in for a precautionary stop, leaving Prost to win both the race and the title.

The Williams team dominated 1987, but McLaren hit back in 1988, with Prost and new team-mate Senna between them winning 15 of the 16 races, and Senna taking the title by 3 points. The positions were reversed in 1989, their crash at Suzuka settling the championship in Prost's favour, but he was again consigned to runner-up spot behind Senna in 1990. A poor season followed, after which he took a year's sabbatical. Driving for Williams in 1993, he replaced reigning champion Mansell, and added seven more victories to his tally to claim his fourth world crown before retiring.

FERRARI'S FINNISH WINNER

B. 17 OCTOBER 1979,
LAPPEENRANTA, FINLAND

GRAND PRIX STARTS: 140*

GRAND PRIX VICTORIES: 17*

POINTS TOTAL: 531*

WORLD CHAMPION: 2007

*TO END OF 2008 SEASON

Kimi Raikkonen had a long line of successes in karting before turning to single seaters in 1999, and it was his outstanding seven wins in ten outings in the 2000 British Formula Renault series that brought him to the attention of F1 bosses. In September 2000 he tested for Sauber, making his championship debut a few months later at the Australian GP, finishing sixth.

Taking over from Hakkinen at McLaren in 2002

Raikkonen was their no. 2 to Coulthard, finishing the year sixth overall. Within a year, he was not only McLaren's front-runner but also its title contender. His only victory in 2003, and his maiden one at that, was at Sepang, but he backed it up with ten podiums to finish only 2 points behind the perennial champion, Schumacher.

In 2004 Raikkonen scored a second win, at Spa, and notched up 45 points but problems with the new car early in the season saw him slip to seventh overall, more than 100 points behind Schumacher.

2005 saw him emerge as a genuine championship winner, taking seven victories, including Spain, Monaco, Canada and Japan. However, reliability problems, yet again, meant that he was unable to lift the title crown, finishing runner-up, 20 points adrift of Fernando Alonso. After wining no races and finishing fifth overall in 2006, Raikkonen made the switch from McLaren to Ferrari. Six wins helped him lift the 2007 title, pipping McLaren duo Hamilton and Alonso by a single point. He set the fastest lap in ten races in 2008, equalling Michael Schumacher's record and putting him third on the all-time list, but could finish only third in the championship.

CARLOS REUTEMANN

RUNNER-UP BY A SINGLE POINT

B. 12 APRIL 1942, SANTA
FE, ARGENTINA

GRAND PRIX STARTS: 146

GRAND PRIX VICTORIES: 12

POINTS TOTAL: 310

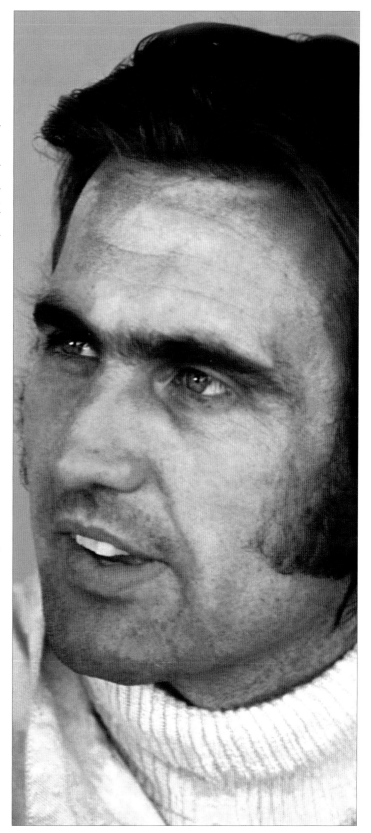

Carlos Reutemann travelled to Europe to compete in F2 in 1970, and two seasons in he took the runner-up spot behind Ronnie Peterson.

He signed for Brabham in 1972, but despite taking pole on his debut, the Argentinian GP, he scored just 3 points that year. The 1973 championship saw Reutemann rise to seventh place, but this was followed by a typical roller-coaster season of wins and dips in form.

In 1975 he peaked with a third place, winning just once, in Germany, but taking five podiums. After a disastrous 1976, Reutemann had two years at Ferrari, culminating in a third place overall in 1978, scoring four wins to finish behind Lotus duo Andretti and Peterson. He joined Andretti the following season but achieved nothing of note with an under-performing car.

His last two campaigns were with Williams. In 1980 he took another third place overall behind team-mate Alan Jones and Piquet; the following year he lost out on the title to Piquet by a single point. Two races into the 1982 season Reutemann quit the sport.

JOCHEN RINDT

POSTHUMOUS CHAMPION

B. 18 APRIL 1942, MAINZ-AM-RHEIN, GERMANY

D. 5 SEPTEMBER 1970

GRAND PRIX STARTS: 60

GRAND PRIX VICTORIES: 6

POINTS TOTAL: 109

WORLD CHAMPION 1970

Jochen Rindt swapped hill climbs and rallies for circuit racing in the early 1960s. He made his championship debut at Zeltweg in 1964 for Brabham, failing to finish that day, but the following year he raced for Cooper alongside Bruce McLaren. His first championship points came in 1965.

Rindt took three podiums in 1966, but then struggled the following season due to an uncompetitive Cooper. This was followed by an unsuccessful year with Brabham, suffering reliability problems. Rindt moved to Lotus in 1969, to partner reigning champion Graham Hill, whom he outscored in a season which produced his maiden victory, at Watkins Glen.

Hill's leg injuries in a crash at the 1969 US GP ended his time at the top of F1, and in 1970 Fittipaldi was drafted in to support Rindt. Rindt won five races out of six in mid-season to lead the title race comfortably, but was tragically killed during practice for Monza. With four races still to run, Jacky Ickx, the only man who could catch him, was unable to bridge the gap. Rindt thus became the first posthumous world champion.

A PROMISING CAREER CUT SHORT

PEDRO RODRIGUEZ

B. 18 JANUARY 1940, MEXICO CITY, MEXICO

D. 11 JULY 1971

GRAND PRIX STARTS: 55

GRAND PRIX VICTORIES: 2

POINTS TOTAL: 71

Pedro Rodriguez's younger brother Ricardo broke into F1 first, but his death in 1962 at the non-championship Mexican GP left Pedro to make the family's name in GP racing.

He was given his first opportunity by Lotus in 1963, and over the next three seasons made sporadic appearances: sixth in the 1964 Mexican GP, seventh a year later and fifth at Watkins Glen, all for Ferrari; in 1966 he drove well in a couple of outings for Lotus but failed to finish. He finally got a full team place with Cooper in 1967, ending the year in sixth place, well ahead of team-mate and future champion, Jochen Rindt.

Rodriguez took sixth again in 1968, this time for BRM. He started the 1969 season with BRM and ended it with Ferrari, gaining points at Monza and Watkins Glen for the latter. 1970 saw him back for a full campaign with BRM, giving the team its first victory in four years at Spa. He finished the year seventh in the championship.

1971 began well, with Rodriguez taking second place at Zandvoort, and scoring in Spain. He was killed, at the age of 31, when his Ferrari crashed in a minor sports-car race at Norisring, Germany.

CONSISTENT SWEDE BECOMES WORLD CHAMPION

KEKE ROSBERG

B. 6 DECEMBER 1948, STOCKHOLM, SWEDEN

GRAND PRIX STARTS: 114

GRAND PRIX VICTORIES: 5

POINTS TOTAL: 159.5

WORLD CHAMPION: 1982

Rosberg had an inauspicious start to his F1 career in 1978, when he struggled to qualify for the series. He ran with Theodore that year, and also ATS.

In 1979 he took over from James Hunt at Wolf but made little impact. The Wolf team merged with Fittipaldi in 1980, and Rosberg found himself partnering the twice world champion, Fittipaldi, outscoring him – albeit by a single point – at the end of the season. Fittipaldi moved upstairs in 1981, giving Rosberg a new partner, Chico Serra.

In 1982 Williams chose Rosberg to replace Alan Jones and when Reutemann quit after two races he was elevated to team leader. Despite winning only once, the Swiss GP, he was consistently in the points, scoring ten times in a season when the best eleven finishes counted. He secured the title ahead of John Watson with fifth place at Caesar's Palace.

Over the next two seasons Rosberg won only twice, not helped by the late arrival of the Williams turbo unit, and struggling to come to terms with it. He finished third in the 1985 championship, but slipped to sixth the following year with McLaren, his final F1 campaign.

JODY SCHECKTER

FERRARI RELIABILITY LEADS TO WORLD CROWN

B. 29 JANUARY 1950, EAST LONDON, SOUTH AFRICA

GRAND PRIX STARTS: 112

GRAND PRIX VICTORIES: 10

POINTS TOTAL: 255

WORLD CHAMPION: 1979

Jody Scheckter's reputation for being exceedingly quick but something of a liability was confirmed at Silverstone in the first lap of the 1973 British GP, when he was responsible for a 20-car pile-up. Ken Tyrell, however, recognised his potential, and signed him from McLaren in 1974 to replace the retired Jackie Stewart.

With victories in Sweden and Britain, Scheckter was in with an outside chance of the title, but he failed to finish at Watkins Glen, and had to settle for third behind Fittipaldi and Regazzoni. He slipped to seventh overall in 1975, though victory in his home GP was the highlight. Scheckter drove Tyrell's new six-wheeled P34 to second place in only its third outing at Monaco, then to victory in Sweden, though it would be the car's sole success.

In 1977 Scheckter joined the new Wolf team and won first time out in the WR1 in Buenos Aires, also taking victories in Monaco and Canada. He stayed in contention with Lauda for most of the year but finished runner-up to him.

Scheckter joined Ferrari after two seasons with Wolf, and the reliability of the car gave him three wins and plenty of points finishes to help him take the title from team-mate Villeneuve. By contrast, 1980 was a disaster; Scheckter picked up just 2 points all year, and retired at the end of it.

SEVEN TIMES WORLD CHAMPION REWRITES THE RECORD BOOKS

MICHAEL SCHUMACHER

B. 3 JANUARY 1969, HURTH-HERMUHLHEIM, GERMANY

GRAND PRIX STARTS: 248

GRAND PRIX VICTORIES: 91

POINTS TOTAL: 1369

WORLD CHAMPION: 1994, 1995, 2000, 2001, 2002, 2003, 2004

Schumacher, in a league of his own, has rewritten the record books. He is the only driver to have taken five championships in a row, surpassing Fangio. His F1 debut came at Spa in 1991, driving for Jordan. He retired before the end of the first lap, but in qualifying seventh he'd already proved that he had talent. Benetton quickly signed him and he rewarded them with a fifth at Monza two weeks later. In his first full season in 1992, he was regularly on the podium, and this, together with a maiden win at Spa, put him third in the championship that year. 1993 gave him another win, plus eight podiums.

1994 saw him take his first title, albeit amid controversy, with Hill in the final race at Adelaide. He retained the title in 1995 with nine wins, casting aside all doubts as to his championship abilities.

In 1996, he moved to Ferrari, whose car was not as fast as Williams, and suffered a temporary setback. He began his dominance of F1 in 2000, taking five consecutive championship titles, his best year being 2004 when he won 12 of the first 13 rounds.

At the beginning of 2005, rule changes were introduced to try to level the playing field and make the racing more competitive. Whether as a result of this or not, Schumacher had a disappointing season, taking just one victory – at Indianapolis – and making five podiums. He finished the season third behind Alonso and Raikkonen.

2006 was to be Schumacher's final season in Formula One and his chances of winning one last championship were slim with Alonso dominating at the beginning of the season. However, in a thrilling reversal of fortunes, Schumacher began to catch up and eventually he and Alonso were neck and neck with just two races to go. Sadly, engine trouble forced Schumacher out of the penultimate race in Japan, which pushed Alonso too far out of his grasp. He may have finished his last championship in second position, but his place among the sports all-time greats had been assured long before.

RALF SCHUMACHER

SEASONED CAMPAIGNER ENDS F1 CAREER

B. 30 JUNE 1975, HURTH-HERMUTHLHEIM, GERMANY

GRAND PRIX STARTS: 180

GRAND PRIX VICTORIES: 6

POINTS TOTAL: 329

Ralf Schumacher rose to prominence in the German F3 championship of 1994, taking third place and then runner-up the next season. A move to Formula Nippon saw him take the title at the first attempt.

He was offered his F1 break in 1997 with Jordan, where he paired with Giancarlo Fisichella. In his second season, alongside Damon Hill, he managed just 14 points, then left to join Williams. He emerged from his brother's shadow in 1999, making the podium at Melbourne – his Williams debut, from eighth on the grid – and taking second place at Monza. Teamed with Jenson Button in 2000, he managed fifth overall in the title race.

He scored his maiden win at Imola in 2001, thus ending a 54-race barren run for Williams. Winning at Montreal, he and Michael became the first siblings to finish one-two in a championship race. His third win that year came on home soil at Hockenheim.

The next two seasons saw him take three wins to give him fourth and fifth in the championship, outscored on both occasions by team-mate Montoya. He slipped to ninth overall in 2004 and announced his intention to drive for Toyota the following season.

For the first 12 races of 2005, he was outraced by team-mate Jarno Trulli, but showed some promise towards the end, taking a third at the Chinese GP. He ended the season sixth overall, 2 points ahead of Trulli. Having totalled just 25 points in the 2006 and 2007 seasons, Schumacher quit F1 to compete in the German touring car series.

FORMULA ONE'S GREATEST TALENT

AYRTON SENNA

B. 21 MARCH 1960, SAO PAULO, BRAZIL

D. 1 MAY 1994

GRAND PRIX STARTS: 161

GRAND PRIX VICTORIES: 41

POINTS TOTAL: 614

WORLD CHAMPION: 1988, 1990, 1991

With 65 pole positions, 41 wins, 80 times on the podium, and 614 points, Ayrton Senna was, to many, the greatest ever talent in F1.

He moved to Britain in 1981 to further his career in four-wheeled competition, after winning a string of karting titles, and within three years he had won the British F3 title. In 1984 he made his F1 debut, testing for Brabham and Williams, but choosing instead to join the smaller Toleman team.

His first point came at Kyalami, and by his sixth race, Monaco, he was chasing race-leader Prost when the race was stopped due to bad weather conditions. Before the end of the season he had signed for Lotus, scoring his first wins at Estoril and Spa, in 1985, and taking a fourth overall in the title race that year.

The next two seasons saw him elevated to third in the championship both times, but Senna wanted more and joined McLaren in 1988. He was teamed with twice-champion, Prost, and a bitter rivalry soon developed. Senna won his first championship in 1988 by 3 points from Prost, but the following season Prost relegated him to runner-up after their clash at Suzuka. Prost then left for Ferrari but the rivalry continued, culminating in yet another clash in Japan at the 1990 championship, and Senna taking the title. He later hinted at his responsibility for the crash.

His third title was won with a comfortable 24-point margin over Mansell, but the Williams car began to dominate after that. Despite this, Senna won three GPs in 1992. In 1993, five wins earned him the runner-up spot to Prost.

Senna joined Williams in 1994, taking pole in the first two rounds but retiring in each. He was on pole again at San Marino, when he crashed fatally at Tamburello, aged 34.

FLYING SCOTSMAN WINS THREE WORLD CROWNS

JACKIE STEWART

B. 11 JUNE 1939, MILTON, SCOTLAND

GRAND PRIX STARTS: 99

GRAND PRIX VICTORIES: 27

POINTS TOTAL: 360

WORLD CHAMPION: 1969, 1971, 1973

Jackie Stewart was a natural behind the wheel, and quickly attracted the attention of some of the sport's major players. Ken Tyrell signed him for his F3 team in 1964, but it wasn't long before he was offered F1 contracts and he signed for BRM at the end of the season.

His championship debut came at the 1965 South African GP, where he took sixth place, winning his first race at Monza before the season was out. He finished a stunning third in his debut season behind Jim Clark and team-mate Graham Hill. He remained at BRM for two more years, but with an uncompetitive and unreliable car, he won just once in that time, at Monaco in 1966.

Stewart was reunited with Tyrell in 1968, a partnership that would yield three world titles. He missed two races in 1968 through injury and finished runner-up to Hill. But the following season, in a Matra MS80, he swept away the opposition, taking the title 26 points clear in the final table. A disappointing 1970 season was followed by Stewart taking his second world title in 1971, winning six of the eleven rounds. Despite four more victories in 1972, Fittipaldi went one better and Stewart had to settle for the runner-up spot.

He added five more victories to his tally the following year to take his third championship brfore the season was out. He planned to retire at the US GP, but the death of team-mate Francois Cevert during qualifying led Tyrell to withdraw, and Stewart retired with immediate effect. His 27 wins set a new world record that was to stand for 14 years.

JOHN SURTEES

CHAMPION ON TWO WHEELS AND FOUR

B. 11 FEBRUARY 1934, TATSFIELD, ENGLAND

GRAND PRIX STARTS: 111

GRAND PRIX VICTORIES: 6

POINTS TOTAL: 180

WORLD CHAMPION: 1964

John Surtees is still the only man to win world championships on both two wheels and four. He landed his first motorcycling world title in 1956 and followed it up with six more championships over the next four years.

He was offered a F1 drive with Lotus in 1960, finishing second to reigning champion Jack Brabham at Silverstone on only his second outing. Surtees joined Yeoman Credit Cooper in 1961, winning just 4 points in a car of variable quality. Rejecting an offer from Ferrari, he remained with Cooper to finish fourth in the 1962 championship, but when Ferrari asked again, he judged the time to be right, and signed up.

1963 gave Surtees his first victory at the Nürburgring, and a fourth place overall. Two more wins the following year took him into the final race, the Mexican GP, in contention for the crown against Hill and Clark. Luck went his way, as they hit problems. Team-mate Lorenzo Bandini allowed him through to take second place, enough to win the championship by a single point.

He sustained severe injuries in a CanAm sports car race in 1965, and in the middle of the following season joined Cooper to finish runner-up. He then spent two years at Honda, followed by a disappointing year with BRM, before forming his own team in 1970. He retired from GP racing in 1972 to manage the business, but results were indifferent and the team folded in 1978.

FROM KARTING TO THE BIG STAGE

SEBASTIAN VETTEL

B. 3 JULY 1987, HEPPENHEIM, GERMANY

GRAND PRIX STARTS: 26*

GRAND PRIX VICTORIES: 1*

POINTS TOTAL: 41*

*TO END OF 2008 SEASON

Lewis Hamilton took the accolades for becoming the youngest ever world champion in 2008, but he was not the only record-breaker among the young bloods that year. It was easy to overlook the enormous strides made by Sebastian Vettel, in his first full season in the elite division.

Vettel was a junior karting star who swept the board when he stepped up to the German Formula BMW Championship in 2004. He locked horns with Hamilton in the Formula 3 Euroseries in 2005, finishing fifth that year and runner-up the next. He went into 2007 as BMW Sauber test driver, while also competing in the Renault World Series. Vettel made his F1 debut at the US Grand Prix, replacing the injured Robert Kubica. Fellow test driver Timo Glock had had a spell with Jordan in 2004, but the team's decision was vindicated as the 19-year-old finished in eighth place, taking over from Jenson Button as the youngest driver to score a championship point.

Vettel was contracted to Red Bull from the end of 2007, but BMW Sauber released him early so that he could join Red Bull's sister outfit Scuderia Toro Rosso, who had lost Scott Speed. He finished fourth in Shanghai in the penultimate race of the year, but it was in 2008 when he really began to show his mettle. He scored in seven of the last nine races, including a maiden victory from pole at Monza. With that success he displaced Fernando Alonso as F1's youngest race winner.

Vettel finished 8th in the championship with a highly creditable 35 points, and it was no surprise when he was named in the Red Bull line-up for 2009, replacing David Coulthard.

GILLES VILLENEUVE

NATURAL RACER A SAD LOSS TO FORMULA ONE

B. 18 JANUARY 1950, ST-JEAN-SUR-RICHELIEU, CANADA

D. 8 MAY 1982

GRAND PRIX STARTS: 67

GRAND PRIX VICTORIES: 6

POINTS TOTAL: 107

Gilles Villeneuve's early forays into four-wheeled motor sport began with Formula Ford, winning an invitation race in 1976, and a year later retaining his Canadian Formula Atlantic title.

At his F1 debut in the 1977 British GP he competed well, despite an ageing McLaren, and finished eleventh. McLaren chose to lose him and he was driving for Ferrari before the season was out, replacing Lauda.

His maiden victory came on home soil in the final round of the 1978 championship. The following year he took two victories at Kyalami and Long Beach, and added a third in the final race at Watkins Glen. Team-mate Scheckter already had the title in the bag by then, Villeneuve having to follow team orders, and he finished runner-up to him in the championship.

The 1980 Ferrari was a disaster, with Villeneuve scoring only 6 points, and his team-mate and reigning champion scoring just a couple. The 1981 model showed little improvement, but Villeneuve managed wins in Monaco and Spain to finish seventh overall.

At San Marino in 1982, Villeneuve was furious when his then team-mate Didier Pironi broke an agreement and passed him on the last lap. At the qualifiers for Zolder two weeks later, the feeling of resentment between the two was palpable. Villeneuve was determined to take pole and in so doing, struck Jochen Mass's March. He was hurled from his Ferrari and killed.

CANADIAN WINS 1997 SHOWDOWN WITH SCHUMACHER

JACQUES VILLENEUVE

B. 9 APRIL 1971, ST JEAN-SUR-RICHELIEU, CANADA

GRAND PRIX STARTS: 165

GRAND PRIX VICTORIES: 11

POINTS TOTAL: 235

WORLD CHAMPION: 1997

Jacques Villeneuve experienced a meteoric rise to become world champion, a feat his father never achieved. He became the youngest ever winner of the Indy Car championship in 1995 and secured a two-year deal with Williams as a result. His maiden victory at the European GP at the Nürburgring in 1996 was followed by three more wins, and he emerged as the only rival to team-mate Damon Hill. Crashing out at Suzuka ended his slim chance

of taking the title, Hill winning when he needed a single point.

The championship title came in 1997, where there were seven wins, and a showdown in the final race at Jerez. Schumacher led the title race by a point and attempted to shunt Villeneuve out of the race, but the Canadian recovered to finish third and take the title.

Villeneuve signed up with BAR at the end of a disappointing 1998 where he had made the podium just twice. The team did not pick up a single point in 1999, Villeneuve suffering 12 DNFs. The next four years saw him make a total of 40 points, and at the end of 2003 he left BAR.

After a short time at Renault at the end of the 2004 season, he moved to Sauber-Petronas for another attempt at the title. The 2005 Championship saw Villeneuve score just nine points with a fourth at San Marino being his best finishing position. He continued to race under the newly-named BMW Sauber in 2006, but a crash in the German Grand Prix left him with injuries, which forced his team to bring in a replacement, Robert Kubica. Villeneuve was being edged out of the team as Kubica put in several impressive performances, finishing on the podium in only his third race. As a result the former champion decided to retire from the sport during the middle of the season.

TRAGEDY IN SEARCH OF 1961 WORLD CROWN

WOLFGANG VON TRIPS

B. 4 MAY 1928, NR. COLOGNE, GERMANY

D. 10 SEPTEMBER 1961

GRAND PRIX STARTS: 27

GRAND PRIX VICTORIES: 2

POINTS TOTAL: 56

Already a member of Ferrari's sports car team in 1956, von Trips gained promotion to the F1 team for the Italian GP, but an accident during practice prevented him from racing. His debut came in Buenos Aires, the first race of the 1957 season, and gave him sixth place, followed by a podium place at Monza. With the deaths of Castellotti and de Portago that year, he was given a full-time seat for 1958, scoring 9 points. He was released at the end of the year, however, driving for much of 1959 in F2 for Porsche.

Back with Ferrari for the last race of the season in the US, he struggled the following year with an uncompetitive car, managing only sixth place overall. In 1961, however, Ferrari had the car to beat with their new 'sharknose' and von Trips' victory at Zandvoort made him the first German to win a post-war GP. A win at Aintree and two second places gave him a real chance of taking the crown.

Four weeks later, he took pole at Monza and clashed with Jim Clark's Lotus on the first lap. His car took to the air before crashing into a side barrier and killing both him and fourteen spectators. He finished a posthumous runner-up in the 1961 championship.

JOHN WATSON

ULSTERMAN NARROWLY MISSES OUT

B. 4 MAY 1946, BELFAST, NORTHERN IRELAND

GRAND PRIX STARTS: 152

GRAND PRIX VICTORIES: 5

POINTS TOTAL: 169

John Watson's racing career began in his native Ulster and by the early 1970s he was competing in F2. Brabham gave him his GP debut at Silverstone in 1973, and he then signed a contract with the Hexagon team for the following year.   Having scored his first championship point at Monaco, Watson followed it up with a fourth in Austria. When Hexagon withdrew from F1, he signed for Team Surtees. They too had withdrawn by the end of the year, and Watson moved on to Penske, scoring his maiden victory, and the team's only success, at the 1976 Austrian GP.

Another move followed Penske's withdrawal at the end of the year, this time to Brabham. A season of erratic results was followed by a marked improvement in 1978, and Watson finished sixth in the title race.

A move to McLaren in 1979 produced just 21 points for Watson over the next two seasons but a new chassis saw a dramatic improvement in performance with Watson's second win coming at Silverstone in 1981. Two further victories the following year helped put him in contention for the title, but second place in the final race left him runner-up to Rosberg in the championship.

McLaren was chasing the turbos in 1983 and Watson was dropped from the team in 1984. He made a brief return the following year before concentrating on sports-car events, establishing a driving school at Silverstone, and TV commentary work.

THE CONSTRUCTORS

WINNERS OF THE INAUGURAL MANUFACTURERS CHAMPIONSHIP

Alfa Romeo was founded in 1907 by Milanese aristocrat Cavaliere Ugo Stella, in partnership with the French automobile firm of Alexandre Darracq. After that collaboration ended, Stella set up a new company, Anonima Lombarda Fabbrica Automobili, in the Portello suburb of his home town.

The first Alfa appeared in 1910, a 24-hp model designed by Giuseppe Merosi. Within a year the company also turned its thoughts to motor sport, Franchini and Ronzoni competing in the 1911 Targa Florio in an Alfa.

Alfa takes on Romeo's name

Nicola Romeo bought the company in 1915, and after helping to support the war effort, Alfa reverted to car production. In 1920 the name of the company was changed to Alfa Romeo, the Torpedo being the first car to bear the famous badge.

In 1923 Alfa driver Enzo Ferrari was instrumental in luring renowned designer Vittorio Jano from Fiat. The first Jano-designed car was the P2, in which Giuseppe Campari and Antonio Ascari enjoyed enormous success. In 1925 Alfa Romeo won the inaugural manufacturers' world championship with the same model.

First monoposto racing car

In 1932 Jano unveiled the Tipo B P3, the first monoposto racing car. It made a victorious debut at that year's Monaco GP, with Tazio Nuvolari at the wheel, and went on to dominate the Grand Prix arena for the next two years.

In 1933 Alfa was nationalised by a Mussolini government keen to showcase the best in Italian design and technology, and the company withdrew from racing. For the next five years Alfa Romeos did compete, Enzo Ferrari running a semi-works team. Auto Union and Mercedes were dominant in this period, though Alfa did enjoy some stunning successes, notably at the Nürburgring in 1935. Nuvolari beat the German powerhouses in their own back yard with the now-

outdated P3. So confident had the organisers been of a home victory that the German national anthem was cued up ready to acclaim the victor. Nuvolari promptly produced his personal copy of the Italian anthem for the post-race honours.

The rise of the Alfetta

Jano was sacked in 1937, and after Alfa regained control of its racing affairs the following year, the marque turned its attention to the voiturette class. Giocchino Colombo designed the famous 158 'Alfetta'. This was a 1.5-litre model, and in 1939 the Italians decided to hold all their races to a 1500cc formula to stave off the German onslaught. Mercedes did produce a one-off car to win that season's Tripoli GP, but in the postwar period the Alfetta was the car to beat. Not that that happened too often, the Alfa enjoying a 26-race winning streak in the late 1940s.

Alfa withdrew from racing in 1949, following the double blow of losing ace driver Jean-Pierre Wimille – killed during practice for the Buenos Aires GP in January that year – and team-mate Count Trossi, who lost his fight against cancer. The marque was back for the inaugural world championship the following year, with the famous '3 Fs' dominating the championship series. Nino Farina pipped Fangio for the title, with Luigi Fagioli third. A year later Fangio lifted the first of his five world crowns in an Alfa 159, essentially the same car but with a two-stage compressor.

Lack of funds causes Alfa to quit

Although Alfa had squeezed home in the 1951 title race, the team bosses knew that without a major injection of funds, it would lose out to Ferrari the following season. No money was forthcoming, so Alfa announced its immediate withdrawal from the sport.

Alfa Romeo did return to Grand Prix racing in 1976, supplying engines to Bernie Ecclestone's Brabham team. In 1978 Niki Lauda scored two wins, one of which was in the famous 'fan' car in its only outing before it was banned. Alfa ran under its own name once again for the next seven years, but failed to recapture the heady successes of the early 1950s. The best return came in 1983, when Andrea de Cesaris scored 15 points to finish eighth in the championship.

ALFA ROMEO TEAM PROFILE	
Country	Italy
Foundation	1910
Years in Formula One:	1950-51, 1979-85
Constructors' cup victories:	0

OPPOSITE ABOVE: *1983 Brazilian Grand Prix, Jacarepagua, Rio de Janeiro. Andrea de Cesaris (Alfa Romeo 183T).*

BELOW: *1951 French Grand Prix, Reims. Race winner Juan Manuel Fangio (Alfa Romeo 159A).*

OPPOSITE BELOW: *From left: Baconin Borzacchini, Enzo Ferrari, Tazio Nuvolari in front of an Alfa Romeo 8C 'Monza' (c.1931/32)*

AUTO UNION

REVOLUTIONARY NEW DESIGN BY FERDINAND PORSCHE

Along with Mercedes, Auto Union dominated motor racing in the 1930s, a period in which Adolf Hitler actively promoted track success and speed records as a means of demonstrating to the world the fruits of German design and engineering.

Auto Union was formed in 1932, an amalgamation of four companies: Audi, Horch, Wanderer and DKW.

Spurred on by the intense domestic rivalry, the company produced a revolutionary new racing car in 1934, designed by Ferdinand Porsche. The 4.4-litre, 16-cylinder engine was mounted behind the driver, and with an output of 300bhp it made a mockery of the new 750kg formula, introduced in an attempt to curb the manufacturers' penchant for increasing engine size year on year.

First win for rear-engined car

At the 1934 German GP at the Nürburgring, Hans Stuck became the first man to drive a rear-engined car to

victory in a championship race. Stuck was a favourite of the new German Chancellor, and although not in the first rank of drivers, he was good enough to cross the line first in the inaugural Swiss GP at Bremgarten, and

at the Czech GP. Mercedes undoubtedly boasted the stronger line-up, prompting Auto Union to sign Achille Varzi. Varzi had had a stellar year with Alfa Romeo in 1934 but didn't achieve the same heights with Auto Union. Victory in the 1935 Tunis GP was one of the highlights, but by 1936 his career was on the wane. However, Auto Union unearthed a new star. Bernd Rosemeyer claimed his first victory in the 1935 Czech GP, and a year later – his first full Grand Prix campaign – he won six races, including the German Swiss and Italian GPs, to become European champion, the most prestigious title in motor sport at that time.

Death of Rosemeyer

By the end of 1937, Rosemeyer had notched 10 wins in 31 Grand Prix starts. He was killed during an attempt to recapture the world speed record from Mercedes in January 1938, and as his replacement Auto Union signed the legendary Tazio Nuvolari. Nuvolari had wanted to join the team three years earlier, but it is said that neither Varzi nor Stuck wanted the greatest driver of the era alongside them. Nuvolari won the Italian and Donington GPs in 1938, while team-mate Hermann Muller drove an Auto Union to victory in the 1939 French Grand Prix.

As Auto Union's base was the East German town of Zwickau, it proved impossible to resurrect the marque as a racing outfit after the Second World War. Its legacy in the modern era is the four-ring logo – representing the merger of the original four companies – which Audi continues to use.

AUTO UNION TEAM PROFILE	
Country of origin:	Germany
Date of foundation:	1932
Years in Formula One:	0
Constructors' cup victories:	0

OPPOSITE ABOVE: *1938 Donington Grand Prix, Donington Park, England. Tazio Nuvolari (Auto Union D-typ) on his way to first position.*

BELOW: *Hans Stuck's Auto Union A-typ in the pit lane at the 1934 French Grand Prix, Montlhery, Paris.*

OPPOSITE BELOW: *Hermann Muller attained fourth position at the 1937 Donington Grand Prix, driving this Auto Union C-typ.*

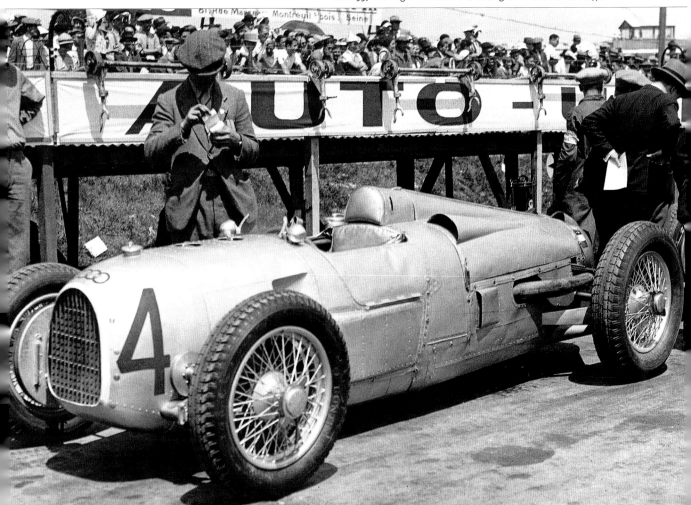

VILLENEUVE SIGNS FOR FLEDGLING BAR TEAM

Tobacco giant BAT entered F1 after buying the Tyrrell team in 1997. British American Tobacco took to the grid as British American Racing, making its debut at the Melbourne curtain-raiser in 1999. One of the team's prime movers was Craig Pollock, whose close association with Jacques Villeneuve helped secure the services of the 1997 world champion. It proved to be a difficult baptism, but things improved with the arrival of Honda power in 2000, Villeneuve finishing fourth on four occasions. His 17 points put him seventh in the championship, ahead of Button's Williams and both Jordans.

In 2001 Villeneuve finally got BAR onto the podium, in Spain and Germany, and there were changes at the top as Dave Richards took the helm. After a hugely disappointing 2002 campaign, Richards drafted in Jenson Button from Renault. Button regularly

outperformed the former champion, whose loss of interest and patience culminated in a dramatic walk-out just before the final race at Suzuka.

Runner-up to Ferrari

Button scored 10 podium finishes in 2004, his 85-point haul taking BAR to the runner-up spot behind Ferrari in the Constructors' race. The Briton was somewhat unlucky in 2005, his third place at Imola chalked off for a technical infringement, which also earned him a two-race ban. He scored 37 points for ninth place, Takuma Sato adding just one to the team effort as BAR slipped to sixth overall.

The highlight of the 2005 season for BAR didn't occur on the track – that was something of a disappointment following the great strides the team had made in the previous campaign. Rather, it was the change of heart on the part of Jenson Button, who committed his future to a team he said offered him the best chance of fulfilling his ambition of becoming Britain's ninth world champion. That decision came with a hefty price tag, Button reportedly having to stump up some £10 million to buy himself out of the contract which should have seen him rejoin Williams in 2006.

Honda buy out BAT

Honda bought out BAT's majority stake at the end of 2005, and the Honda Racing F1 team took its place on the grid the following season. It was the first time since 1968 that Honda had lined up on the constructors' roster. Rubens Barrichello joined from Ferrari, replacing Sato, and predicted great things for the new concern. He finished seventh in 2006, one place behind Button, who put the team on top of the podium at the Hungarian GP. A combined total of 86 points placed Honda a creditable fourth in the Constructors' championship. Fortunes dipped dramatically over the following two seasons, the same drivers accumulating just 20 points between them. In December 2008 Honda announced that it was quitting the sport and put the team up for sale. Following an 11th-hour buy-out, the new Brawn GP team debuted at the Australian GP.

BAR TEAM PROFILE	
Country of origin:	United Kingdom
Date of foundation:	1997
Years in Formula One:	1999-2005
Constructors' cup victories:	0

HONDA TEAM PROFILE	
Country of origin:	Japan
Years in Formula One:	1964-1968
	2006-2009
Constructors' cup victories:	0

OPPOSITE ABOVE: *Rubens Barrichello, BAR Honda 007 (Formula One testing, Jerez, Spain, January 2006)*

BELOW: *Olivier Panis, BAR Honda 003. (Formula One testing, Silverstone, England, January 2001).*

OPPOSITE BELOW: *Dave Richards.*

FASHIONING A GEAR CHANGE IN MOTOR SPORT

The famous fashion house entered Formula One as a sponsor to Tyrrell in 1983. Just two years later it decided to take the plunge into team ownership, buying out Ted Toleman's outfit. Toleman had hardly set the F1 world alight in its five years at the top, its main claim to fame being a couple of podium finishes for the young Ayrton Senna in 1984.

Toleman designer Rory Byrne stayed on with the new concern, and his BMW-powered B186 was competitive from the outset. In the penultimate round of the 1986 season Gerhard Berger, helped by a shrewd tyre strategy, gave Benetton its maiden success on a bumpy Mexico City track.

1987 saw the beginning of a long-term deal with Ford. Thierry Boutsen finished fourth in the 1988 title race, Alessandro Nannini taking sixth the following year. The Italian won the controversial 1989 Japanese GP, inheriting maximum points after Senna was disqualified for chopping a chicane following a clash with Prost. Flavio Briatore took over as team principal that year, and with three-times champion Nelson Piquet spearheading the line-up, Benetton had their best season to date in 1990. The Brazilian won the last two races of the season for a share of third in the title race.

Schumacher snatched from Jordan

Piquet stayed on for '91, and performed creditably again, but more significant was the arrival of Michael

Schumacher. His signature infuriated Eddie Jordan, for whose team the German wunderkind had made an impressive debut at Spa, qualifying seventh.

Schumacher hung onto Williams' coat-tails in '92, but the active suspension of the FW14B made Mansell unstoppable. He did take his maiden win at Spa, though, and with another victory plus eight podiums in 1993, Benetton continued to narrow the gap on Williams.

Following Senna's death at Imola in 1994, Schumacher pipped the Brazilian's Williams team-mate Damon Hill for the title. It wasn't plain sailing: there was a ban for ignoring a black flag at Silverstone; disqualification at Spa for skidblock wear which infringed the rules; and the clash with Hill at the Adelaide decider which took both men out and preserved the German's one-point advantage.

Nine wins brings championship double

Benetton switched to Renault power in 1995 and Schumacher delivered a more emphatic, less controversial second championship, winning nine races. With Johnny Herbert playing a useful supporting role, Benetton won its only Constructors' title that year.

The team slipped after Schumacher departed to Ferrari in 1996, and the loss of technical wizards Rory Byrne and Ross Brawn to Maranello was also a severe blow. The withdrawal of Renault in 1997 also impacted on performances. In 2000, however, Renault decided to return to F1 as a full works team, and to that end purchased Benetton. Fisichella and Button picked up 10 points between them in the 2001 Benetton-Renault, the last campaign before Renault assumed total control and the Benetton name disappeared.

BENETTON TEAM PROFILE

Country of origin:	United Kingdom
Date of foundation:	1986
Years in Formula One:	1986-2001
Constructors' cup victories:	1995

OPPOSITE ABOVE: *Jarno Trulli, Benetton (Formula One testing at the Circuit de Catalunya, Barcelona, Spain, January 2002).*

BELOW: *Thierry Boutsen (Benetton B187 Ford).during the 1987 French Grand Prix (Paul Ricard, Le Castellet).*

OPPOSITE BELOW: *Michael Schumacher (Benetton Renault) first position with team boss Flavio Briatore, celebrate taking his second successive drivers' world championship on the podium at the 1995 Pacific Grand Prix, Tanaka International, Aida, Japan.*

BRABHAM

THE DETERMINED AUSTRALIAN

After winning successive world titles with the rear-engined Cooper, Jack Brabham's thoughts turned to running his own team. He left Cooper at the end of 1961 and, with friend and fellow Antipodean Ron Tauranac as chief engineer, entered the fray at the Nürburgring the following season. The Climax-powered BT3 failed to go the distance that day, but within two years Jack was back on top of the podium, this time as a team boss. Dan Gurney gave the marque its maiden success, at Rouen in 1964, and also took victory in Mexico that year.

When Gurney competed in the 1965 Indy 500, Brabham drafted Denny Hulme into the team for the Monaco GP, the Kiwi having competed in Formula Junior events for Brabham. Following Gurney's departure to set up his Eagle team, Hulme took the no. 2 seat on a permanent basis.

Repco deal

There were no wins in 1965, a Lotus-BRM-dominated season, but with the introduction of the new 3-litre formula for 1966, the Brabham team came to the fore. Jack cut an engine deal with an Australian company which supplied parts under the Repco name. Brabham became the first man to take a Grand Prix victory in a car bearing his own name when he crossed the line first at Reims. Three more wins brought him his third world crown, and Hulme's valuable contribution helped the team lift the Constructors' title. Brabham had just turned 40, and at Zandvoort he took time out to poke

fun at himself by appearing with false beard and walking stick. He won the race.

Denny Hulme retained the title for the stable, despite the arrival of the new Cosworth DFV to power the Lotus cars. Hulme won just twice, Monaco and Germany, but consistency put him ahead of his boss and Clark in the final table.

Belgian Jacky Ickx gave Brabham the runner-up spot in '69, albeit a long way off the pace set by Stewart

in the Matra-Ford. Jack called it a day the following season. He should have signed off with a fourth victory in the British GP, heading the Lotus 72 of ex-Brabham driver Jochen Rindt by a street at Brands Hatch. But his BT33 died and he coasted through for second. It was later found that the engine had been left to run rich after starting from cold, and thus used four gallons more than it should. The mechanic who no doubt got it in the neck that day was none other than future McLaren supremo Ron Dennis.

'Fan car' banned

Tauranac bought the company – Motor Racing Developments – but it soon changed hands again, former F3 driver Bernie Ecclestone stepping up to the role of team boss. Gordon Murray was promoted from assistant to Brabham's chief designer. The Murray-designed BT44 scored three wins in 1974, with Carlos Reutemann at the wheel. Reutemann's third place in 1975 was Brabham's best effort of the decade, and the team hoped that switching from Cosworth to Alfa Romeo power, and signing Lauda from Ferrari, would put it on top again. The Austrian joined in 1978, the year of the BT46B, the famous 'fan car'. It swept to victory on its debut in Sweden – and was then promptly

banned by the FIA, who ruled that the fans were there to suck air from underneath the car rather than cool the engine.

Brazilian tyro Nelson Piquet made his debut for Brabham that year, and it was he who gave the team their final two championships, in 1981 and 1983. Brabham reverted to Cosworth power, while Murray was again producing innovative designs. For 1981 he devised an ingenious hydraulic system whereby the car sank during the race – improving ground-effect and cornering speed – but complied with the regulation 6cm height between ground and bottom of the car for the mandatory tests. Piquet edged Williams duo Reutemann and Jones that season, and two years later pipped Renault and Prost, Brabham by now running a BMW unit.

In 1986 Piquet joined Williams and Riccardo Patrese notched just two points in a miserable campaign. To compound the misery, Murray departed to McLaren. Ecclestone withdrew at the end of 1987, though Brabham reappeared on the grid two years later, having been bought by Swiss financier Joachim Luithi. He was soon in jail for tax evasion. The team struggled on until 1992, when the Brabham name finally disappeared for good.

BRABHAM TEAM PROFILE

Country of origin:	United Kingdom
Date of foundation:	1962
Years in Formula One:	1962-1987, 1989-1992
Constructors' cup victories:	1966, 1967

OPPOSITE ABOVE: *Niki Lauda wins the 1978 Swedish Grand Prix. at Anderstorp in the controversial Brabham Alfa fan car, making its debut and last outing before being banned.*

BELOW: *Jack Brabham (Brabham BT3 Climax) competes in the German Grand Prix at the Nürburgring, August 1962.*

OPPOSITE BELOW: *Jack Brabham celebrating victory in the 1966 French Grand Prix, at Reims.*

LONG WAIT FOR FIRST VICTORY

BRM

The roots of BRM go back to the early 1930s, when Raymond Mays and Peter Berthon founded English Racing Automobiles, a concern which sought commercial backing for its racing ventures. Mays and Berthon left ERA in 1939, but the same idea underpinned their new project: to attract sponsors and fund a British Grand Prix car capable of taking on the world's finest. British Racing Motors was born.

To comply with the Grand Prix regulations of the day, the car was fitted with a V-16 1.5-litre supercharged engine. Launched in December 1949, the BRM was hailed as a world-beater – which made the subsequent fall from grace the more dramatic. The teething troubles were endless, but under pressure from the backers, Mays was forced to enter the car for the 1950 International trophy meeting at Silverstone. It was an unmitigated disaster, Raymond Sommer being left on the grid with a broken driveshaft.

Figure of fun

BRM became a figure of fun, something Reg Parnell's fifth place in the 1951 British GP couldn't reverse. Retirements made that result somewhat flattering. The final straw came with a change in the Grand Prix formula, which rendered the car effectively obsolete. In 1952 a sorry chapter was closed when the BRM Trust was sold to industrialist Sir Alfred Owen for a knockdown price.

Over the next six years rival British marques Cooper, Connaught, HWM – and particularly Vanwall –

all outperformed BRM in championship races. Harry Schell and Jean Behra both got on the podium at Zandvoort in 1958, easily BRM's best day thus far, and a year later on the same circuit, Jo Bonnier gave the marque its maiden success.

The 1960s were BRM's heyday, particularly the 1.5-litre era which ran from 1961 to 1965. There was a championship double in 1962, with BRM finishing runner-up in the Constructors' race for the following three seasons too. The team began the 1962 campaign still looking for a second victory, and under severe pressure from Owen to deliver. Graham Hill had amassed just 7 points from the previous two championships, but the development of a new mid-engined V-8 unit promised much.

Four wins for Hill

Hill scored three victories and two second-places with the best five scores to count. Even so, he went to Kyalami in December knowing that a Jim Clark victory could still rob him of the title. That proved academic as the Lotus fell by the wayside and Hill took his fourth win of the year.

In 1964, another final race shoot-out, Hill went to Mexico City leading Ferrari's John Surtees by 5 points, and Clark by 9. Hill was cruising in third when he

tangled with Surtees' team-mate, Lorenzo Bandini. Clark's engine gave out, and Bandini allowed Surtees through to take second place and the 6 points he needed to snatch the crown for Ferrari.

Debut for Stewart

BRM gave Jackie Stewart his first taste of F1 in 1965. The Scot won at Monza, and Hill added two more wins to the BRM tally, but Clark ended the year with a perfect score from his best six races.

The introduction of the 3-litre formula in 1966 marked the beginning of a long slow decline for BRM. There were four more wins for the stable in the early 1970s. One of those fell to Jo Siffert in Austria in 1971, helping him to a share of fourth place in the championship. That would be the best return in the post-Hill era, and BRM made its swansong appearance six years later, at Kyalami.

OPPOSITE ABOVE: *Niki Lauda (BRM P160E) in action during the 1973 Swedish Grand Prix, Anderstorp.*

BELOW: *Jo Bonnier (BRM P25) driving to victory in the 1959 Dutch Grand Prix at Zandvoort. This was the first Grand Prix win for BRM.*

OPPOSITE BELOW: *Raymond Mays, one of the co-founders of BRM, pictured at the 1951 British Grand Prix, Silverstone.*

BRM TEAM PROFILE	
Country of origin:	United Kingdom
Date of foundation:	1948
Years in Formula One:	1951, 56-77
Constructors' cup victories:	1962

THE REAR-ENGINE REVOLUTION

John Cooper made his name making low-cost cars with chain-driven motorcycle engines for the budget Formula 500 series of the postwar era. He competed in such events, along with the likes of Moss and Ecclestone, but it would be as an innovative manufacturer that Cooper would scale the heights.

The natural home for the 500cc engine was behind the driver, and when Cooper turned his thoughts to competing against Ferrari, Maserati and the other giants, he decided to apply the same principle. The Cooper garage in Surbiton would be the launchpad for the rear-engined revolution.

1955 was a key year, not so much for a breakthrough on the track but for Jack Brabham's arrival from Australia to try his hand against the best drivers in the business. He gravitated towards the Cooper stable and this combination would go on to dominate the field. Brabham stole the show at Monaco in 1957, running third in his underpowered Cooper-Climax before suffering a fuel pump problem. He pushed the car over the line for sixth place.

Moss provides maiden victory

Stirling Moss had the honour of giving Cooper its first victory, at the 1958 Argentina GP, though this was for Rob Walker's stable. Maurice Trintignant then gave

Cooper its second win, in Monaco, for the same privateer outfit. At that season's Nürburgring race Cooper and Brabham noted the performance of Kiwi Bruce McLaren – winner of the F2 race and fifth overall

– and signed him to the F1 team for 1959. Another piece of the jigsaw was thus slotted into place.

Brabham gave the latest T51 model a winning debut at the 1959 Monaco GP. A new 2.5-litre Climax engine finally gave the car the power it needed to compete with the best, and at 458kg it had a considerable weight advantage over the front-engined opposition. Brabham also won at Aintree, and in the decider at Sebring had to resort to muscle power once again, pushing the T51 across the line for fourth place. He took the title by 4 points from Brooks' Ferrari. Moss had given Rob Walker two wins that year in a T51, and McLaren's victory in the US meant a Cooper had taken the chequered flag in five of the eight European rounds.

Five wins for Brabham

The marque was even more dominant the following year, winning six out of nine, Brabham reeling off five straight victories mid-season. He duly claimed his second crown, McLaren taking the runner-up spot. Cooper comfortably retained the Constructors' Cup.

Cooper struggled with the introduction of the new 1.5-litre formula in 1961, and although McLaren took third in the '62 championship, and Jochen Rindt matched that four years later, the Surbiton stable fell behind the pace set by other marques. Pedro Rodriguez gave the marque its final victory in South Africa, the opening round of the 1967 championship, but the Maserati engine was no match for the Brabham-Repco, and Lotus upped the stakes even further by rolling out the Cosworth DFV that season. Cooper withdrew the following year, though the lineage of F1 success continued through the teams set up by Brabham and McLaren.

OPPOSITE ABOVE: *Alan Rees (Cooper T81 Maserati) achieved ninth position in the 1967 British Grand Prix at Silverstone.*

BELOW: *Stirling Moss driving a Cooper Alta in the 1953 Daily Express Meeting, also at Silverstone.*

OPPOSITE BELOW: *John Cooper, founder of the marque.*

DELAGE

SETTING THE STANDARDS

Delage enjoyed huge success in the 1920s, a period in which French marques were in the vanguard of motor sport. The company was founded by ex-Peugeot engineer Louis Delage in 1905, and within a few years it was building its own engines and body parts, and competing in Grand Prix events. Rene Thomas won the 1914 Indianapolis 500 in a Delage, averaging over 82 mph. A decade later the same man drove a Delage to a new world record of over 143 mph, eclipsing the previous mark by 10mph.

Hot work for Benoist

Delage virtually swept the board at the two prewar British Grands Prix, run at Brooklands in 1926 and 1927. Robert Senechal and Louis Wagner shared the spoils in the inaugural race, with Robert Benoist also needing temporary respite on his way to taking third. One of the reasons for the shared drives was a design problem which had the exhaust pipe running too close to the drivers' feet. Trays of iced water were kept on hand to cool the scorched and blistered soles.

In 1927 Delage fielded the 15-S8, which not only had a superb straight-eight engine, but also gave the drivers considerably more comfort as the exhaust system had been rerouted. There was a clean sweep at Brooklands, Benoist this time coming out on top. It was a golden year for both driver and manufacturer, as they also won the French, Spanish and Italian Grands Prix. Benoist received the Legion d'Honneur for his remarkable achievements.

By the 1930s, Italian and German marques had taken over, and Delage, in financial difficulties, withdrew from motor sport. The company went into liquidation in 1935, though the name lived on until the early 1950s, produced by Delahaye.

DELAGE TEAM PROFILE

Country of origin:	France
Date of foundation:	1905
Years in Formula One:	o
Constructors' cup victories:	o

OPPOSITE ABOVE: *1936 Junior Car Club 200 mile race, Donington Park, England. Dick Seaman, the winner, driving a Delage 15S8.*

BOTTOM: *1926 British Grand Prix, Brooklands. Robert Senechal/Louis Wagner (Delage 15S8) leads Albert Divo (Talbot 700) (Senechal/Wagner finished in first position).*

BELOW: *Edmond Bourlier (Delage 15S8), driving to second position in the 1927 French Grand Prix, Montlhery, Paris.*

OPPOSITE BELOW: *1932 British Empire Trophy, Brooklands, Great Britain. The winner was John Cobb, seen here at the wheel of the Delage V12/LSR that he drove.*

THE STANDARD BEARERS OF F1

No marque encapsulates the glamour, style and thrill of Grand Prix racing like Ferrari. It is the only constructor to have contested every world championship, but the magic of Ferrari is not based on mere longevity, or even success on the track. When Michael Schumacher lifted the title in 2000, the beginning of a five-year period of domination, it ended a 21-year barren streak; yet even when Ferrari found race victories, let alone championships, hard to come by, it remained the brand with the greatest cachet in motor sport.

Enzo Ferrari enjoyed moderate success as a driver with Alfa Romeo in the 1920s. At a race in Ravenna in 1923, an Italian couple presented him with a badge which their fighter pilot son had carried with him during WWI. It bore the famous prancing horse motif – an emblem of spirit and power – which would become synonymous with Ferrari.

Split with Alfa

Enzo Ferrari's first foray into team ownership came in the 1930s, when he began running semi-works Alfas from a base in Modena. With the legendary Tazio Nuvolari at the wheel he enjoyed some success against the mighty German marques which dominated that era. By 1939 Ferrari harboured plans to go his own way, but the outbreak of war deferred the appearance of the first true Ferrari for almost a decade. The debut came at the 1948 Monaco GP, Ferrari running a remodelled V12 sports car.

In 1949 Ferrari signed Alberto Ascari and Luigi Villoresi from rivals Maserati, further strengthening a driver line-up that already included Raymond Sommer and Giuseppe Farina. Farina departed to Alfa for the

inaugural world championship the following year and lifted the title. Ascari finished fifth in what was a transitional season, Ferrari moving from the supercharged 125 to an unblown 4.5-litre unit. By the end of the year it was on the pace with the dominant Alfa 158, and being less thirsty than the supercharged Alfetta, things looked good for 1951. Alfa squeezed home in that title race too, but this time with Ascari and Jose Froilan Gonzalez breathing down their necks. The 'Pampas Bull' gave Ferrari its first championship win that year, at Silverstone. Ascari won the next two rounds to complete a hat-trick for the marque.

Ascari dominant

Alfa's withdrawal left the way clear, and a Ferrari crossed the line first in every European round of the 1952 championship, Ascari becoming the team's first world champion. Five more victories in 1953 saw him retain his crown.

Ferrari fell behind when the 2.5-litre formula was introduced in 1954, but the arrival of Fangio two years later gave the marque its third championship. That was with a modified version of the Vittorio Jano-designed Lancia D50, Ferrari having taken the car over when Lancia withdrew from F1 in 1955. Lancia-Ferraris also appeared in 1957, but it was in the new Dino 246 that Mike Hawthorn pipped Stirling Moss to lift the 1958 title.

'Sharknose'

Ferrari was one of the last to embrace the rear-engined revolution, but in 1961, with the introduction of the 1.5-litre formula, it ruled the roost with the new V6 'sharknose'. Phil Hill and Wolfgang von Trips fought a thrilling championship duel, which the American won after von Trips' fatal accident in the penultimate round at Monza. That took the gloss off Ferrari's first Constructors' title, three years after the introduction of that award.

John Surtees snatched the title from Graham Hill and Jim Clark in Mexico, the climax of the 1964 season, but when the 3-litre era arrived in 1966, Ferrari struggled. In 1970 Jacky Ickx gave Ferrari the runner-up spot when he failed to overhaul Jochen Rindt's points total, the Austrian having lost his life at Monza. Clay Regazzoni finished third that year, and four years later it was the Swiss's turn to narrowly miss out as Fittipaldi got the better of him in a final-race decider.

The Lauda era

Niki Lauda was Ferrari's unheralded second-string at the start of that year; by the end he had established his racing credentials, and in 1975 he cruised to the title,

FERRARI TEAM PROFILE

Country of origin:	Italy
Date of foundation:	1946
Years in Formula One:	1950 to date
Constructors' cup victories:	1961, 1964, 1975, 1976, 1977, 1979, 1982, 1983, 1999, 2000, 2001, 2002, 2003, 2004, 2007, 2008

OPPOSITE ABOVE: *2006 Scuderia Ferrari 248 F1 Launch, Mugello, Italy. 24 January 2006.*

BELOW: *Luigi Villoresi (Ferrari 375) competing at the 1951 French Grand Prix, Reims-Gueux.*

OPPOSITE BELOW: *Scuderia Ferrari boss Enzo Ferrari stands with his chief designer Mauro Forghieri, as they look over the Ferrari 312 chassis at the 1967 Italian Grand Prix, Monza.*

Ferrari's first in 11 years. Lauda lost out by a single point to James Hunt in the famous 1976 Ferrari-McLaren battle, in which the Austrian recovered from the horrific fireball crash at the Nürburgring. Consistency brought Lauda and Ferrari another championship in 1977, and two years later the team scored a championship one-two, emulating the successes of 1952 and 1961. This was the dawn of the ground-effect era, and although the Ferrari 312T4 wasn't at the head of the new game, it was strong and reliable, and in Gilles Villeneuve and Jody Scheckter the team boasted a hugely talented driver line-up. The South African took the championship, garnering 4 more points than his Canadian team-mate.

Enzo's death

There were two Constructors' titles in the 1980s, but by the time Enzo Ferrari died – in 1988 at the age of 90 – McLaren and Williams were enjoying greater success. Alain Prost did win five races in 1990, the year in which he clashed with former McLaren team-mate Senna at Suzuka, an incident which handed the crown to the Brazilian. Prost was driving the John Barnard-designed Ferrari 641 that year, but it was over the next decade that the team would lay the groundwork that would put Ferrari back to the forefront of F1. Frenchman Jean Todt, who had led Peugeot to a string of sports car titles, joined as team principal in 1993. A trio of ex-Benetton men, who had won back-to-back world championships in 1994 and 1995, were then recruited to the Maranello cause. Rory Byrne took over from Barnard as chief designer, Ross Brawn was installed as technical director, and in Michael Schumacher the team had the man who had succeeded Prost and Senna as the best in the business.

Five-year juggernaut

In 1997 Schumacher went a step too far in trying to secure his first title with Ferrari, failing in his attempt to take Jacques Villeneuve out in the decider at Jerez. Three years later Schumacher won nine races as Ferrari edged McLaren into the minor placings. There was yet another Constructors' title, too, Maranello's first double for 21 years. For the next four years Ferrari pulverised the opposition. Apart from 2003, when the team's winning margin was 2 points in the Drivers' championship and 14 in the Constructors' race, the gaps were enormous. In 2002 Schumacher notched a record 144 points to take the title in the shortest time ever, and Ferrari became the first team to break the 200-point mark. Two years later the team raised the bar still further as the champion scored 148 points and Ferrari 262, more than double the total of runners-up BAR. After ceding the crown to Renault for two years, Ferrari was back on top in 2007, Kimi Raikkonen's championship victory helping Maranello secure yet another double. Celebrations began when Felipe Massa took the chequered flag in the final race at Interlagos in 2008, but the champagne went flat as the team learnt that Lewis Hamilton had snatched fifth place at the death, and with it the title by a single point. A 16th Constructors' championship softened the blow, Ferrari stretching its lead over Williams to seven in the all-time list.

OPPOSITE: *Michael Schumacher, testing the Ferrari 248, Mugello, Italy, January 2006.*

BELOW: *Niki Lauda (Ferrari 312T) on his way to winning the 1975 Monaco Grand Prix, Monte Carlo. One of the victories that delivered a long awaited Drivers' championship to Ferarri.*

JAGUAR

SHORT-LIVED PERIOD AS F1 TEAM

In 1997 three-times world champion Jackie Stewart entered F1 as a team boss, partnered, unsurprisingly, by Ford, with whom he had enjoyed such spectacular success three decades earlier. The highlight for the fledgling team came with Johnny Herbert's victory at the 1999 European GP. A year later Ford bought Stewart out and entered the 2000 championship rebranded as Jaguar, which was a Ford subsidiary. There were high hopes for the Milton Keynes-based team as the blue-and-white livery of Stewart-Ford gave way to the green of Jaguar, but the next five years were to be fraught with disappointment. Personnel changes – including Stewart's departure as team principal before the start of the 2000 season – didn't help.

Irvine delivers first podium

Eddie Irvine, runner-up to Schumacher in 1999, arrived from Ferrari, but his 4 points represented the entire haul for the debut season. Irvine did give the team its first podium finish, at Monaco in 2001, and the

Ulsterman repeated that achievement at Monza a year later, but the successes were few and far between; Jaguar's return for those two campaigns was just 17 points.

Mark Webber and Christian Klien between them could manage just five sixth-place finishes in the following two seasons. That meant a five-year haul of

just 49 points from 85 races. In September 2004 it was announced that the team was being sold to one of its sponsors, Red Bull, the energy drink company owned by Austrian billionaire Dietrich Mateschitz.

OPPOSITE ABOVE: *Qualifying action on the Sunday morning of the 2004 Japanese Grand Prix, Suzuka. Pictured is Christian Klien, Jaguar R5.*

BELOW: *Johnny Herbert (Jaguar R1) during Saturday qualifying for the 2000 Belgian Grand Prix, Spa-Francorchamps. He completed the race in eighth position.*

OPPOSITE BELOW: *Eddie Irvine gave Jaguar their first podium finish by coming third at the 2001 Monaco Grand Prix.*

RIGHT: *Jaguar team principal, Tony Purnell, fields the many questions about the future of his team, prior to the Chinese Grand Prix, (Shanghai) in September 2004.*

JAGUAR TEAM PROFILE

Country of origin:	United Kingdom
Date of foundation:	1999
Years in Formula One:	2000-2004
Constructors' cup victories:	0

THE CHARISMATIC IRISHMAN

JORDAN

A number of top drivers got their big break with Eddie Jordan's team, including Barrichello, Irvine, and both Schumacher brothers. Jordan entered F1 in 1991, a decade after the enterprising, charismatic Irishman established his outfit. It was a respectable debut, Andrea de Cesaris and Bertrand Gachot both getting in the points in Montreal, in what was only the fifth outing for Gary Anderson's impressive Jordan 191. When Gachot was jailed following an altercation with a taxi driver, Jordan fielded a new young tyro at Spa, Michael Schumacher. The future champion retired after outqualifying de Cesaris, and was soon being wooed by Benetton, much to the annoyance of the Jordan boss.

Yamaha power proved underwhelming in 1992, and a Hart V-10 unit was secured for the following season, as was Rubens Barrichello. With better luck the Brazilian might have garnered more than the 2 points for fifth at Suzuka. Just behind him that day was Eddie Irvine, who marked his F1 debut by trading blows with Senna as well as scoring a point.

Barrichello puts Jordan on podium

Only drivers from the big four – Benetton, Williams, McLaren and Ferrari – finished ahead of Barrichello in '94, his 19-point haul including third place at the Pacific GP, Jordan's first podium finish. He also gave the team its first pole, at Spa, where he had a spell in front before spinning off. Irvine might have been up with his team-

mate had he not been hit with a three-race ban for his part in a pile-up at the season's curtain-raiser at Interlagos.

Peugeot provided the power for the next three years, but it was when Jordan switched to a Mugen-Honda unit in 1998 that the team registered its first victory. Damon Hill won an accident-littered race at Spa, with team-mate Ralf Schumacher making it a famous one-two. It would be Hill's 22nd and final victory, while Jordan's first had come at the 259th attempt.

Frentzen takes third in title race

Things got even better in 1999 as Heinz-Harald Frentzen arrived from Williams, with Schumacher going in the opposite direction. Frentzen won at Magny-Cours and Monza and finished third in the championship,

behind Hakkinen and Irvine. Only McLaren and Ferrari headed Jordan in the Constructors' race.

1999 was to be Jordan's high watermark. The team's only other victory came in the 2003 Brazilian GP, where in the confusion of a red-flagged race Fisichella was awarded second place to Raikkonen. A subsequent FIA inquiry reversed that decision, and the Finn did the presentation honours at the next race. It was Fisichella's maiden success.

Early in 2005 it was announced that the team was being taken over by the Midland Group. It continued to run as Jordan for the duration of that season, but a colourful 15-year chapter was brought to an end as MF1 Racing took its place on the grid at the start of the 2006 series.

JORDAN TEAM PROFILE	
Country of origin:	United Kingdom
Date of foundation:	1981
Years in Formula One:	1991-2005
Constructors' cup victories:	0

OPPOSITE ABOVE: *Nick Heidfeld, Jordan Ford EJ14. Formula One testing Imola, Italy, February 2004.*

BELOW: *Heinz-Harald Frentzen, (Jordan 199 Mugen-Honda) driving to victory in the 1999 French Grand Prix, Magny-Cours.*

OPPOSITE BELOW: *Eddie Jordan sits in the cockpit of an EJ13 as the team celebrated its 200th Grand Prix at the 2003 Brazilian Grand Prix, Interlagos, Sao Paulo.*

CHAPMAN THE GREAT INNOVATOR

LOTUS

It is rare for an F1 marque to rise to the top of the sport, then, after a period in the doldrums, sweep all before it once again. That is exactly what Lotus did in the '60s and '70s, though it actually competed at the top level in five decades.

The man behind Lotus was Colin Chapman, one of the greatest innovators in the history of motor sport. In 1954, two years after founding Lotus, he drove a Mark 8 model to victory on the undercard to the British GP. With its spaceframe chassis, the Lotus 8 was beautifully engineered, a sign of things to come when Chapman made his bow in F1 four years later.

The debut season saw Graham Hill and Cliff Allison compete in the Lotus 12, Chapman's first single-seater. Allison outshone the future champion, taking fourth at Spa, then, in the new Lotus 16, vying for the lead at the Nürburgring when his radiator sprang a leak.

Chapman follows Cooper's lead

Hill and new partner Innes Ireland suffered a string of retirements in 1959, but the next generation model, the Lotus 18, became a serious contender. Chapman, noting Cooper's success, saw that rear-mounted engines represented the way forward. It was Moss who gave the marque its maiden win, however, driving a Rob Walker Lotus 18 to victory at Monaco in 1960. Team Lotus fielded a number of drivers that year, and although Ireland earned plaudits for 18 points and fourth in the championship, it was a young Scot, with eight points from six outings, who would have a much greater impact on Lotus and F1. Over the next 8 years, until his

death in an F2 race at Hockenheim in 1968, Jim Clark and Lotus formed a formidable partnership. Apart from winning the title in 1963 and 1965, on both occasions with perfect scores, Clark might also have won in 1962 and '64 had his car been more reliable.

First monocoque

Chapman consistently produced vehicles worthy of the greatest driver of the era. In 1962 he introduced the Lotus 25, the first F1 car with a monocoque chassis. It was both lighter and more rigid, and, unsurprisingly, was soon copied by other chassis designers. Its arrival signalled the death-knell for the spaceframe chassis.

In 1967 the Lotus 49, with a new Ford engine was unveiled. With a little prodding from Chapman, Ford had agreed to add some glamour to their brand by producing a racing engine. For one year it was agreed that Lotus would have exclusive use of the Cosworth DFV unit, and at Zandvoort '67 Clark gave the engine the first of over 150 victories. After the Scot's death the following year, Graham Hill gave Lotus its third championship, and the 49 was also the vehicle for the last privateer GP victory, Jo Siffert winning at Brands Hatch for Rob Walker.

Chapman was at the forefront of experiments with wings and stalk-mounted aerofoils. There were safety concerns over the earliest modifications, but it was the birth of the downforce era which would soon become common F1 currency.

Jochen Rindt became the sport's first posthumous champion in 1970, taking five wins in the wedge-shaped Lotus 72 before losing his life at Monza. Chapman was already grooming a new young star, Emerson Fittipaldi, and two years later the Brazilian became F1's youngest champion in the latest incarnation of the 72 model.

Ground-effect revolution

The final golden period came six years later, when the Lotus 79 came on stream and Mario Andretti and Ronnie Petersen took a championship one-two. Chapman's design created a vacuum which literally sucked the car onto the track; soon all F1 marques were studying the 'ground-effect' principle.

Chapman gave Nigel Mansell his debut in 1980, but succumbed to a heart attack before his latest protégé topped the podium. Elio de Angelis and Ayrton Senna brought Lotus some respectable results in the mid-'80s but the marque never recaptured the heights it had attained under its inspirational leader, and folded in 1994.

LOTUS TEAM PROFILE	
Country of origin:	Great Britain
Date of foundation:	1956
Years in Formula One:	1958-1994
Constructors' cup victories:	1963, 1965, 1968, 1970, 1972, 1973, 1978

OPPOSITE ABOVE: *Mario Andretti (Lotus 79 Ford) on his way to winning the 1978 Belgian Grand Prix, Zolder. The car won in its maiden Grand Prix.*

BELOW: *Cliff Allison, in a Lotus 12 Climax at the 1958 Belgian Grand Prix, Spa-Francorchamps.*

OPPOSITE BELOW: *Jim Clark (Team Lotus) with team boss Colin Chapman pictured at the 1963 Dutch Grand Prix, Zandvoort.*

THE FAMILY BUSINESS

One of the most famous names in motor sport was born in 1914 when Alfieri Maserati, along with brothers Ernesto and Ettore, founded a garage business in Bologna. It would be 12 years before the company built its first racing car, the Tipo 26, which sported an 8-cylinder, 1.5-litre supercharged engine. It made its debut at the 1926 Targa Florio, with Alfieri himself at the wheel. He finished ninth overall in what was a Formula Libre event, winning the 1500cc class. This race also saw the famous trident badge, a design inspired by a statue of Neptune in the main square at Bologna, adorn a Maserati for the first time.

Alfieri Maserati died in 1932, aged 44. This was a decade in which the marque scored a number of Grand Prix victories, with the likes of Nuvolari and Varzi at the wheel, though the era was dominated by Alfa Romeo, Mercedes and Auto Union.

OSCA founded by Maserati family

Financial pressures caused the remaining brothers to sell out to the Orsi family in 1937, though they secured a contract to continue working for the company for the next decade. The company relocated to Modena and focused its attention on building road cars, though Maseratis did win the Indianapolis 500 in 1939 and 1940. When the contract expired, the brothers were keen to return to racing in their own right and a new company, OSCA, was formed in 1947.

The Maserati 4CLT won on its first outing, the 1948 San Remo GP, with Alberto Ascari at the wheel.

Ascari and Luigi Villoresi were the works drivers, and they dominated that year's British GP, despite arriving late and having to start from the back of the grid. Maserati suffered a huge blow when Enzo Ferrari signed both drivers for 1949. That year Baron Emmanuel de Graffenried won at Silverstone with a privately entered Maserati, and in the early years of the world championship Maseratis would be the popular choice for privateers keen to slug it out with the works teams. Stirling Moss was among those who took this route.

Fangio scores maiden win

Ferrari dominated the 1952 and 1953 championship races, which were run to an F2 formula, but by the back end of the latter season Fangio, Gonzalez and Marimon were pushing hard for Maserati. The marque finally scored its maiden victory at Monza, Fangio coming out on top after a thrilling duel with Ascari, though the latter already had his second title in the bag.

Fangio won the first two rounds of the 1954 championship in the famous 250F, one of the most successful cars of the 2.5-litre era, but he was merely biding his time until his new employers, Mercedes, were ready with their new hardware.

For the 1957 season Maserati managed to re-sign the four-times world champion. It would be a glorious F1 swansong for both driver and manufacturer. Fangio won four of the seven European races to relegate Stirling Moss to second place in the title race for the third year running. But within a year a funding crisis led Maserati to withdraw from F1 and concentrate on its road car operation.

OPPOSITE ABOVE: *Juan Manuel Fangio (Maserati 250F) en route to victory in the 1957 German Grand Prix, Nürburgring.*

BELOW: *Jose Froilan Gonzalez (Maserati A6GCM), competing in the 1952 Italian Grand Prix, Monza.*

OPPOSITE BELOW: *Juan Manuel Fangio (Maserati), first, and Mike Hawthorn (Ferrari), second on the podium at the 1957 German Grand Prix.*

MASERATI TEAM PROFILE	
Country of origin:	Italy
Date of foundation:	1926
Years in Formula One:	1950-1958
Constructors' cup victories:	0

FRANCE MAKES ITS MARK

MATRA

Matra takes its name from French aerospace company Mécanique Avion Traction. Matra boss Marcel Chassagny provided hardware and financial support for the racing ventures of a friend, Rene Bonnet. When the latter got into financial difficulties in 1964, company executive Jean-Luc Lagardere saw it as an opportunity to go down the works path. Matra Sport was formed.

After a brief flirtation with F3 and F2, Matra, with backing from Elf, took the step up to the top division in 1968. The team ran its own V12-powered car, Jean-Pierre Beltoise heading the Matra Sports entry. The company also supplied a car to Ken Tyrrell and his young star, Jackie Stewart, who operated as Matra International. Stewart, running on Cosworth power, fared much the better, though his three wins weren't enough to wrest the title from Graham Hill and Lotus.

Championship at second attempt

For 1969 Matra concentrated on sports cars, leaving Tyrrell and Stewart to fly the company flag in F1. The Scot took six victories to give Matra the championship at only the second attempt. Beltoise, Stewart's team-mate that year, provided able support, his contribution helping put Matra well clear of Brabham and Lotus in the Constructors' race.

At the end of the year Matra's automotive division was sold to Chrysler France, and politics dictated that Matra couldn't compete with the Ford DFV. The company's insistence on using its own V12 unit was enough to end the deal with Tyrrell. Matra

immediately went on the slide, Beltoise only just making the top ten in 1970.

Powering Ligier to victory

Chris Amon spearheaded Matra's next two campaigns. The New Zealander won first time out in 1971, in Argentina, though this was a non-title race as a precursor to that country's return as a championship

venue. Third place in Spain was his best effort when it counted. On top of the podium that day was the man Matra had let go and who was now on his way to a second title with Tyrrell.

There was another lone podium for Amon in 1972, when the team wound down its F1 operation by fielding just one car. Matra disappeared from the grid at the end of the year, concentrating its efforts on sports cars. That brought a return to winning ways, Henri Pescarolo and Graham Hill winning at Le Mans, Matra retaining the 24-hour classic title in the following two years. In 1973 and 1974 Pescarolo was partnered by Gerard Larrousse.

In 1974 Matra announced it was quitting the sport and designer Gerard Ducarouge joined the new Ligier team, which also took over the Matra V12 engines. Matra powered Jacques Laffite to Ligier's

maiden victory, at Anderstorp in 1977, and the Frenchman also won in Austria and Canada four years later.

MATRA TEAM PROFILE	
Country of origin:	France
Date of foundation:	1964
Years in Formula One:	1968-1972
Constructors' cup victories:	1969

OPPOSITE ABOVE: *Chris Amon (Matra-Simca MS120C) in action during the 1972 South African Grand Prix at Kyalami.*

BELOW: *Jackie Stewart (Matra MS10 Ford) on his way to winning the 1968 Dutch Grand Prix, Zandvoort.*

OPPOSITE BELOW: *Jackie Stewart (Matra Ford) leaves the podium after the 1968 Dutch Grand Prix. He won despite wearing a plaster cast on his right hand.*

DENNIS BUILDS ON MCLAREN'S DREAM

Bruce McLaren was F1's youngest ever race winner until Fernando Alonso's victory in Hungary in 2003. A protégé of fellow Antipodean Jack Brabham, McLaren followed in the footsteps of the three-times champion by establishing his own team in 1966. It was the start of the 3-litre era, and McLaren struggled to find a unit that would do justice to the Robin Herd-designed M2B. While 'Black Jack' won his third world crown with the superb Brabham-Repco, the Kiwi had just 3 points to show for his season's efforts.

It was an inauspicious start, but better times lay ahead. In 1968 he signed reigning champion and compatriot Denny Hulme – from Brabham. Although Hulme would win in Italy and Canada, and finish third to McLaren's fifth in the championship, it was the team boss who gave the team its maiden victory, at Spa. He was helped by the fact that Jackie Stewart's Matra-Ford ran out of juice with the line almost in sight, but McLaren was on its way. Hulme scored the only victory of 1969, though McLaren's consistency put him third behind Stewart and Ickx in the title race.

McLaren killed at Goodwood

McLaren had contested just three rounds of the 1970 championship – finishing second at Jarama – when he was killed while testing one of his CanAm cars at Goodwood. He was 33. Hulme battled on for fifth place in the championship.

Teddy Mayer, with whom McLaren had formed Bruce McLaren Motor Racing Ltd in 1963, took the reins for the next decade, and it was under his leadership that the team won its first Drivers' and Constructors' titles. In 1972 the team, now backed by Yardley, was competitive again, the pick of the bunch apart from Fittipaldi in the Lotus 72D and Stewart's Tyrrell-Ford. It was a similar story in 1973, though Gordon Coppuck's M23, which made its debut at Kyalami, looked a winner. And with Fittipaldi at the wheel in 1974, it was. Now running as Marlboro Team Texaco, McLaren did the double, edging Regazzoni and Ferrari in both championships. The Brazilian won only three races but was consistently in the points.

Ferrari got their revenge in '75, but a year later the M23 was still the car to beat, this time in James Hunt's hands. Hunt's third place in torrential conditions in Japan was enough to pip Lauda by a single point.

Dennis takes over

McLaren was behind the game in the ground-effect era, and it would be eight years before the team was back on top. Ron Dennis and designer John Barnard were the key men in McLaren's spectacular run of success in the 1980s. Dennis had been running Marlboro's F2 team, Project 4, and in 1980 the sponsor brokered the deal which saw the two outfits merge. Dennis brought Barnard with him, and the latter produced MP4/1, F1's first carbon fibre monocoque. Lauda was coaxed out of retirement, TAG-Porsche came on board to provide the turbo unit, and in 1984 this combination took the title. Lauda won by half a point from team-mate Prost, with the rest nowhere, the duo between them winning 12 races.

Prost made it a McLaren hat-trick by winning in 1985 and 1986, though in the latter season the Williams-Honda, which ran away with the Constructors' championship, was the class act of the field. By 1988 McLaren had the benefit of Honda power, and went on to win four successive titles, Senna lifting three of them, Prost the other.

Mercedes deal

Honda's withdrawal in 1992 put McLaren on the back foot for a couple of seasons, though Senna still managed five wins and the runner-up spot with Ford power in '93. A new era dawned in 1995, when Mercedes, back in F1 as an engine supplier, agreed a deal with Dennis's team. It would be two years before the new partnership registered a win, Coulthard's victory in the 1997 curtain-raiser ending a four-year barren spell. But Mika Hakkinen won 13 races in the following two campaigns to win back-to-back titles, Coulthard weighing in with three victories as he finished third and fourth.

McLaren came closest to halting the Schumacher-Ferrari five-year juggernaut when Kimi Raikkonen lost out by just 2 points in 2003. In 2005 the Iceman was dogged by ill luck yet still managed seven wins in the MP4/20. McLaren won 10 of the 19 races but missed out to Alonso and Renault in both championships.

It was all change for 2007, Raikkonen moving to Ferrari and team-mate Juan Pablo Montoya quitting F1 altogether. The team paired double world champion Fernando Alonso with rising British star Lewis Hamilton, and looked set to record a famous double. Raikkonen spoiled the party by snatching a dramatic one-point victory in the final race, while a spying scandal cost the team the Constructors' cup. A frosty relationship between Alonso and Hamilton resulted in the two-time champion returning to Renault after just one year, with Heikki Kovaleinen travelling in the opposite direction. A dramatic finale to the 2008 season saw Hamilton snatch the title from Ferrari's Felipe Massa. It brought McLaren a 12th drivers' championship, putting the team three wins behind Ferrari in the all-time list. In the close season Ron Dennis announced that he was stepping down from the role of team principal, handing over to Martin Whitmarsh after 27 years at the helm.

McLaren Team Profile	
Country of origin:	United Kingdom
Date of foundation:	1966
Years in Formula One:	1966 to date
Constructors' cup victories:	1974, 1984, 1985, 1988, 1989, 1990, 1991, 1998

Opposite above: *Pedro de la Rosa, McLaren Mercedes MP4-21 in action during Formula One testing, Barcelona, Spain, January 2006.*

Below: *Bruce McLaren (McLaren M2B-Serenissima), pictured at the 1966 British Grand Prix, Brands Hatch. This was the team's first season in Formula One.*

Opposite below: *Bruce McLaren, team founder.*

SHORT-LIVED BUT SPECTACULAR

In the early years of the 20th century Austrian Daimler dealer Emil Jellinek raced the imported cars under his daughter's name – Mercedes. The famous marque appeared at the birth of Grand Prix racing, the 1906 French GP, staged at Circuit de la Sarthe. Although there was no German victory that day, it wasn't long before the famous three-pointed star, symbolising mastery of land, sea and air, made its mark on motor sport's premier events.

Daimler employee Christian Lautenschlager was the first Mercedes star, winning the 1908 French GP at Dieppe. He kept his factory job and raced only sporadically, which made his celebrated victory in the 1914 French GP – a seven-hour marathon staged at Lyon – all the more remarkable.

Rivalry with Auto Union

After Hitler's rise to power in 1933, Mercedes took up the challenge laid down by the Fuhrer to build world-beating racing cars. It was a propaganda war which also sparked intense internal rivalry between Mercedes and Auto Union. The two German marques dominated Grand Prix racing from 1934 to the outbreak of WWII, and also vied with each other for the land speed record.

The new era began when the Hans Nibel-designed W25 was unveiled at the 1934 Eifel GP at the Nürburgring. It transgressed the new 750 kg weight

limit and team boss Alfred Neubauer is said to have ordered the paintwork to be stripped, leaving the gleaming aluminium bodywork on show; the legend of the Silberpfeile – Silver Arrows – was born.

Caracciola takes three European titles

The undoubted star of this era was, like Lautenschlager, a former company employee. Rudolf Caracciola was crowned European champion three times between 1935 and 1938, losing out to Auto Union's Bernd Rosemeyer in 1936. Caracciola's cv included five victories in his home Grand Prix. So disenchanted were the Italians with being reduced to also-rans that in 1939 they ran their races to a 1500cc formula. Mercedes responded by building a scaled-down version of their Grand Prix car and scored a one-two victory. This model never raced again.

Neubauer still the mastermind

Mercedes made a dramatic return to Grand Prix racing in 1954, four years after the inception of the world championship. Neubauer was still at the helm, and Fangio was recruited to head the driver line-up, though the 1951 champion had a couple of outings for Maserati as the new W196 wasn't quite ready for action. Fangio and Karl Kling made it a triumphant return, finishing first and second when the W196 made its debut at Reims. Fangio went on to win three of the next four races, the W196 appearing both in streamlined and open-wheeled form during the course of the season.

Silverstone was the only circuit which didn't suit the car, and even here Fangio picked up points for fourth place.

Withdrawal follows Le Mans tragedy

Fangio was joined by Moss in 1955, and the season developed into a two-horse race. Maurice Trintignant's win for Ferrari at Monaco prevented a clean sweep for Mercedes. The British GP at Aintree saw the W196 at its most dominant, Karl Kling and Piero Taruffi following Moss and Fangio home to give Mercedes the top four finishers. The lustre of that triumph was tarnished by events at Le Mans a month earlier, where Pierre Levegh's Mercedes 300 SLR ploughed into a spectators' enclosure, causing over 80 fatalities. Four F1 races were cancelled as a result, and although Fangio comfortably retained his crown, Mercedes withdrew from racing at the end of the year.

Mercedes returned to the sport as engine supplier to the fledgling Sauber team in 1993, switching to McLaren two years later. It was the beginning of a highly successful partnership which brought Mika Hakkinen successive world championships in 1998 and 1999.

MERCEDES TEAM PROFILE	
Country of origin:	Germany
Date of foundation:	1901
Years in Formula One:	1954-1955
Constructors' cup victories:	0

OPPOSITE ABOVE: *Winner of the 1955 British Grand Prix at Aintree was Stirling Moss, driving a Mercedes Benz W196.*

BELOW: *Rudolf Caracciola leads Luigi Fagioli (both Mercedes-Benz W25) and Hans Stuck (Auto Union A-typ) in the 1934 French Grand Prix held at Montlhery, Paris.*

OPPOSITE BELOW: *The team boss from the 1930s, Alfred Neubauer, was still at the head in 1955, the year that the Mercedes team withdrew from F1.*

THE SMALL POPULAR TEAM

Giancarlo Minardi's Faenza-based team was held in high regard during the 20 years in which it competed, F1 fans recognising the achievements of the tiny Italian outfit in a sport dominated by teams with telephone-number budgets.

In 1979 Minardi began building its own cars for the European Formula Two championship, and six years later, as F2 was superseded by F3000, Minardi made the decision to step up to the top table. Pierluigi Martini gave the team its first outing at the 1985 curtain-raiser in Brazil. Minardi ran an outdated Cosworth engine to begin with, and even the introduction of must-have turbo power failed to improve matters significantly.

Martini was dropped from the team, but both he and the Cosworth unit were reinstated for 1988 and they gave Minardi its first point, at the 1988 Detroit GP. A year later Martini and Spain's Luis Perez Sala both scored at Silverstone, and Minardi squeezed into the top ten in the Constructors' race.

Martini on front row

On the opening round of the 1990 series, in Phoenix, Martini put the M189 on the front row of the grid, alongside the McLaren of pole-sitter Gerhard Berger. A year later he took M191, now using Ferrari power, to fourth place at both San Marino and Estoril. That

helped Minardi to finish seventh in the Constructors' championship, which would be its best showing.

The next decade saw a succession of changes, both in engine suppliers and drivers, and Minardi became a perennial also-ran, though Christian Fittipaldi

did match Martini's achievement by taking fourth at Kyalami in '93. When Hungarian driver Zsolt Baumgartner finished eighth at Indianapolis in 2004, Minardi fans cheered their first point since Mark Webber's fifth spot at Albert Park two years earlier.

Stepping stone for future stars

Minardi was an early stepping stone for a number of top drivers, including Fisichella, Trulli and 2005 world champion Fernando Alonso. Financial constraints have always impinged on track performances, however,

something not even the deep pockets of airline boss Paul Stoddart, who bought Minardi in 2001, managed to reverse.

In September 2005 the team was sold to Red Bull, which announced it would race two teams in 2006. Die-hard fans petitioned the new owners to retain the Minardi name, but commercial imperatives meant that the new outfit would take to the grid as Squadra Toro Rosso – Team Red Bull – signalling the end of an era for a much-loved F1 minnow.

Opposite above: Christijan Albers (Minardi Cosworth PS05), in action at the 2005 USA Grand Prix, Indianapolis.

Below: Pierluigi Martini (Minardi M185 Motori Moderni) attempting to qualify for the 1985 Monaco Grand Prix, Monte Carlo, during the team's maiden F1 season.

Opposite below: Paul Stoddart marks the last race for the Minardi F1 team at the Chinese Grand Prix, October, 2005.

MINARDI TEAM PROFILE	
Country of origin:	Italy
Date of foundation:	1985
Years in Formula One:	1985-2005
Constructors' cup victories:	0

THE CHARGE FOR THE TOP

Just one year on from the eleventh-hour deal which saw Red Bull take over Jaguar's F1 berth, the famous energy drink company repeated the trick with Minardi in 2005. Billionaire owner Dietrich Mateschitz added the Italian minnow outfit to his stable, giving Red Bull two entrants for the 2006 campaign. Much to the chagrin of Minardi fans, who had hoped to see the famous name preserved, it was announced that the latest phoenix-like transformation would see a new name on the grid: Scuderia Toro Rosso.

The rise of Red Bull has been one of the most dramatic events in F1 in recent years. The company gave backing to the defunct Arrows team, and also sponsored the Swiss-based Sauber outfit. Having made the step up from Jaguar sponsor to team owner in 2005, Red Bull made an immediate impact. David Coulthard proving that there was life after McLaren, by finishing fourth at the Melbourne curtain-raiser.

DC ended the year with a creditable 24 points, just 4 adrift of Williams' Nick Heidfeld. Christian Klien provided able support with 9 points, helping Red Bull to seventh place in the Constructors' race, ahead of the much more established Sauber, Jordan and Minardi outfits and just 4 behind BAR.

Newey joins from McLaren

At the end of the year Red Bull showed their determination to break into the sport's top echelons by drafting in Adrian Newey. The designer of six world championship-winning cars in his time with Williams and McLaren ended his eight-year association with Ron

Dennis's team, seeking fresh pastures with a smaller but no less ambitious contender. Newey worked with Coulthard at both McLaren and Williams, and his arrival was a major coup for Red Bull as the team prepared for the new 2.4-litre, V-8 era. Delighted team boss Christian Horner said that the pieces were falling into place for Red Bull to be on top of the podium by 2008.

That looked to be a realistic possibility as Coulthard gave the team a maiden podium at the 2006 Monaco GP, but breaking through from a midfield position has proved elusive. Mark Webber was in the points in nine races in 2008, though fourth in Monaco was his best finish, while Coulthard gave Red Bull its third podium in Montreal.

Red Bull's sister team registered a solitary point in its debut season, and fared little better in 2007, when Sebastian Vettel took over from Scott Speed mid-season. 2008 saw a much stronger showing from Scuderia Toro Rosso, Vettel scoring in nine races and taking victory from pole at Monza. His 35-point haul put him eighth in the championship and helped the supposed second-string outfit to outperform the A-team.

RED BULL TEAM PROFILE

Country of origin:	United Kingdom
Date of foundation:	2004
Years in Formula One:	2005 to date
Constructors' cup victories:	0

TORO ROSSO TEAM PROFILE

Country of origin:	Italy
Date of foundation:	2004
Years in Formula One:	2006 to date
Constructors' cup victories:	0

OPPOSITE ABOVE: *David Coulthard, Red Bull Racing Cosworth RB1, at the 2005 Japanese Grand Prix, Suzuka.*

ABOVE: *David Coulthard again, at the 2005 Monaco Grand Prix, Monte Carlo.*

OPPOSITE BELOW: *Red Bull boss Dietrich Mateschitz and team manager Tony Purnell, chat by the side of the RB01, during Formula One Testing, November 2004, Barcelona, Spain.*

BUILDING ON A LEGEND

The Renault brothers manufactured and raced cars in the great city-to-city spectaculars that predated the Grand Prix era. Marcel Renault was among those who lost their lives in the infamous Paris-Madrid race of 1903, one of several tragic incidents which helped usher in the age of circuit racing. It was a Renault which crossed the line first in the inaugural Grand Prix, staged at Le Mans in 1906. Only 11 of the 32-car field went the distance in the two-day race, Ferenc Szisz's 90-hp Renault coming out on top.

Renault departed the racing scene for almost 70 years, the team not making its F1 debut until 1977. Jean-Pierre Jabouille had a few fruitless outings that season, failing to take the turbo-charged RS01 the distance in an era dominated by 3-litre, normally-aspirated units. Jabouille and the team notched just 3 points in 1978, but the breakthrough was only one year away. After a few unsuccessful outings for the old RS01, the new RE10 appeared. Jabouille won from pole position at the team's home GP, at Dijon, team-mate Rene Arnoux taking third. Although there were no further victories, a Renault headed the grid on four more occasions; it was the dawn of a new era as rival manufacturers took another look at the potential of turbo power.

Prost's maiden victory

Alain Prost came within 7 points of champion Nelson Piquet in 1981, giving Renault another success at the French Grand Prix in Dijon – his maiden victory – and

also crossing the line first at Zandvoort and Monza. Two years later the same drivers fought the title race to the wire. Prost went into the final race, Kyalami, with a 2-point cushion, but his turbo blew up and third place for the Brazilian's Brabham was enough to snatch the crown.

Prost was openly critical of the team's failure to maintain the advantage it had enjoyed over its rivals. He departed for a highly successful stint at McLaren, while Renault, after two indifferent seasons, quit the sport. It did continue as an engine supplier, however, and its units powered Williams and Benetton to a string of world titles in the 1990s.

Benetton buy-out

Renault returned as a works team after buying out Benetton in 2000, with Flavio Briatore heading the new enterprise. Jenson Button and Jarno Trulli were feeding off scraps in 2002, a year dominated by Ferrari, but in 2003 Fernando Alonso became the youngest ever pole-sitter, at Sepang, then in Hungary took over from Bruce McLaren as F1's youngest winner.

Jarno Trulli won at Monaco in 2004, but was dropped at the end of the season, Giancarlo Fisichella arriving to partner Alonso. 2005 was a season of glorious triumph: 15 podiums, including seven wins, helped Alonso become F1's youngest champion in the 56-year history of the event. The last of those, at Shanghai, clinched the Constructors' title for Renault, who edged McLaren by 9 points. The reigning champions continued to dominate the table in 2006, although Ferrari began to close the gap and even inched ahead late in the season. The competition went down to the last race in Brazil, but Renault managed to retain its title by just five points. The team slipped down the rankings in 2007, when Alonso left to join McLaren, but he returned a year later and gave Renault two more wins in 2008.

RENAULT TEAM PROFILE	
Country of origin:	France
Date of foundation:	1898
Years in Formula One:	1977-1985, 1989-1997, 2002 to date
Constructors' cup victories:	2005, 2006

OPPOSITE ABOVE: *Giancarlo Fisichella during testing at Jerez.*

BELOW: *British Grand Prix, Silverstone, England, July 1977. Jean-Pierre Jabouille in Renault's debut race.*

OPPOSITE BELOW: *Shanghai 2005: Fernando Alonso celebrates Renault's Constructors' championship victory with Flavio Briatore, the Renault F1 managing director.*

BMW SAUBER

THE SWISS SEARCH FOR A BREAKTHROUGH

Peter Sauber's Mercedes-backed team made the step up to F1 in 1993, after a highly successful period in sports cars which culminated in a world championship-Le Mans double in 1989. The team was in the points on its very first outing, Kyalami 1993, where Finnish driver JJ Lehto brought the Sauber C12 home fifth, albeit two laps behind Senna and Prost. Lehto took a fine fourth at Imola, and team-mate Karl Wendlinger matched that at Monza, helping Sauber to a share of sixth place in the Constructors' championship. It would set the pattern for the next 13 years: solid midfield consolidation without really threatening to make a major breakthrough.

Heinz-Harald Frentzen took Lehto's seat in 1994, and in his two spells with the team the German would become its most successful driver, notching 48 points in five seasons.

Switch to Ferrari power
In 1997, after running a works Ford engine for two years, Sauber began using Ferrari power, rebadged as Petronas for sponsorship reasons. It was during this long association that Sauber had its best return, Nick Heidfeld and Kimi Raikkonen between them scoring 21 points in 2001. That lifted Sauber to fourth in the table, ahead of Jordan, BAR and Benetton, although the gap between the big three and the rest of the field was immense. Indianapolis 2003 saw Sauber lead a Grand

Prix for the first time in its history, Frentzen eventually finishing third to equal the team's best showing.

In the summer of 2005 Peter Sauber sold out to BMW, the latter bringing to an end its partnership with Williams and giving F1 a new name on the grid for 2006. It was also announced that Ferrari were taking up their long-term option on Felipe Massa, who would be replacing Barrichello at Maranello. Having promoted the careers of Raikkonen, Heidfeld and Massa, Sauber proved to be a shrewd judge of new talent in its 13-year involvement with the sport.

A new young star, Robert Kubica, partnered Nick Heidfeld as BMW Sauber led the charge to catch front-runners Ferrari and McLaren in 2007. The team took second in the Constructors' championship, following a spying row that saw McLaren's points haul expunged. The duo carried on in the same vein in 2008. Kubica got on the podium seven times and topped it in Montreal, the team's maiden success. Heidfeld recorded four second-place finishes, including following his team-mate home in Canada. Kubica ended the season level with Raikkonen, edged out of third place on race wins, while 135 points put the team third behind Ferrari and McLaren in the Constructors' championship.

SAUBER TEAM PROFILE

Country of origin:	Switzerland
Date of foundation:	1970
Years in Formula One:	1993 to date (as BMW Sauber)
Constructors' cup victories:	0

OPPOSITE ABOVE: *Felipe Massa, Sauber Petronas C23, Formula One testing April 2004, Barcelona, Spain.*

BOTTOM: *Karl Wendlinger (Sauber C12 Ilmor) on the way to finishing fourth at the 1993 Italian Grand Prix, Monza.*

BELOW: *Nick Heidfeld, Sauber Petronas C22, leads the pack during the 2003 United States Grand Prix, Indianapolis.*

OPPOSITE BELOW: *Peter Sauber*

CORPORATE GIANT ENTERS THE FRAY

The world's third biggest motor manufacturer had a proud record in rallying, with a string of world championships to its name, when it entered the F1 fray in 2002. Like Ferrari, Toyota manufactured its own chassis and engines, yet even with the backing of such a huge corporation, there was no guarantee of success in such a specialised field.

Mika Salo got the team off to an excellent start, finishing sixth at Melbourne, Toyota's very first F1 outing. He and Allan McNish were dropped for 2003, Olivier Panis and Cristiano da Matta taking over the driving duties for the next two seasons. In 2003 the duo accumulated 16 points, enough to put Toyota ahead of Jordan in the final shake-up.

Breakthrough season

2004 was targeted as the breakthrough year, the team confidently predicting regular points finishes. In fact, Panis and da Matta garnered just 9 between them; the prediction was a year out. For it was 2005 which saw Toyota really start to come good. Ralf Schumacher and Jarno Trulli were signed, and they scored an aggregate 88 points in the TF105. That put them sixth and seventh respectively in the title race; only the McLaren and Renault men, plus seven-times champion Michael Schumacher, finished ahead of them. Toyota failed to get into the points in just two races, but a maiden victory was still proving elusive. Although the new TF106 was unveiled early in 2006, it failed to help Toyota achieve its aim to end the competition as one of the top three constructors.

Schumacher and Trulli fared little better in 2007, managing just 13 points between them. GP2 champion Timo Glock was drafted in to replace Schumacher for 2008, and he recorded the team's best result of the year, second place at the Hungarian GP.

TOYOTA TEAM PROFILE

Country of origin:	Japan
Date of foundation:	2001
Years in Formula One:	2002 to date
Constructors' cup victories:	0

OPPOSITE ABOVE: *Jarno Trulli at the wheel of the new Toyota TF106 (Formula One testing, Jerez, Spain, January 2006).*

ABOVE: *Toyota again finished in the points with a sixth place for Mika Salo at the 2002 Brazilian Grand Prix, Interlagos. (He finished sixth at Melbourne on the Toyota F1 debut).*

OPPOSITE BELOW: *Jarno Trulli, Toyota TF105, on the podium, celebrates taking second position at the 2005 Malaysian Grand Prix, Sepang, Kuala Lumpur. (He repeated the feat at the next Grand Prix in Bahrain).*

TYRRELL

BREAKING INTO THE BIG TIME

Ken Tyrrell was among the crop of young drivers to come to prominence in the 500cc Formula Three era of the 1950s, a shoestring class which brought racing within the reaches of the likes of Stirling Moss and Peter Collins. Tyrrell founded his own team in 1960, but the key date came four years later, when his long association with Jackie Stewart began. Although Stewart made his F1 debut with BRM in 1965, he continued to drive for Tyrrell when commitments allowed. In 1968 the two embarked on their first joint F1 adventure, in a Matra-Ford. Matra were new to the sport, and as well as running their own V-12 powered car, they supplied one to Tyrrell. The works car, driven by Jean-Pierre Beltoise, fared much worse than the Tyrrell version, which had been fitted with the Ford Cosworth DFV. Stewart missed out to Graham Hill in the title race, though at the Nürburgring that year he finished four minutes ahead of his rival, the biggest margin of victory in championship history.

Six wins brings championship double

Stewart and Matra-Ford swept the board the following year, winning six of the 11 rounds for a championship double. 1970 saw Matra receive backing from Chrysler France, making it politically impossible for the cars to use Ford power. With that door closed, Tyrrell ran a March that season, an interim arrangement while its

own car was being developed. The Tyrrell 001 was on the grid before the end of the year, but it was 1971 when it came into its own. Stewart added six more wins to his tally, while second-string Francois Cevert took what would be his only career victory in the final round, Watkins Glen. Tyrrell also took the Constructors' title in what was its first full season running its own car.

Clark's record broken

There were four more wins in 1972 but Stewart was hampered by an ulcer and had to be satisfied with the runner-up spot behind Fittipaldi and Lotus. Those positions were reversed in 1973, a season in which the Scot set a new mark of 27 victories, beating Jim Clark's record. Watkins Glen would have been Stewart's 100th Grand Prix, and thoughts of bowing out at the top were crystallized as Cevert was killed during qualifying.

Having lost both his star and the heir apparent, Tyrrell gave Jody Scheckter and Patrick Depailler their first full season in F1. They finished third and fourth in the 1976 title race – the year of the famous P34 six-wheeler – with a one-two at Anderstorp the crowning moment. It was soon back to a conventional arrangement, but over the next 20 years successes were sporadic. Depailler did win at Monaco in 1978, a welcome victory after eight second-places, while Michele Alboreto had the honour of giving the Cosworth DFV its final victory at Detroit in 1983. But Tyrrell was consigned to a midfield position, and in 1997 the team was bought by British American Tobacco, who joined the circus as BAR two years later.

Tyrrell Team Profile	
Country of origin:	United Kingdom
Date of foundation:	1960
Years in Formula One:	1970-1998
Constructors' cup victories:	1971

OPPOSITE ABOVE: *Jody Scheckter at the controls of his six-wheeled Tyrrell P34 Ford in the 1976 Swedish Grand Prix, Anderstorp. (This was to be the car's only GP win.)*

BELOW: *Michele Alboreto (Tyrrell 011 Ford) gives Tyrrell their final Grand Prix win at Detroit, Michigan, USA, June 1983.*

OPPOSITE BELOW: *Ken Tyrrell with Jackie Stewart. A formidable partnership for the Tyrrell team.*

VANWALL

INAUGURAL CONSTRUCTORS' CHAMPIONS

Vanwall took its place in the history books as winner of the inaugural Consctructors' Cup in 1958, and ran Mike Hawthorn's Ferrari mightily close in that year's Drivers' championship.

Team owner Tony Vandervell was an industrialist and fervently patriotic racing fan who was one of the early backers of the ill-fated BRM project. His frustration with that, and determination to see a British racing car take on the world, led him to acquire a Ferrari 125 in 1949. In adapted form, these 'Thinwall Specials' – the name taken from the revolutionary bearings made by Vandervell's company – took to the track, Reg Parnell finishing fourth at Reims in the 1951 French GP.

'Vanwall Special'

By then Vandervell decided to sever all links with BRM and Ferrari and build his own car. Norton, with some input from Rolls-Royce, worked on a new engine, Cooper was commissioned to provide the chassis. Unveiled in 1954 and dubbed the 'Vanwall Special', the car made its debut at the prestigious International Trophy meeting, held at Silverstone. It was running in fifth place in the final when an oil pipe broke, but the signs were encouraging.

Peter Collins was behind the wheel at that year's British Grand Prix. It was another retirement, but once again, there had been much to commend the performance.

A 2.5-litre Vanwall – the 'Special' had now been dropped – appeared in 1955, but neither Mike Hawthorn, Ken Wharton or Harry Schell got into the points in a Mercedes-dominated year. A frustrated Hawthorn decamped mid-season.

'C'est une bombe!'

Stirling Moss, open to offers after Mercedes' withdrawal from the sport, tested a Vanwall but opted to join Maserati for 1956. Vandervell also tried to sign Fangio, but in the end Harry Schell was retained and Maurice Trintignant joined the team for a two-pronged attack. Colin Chapman was brought in to improve the chassis, which became a spaceframe layout, and Frank Costin

designed new bodywork with better aerodynamics. Trintignant's verdict when he saw the new car: 'Ça alors, *c'est une bombe!'*

Moss, not on Maserati duty, gave the car a victorious debut at the 1956 International Trophy, outclassing the much-vaunted Lancia D50s run by Ferrari. The rest of the season didn't match that standard, but it was a shot across the bows of the rivals.

Victory at Aintree

The teething troubles addressed, Vandervell turned his thoughts to the driver line-up for 1957. Schell and Trintignant were both released; in came Moss, along with Tony Brooks, the cream of British talent. Moss finished runner-up – again – to Fangio, with Brooks taking fifth in the title race. The highlight was the British GP at Aintree. Moss took pole, Brooks third, with new young star Stuart Lewis-Evans making it three Vanwalls in the first six on the grid. Moss was running well until a technical glitch occurred. Brooks, still recovering from injury, gladly handed over his car and Moss tore through the field from ninth to become the first Briton

to win the home Grand Prix in a British car. With better luck, Lewis-Evans might have made it a Vanwall one-two.

Moss also won the two Italian races, Pescara and Monza. In the latter, Brooks set the fastest lap and Lewis-Evans took pole. 1958 couldn't come quickly enough.

Lewis-Evans killed in fireball crash

Vanwall again gave the curtain-raiser in Argentina a miss, Moss winning in a Rob Walker Cooper. He and Brooks then shared six victories in the European races to take the title race to the wire. Mike Hawthorn, with just a single win to his name, pipped Moss by a point in a championship decided by the best six scores. That disappointment paled beside the death of Lewis-Evans, who died from burns suffered in the Moroccan GP, where Hawthorn's fifth second place of the season clinched the crown for Ferrari.

For Vandervell, who was not in the best of health, this was a crushing blow, and in January 1959 it was announced that Vanwall was withdrawing from competition.

VANWALL TEAM PROFILE	
Country of origin:	United Kingdom
Date of foundation:	1949
Years in Formula One:	1954-1960
Constructors' cup victories:	1958

OPPOSITE ABOVE: Stirling Moss (Vanwall) won the 1958 Moroccan Grand Prix, (Ain-Diab, Casablanca).

BELOW: Harry Schell leads Stirling Moss (both Vanwall) in the 1956 International Trophy, Silverstone, Great Britain. Moss finished in first position.

OPPOSITE BELOW: Tony Vandervell celebrates winning the 1957 British Grand Prix, at Aintree, England.

WILLIAMS

FRANK WILLAMS' TEAM THIRD ON ALL-TIME LIST

Frank Williams first made his mark on Formula One as a privateer, running a Ford-powered Brabham for his friend Piers Courage in the 1969 championship. In only the car's second outing, at Monaco, Courage followed home the reigning champion and Monaco king Graham Hill to give Williams his first points at the sport's top table. There was another podium finish at Watkins Glen, and the team also collected points at Silverstone and Monza to round out a fine debut season.

Williams was deeply affected by Courage's death in a fireball accident at Zandvoort in 1970. The next few years were somewhat thin, Williams' drivers scratching for the odd championship point against the powerhouse works teams. In 1974 he ran his own chassis for the first time, his driver line-up that year including rookie Jacques Laffite. The Frenchman's second place at the Nürburgring in 1975 gave Williams his first podium as a constructor. The team was struggling to keep its head above water, however: a situation which led to a collaboration with Austrian oil magnate Walter Wolf in 1976. That quickly disintegrated, and Williams re-entered the fray the following year, founding Williams Grand Prix Engineering. More significantly, he brought in Patrick Head as chief designer; thus was born a partnership which would go on to win seven Drivers' championships and nine Constructors' titles.

First championship

After a transitional year, the new Williams FW06 was soon in the points, with Alan Jones at the wheel. In 1979 Jones was a title contender, though it was team-mate Clay Regazzoni who gave Williams its first win, at Silverstone. This was in Head's superb FW07, the class act in the field in the new ground-effect era. Jones went on to win four of the next five races. Had the FW07 been available for the early rounds, Jones may well have beaten Jody Scheckter, who took the title with just 11 more points than the Australian.

Williams' first championship was deferred only one year, Jones picking up in 1980 where he left off the previous season, taking the chequered flag five times on his way to the title. Had Jones and Carlos Reutemann

played a cannier team game, Williams might have won in '81, but their frosty relationship helped Nelson Piquet lift the crown. Williams at least retained the Constructors' title. Consistency brought Keke Rosberg the 1982 championship, the last hurrah for the Cosworth engine.

Williams entered the turbo era with Honda engines, and by 1986 the car was the pick of the bunch, winning nine of the 16 rounds. Unfortunately, those were shared between Mansell and Piquet, to Alain Prost's advantage.

That year the team was left reeling as Frank Williams was involved in a car crash which left him confined to a wheelchair. The team boss returned as committed and indefatigable as ever, and saw Piquet and Mansell at the top of the tree in 1987.

Record for Mansell as Williams dominate

The loss of the superb Honda unit brought a dip in fortune, but a deal with Renault in 1989 put Williams back on top. Mansell, returning from a spell at Ferrari, finished runner-up to Prost in 1991; a year later, the FW14, now with active suspension, was unstoppable. Mansell scored a record-breaking nine wins, and had the title sewn up with five races to spare.

Mansell departed to Indycars, and Prost ended a year's sabbatical, returning to F1 with Williams and claiming his fourth world crown. The Professor's no. 2 that year was Damon Hill, promoted from test driver. In 1994 Hill found himself carrying the fight after Senna's spell with the Didcot team was so tragically cut short at Imola. Hill missed out by a single point to Schumacher, following the controversial clash which took them both out of the Adelaide decider. In 1996 the championship developed into a Williams two-horse race, Hill edging out Jacques Villeneuve. The Canadian went one better than his mercurial father by winning the 1997 title, nursing his FW19 to the line despite Schumacher's best efforts to prevent him from doing so.

In 2000 Williams began using BMW engines, and over the following four seasons Juan Pablo Montoya and Ralf Schumacher added 10 more victories to the team's roll of honour. It currently lies third in the all-time list of Drivers' and Constructors' championships. Only Ferrari and McLaren – both active in F1 for considerably longer – have delivered more titles than Frank Williams' team. In 2007 Williams turned to Toyota power, bringing the curtain down on Cosworth's long, proud history in F1.

OPPOSITE ABOVE: *The Williams FW27 Cosworth being tested in Barcelona, Spain in December 2005 in preparation for the 2006 season.*

BELOW: *Jacques Villeneuve in the Williams FW19 Renault, forging ahead to win the Luxembourg Grand Prix at the Nürburgring, Germany in 1997. Villeneuve's title, which he won by 3 points, was the last world crown for the Williams' team.*

OPPOSITE BELOW: *Frank Williams in 1971, three years after he set up his team, which would become one of the major forces in Formula One.*

WILLIAMS TEAM PROFILE

Country of origin:	United Kingdom
Date of foundation:	1968
Years in Formula One:	Since 1973
Constructors' cup victories:	1980, 1981, 1986, 1987, 1992, 1993, 1994, 1996, 1997

THE CIRCUITS

BUENOS AIRES

Although the Argentine Grand Prix no longer features as part of the Formula One world championships, the last having taken place in 1998, 20 such races were held, somewhat intermittently, from 1953 until that time, and all were staged near Buenos Aires at the Autódromo Oscar Alfredo Gálvez, or the Autodrome, as it is perhaps more commonly known.

Situated on a flat expanse of former marshland, the circuit was constructed in 1952 with the blessing of Argentine president Juan Perón, on the back of the success of native countryman Juan Manuel Fangio, who had taken the world championship title the previous year, and who would go on to do so on four consecutive occasions during the 1950s, taking first place in the Argentine Grand Prix three times in the process.

Fangio was also to win the inaugural race held at the Autodrome in 1952, the Perón Cup, but it would be the Italian Alberto Ascari who would triumph in the first Formula One race to be held there in 1953, which was in fact also the first Formula One competition ever to be staged outside Europe. Having completed 36 laps, Fangio had been forced to retire his Maserati due to transmission failure.

However, Fangio was to win at home in 1954, 1955 and 1957, with first place being claimed by the Italian Luigi Musso in 1956. Following a highly distinguished career, Fangio was to retire at the age of almost 50, and his last appearance at his home circuit took place in 1958, when the win would be taken by Britain's Stirling Moss.

Following the exile of president Perón in 1955, the political climate in Argentina became increasingly unstable, and 1960 was to bear witness to the last

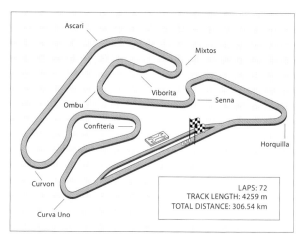

LAPS: 72
TRACK LENGTH: 4259 m
TOTAL DISTANCE: 306.54 km

Argentine Grand Prix for over ten years until its return in 1972. The world champion, Jackie Stewart, would take top place on the podium on that occasion, but the race marked the emergence of a new homegrown talent, Carlos Reutemann, who made his auspicious world championship debut by taking pole position.

With the exception of 1976, the Argentine Grand Prix continued to be a regular fixture until the 1980s, with Reutemann seeing second place success at the Autodrome in 1979 and 1981, but the outbreak of the Falklands War in 1982, and Reutemann's retirement, would ensure that he was never to win at home.

By the time the race returned to Argentina in 1995, the circuit had been purchased by a private consortium, and in the wake of Ayrton Senna's death in 1994, a process of safety-conscious modernisation had been set in motion throughout Formula One. For the Autodrome, this meant the replacement of many of its high-speed, sweeping curves with a tightly twisting infield section, but the circuit remained exciting, and as Jean Alesi and Michael Schumacher proved in 1995 and 1997 respectively, with costly mistakes at the first corner, it could still be a challenging circuit for the drivers.

Damon Hill took the win for Williams in 1995, and again in 1996, during what would become his championship season, and the following year, that team's success was continued at the Autodrome by Canadian Jacques Villeneuve.

At the start of the 1998 season, with Reutemann a state senator, it was hoped that the future of the Argentine Grand Prix was secure, but with the organisers of the race facing increasing financial difficulties, 1998 would herald the last championship race to be held at the Autodrome, which was won by Michael Schumacher.

LEFT: *1979 Argentinian Grand Prix, Buenos Aires, Argentina.*

218

ALBERT PARK

AUSTRALIA

Located just south of central Melbourne, the Albert Park circuit has been home to the Australian Grand Prix, which had been previously based at Adelaide, for just ten years, during which time it has probably become best known as the opening venue for the Formula One world championship season.

The circuit, which is essentially street-based, and which is situated around a small man-made lake in Albert Park, was opened in 1996 after considerable expense, and improvement of the road sections, resulting in a smooth and rather picturesque course, but it has not been without its detractors; notably local residents who have objected to the encroachment of the race on a public park, and the disruption that the event causes to their lives each year. However, the government and the race organisers have claimed that the improved amenities and economic benefits far outweigh such perceived costs, and it remains something of a favourite amongst drivers and fans alike.

In the inaugural race in 1996, the Canadian Jacques Villeneuve caused a sensation by coming incredibly close to securing a win on his debut; a feat only achieved once before, in 1961 by Giancarlo Baghetti, but he was forced to slow by a drop in oil pressure, allowing Williams team-mate Damon Hill to take the first win in what was to become his world championship year. That race was also notable for a spectacular first-lap crash by Martin Brundle.

After qualifying by a huge margin in 1997, Villeneuve once more looked set to dominate, but at the first corner he was sent out of the race by Eddie Irvine. Heinz-Harald Frentzen, who had been looking strong in second, crashed in the final stages, and technical problems for Damon Hill meant that he didn't even start the race, all of which provided the opportunity for David Coulthard to secure victory for McLaren.

McLaren's success continued at Albert Park in 1998, with a win from Mika Hakkinen, who would become world champion that year, but from 1999 to 2002, Ferrari would overshadow the competition, first with a win from Eddie Irvine, and then with three consecutive victories by Michael Schumacher.

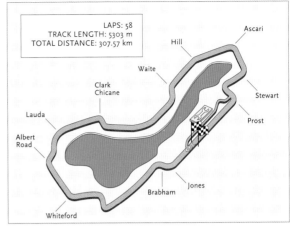

The race was marred by tragedy in 2001, when a marshal was killed by a flying tyre following a crash between Ralf Schumacher and Jacques Villeneuve, but in 2002 there was cause for celebration amongst the crowd, with Australian Mark Webber putting in a performance which saw him finish a surprising fifth in his Minardi, a result, which in Australia at least, eclipsed Michael Schumacher's win.

Coulthard interrupted Schumacher's winning run for a year by securing his second victory at Albert Park in 2003, and Italian Giancarlo Fisichella took first place for Renault in 2005.

Despite being constrained within a city park, the Albert Park circuit is amongst the longest and most distinctive in Formula One, and with 16 corners, several chicanes and only one major straight, there is often little room for overtaking, but the venue still offers the opportunity for both high-speed action and impressive cornering manoeuvres.

BELOW: *2005 Australian GP, Albert Park, Melbourne.*

OSTERREICHRING

AUSTRIA

The first Austrian Grand Prix was held in 1964 at Zeltweg Airfield, but despite its success, the course was deemed to be unsafe, and the race was removed from the Formula One calendar until 1970, and the completion of a purpose-built circuit: the now legendary Osterreichring, which was also located close to Zeltweg. The Austrian Grand Prix was staged at that venue consecutively for 18 years until 1987, when it became regarded as too dangerous. For a decade, the race was once more to disappear from the world championships, but following major modernisation, which included several changes to the layout of the track, the circuit reopened as the A1-Ring, and went on to host the Austrian Grand Prix from 1997 to 2003.

Straddling the municipalities of Zeltweg and Spielberg, set high in the Styrian mountains, the Osterreichring was notable for both its dramatic scenery and changes in elevation, but was perhaps best known for its speed and sweeping curves.

The circuit was a real test of a driver's mettle and abilities, with the first curve, Hella-Licht, being approached up a long steep gradient, so as to render the apex invisible until it was reached, at speed, and tragically, in 1975, it was to claim the life of American driver Mark Donohue, who despite remaining conscious after crashing, was to die of his injuries in hospital. That year, driving conditions had been made all the more difficult by torrential rain, turning the race into something of a lottery, and the win was claimed by Vittorio Brambilla, who had been leading the field when the race was cut short. However, even his win was not without incident, as he was to crash into the barriers after seeing the chequered flag.

Throughout the 1970s, the Osterreichring became known for producing unpredictable results, with several first-time winners, including Jo Siffert in 1971, and in the years between 1975 and 1977, Vittorio Brambilla, John Watson, and Allen Jones. In 1979, Jones would triumph there again, the year before he would become world champion. Another surprise result came in 1982, with one of the closest ever finishes in Grand Prix history, with just 0.08 seconds separating Keke Rosberg and the winner, Elio de Angelis.

Frenchman Alain Prost notched up three wins at the circuit during the 1980s, first in 1983, and then again during his championship seasons of 1985 and 1986, with Niki Lauda taking the win in 1984, in what was his championship year, and the last Austrian Grand Prix to be held at the majestic Osterreichring, in 1987, was won by Briton Nigel Mansell.

The circuit was then abandoned for almost ten years, mainly due to concerns over its safety, before being rebuilt during the mid-1990s, and reopened as the A1-ring; named after A1, the mobile phone company that was its sponsor. In order to be reaccepted by Formula One, the circuit's length had been reduced, the sweeping curves had been cut short or bypassed, and a slower, twisting infield section inserted.

From the outset, the circuit seemed to many to be a shadow of its former self, but the inaugural race was to throw up a number of surprises. Jacques Villeneuve, who required the win in order to stay in the running for the championship, began in pole position, but was threatened first by Mika Hakkinen and then the rookie Italian driver Jarno Trulli. Hakkinen and Trulli however were to go out of the race with engine failure, whilst Michael Schumacher, ten points clear of Villeneuve at the start of the race, was penalised for failing to notice the flags that signalled a dramatic collision between Eddie Irvine and Jean Alesi, and Villeneuve went on to win the race by three seconds from David Coulthard.

Coulthard succeeded in winning at the A1-Ring in 2001, with Michael Schumacher victorious in the subsequent final two competitions held there in 2002 and 2003, although in 2002 the Austrian Grand Prix was shrouded in controversy after the Ferrari team ordered Rubens Barrichello to deliberately hand victory to Schumacher.

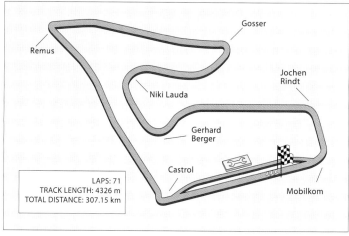

LAPS: 71
TRACK LENGTH: 4326 m
TOTAL DISTANCE: 307.15 km

SAKHIR

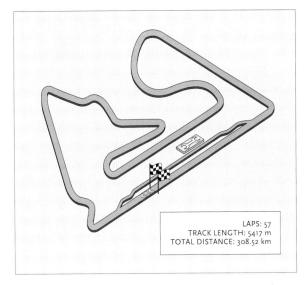

LAPS: 57
TRACK LENGTH: 5417 m
TOTAL DISTANCE: 308.52 km

The Bahrain Grand Prix is amongst the most recent to have been added to the world championships, and is the first Formula One event to take place in the Middle East. Its home is the Bahrain International Circuit at Sakhir, which is also amongst the most recently constructed of venues, and is remarkable not only for its impressive, world-class facilities, but also for the feat of engineering involved in its construction, which took little more than a year to complete. Designed by Formula One's favoured architect, Hermann Tilke, the man behind new tracks in Malaysia, China and Turkey, the venue has a capacity of some 50,000 spectators, incorporates six individual tracks (two of which are configured to Formula One standard), media and medical centres, and the striking eight-storey Sakhir Tower, which incorporates the Bahrain Motor Federation, International Circuit Management offices, a restaurant and several hospitality suites, and provides views of the entire circuit.

The project was a national concern for Bahrain, which fought off competition from other Middle Eastern countries such as Egypt, and was instigated and backed by the Honorary President of the Bahrain Motor Federation, Crown Prince, Shaikh Salman bin Hamad Al Khalifa, and despite fears that the circuit would not be ready in time for 2004, the inaugural Bahrain Grand Prix took place on 4 April that year, and the FIA awarded it the 'Best Organised Grand Prix'.

Although there were concerns over the dusty conditions, which had been blamed for causing spins during practice, 17 cars finished the race in 2004, with only three retirements, and Ferrari took the top two places on the podium, with Michael Schumacher in first, and Rubens Barrichello second, whilst young Briton, Jenson Button took third place in his BAR. Another first followed, with the celebratory champagne replaced with lemonade and rosewater, this being a Muslim country.

The 2005 race saw the highest ever temperatures at a Grand Prix, with an air temperature of 42°c, and track temperatures reaching 56°c, which no doubt accounted for several of the eight retirements.

Fernando Alonso and Michael Schumacher, starting the race in pole and second

positions respectively, battled it out in the opening laps, until Schumacher was forced into the pits after overshooting a corner, which remarkably made this his first technical retirement since 2001.

Alonso went on to take victory, bringing Renault their 100th Grand Prix win, whilst amazingly Ferrari were left without points for the first time in almost two years.

The track itself is comprised of 12 corners, and an impressively long straight, providing plenty of opportunities for overtaking, and although some detractors have commented that the layout does not live up to some of the other new courses, such as Sepang in Malaysia for example, it remains an interesting and impressive venue, which is enhanced by its unique desert location and Arabian flavour.

SPA-FRANCORCHAMPS

BELGIUM

Widely regarded as the greatest Formula One circuit of all time, Spa-Francorchamps, the home of the Belgian Grand Prix, is also amongst the most historic of the world championship venues, having been constructed in 1921 and first used for Grand Prix racing in 1925, and although it has undergone various transformations over the years, its reputation as a classic circuit has remained largely unscathed.

The long, flowing track is set in the tree-lined hills of the Ardennes, and was originally an incredibly fast course, comprised mainly of slender public roads that left little room for error, and despite having been reduced by about half its original length from over 14km (8.7 miles) to almost 7km (4.4 miles), it still remains the longest circuit in F1.

Several corners have also been inserted, making for a slower, but perhaps more demanding course, but the one thing that has always posed a major difficulty for drivers at Spa is the weather, for whilst conditions may be dry on one part of the track, it can be pouring with rain on another, and at one time, the Belgian Grand Prix had seen rain on 20 consecutive occasions. All this, coupled with several changes in elevation, combines to make Spa-Francorchamps probably the most challenging circuit on the Formula One calendar.

As if to illustrate this point, only a handful of drivers have ever taken first place at Spa more than twice, and all of them have been world championship drivers. Argentine legend Juan Manuel Fangio secured three victories, in 1950, 1954 and 1955, and during the 1960s, Briton Jim Clark won on four consecutive occasions, from 1962 to 1965. However, in spite of his triumphs there, Clark hated Spa, and with good reason. In 1958, on his first outing to the circuit, he had witnessed the death of Archie Scott-Brown, and two years later, during his first Grand Prix at the course, he narrowly avoided collision with wreckage after Chris Bristow's fatal crash, and also lost his team-mate, Alan Stacey.

The great Jackie Stewart also famously loathed Spa, and following a terrifying accident on the first lap in 1966, when a sudden downpour had caused eight cars to spin, resulting in Stewart finding himself upside-down in a ditch with petrol leaking onto him, and requiring rescuing by fellow drivers Bob Bondurant and Graham Hill, he began a lifelong campaign to improve safety in Formula One.

After 1970, it was decided that it was too dangerous to continue hosting Formula One events at Spa, and the Belgian Grand Prix was instead alternated between Zolder and Nivelles.

Following a major overhaul of the track, which included the addition of several chicanes, wider run-off areas and an improved surface, the race returned to Spa in 1983, and after being held once more in Zolder in 1984, it has remained at Spa since 1985. Ayrton Senna was victorious on that occasion, the first of his five wins at the circuit, the remaining four being achieved in the consecutive years between 1988 and 1991, and only Michael Schumacher has won more times at Spa-Francorchamps, claiming six wins from 1992 to 2002.

The historic circuit was omitted from the 2006 calendar at the last moment because planned upgrades were not completed on time. The local government, keen to maintain Spa's place on the Formula One circuit, stepped in to complete the renovations and the course was reinstated for 2007.

OPPOSITE: *1991 Belgian Grand Prix, Spa-Francorchamps, Belgium. A view looking down towards Pouhon on the circuit, situated amongst the hills of the Ardennes Forest.*

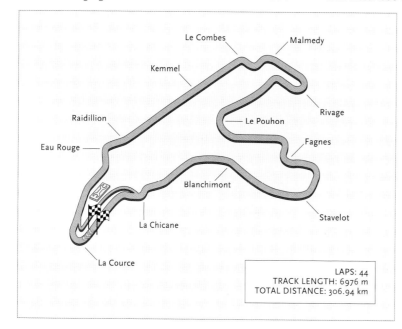

Le Combes
Malmedy
Kemmel
Raidillion
Le Pouhon
Rivage
Eau Rouge
Fagnes
Blanchimont
La Chicane
Stavelot
La Cource

LAPS: 44
TRACK LENGTH: 6976 m
TOTAL DISTANCE: 306.94 km

INTERLAGOS

With a carnival atmosphere that is perhaps unmatched in the world championships, with the possible exceptions of Monza and Imola, the Brazillian Grand Prix holds a special place in the hearts of Formula One fans, and no doubt the drivers too, but it is also regarded as one of the most challenging events on the calendar, and the Interlagos circuit presents drivers with a unique combination of difficulties.

In addition to the extreme heat and humidity, Interlagos is one of the few circuits to be raced in an anti-clockwise direction, meaning that most of the corners are left-handed, and the drivers are subjected to sustained G-force on the left side of the body that can be rapidly draining, and despite improvements, the track is also notoriously bumpy, creating problems for both drivers and their cars alike. In addition, there are several changes in elevation, tricky corners, and only two real opportunities for overtaking; at the end of the pit straight, and at the end of the long back straight, the Reta Oposta.

Facilities, organisation and safety have also come under scrutiny at Interlagos on numerous occasions, notably in 2000 when advertising hoardings fell onto the track three times during qualifying, and in 2004 during practice when a dog got onto the track. Nevertheless, the venue has thrown up some highly memorable and exciting encounters, and Brazil itself has spawned multiple world champions.

Although constructed in the late 1930s, the first world championship Brazilian GP was held at Interlagos in 1973, the year after native Emerson Fittipaldi claimed the first of his two world championships, the second coming in 1974, and he was to secure victory in the first two

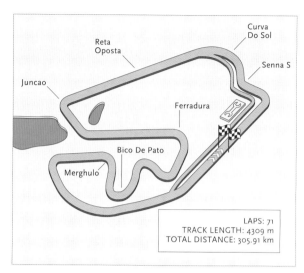

LAPS: 71
TRACK LENGTH: 4309 m
TOTAL DISTANCE: 305.91 km

Formula One Grand Prix races at Interlagos. Brazilian success was continued in 1975 by Carlos Pace, after whom the circuit would become officially named following his tragic death in a plane crash just two years later.

At the end of the 1970s, the Brazilian Grand Prix moved to Jacarepaguá in Rio de Janeiro, home of another Brazilian champion, Nelson Piquet, where it would remain until returning to a modernised Interlagos in 1990.

By that time the circuit had been shortened to a little over half its original length, and the incredibly fast opening section moderated by the addition of 'Senna's S' curve, but as with Spa-Francorchamps in Belgium, general opinion seems to suggest that despite such changes, it remains one of the all-time classic circuits.

Further home victories were assured in 1991 and 1993 by Ayrton Senna, and then from 1994 to 2000, a pattern emerged whereby whoever won at Interlagos went on to become world champion, with wins from Michael Schumacher in 1994, 1995 and 2000, Damon Hill in 1996, Jacques Villeneuve in 1997 and Mika Hakkinen in 1998 and 1999. 2001 was notable for the dramatic arrival of Colombian Juan Pablo Montoya, who would go on to win at Interlagos in 2004 for Williams and 2005 for McLaren, and in 2005 Fernando Alonso made history there, with his third place enough to secure his position as the youngest Formula One world champion of all time. Felipe Massa won at Interlagos in 2006, the first Brazilian to win on home ground since Senna in 1993. He might have won in 2007, too, but allowed team-mate Kimi Raikkonen to take victory, and with it, the championship. The 2008 race eclipsed previous dramatic finales as Lewis Hamilton snatched fifth place in the closing seconds to take the title from race winner Massa.

LEFT: *2003 Brazilian Grand Prix, Interlagos, Brazil.*

MONTREAL

CANADA

Following the first Canadian Grand Prix in 1967, which was held at Ontario's Mosport Park, the event alternated between that venue and Quebec's Mont Tremblant until 1971, when safety concerns about the latter saw it moved back to Mosport Park until 1977. The race was then moved to its current location on the Île de Notre Dame, a man-made island in the St. Lawrence River, Montreal.

Designed by Roger Peart, the circuit presents a combination of long, fast straights and tight, slow corners and chicanes, and although it is not an over-demanding course for drivers, with good opportunities for overtaking at the hairpin and last chicane particularly, it can be hard on the cars, and after Monza it is regarded as the most hardwearing on the brakes.

The race therefore often becomes a battle of attrition, but that is not to say that it is not capable of producing some exciting, action-packed encounters, or that the drivers always have an easy time of it, and many experienced drivers have been caught out at Montreal.

The first Canadian Grand Prix held there, in 1978, was won by Gilles Villeneuve, the home-grown talent and former snowmobile racer who had single-handedly ignited interest in Formula One in Canada during the late 1970s, and it also provided the first Grand Prix win of his career. It was fitting then, that after his tragic death in qualifying for the 1982 Belgian Grand Prix, the venue was renamed the Circuit Gilles Villeneuve in his memory.

Sadly a terrible accident also occurred during the Canadian Grand Prix that year, when Villeneuve's team-mate, Didier Pironi stalled and was crashed into by Riccardo Paletti, who would later die from his injuries in hospital.

The course has changed relatively little over the years, although in an attempt to improve safety, the early 1990s saw the addition of a new corner in front of the pits and also a chicane, but in 1997 the race was brought to an early conclusion after Oliver Panis spun

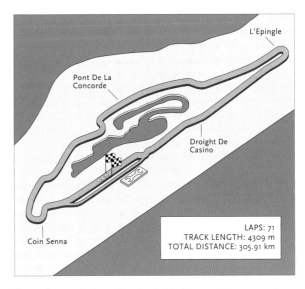

LAPS: 71
TRACK LENGTH: 4309 m
TOTAL DISTANCE: 305.91 km

from the track, breaking both his legs, and in 1999, the wall after the final chicane, which famously bears the slogan 'welcome to Quebec', put former world champions Michael Schumacher, Damon Hill and Jacques Villeneuve, son of Gilles, out of the race. However, between 1994 and 2004, Schumacher dominated the circuit, notching up a total of seven victories there. Robert Kubica's victory for BMW Sauber in 2008 brought to an end Montreal's 31-year run as a Formula One venue. The Circuit Gilles Villeneuve was dropped from the schedule to accommodate the new Abu Dhabi GP for 2009.

BELOW: *1997 Canadian Grand Prix, Montreal, Canada.*

SHANGHAI

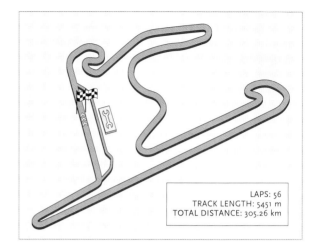

LAPS: 56
TRACK LENGTH: 5451 m
TOTAL DISTANCE: 305.26 km

Like the Bahrain Grand Prix, the inaugural Chinese Grand Prix became a new addition to the Formula One world championships in 2004, and the event took place at a brand new, state-of-the-art circuit, where no expense had been spared in its development and construction; announcing China's arrival as a player on the Formula One world stage.

As at Bahrain, the Shanghai International Circuit was designed by renowned architect Hermann Tilke, who is also responsible for Sepang in Malaysia and Istanbul Park in Turkey, and boasts superlative facilities for both spectators and teams alike, with approximately half of the venue's area occupied by a superb track, and the remainder home to a complex that houses entertainment and commercial areas, with provision for exhibitions and conventions.

A delight for fans, the circuit boasts a capacity of 200,000, with permanent seating for almost 50,000 spectators, some 29,000 of which are located in the grandstand, from where around 80 per cent of the track is visible, and the course itself is comprised of 14 corners, divided equally into right and left hand turns, and two major straights, providing plenty of opportunities for overtaking, but also requiring rapid changes between acceleration and deceleration that are demanding for both the drivers and their cars.

Rubens Barrichello won the Inaugural Chinese Grand Prix in 2004 for Ferrari, and his second successive victory of the season, having led for most of the race, with young Briton Jenson Button keeping the pressure on to finish just over a second behind in his BAR, whilst Michael Schumacher failed to secure any points for only the second time that year.

Then in 2005 the race brought an end to the season and a double triumph for Fernando Alonso and his Renault team, with Alonso having won the FIA Formula One Drivers World Championship, and clinching the Constructors' title for Renault. In an impressive performance, Alonso led for the entire 56 laps.

The most expensive Formula One facility ever constructed, at a cost of US$240 million, Shanghai International Circuit is certainly a spectacular venue, and the layout has also received a generally positive response from drivers, mainly for the variety it offers, but in spite of this, it has its critics, who claim that no amount of money could have transformed what was formerly flat marshland into a classic circuit such as Suzuka in Japan or Belgium's Spa-Francorchamps.

LEFT: *Shanghai, China, 2004: one end of the impressive complex that spans the start/finish straight at the Shanghai circuit.*

MAGNY-COURS

As the birthplace of Grand Prix motor racing, France can lay claim to the oldest international race, with the first French Grand Prix having taken place in 1906. The race was then included in the first world championships in 1925, and has been part of the annual Formula One competition since its inception in 1950, apart from 1955. The French Grand Prix has been held at numerous venues throughout the country since that time, but its home since 1991 has been the Circuit de Nevers Magny-Cours.

Formerly known as the Circuit Jean Behra, the Circuit de Nevers Magny-Cours, or simply Magny-Cours as it is more commonly known, was first constructed in 1959, and was home to a racing school that spawned drivers such as Jacques Laffite and François Cévert. However, the track fell into disrepair, and it was not until it was modernised during the 1980s at the behest of President Mitterrand, that the circuit began to attract the attention of the Fédération Internationale de l'Automobile (FIA), and international racing events began to return.

As part of the process of redesign and redevelopment, inspiration was drawn from many of the existing major circuits, particularly regarding corners, and most are named after other circuits, such as the Adelaide hairpin and Estoril corner.

The track is renowned for its smooth, fast surface, and the layout offers a mixture of long straights, and both fast and technical turns, demanding rapid transitions between acceleration and deceleration, which are testing for even experienced drivers, but despite this, many within the Formula One community, drivers and fans alike, regard the circuit as rather average, with few overtaking opportunities, and a somewhat lacklustre atmosphere and facilities, which is no doubt due in part to the remote location of the venue.

In recent years however, there has been something of an improvement in both facilities and the quality of racing at Magny-Cours, although it is has often been poor weather that has made for the more interesting encounters.

British legend Nigel Mansell took victory in the first two races at Magny-Cours in 1991 and 1992, the latter being his world championship season, followed by French hero Alain Prost in 1993, Michael Schumacher in 1994 and 1995, and

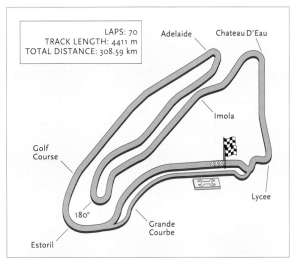

LAPS: 70
TRACK LENGTH: 4411 m
TOTAL DISTANCE: 308.59 km

Adelaide — Chateau D'Eau — Imola — Lycee — Grande Courbe — Estoril — 180° — Golf Course

Damon Hill in 1996, all of which were championship years for the drivers in question. Schumacher has since repeated the pattern in 2001, 2002 and 2004, and has notched up a total of seven wins at the circuit.

In 2002 the length of the pitlane was reduced due to changes at the final corner and chicane, which were designed to increase overtaking, and although it had little effect in that respect, the shorter pit stop times enabled Schumacher to win in 2004 with an unprecedented strategy of four pit stops. Economic reasons were cited for the omission of Magny-Cours from the 2009 calendar. It meant that there would be no French Grand Prix for only the second time in the championship's 60-year history.

BELOW: *Fernando Alonso Renault R25 crosses the line to take victory in the 2005 French Grand Prix, Magny-Cours.*

HOCKENHEIM

GERMANY

Hockenheim, or the Hockenheimring, to give it its full title, was originally constructed in 1936 as a test track for Mercedes-Benz. It was nearly 8km in length, and comprised simply of two long straights connected by two long bends, but following WWII, a new Hockenheim was built, with a tightly twisting stadium section, where the grandstands are situated, and a long, fast, forested 'country' section, composed of long straights separated by chicanes. Further modifications were made for safety reasons in 2001, reducing the track's overall length to around 4.5km (3 miles).

With the exception of the 1985 season, Hockenheim has been home to the German Grand Prix, which was previously held at the Nürburgring, since 1977, whilst that venue has gone on to become the home of the European, or Luxembourg Grand Prix. However, the first Formula One Grand Prix to take place at Hockenheim was in 1970, two years after the legendary Jimmy Clark tragically lost his life there during a Formula Two competition, and a corner at the circuit, the Jim Clark Kurve, has since been dedicated in his honour.

The 1970 race was won by Austrian Jochen Rindt, as part of his world championship campaign, and

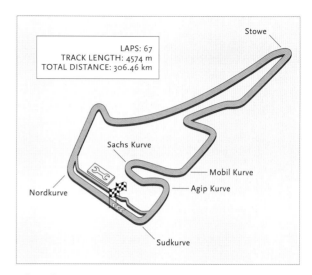

LAPS: 67
TRACK LENGTH: 4574 m
TOTAL DISTANCE: 306.46 km

Stowe, Sachs Kurve, Mobil Kurve, Agip Kurve, Nordkurve, Sudkurve

when the event returned to Hockenheim in 1977, it was also to be won by that season's world champion, and furthermore, by another Austrian, the great Niki Lauda.

Only three drivers have won the German Grand Prix at Hockenheim more than twice, the Brazilians Nelson Piquet and Ayrton Senna, and Germany's golden boy, Michael Schumacher, all of whom have stood at the top of the podium there on three occasions, most recently for Schumacher in 2004.

After the 2001 German Grand Prix, with safety in mind, well-known circuit architect Hermann Tilke was brought in to redesign the course, focusing on the fast forested sections, where drivers had previously powered past the trees at over 320km/h (200mph), and which were particularly dangerous in wet conditions. This section was truncated, and new corners were added, reducing the circuit's overall length, which required an increase in laps from 45 to 67.

The modifications have been criticised by some, who believe that they detract from Hockenheim's character, but it is largely agreed that they were necessary, and the addition of a hairpin, with opportunities for overtaking, has no doubt placated some disgruntled fans.

Regardless of the changes, the German Grand Prix at Hockenheim remains one of the highest attended races on the Formula One calendar. Hockenheim missed out in 2007 as the FIA ushered in a new era in which the circuit would alternate with Nurburgring for Germany's championship round.

LEFT: *1979 German Grand Prix, Hockenheim, Germany. Alan Jones (Williams FW07 Ford) leads into the Nordkurve at the start.*

NÜRBURGRING

The original Nürburgring was an awesome circuit, which wound its way through the Eifel Mountains, around the village and castle of Nürburg, for a distance of over 28km (17 miles), and was the setting for the first German Grand Prix in 1927. However, today's Nürburgring, which was constructed in the 1980s and is now the home of the European Grand Prix, is a meagre shadow of that former classic track.

The ADAC Eifelrennen road races began in the region in the early 1920s, but quickly came to be regarded as too dangerous and unpractical, and so the construction of a purpose built racing track got underway in 1925. The result was the first incarnation of the Nürburgring, an immense circuit with 174 bends, which could be divided into two sections; the Nordschleife, or Northern Loop, which was over 22km (14 miles) in length, and the shorter Südschleife, or Southern loop, of almost 8km (5 miles). There was also a much shorter track around the pit area that could be used for small events and practice.

The first German Grand Prix was held at the circuit in July 1927 and utilised the full Ring, but after 1929, only the Nordschleife would be used for such events, whilst minor races and motorcycle competitions were primarily confined to the Südschleife.

Following WWII, motor racing returned to the Nürburgring during the 1950s and the Nordschleife section became home to the German Grand Prix, which was now included in the F1 world championships, featuring such greats as Alberto Ascari, Juan Manuel Fangio, Jackie Stewart, Stirling Moss and John Surtees.

Throughout the 1960s, as F1 cars became increasingly powerful, and the sport more dangerous, there was mounting pressure to improve the safety of circuits, and in 1970 drivers decided to boycott the German Grand Prix, with the result that it was moved to Hockenheim that year. Improvements were made, and the race returned to the Ring until 1976.

Ironically, Nicky Lauda, who was world champion at that time, and who had been attempting to organise a boycott of the 1976 German Grand Prix due to safety concerns, crashed on the second lap of that race and was lucky to survive. As a result, it would be the last Formula One Grand Prix to be held at the old Nürburgring, and construction of the new circuit began in 1981.

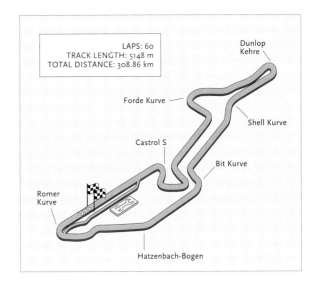

LAPS: 60
TRACK LENGTH: 5148 m
TOTAL DISTANCE: 308.86 km

Dunlop Kehre
Forde Kurve
Shell Kurve
Castrol S
Bit Kurve
Romer Kurve
Hatzenbach-Bogen

The new, shorter Nürburgring was built around the old pits area, and opened in 1984 to hold the European Grand Prix, which returned in 1995 and 1996, and has remained there since 1999, when Briton Johnny Herbert was to seize Stewart's first and only win, before their sale to Ford.

Although incomparable to the old Nürburgring, the GP-Strecke, as today's circuit is also known, is regarded as a fairly challenging and technical course, with few overtaking opportunities, a slippery surface, and a first corner that is notorious for having ended many a driver's race on the first lap.

The European Grand Prix was discontinued at the end of the 2006 season and now only one Grand Prix will take place in Germany each year, at Hockenheim and Nurburgring alternately. It was the latter's turn to host the 2007 event, but as Hockenheim held the naming rights to the German Grand Prix, the race went ahead under the European GP banner.

BELOW: *2001 European Grand Prix, Nürburgring.*

SILVERSTONE

GREAT BRITAIN

The Silverstone circuit is located at a former WWII airfield, RAF Silverstone, which straddles the counties of Northamptonshire and Buckinghamshire, and is known as 'The Home of British Motor Racing'. But Silverstone occupies a unique position, not only in terms of British motor sport, but indeed in the history of Formula One, for it was the venue for the first ever Formula One world championship Grand Prix in 1950.

Before the construction of a dedicated circuit, organisers made use of the perimeter track around the airfield, and for the inaugural race, spectators were held back by rope, and corners were marked by oil drums. Much has changed since those days, and over the years Silverstone has undergone a process of seemingly continuous modification, but one thing remains the same: Silverstone will always be regarded as a cradle of world motor racing.

The British Grand Prix was held at the circuit from 1950 until 1954, before alternating with Aintree, best known as a horse-racing course and home of the Grand National, until 1964 when it instead began to alternate between Silverstone and Brands Hatch. But from 1987, Silverstone has been the permanent home of the British Grand Prix.

In 1950, every Grand Prix was won by Alfa Romeo, as team-mates Juan Manuel Fangio and Giuseppe Farina battled it out, but Ferrari quickly emerged as challengers, winning their first championship Grand Prix at Silverstone in 1951, and the next three consecutive races

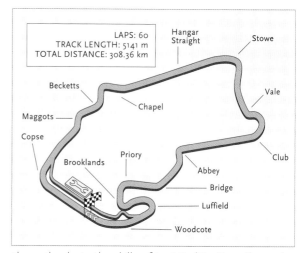

LAPS: 60
TRACK LENGTH: 5141 m
TOTAL DISTANCE: 308.36 km

there, thanks to the skills of José Frolián González and Alberto Ascari, and the fuel economy of the Ferrari 375.

During the 1960s, British legend Jim Clark was to win the British Grand Prix five times for Lotus, with three of those victories achieved at Silverstone, but McLaren were to dominate the circuit in the 1970s, with wins from Peter Revson, Emerson Fittipaldi and James Hunt.

The first major changes to the established layout came in 1987, when the British Grand Prix moved to Silverstone for good, with the addition of Bridge Bend before the final Woodcote kink, and the removal of the chicane for reasons of safety, and the race that year was won by local hero Nigel Mansell, following an epic battle with team-mate Nelson Piquet.

Mansell would triumph again in 1991 and 1992, the latter being his championship year, and in 1991 further modifications had been made, with the notorious Maggotts and Stowe corners being eased. Several further changes were made during the 1990s, including improved access and facilities for spectators, but despite this, in recent years the track has come under criticism, and the 2005 event came close to being removed from the Formula One calendar.

The wrangling between Silverstone's owners the British Racing Drivers Association and the F1 executive was settled amicably on that occasion, but the future of the race was guaranteed only until 2009. Midway during the 2008 season it was announced that the following year would be Silverstone's last as host of the British Grand Prix, for a decade at least. The contract was awarded to Donington Park, which would take its place on the schedule from 2010.

LEFT: *1994 British Grand Prix, Silverstone.*

BRANDS HATCH

GREAT BRITAIN

Although Silverstone claims the title as 'The Home of British Motor Racing', Brands Hatch has played host to a number of world championship events, including both the British and European Grand Prix, and whereas the circuit at Silverstone is flat, and some have said,characterless, Brands Hatch is situated within a natural amphitheatre that offers both excellent views for spectators, and a more varied course for the drivers.

During the 1920s and '30s, the fields at Brands Hatch were used by cyclists, cross-country runners and motorcyclists, and a rudimentary circuit was developed, but the land was used as a depot for military vehicles during WWII, and was heavily bombed.

However, after the war, there was still a desire to see the land used as a racing circuit, and in 1947, Brands Hatch Stadium Ltd. was established, with the result that by 1950, a track suitable for car racing had been created, and Formula Three events began to be held. In 1953 a motor racing club and school was formed, and throughout the 1950s, there were further developments, including the lengthening of the track, the creation of Druid's Bend, and the addition of pits, banks for spectators and a grandstand.

The first non-championship Formula One event was held in 1960, which was won by Jack Brabham, before the circuit was purchased by Grovewood Securities, and placed under the management of John Webb, who successfully negotiated to host the British Grand Prix, alternating with Silverstone. So, in 1964, the first world championship Formula One race was held at Brands Hatch, which was won by Jim Clark. Brabham took victory two years later and Jo Siffert in 1968. However, by that time, the circuit had claimed the lives of three drivers, and after Siffert tragically lost his life in 1971, a major overhaul took place.

The British Grand Prix continued to alternate between Brands Hatch and Silverstone up until 1986, and Brands Hatch was also to play host to the European Grand Prix in 1983 and 1985. On the first of these occasions, the event was hurriedly scheduled to replace the cancelled New York Grand Prix, but was nevertheless highly successful, and in 1985, the race would return, providing Nigel Mansell with his first Grand Prix win.

The following year, Mansell would triumph again, taking first place in the last British Grand Prix to be held at Brands Hatch, before the event moved permanently to Silverstone.

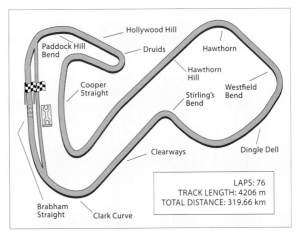

LAPS: 76
TRACK LENGTH: 4206 m
TOTAL DISTANCE: 319.66 km

In 1986, Brands Hatch was sold to John Foulston, and Brands Hatch Leisure was created, but sadly Foulston was to die soon afterwards whilst testing an indycar at Silverstone, and John Webb took over the running of the company until 1990.

During that time, the track saw further modifications, including the addition of a chicane and Dingle Dell Corner, and the tightening of Westfield and Graham Hill Bend, and in the late 1990s trackside facilities were also improved.

In 1999 it was announced that Brands Hatch would hold the 2002 British Grand Prix, but the company was sold once more, and unfortunately the new owners failed to secure planning permission to bring the circuit up to the required standard. Although not staging the British Grand Prix, Brands Hatch continues to host several notable events, such as the World Superbike Championships, the A1 Grand Prix, and touring car series, and also holds testing and public track days.

BELOW: *1986 British Grand Prix, Brands Hatch. Nelson Piquet leads away from Nigel Mansell.*

HUNGARORING

HUNGARY

The first Hungarian Grand Prix was held in 1936, but the political climate of Eastern Europe ensured that the event would not return for 50 years, and therefore, when it did so in 1986, it represented a major coup for the Formula One world championships and Bernie Ecclestone. It was also the first Formula One Grand Prix to be held behind the Iron Curtain. The race has since become a regular fixture on the Formula One calendar however, with its home at the Hungaroring, near Budapest.

The circuit was constructed in just eight months in 1985, in a natural amphitheatre in the rolling Hungarian hills, which offers spectators with probably the best visibility of any track in the championships. However, there is relatively little change in elevation in the track itself, and the tightly twisting layout offers few opportunities for overtaking, which has frequently resulted in rather processional events.

The race is also held at the height of summer, and the circuit is little used for the rest of the year, ensuring that conditions are invariably hot and dusty, turning racing into something of an endurance test for both the drivers and their vehicles, but despite all this, the Hungaroring has produced some memorable races and some important results.

Nelson Piquet won the first race for Williams in 1986, beating fellow Brazilian Ayrton Senna in his Lotus,

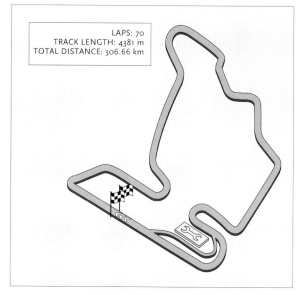

LAPS: 70
TRACK LENGTH: 4381 m
TOTAL DISTANCE: 306.66 km

with the two well ahead of the rest of the pack, and would claim victory again the following year, in his third and final world championship season, but Senna would stand at the top of the podium in 1988 for McLaren, after beating team-mate Alain Prost by just half a second.

In 1989, Nigel Mansell put in an impressive performance to win, having started the race from 12th place on the grid, and then 1990 saw another incredibly close finish, with Thierry Boutsen keeping Senna at bay to win by 0.288 seconds.

Senna won again in 1991 and 1992, but Mansell's second place was enough to secure him the 1992 world championship title.

Damon Hill won in 1993 and 1995 for Williams, the former being his first Grand Prix victory, and then almost pulled off a surprise win for the Arrows team in 1997, after qualifying in third and taking the lead from Michael Schumacher, before suffering gearbox problems that pushed him back to second place, and saw former team-mate Jacques Villeneuve snatch the win for Williams in the final lap.

Other notable races include Schumacher's third win at the Hungaroring in 2001, which provided his fourth world title, whilst also equalling Alain Prost's record of 51 Grand Prix wins, and then in 2003, after some modifications to the circuit, which were designed to improve overtaking, Fernando Alonso became the first Spaniard to win a Grand Prix, and the youngest driver ever to do so, at the age of 22 years and 26 days.

LEFT: *1997 Hungarian Grand Prix. Damon Hill at Turn 12, followed by Eddie Irvine.*

SAN MARINO

Whilst the circuit at Imola has only been home to world championship Grand Prix racing since 1980, it has quickly become one of the best-loved on the Formula One calendar, largely on account of the Italian Ferrari fans, or tifosi, who guarantee a race day atmosphere that is almost without equal. However, the tragic events of 1994, when Roland Ratzenberger and Ayrton Senna lost their lives at Imola on consecutive days, has had lasting implications both for the circuit and the whole of Formula One.

Although most commonly referred to as Imola, after the nearby town of that name, the circuit is actually named the Autodromo Enzo e Dino Ferrari, in honour of Ferrari founder Enzo Ferrari, who passed away in 1988, and his son Dino, who died at a tragically young age during the 1950s. The circuit is fairly close to the Ferrari factory at Maranello, and the surrounding area is also home to the car manufacturers Maserati and Lamborghini, and so the construction of a test track for prototypes, which incorporated some public roads, was begun in 1950, to be first used in 1952 by Ferrari.

Motorcycle racing began at the circuit in 1953, and then car racing the following year, but it was not until 1963 that the venue first played host to Formula One, with a non-championship event that was won for Lotus by Jim Clark. The circuit was notoriously fast and flowing, and in 1973 and 1974, chicanes were added as a safety measure, before Formula One returned in 1979, with another non-championship race, which was won on this occasion by Niki Lauda in a Brabham-Alfa Romeo.

The first championship event was held in 1980, as Imola hosted the Italian Grand Prix, which had been moved from its usual home at Monza, due to a pileup at the start line in 1978, in which Sweden's Ronnie Peterson had been killed. The race was won by Nelson Piquet, also in a Brabham.

Formula One returned to Imola in 1981, with the San Marino Grand Prix, which is named after the nearby principality of San Marino, and the race has remained an annual fixture ever since, providing Italy with two Grand Prix events each year, much

to the delight of Ferrari fans, who regard Imola as their team's home circuit.

Unusually, the race is run in an anti-clockwise direction, forcing drivers to endure increased G-forces on the opposite side of the body to that which they are used to, and changes in gradient present a further difficulty. Until recently however, the greatest challenge faced by drivers at Imola came in the form of demanding corners such as Tamburello, Tosa and Piratella. However, his was to change as the dangers of the track, and the need for modifications became increasingly apparent.

Gerhard Berger was lucky to survive a crash at Tamburello in 1989, as was Rubens Barichello at the final corner, Variante Bassa, during practice in 1994. Then, tragedy struck the following day, as Roland Ratzenberger was killed at the Villeneuve corner during qualifying, and the horror continued on race day with the death of three-times world champion Ayrton Senna, who ploughed into the wall at Tamburello during lap seven.

In 1995, more chicanes were added, existing ones modified, and a wide-ranging review of all Formula One circuits began, and although it has been suggested that Imola and other tracks subsequently lost some of their flow and character, it is widely accepted that this was necessary in order to avert further tragedy at that circuit, and within the sport in general.

In recent years there has been some discussion concerning the future of the San Marino Grand Prix, particularly due to deteriorating facilities as well as the fact that Italy already hosts a Grand Prix at Monza. Although the 2006 Grand Prix went ahead at Imola, it was omitted from the 2007 season and its future still remains in question.

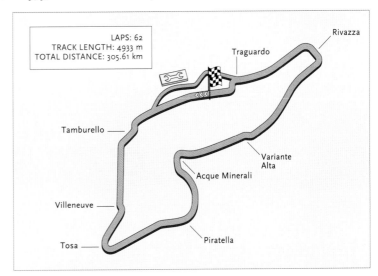

LAPS: 62
TRACK LENGTH: 4933 m
TOTAL DISTANCE: 305.61 km

Rivazza

Traguardo

Tamburello

Variante Alta

Acque Minerali

Villeneuve

Piratella

Tosa

MONZA

Despite numerous changes over its long and auspicious history, Monza, or the Autodromo Nazionale di Monza, remains widely regarded as one of the world's greatest motor racing circuits, and one of Formula One's spiritual homes, for it has played host to every Italian Grand Prix, bar one, since the inception of the world championships in 1950, and the combination of the circuit's history, recent heroes such as Michael Schumacher, and the Italian Ferrari fans, or Tifosi, as they are known, makes for an atmosphere that is practically unknown anywhere else in the Formula One calendar, with the possible exception of the San Marino Grand Prix at Imola.

The original circuit, which was constructed in 1922 in a park outside Milan, was comprised of a road course and a high-speed, banked, oval track, and officially opened to hold the second Italian Grand Prix in September of that year, the first having been held in 1921 at Brescia. The race was dominated by Fiat, who took the top four places.

Sadly, tragedy first struck at Monza in 1928, when Emilio Materassi's steering failed, resulting in one of the worst Grand Prix accidents of all time. Materassi was killed instantly as his car collided with the barrier, and over 20 spectators were killed by flying debris as his vehicle broke apart. As a result, racing was restricted to the high-speed track until 1932, and after Giuseppe Campari, Baconin Borzacchini and Count Czaikowski lost their lives in 1933, the layout was modified by the removal of the longer straights and the addition of two chicanes. Further alterations were made in 1938 and 1939, with the addition of two bends, whilst the track was also resurfaced and new stands were constructed.

During WWII, the circuit was used to house military vehicles, and was badly damaged by bombing, and although Formula One racing began in 1950, a full renovation did not occur until 1955. The first race was won by Italian Giuseppe Farina, and the two subsequent races by fellow countryman Alberto Ascari, with Argentine legend Juan Manuel Fangio taking the next three wins. Then for the rest of the decade, Britons dominated the circuit, with three wins by Stirling Moss, and one from Tony Brooks.

In 1960 and 1961, victory went to American Phil Hill for Ferrari, but the 1961 race was marred by another tragedy, when a collision between Jim Clark and Wolfgang von Trips resulted in the death of the latter and 11 spectators.

Improvements were made, including the addition of run-off areas and new safety walls, and chicanes replaced the banked curves. As speeds continued to increase, two further chicanes were added in 1972, but following the deaths of five motorcyclists in 1973, these were reconstructed, and another added in 1976.

Throughout the 1970s and '80s, improvements continued with safety in mind, and although Monza is still an incredibly fast track, the 1971 race remains the fastest on record, completed at an average of 242.616 km/h (150.755mph) by Briton Peter Gethin. That race also produced the closest finish of all time, with Gethin beating Ronnie Peterson by 0.01 seconds.

More chicanes were added after the deaths of Ayrton Senna and Roland Ratzenberger at Imola in 1994, and in 2000, the first chicane on the main straight was adjusted with the hope of reducing accidents. However, that same year a marshal was killed after a pileup at the second chicane.

Despite all the efforts to reduce the overall speed at Monza, the long straights still ensure that drivers are going flat-out for much of the race, and in qualifying in 2002, Juan Pablo Montoya completed the fastest ever lap in Formula One, with an average speed of 259.827km/h (162.392mph).

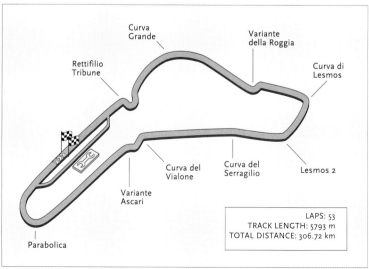

Curva Grande
Variante della Roggia
Rettifilio Tribune
Curva di Lesmos
Curva del Vialone
Curva del Serragilio
Lesmos 2
Variante Ascari
Parabolica

LAPS: 53
TRACK LENGTH: 5793 m
TOTAL DISTANCE: 306.72 km

SUZUKA

JAPAN

The Japanese Grand Prix was first held at the Fuji Speedway in 1976, but following a collision between Gilles Villeneuve and Ronnie Peterson in 1977 that resulted in the death of a marshal, the race then moved to Suzuka, where it has remained since 1987.

The circuit was designed by Dutchman John Hugenholtz in 1962 as a test track for Honda, and is unique in Formula One for its location and layout, consisting of a figure-of-eight contained within a theme park. The course is also amongst the longest in Formula One, and boasts several other challenging features, including a downhill start, a variety of fast, sweeping corners and tight chicanes, and an equal number of left and right-hand corners, a characteristic that was unique until the construction of the new Shanghai International Circuit in China.

Suzuka is generally regarded as one of the all time great circuits by both drivers and spectators alike, with plenty of technical challenges for the drivers, but also several opportunities for overtaking, both of which make for exciting racing.

Further excitement is provided by the fact that Suzuka oftenhost to the last or penultimate race of the calendar, and around half of the encounters at the circuit have been world championship deciders.

The first race at Suzuka was one such affair, with victory being taken by Gerhard Berger for Ferrari, but the championship being handed to Nelson Piquet by Williams team-mate Nigel Mansell, after he crashed during practice.

Then in 1989 and 1990 came the highly controversial championship battles between Ayrton Senna and Alain Prost, which witnessed them colliding during both encounters. In 1989 Prost swerved into Senna as he attempted to pass, taking them both out and ensuring Senna would not take the title, then in 1990 Senna forced Prost off the track at the first bend in a move that he later admitted was deliberate, and which had ensured him the championship.

More recently, and certainly more sportingly, much of the entertainment has been provided by the competition between Michael Schumacher and Mika Hakkinen, with Schumacher's win in 2000, in wet conditions, being notable for providing both his third world title and his first for Ferrari, whilst in 2003, first

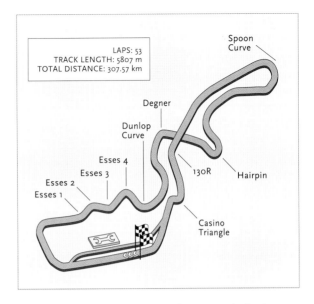

LAPS: 53
TRACK LENGTH: 5807 m
TOTAL DISTANCE: 307.57 km

place went to his team-mate Rubens Barrichello, but Schumacher battled to gain the point that gave him his sixth world championship title, beating the record that Argentine legend Juan Manuel Fangio had held since 1957. In 2007 Suzuka lost its place on the schedule as the Japanese GP returned to the rebuilt Fuji Speedway. Suzuka returned to the calendar in 2009 under a deal by which the Japanese Grand Prix will alternate between the two circuits.

BELOW: *Japanese Grand Prix, 1997, Suzuka, Japan. A view of the Suzuka circuit, on the left showing the Dunlop Curve to the Degna Curve and on the right the notorious Casio Triangle Chicane to 130R.*

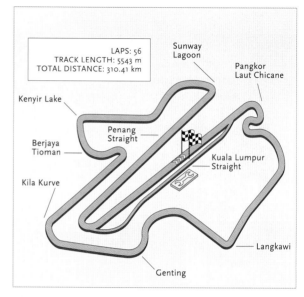

SEPANG

MALAYSIA

The Sepang International Circuit, which is located near Kuala Lumpur in Malaysia, was the first of the new, ultra-modern Formula One venues to be designed by Hermann Tilke, the architect who has since been responsible for similar projects in China, Bahrain and Turkey, and it made a substantial impression when it opened in 1999 to host the inaugural Malaysian Grand Prix.

Not only are the pit, media and corporate facilities superb, but the track has also been constructed with spectators well in mind. The venue has a capacity of 80,000 fans, some 30,000 of which can be accommodated in a back-to-back grandstand area positioned between the two principal straights, whilst all the grandstand areas, including the cheaper seats in the Hillstand, provide good viewing opportunities and are well serviced by amenities.

Just as importantly perhaps, the track itself offers the possibility of exciting racing, with a variety of high-speed sections and slower, more tightly twisting areas, five left and ten right-hand turns, and an average width of 16 metres that is designed to encourage overtaking. So although the layout is challenging, it has been well received by both the drivers and spectators alike.

The weather conditions at Sepang add further variety, with the possibilities of blazing heat, high humidity and tropical downpours, but there have been even more unpredictable factors affecting race results, and perhaps none more so than during the first race at

Sepang in 1999.

Michael Schumacher made a triumphant return, after sustaining a broken leg at Silverstone earlier in the year, by dominating the race for Ferrari, before handing victory to team-mate and championship-hopeful Eddie Irvine, only for both to be disqualified on a technicality, giving Mika Hakkinen the win. However, the decision was later overruled and Irvine was reinstated as the winner.

Then in 2001, the weather came into play, and Schumacher and Rubens Barrichello, both in Ferraris, looked to be out of the race after spinning off in the wet at the same point, but they made miraculous recoveries to end the race in first and second places respectively.

Schumacher secured his third victory at Sepang in 2004, in a race that was also notable for a record lap by Juan Pablo Montoya, who completed the circuit in just 1 minute, 34.233 seconds.

The creation of the circuit was largely driven in the mid-1990s by the then Malaysian Prime Minister, Dr Mahathir Mohamad, with the specific intention of bringing Formula One to a country whose automotive industry was burgeoning; with an oil industry that was putting a great deal of investment into Sauber, and the purchase of Lotus Engineering by Malaysia's Proton, and most would probably agree that in its short history, the Malaysian Grand Prix at the Sepang International Circuit has proved a welcome addition to the Formula One calendar.

RIGHT: *Malaysian Grand Prix, Sepang, 2000.*

MONACO

No venue on the F1 calendar captures the glamour, excitement and romance of the sport as much as Monaco. For many years it was the only street circuit in the annual circus, and although the likes of Valencia and Singapore have now joined the schedule, Monaco retains its unique place in the fabric of the championship, and in the affection of motor racing fans.

Monte Carlo, home of the super-rich yacht and casino set, staged its first Grand Prix on 14 April 1929. William Grover-Williams took victory in a Bugatti 35B in that inaugural race, the first to be staged in an urban setting. In the 1930s the likes of Achille Varzi and Tazio Nuvolari joined battle around the principality's harbourside streets, while the 1948 race saw Ferrari make its bow as a constructor.

Monaco hosted the second round of the inaugural world championship, on 21 May 1950. Juan Manuel Fangio emerged the victor after a pile-up on the opening lap which took out over half the field.

After a four-year gap, the championship returned to the principality in 1955, and has been a fixture on the calendar ever since. That year is chiefly remembered for double world champion Alberto Ascari's unscheduled dip into the harbour while leading the race. He survived

that spectacular crash only to be killed during practice four days later.

Graham Hill's name became forever associated with the circuit after five wins in seven years in the 1960s. It could have been an even better record had he not suffered engine failure while heading the field in 1962.

Despite its reputation as a processional race with overtaking nigh on impossible, Monaco has had more than its share of thrilling encounters. In 1967 Denny Hulme claimed his first GP victory in the street classic en route to the world title. That race saw a fireball accident involving the Ferrari of Lorenzo Bandini, who died from his appalling injuries. Three years later Jack Brabham, with Jochen Rindt hard on his tail, miscalculated the braking at the final bend, handing victory to the Austrian ace. Ronnie Peterson won an accident-littered race for Lotus in 1974, while in 1982 Riccardo Patrese claimed his maiden victory in a spectacular battle which saw the lead change hands four times in the last three laps.

From 1984, Alain Prost and Ayrton Senna divided the Monte Carlo spoils for a decade. When torrential rain caused the 1984 race to be halted at half distance, Senna, from 13th on the grid, was bearing down on leader Prost. This was the race when the Brazilian rookie, driving for Toleman, truly announced himself on the world stage.

Senna's six Monaco victories made him the new king of the principality. Michael Schumacher's first win there came just after Senna's death, in 1994, and he has since racked up four more victories, putting him joint second in the all-time list.

Monaco may be the slowest of the championship venues – Loews is a sedate 30mph hairpin – but, as Ascari proved in 1955, there is no room for error. This demanding circuit, largely unchanged in the past 70 years, is one in which minor mistakes invariably extract a heavy price.

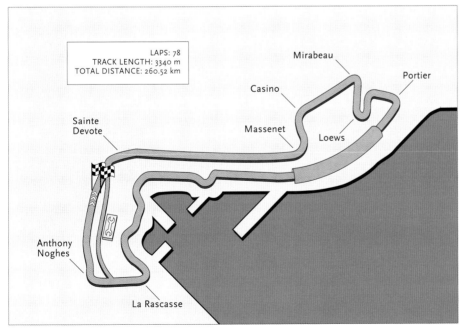

LAPS: 78
TRACK LENGTH: 3340 m
TOTAL DISTANCE: 260.52 km

Mirabeau

Casino

Portier

Sainte Devote

Massenet

Loews

Anthony Noghes

La Rascasse

KYALAMI

SOUTH AFRICA

South Africa had played host to top motor racing events from as early as 1934, with races being held at the Prince George Circuit in East London, and following WWII, at Gunner's Circle in Cape Town and Grand Central in Johannesburg. In 1960, the first modern South African Grand Prix was held at the reconstructed East London circuit, and from 1962 to 1966 the race became part of the Formula One world championships.

However, following the formation of the South African Motor Racing Club, the planning and construction of a new circuit, to be known as Kyalami, began in early 1961, and by the end of the year, the work was complete.

Jim Clark won the first race held there in 1961, the Rand Grand Prix, but it was not until 1967, after upgrading of the track, that Kyalami would host its first Formula One world championship South African Grand Prix. That race was won by Pedro Rodriguez, with John Love narrowly missing out on a home win.

The following year, Jim Clark scored the final Grand Prix win of his illustrious career, as did Jack Brabham in 1970, whilst 1971 was to bring Mario Andretti's first Grand Prix victory.

Then in 1974, tragedy struck with the death of Peter Revson during testing, and again in 1977 when Welshman Tom Pryce was killed after colliding with a marshal who was crossing the track.

The 1979 race was notable for a fine performance from Gilles Villeneuve, who defeated local hero Jody Scheckter in wet conditions, but Scheckter would go on to become South Africa's first and only world champion that same year.

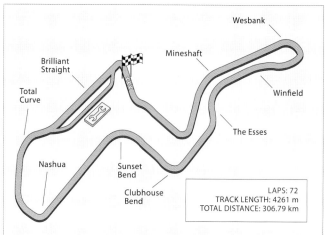

LAPS: 72
TRACK LENGTH: 4261 m
TOTAL DISTANCE: 306.79 km

From 1982 to 1984, Alain Prost provided much of the entertainment: he recovered from a puncture to win in 1982, there was an exciting showdown with Nelson Piquet the following year, when Piquet's third place proved enough to provide his second championship title; and in 1984, having started at the back of the grid in the spare car, Prost finished second. Then in 1985, Nigel Mansell was to claim his second Grand Prix victory, just weeks after his first in the European Grand Prix at Brands Hatch.

However, in 1985, amid growing political unrest and violence in the country, and increasing anti-apartheid feeling elsewhere, France forbade the Renault and Ligier teams from attending the Grand Prix, and the event proved to be a financial disaster. A state of emergency was then declared, and the South African Grand Prix was withdrawn from the Formula One calendar.

The event returned to Kyalami in 1992, as the apartheid system was breaking up, and was again won by Mansell, this time contributing to his championship title, but in the intervening years, the circuit had undergone major modifications, and famously challenging sections such as Crowthorne Corner, Barbecue Bend and Jukseki Sweep, had suffered most.

The circuit was now incorporated in a commercial and residential district, and had been transformed from a fast and majestic track to a narrow, ribbon-like configuration that was to result in processional races, and despite the return of political stability to South Africa, continued financial problems and a less desirable circuit ensured that the 1993 race, which was won by Prost, would be the last Formula One championship Grand Prix to be staged at Kyalami.

LEFT: *South African Grand Prix, 1977, Kyalami, South Africa.*

CATALUNYA

SPAIN

Although Spain, and Catalonia in particular, have a well established tradition of motor racing, and a long history of hosting Formula One events, the Circuit de Catalunya in Barcelona, the current home of the Spanish Grand Prix is a relatively modern venue, which was constructed in the early 1990s and, whilst it boasts good facilities and has produced some memorable encounters it has, however, been somewhat eclipsed by the new generation of circuits.

The first major motor racing competition to be held in Spain was probably the Catalan Cup, a road race that was staged in Sitges, close to Barcelona, in 1908, before the first Spanish Grand Prix took place in 1913, near Madrid. A permanent circuit was then constructed at Sitges, the Sitges-Terramar, but Grand Prix racing was to move to Lasarte after 1923.

Between 1936 and 1945, the Spanish Civil War and WWII were to put an end to such events, but the Grand Prix returned to Barcelona at the Pedralbes Circuit in 1946.

In 1951, Pedralbes was to host its first Grand Prix as part of the world championships, an event that was won by the unstoppable Juan Manuel Fangio, but by 1955, the circuit had been removed from the competition due to concerns over safety.

During the 1960s and '70s, racing alternated between the circuits of Jarama near Madrid, and Montjuich Park in Barcelona, but the latter was dropped after a tragic accident in 1975, which resulted in the deaths of five spectators, and the Spanish Grand Prix moved to Jarama until 1981.

The race then fell from the Formula One calendar, but returned at the new Jerez circuit in southern Spain in 1986, producing the second closest finish of all time, with just 0.050 seconds separating winner Ayrton Senna and Nigel Mansell.

Jerez held its last Spanish Grand Prix in 1990, by which time the construction of the Circuit de Catalunya was well underway, and in 1991, the race returned to make its permanent home in Barcelona.

In a duel reminiscent of the 1986 event, Mansell and Senna battled it out once more, at one point driving side by side down the entire length of the front straight, with Mansell taking the lead, and this time the win.

Mansell triumphed again in 1992, his championship season, and in 1994 another Briton, Damon Hill, would take the win. However, that race was probably most notable for Michael Schumacher's feat of achieving second place with only fourth gear for much of the race.

Schumacher claimed victory in 1995 and 1996, the latter being his first Grand Prix win for Ferrari, and then between 1998 and 2000, Mika Hakkinen scored three consecutive wins. In 2001, Hakkinen again looked set to take first place, but his clutch gave out on the final lap and Schumacher was handed the win, the first of four uninterrupted victories up until 2004.

The circuit itself is quite fast and is varied in terms of its corners, but none are particularly challenging, and there are few opportunities for overtaking, other than at the first, Elf, which has led some to describe the circuit as bland. However, most criticism stems not from the circuit's layout, but from the fact that it is used so often for Formula One testing that the drivers are completely familiar with it so racing at Barcelona has an air of predictability and a lack of atmosphere. However, since the arrival of the young Fernando Alonso onto the Formula One scene the Spanish, at least, have a great deal to be excited about. Spain boasted two races on the schedule in 2008 as the new Valencia Street Circuit was added to the calendar under the European Grand Prix banner formerly held by the Nurburgring.

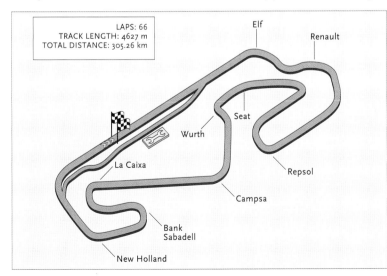

LAPS: 66
TRACK LENGTH: 4627 m
TOTAL DISTANCE: 305.26 km

Elf
Renault
Seat
Wurth
La Caixa
Repsol
Campsa
Bank Sabadell
New Holland

ISTANBUL

TURKEY

The Turkish Grand Prix was added to the Formula One roster in 2005, when the newly built Istanbul Park circuit was unveiled. It is one of the latest of racetrack architect Hermann Tilke's stunning new venues, which also include international circuits at Sepang in Malaysia, Shanghai in China, and in Bahrain.

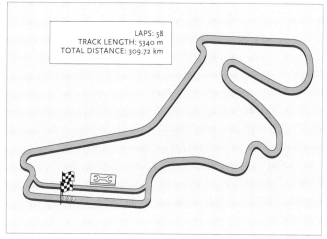

LAPS: 58
TRACK LENGTH: 5340 m
TOTAL DISTANCE: 309.72 km

As with those tracks, Istanbul Park boasts cutting edge design and technology, and superb facilities, with a capacity of over 155,000, a main grandstand that can house around 25,000 spectators, two seven-storey VIP towers, hospitality areas, and excellent facilities for the teams and drivers.

However, the track's layout, and primarily the fact that races are run in a counter-clockwise direction, sets Istanbul Park apart, even from Tilke's other recent creations. It is one of only three circuits that are raced counter-clockwise, the others being Interlagos in Brazil and Imola in Italy, presenting drivers with an increased physical challenge in terms of G-force, and interestingly, there are also several changes in elevation; the track having been constructed on four main levels.

Unlike almost all of Tilke's circuits, Istanbul Park lacks a continuous, long straight, and instead the straight is broken by a major kink, which has raised some concerns about overtaking, but overall the circuit has garnered high praise from drivers and fans alike, particularly for its challenging corners, and for Turn 8 specifically, which has already prompted comparisons with parts of the old Nürburgring, Eau Rouge at Spa-Francorchamps and the 130R at Suzuka.

Some drivers, though, have criticised the circuit for being more of a test of machine than man, and have suggested that it is a rather easy track to learn.

Nevertheless, Turn 8 caught out a number of drivers during the Inaugural Turkish Grand Prix, which took place on 21 August 2005, with several cars spinning from the track at this point, during both qualifying and racing.

Notably, Juan Pablo Montoya lost control there whilst attempting to lap Tiago Monteiro with just two laps remaining, enabling Fernando Alonso to take second place, with Kimi Raikkonen, who had began the race in pole position, securing the win.

It was his McLaren team-mate Montoya who set the pace however, recording a fastest lap of 1 minute 24.77 seconds, and Istanbul Park looks set to become an exciting fixture on the Formula One world championship calendar.

LEFT: *Spanish Grand Prix, 1995, Catalunya, Barcelona, Spain. Johnny Herbert (Benetton B195 Renault) second position on the start/finish straight.*

OPPOSITE: *Turkish Grand Prix, Istanbul, Turkey, 21 August 2005.*

INDIANAPOLIS

UNITED STATES

The Indianapolis Motor Speedway is one of the most famous and historic of all motor racing circuits, and is in fact the second oldest in the world, with racing having begun there in 1909. Today it is also the world's largest sports venue, with a capacity in excess of 400, 000 spectators, and whilst it is best known as the home of the Indianapolis 500 race, the circuit has hosted the United States Grand Prix as part of the Formula One world championships since 2000, and when the championships first began in 1950, it was the inclusion of the results from the 500 that warranted the 'World' title.

The first race in 1909 was something of a disaster, however, as the asphalt and stone surface broke apart, resulting in several crashes and four deaths. This led to the entire track being paved with over three million bricks, and provided the circuit's alternative name; 'The Brickyard'.

Racing returned in 1911, with the first Indianapolis 500, a 500 mile (804.672km) race, which was won by Ray Harroun. The drivers shared a purse of over $27,500, and the dramatic event was witnessed by some 77,000 spectators, setting the future tone of the race as one which involved big money, big crowds, plenty of excitement, and sadly also tragedy, with a number of accidents, and the death of one mechanic. However, the race quickly attracted international interest and European drivers were soon amongst the winners.

During the 1920s and '30s, speeds were beginning to increase, as did the number of fatalities, and parts of the track were surfaced with tarmac to improve safety, and then a major overhaul took place following WWII, as the circuit had fallen into disuse.

Between 1950 and 1960, with the circuit's condition and reputation restored, the Indianapolis 500 became part of the Formula One world championships, despite the fact that Alberto Ascari was the only Formula One driver to compete in the event, and none of the Indy drivers took part in the European Grand Prix races, but after 1960, by which time the track had been almost completely asphalted, several Formula One drivers began to compete in the 500.

At the same time, the US began to host its own Grand Prix as part of the world championships at Watkins Glen, an arrangement that continued up until 1980, but it was not until the year 2000 that Formula One returned to Indianapolis: the first time the US had hosted a Formula One Grand Prix since 1991, and the first non-oval event to take place at the speedway, being run on an infield road circuit.

Unusually for an American event, but not for Formula One, the race was run in a clockwise direction, and it proved to be a great success, with probably the largest crowd ever to attend a Formula One race there to witness Michael Schumacher's win: the second of four consecutive victories to end the season and provide him with his third world title.

In 2001 and 2002 Schumacher had to settle for second place, on the first occasion to Mika Hakkinen in the McLaren, and then to Ferrari team-mate Rubens Barrichello the following year. It seemed that Schumacher, who was set to win, attempted to create a draw with Barrichello, instead losing out to him by 0.011 seconds, the second closest finish of all time.

In 2003 Schumacher was back on top, with a win that brought him a step closer to securing his historic sixth world title at the end of the season, whilst fellow German Heinz-Harald Frentzen scored his first podium position since the 2000 US Grand Prix by finishing in third place.

The race was moved forward to June from its traditional September slot in 2004, and Ferrari scored first and second place with Schumacher and Baricello, and it remained at that point in the calendar for 2005, when the feat was repeated.

However, the 2005 Grand Prix was something of a fiasco, with only six cars starting the race, after seven teams withdrew amidst controversy over tyre safety. Every car also

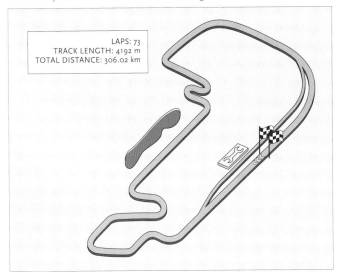

LAPS: 73
TRACK LENGTH: 4192 m
TOTAL DISTANCE: 306.02 km

completed the race, an occurrence that has only been witnessed once before in the history of Formula One. The event was also historic for providing the first podium place for a Portuguese driver, with rookie Tiago Monteiro taking third for Jordan.

There were concerns that the controversial events prior to the race had placed the future of the US Grand Prix at Indianapolis in serious jeopardy, but the race remained scheduled for 2006. However, it was once again mired in calamity as seven drivers were forced to retire during the first lap. Montoya went into

the back of his team-mate Raikkonen, who in turn clipped Button. Heidfeld, Klein, Montagny and the new American driver, Scott Speed, were all caught up in the crash and forced to retire without completing a lap. Indianapolis was omitted from the 2008 race calendar, and following the exclusion of the Canadian Grand Prix a year later it meant that the F1 circus would no longer visit the North American continent.

BELOW: *United States Grand Prix, Indianapolis. 2004.*

WATKINS GLEN

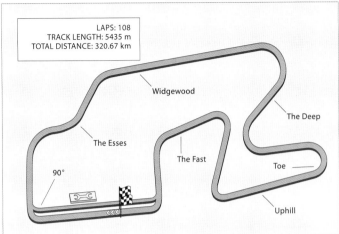

LAPS: 108
TRACK LENGTH: 5435 m
TOTAL DISTANCE: 320.67 km

Widgewood

The Deep

The Esses

The Fast

Toe

90°

Uphill

The US has a well-established tradition of motor racing. Today it is the Indianapolis Motor Speedway circuit that is the home of the United States Grand Prix, but Watkins Glen International in upstate New York also has an illustrious history, and played host to the United States Grand Prix on 20 consecutive occasions between 1961 and 1980.

Grand Prix racing first began in the area in 1948 with the Watkins Glen Grand Prix which was run on local roads, but after a spectator was killed in 1952 the race was moved out of the town to a wooded hill nearby. The course still used existing roads, but with the foundation of the Watkins Glen Grand Prix Corporation, better organisation and safety were assured.

However, three years later, construction of a permanent racetrack got underway, and in 1957, it began to hold the international Formula Libre race, which attracted the likes of Stirling Moss, Jack Brabham, Phil Hill and other great drivers of the day.

In 1959 and 1960 respectively Formula One events took place at Sebring in Florida and Riverside, California, but these were largely unsuccessful, and organisers began to look elsewhere for suitable venues.

So it was that in 1961, Watkins Glen was to stage its first Formula One Grand Prix as part of the World Championships. Following the death of Count Wolfgang von Trips during the previous race at Monza, Ferrari had withdrawn its team from the rest of the season, including the world champion, American Phil Hill, and the race was won by Briton Innes Ireland, who scored the only Grand Prix win of his career, and the first for the Lotus team. Somewhat unexpectedly, however, Ireland was sacked just weeks later and Jim Clark took over as their top driver, winning the US Grand Prix at Watkins Glen the following year. It was an achievement Clark would repeat in 1966 and 1967, but in the intervening years Graham Hill scored three consecutive wins for BRM. Unfortunately in 1969, Hill was to break both his legs at 'The Glen', in an accident that no doubt foreshortened his career. Jochen Rindt took the win for Lotus that year, and although tragically he would lose his life at Monza the following season, the Lotus team secured another victory at Watkins Glen in 1970 with Emerson Fittipaldi, in what was only his third Grand Prix.

The circuit underwent an extensive modification prior to the 1971 outing, being widened and resurfaced, and extended by just over a mile with the addition of the four-cornered 'Boot' or 'Anvil' section. The win that year was a Grand Prix first for François Cévert, but tragedy befell him two years later when he was killed at the circuit.

As the cars became faster during the 1970s, a series of accidents continued to tarnish the formerly bright reputation of Watkins Glen, and against a backdrop of increasing financial problems the venue was dropped from the Formula One calendar after the 1980 US Grand Prix, which was won by Alan Jones for Williams, their first and only victory at the circuit.

Watkins Glen was closed in 1981; a shame for a historic venue that had on three occasions won the Driver's Association award for the best staged Grand Prix, but it was reopened in 1984, and although Formula One has never returned, the circuit continues to host all manner and class of road racing events, including vintage racing and the NASCAR championships.

LEFT: *Watkins Glen, New York, USA.*

STATISTICS

THE DRIVERS' WORLD CHAMPIONSHIP

1950

	Driver	Country	Car	Points
1	Giuseppe Farina	Italy	Alfa Romeo	30
2	Juan Manuel Fangio	Argentina	Alfa Romeo	27
3	Luigi Fagioli	Italy	Alfa Romeo	24
4	Louis Rosier	France	Lago-Talbot	13
5	Alberto Ascari	Italy	Ferrari	11
6	Johnnie Parsons	USA	Kurtis Offenhauser	8
7	Bill Holland	USA	Deidt Offenhauser	6
8	Prince Bira	Thailand	Maserati	5
9	Mauri Rose	USA	Deidt Offenhauser	4
	Reg Parnell	Great Britain	Alfa Romeo, Maserati	4
	Louis Chiron	Monaco	Maserati	4
	Peter Whitehead	Great Britain	Ferrari	4

1951

1	Juan Manuel Fangio	Argentina	Alfa Romeo	31
2	Alberto Ascari	Italy	Ferrari	25
3	Jose-Froilan Gonzalez	Argentina	Lago-Talbot and Ferrari	24
4	Giuseppe Farina	Italy	Alfa Romeo Alfetta	19
5	Luigi Villoresi	Italy	Ferrari	15
6	Piero Taruffi	Italy	Ferrari	10
7	Lee Wallard	USA	Kurtis Offenhauser	9
8	Felice Bonetto	Italy	Alfa Romeo	7
9	Mike Nazaruk	USA	Kurtis Offenhauser	6
10	Reg Parnell	Great Britain	Ferrari, BRM	5

1952

1	Alberto Ascari	Italy	Ferrari	36
2	Giuseppe Farina	Italy	Ferrari	25
3	Piero Taruffi	Italy	Ferrari	22
4	Rudi Fischer	Switzerland	Ferrari	10
	Mike Hawthorn	Great Britain	Cooper Bristol	10
6	Robert Manzon	France	Gordini	9
7	Troy Ruttman	USA	Kuzma Offenhauser	8
	Luigi Villoresi	Italy	Ferrari	8
9	Jose-Froilan Gonzalez	Argentina	Maserati	6
10	Jim Rathmann	USA	Kurtis Offenhauser	6

1953

1	Alberto Ascari	Italy	Ferrari	34.5
2	Juan Manuel Fangio	Argentina	Maserati	28
3	Giuseppe Farina	Italy	Ferrari	26
4	Mike Hawthorn	Great Britain	Ferrari	19
5	Luigi Villoresi	Italy	Ferrari	17
6	Jose-Froilan Gonzalez	Argentina	Maserati	13.5
7	Bill Vukovich	USA	Kurtis Offenhauser	9
8	Emanuel de Graffenried	Switzerland	Maserati	7
9	Felice Bonetto	Italy	Maserati	6.5
10	Art Cross	USA	Kurtis Offenhauser	6

1954

1	Juan Manuel Fangio	Argentina	Maserati Mercedes-Benz	42
2	Jose-Froilan Gonzalez	Argentina	Ferrari	25.14
3	Mike Hawthorn	Great Britain	Ferrari	24.64
4	Maurice Trintignant	France	Ferrari	17
5	Karl Kling	Germany	Mercedez-Benz	12
6	Bill Vukovich	USA	Kurtis Offenhauser	8
	Hans Herrmann	Germany	Mercedes-Benz	8
8	Jimmy Bryan	USA	Kuzma Offenhauser	6
	Giuseppe Farina	Italy	Ferrari	6
	Luigi Musso	Italy	Maserati	6
	Roberto Mieres	Argentina	Maserati	6

1955

1	Juan Manuel Fangio	Argentina	Mercedes-Benz	40
2	Stirling Moss	Great Britain	Mercedes-Benz	23
3	Eugenio Castellotti	Italy	Lancia, Ferrari	12
4	Maurice Trintignant	France	Ferrari	11.33
5	Giuseppe Farina	Italy	Ferrari, Lancia-Ferrari	10.33
6	Piero Taruffi	Italy	Ferrari, Mercedes-Benz	9
7	Bob Sweikert	USA	Kurtis Offenhauser	8
8	Roberto Mieres	Argentina	Maserati	7
9	Tony Bettenhausen	USA	Kurtis Offenhauser	6
	Jean Behra	France	Maserati	6
	Luigi Musso	Italy	Maserati	6

1956

1	Juan Manuel Fangio	Argentina	Lancia-Ferrari	30
2	Stirling Moss	Great Britain	Maserati	27
3	Peter Collins	Great Britain	Ferrari, Lancia-Ferrari	25
4	Jean Behra	France	Maserati	22
5	Pat Flaherty	USA	Watson Offenhauser	8
6	Eugenio Castellotti	Italy	Lancia-Ferrari	7.5
7	Sam Hanks	USA	Kurtis Offenhauser	6
	Paul Frere	Belgium	Lancia-Ferrari	6
	Francesco Godia	Spain	Maserati	6
10	Jack Fairman	Great Britain	Connaught -Alta	5

1957

1	Juan Manuel Fangio	Argentina	Maserati	40
2	Stirling Moss	Great Britain	Maserati, Vanwall	25
3	Luigi Musso	Italy	Lancia Ferrari	16
4	Mike Hawthorn	Great Britain	Lancia Ferrari	13
5	Tony Brooks	Great Britain	Vanwall	11
6	Harry Schell	USA	Maserati	10
	Masten Gregory	USA	Maserati	10
8	Peter Collins	Great Britain	Lancia Ferrari	8
	Sam Hanks	USA	Epperly Offenhauser	8
10	Jean Behra	France	Maserati	6

1958

1	Mike Hawthorn	Great Britain	Ferrari Dino	42
2	Stirling Moss	Great Britain	Cooper, Vanwall	41
3	Tony Brooks	Great Britain	Vanwall	24
4	Roy Salvadori	Great Britain	Cooper	15
5	Peter Collins	Great Britain	Ferrari Dino	14
	Harry Schell	USA	Maserati	14
7	Luigi Musso	Italy	Ferrari Dino	12
	Maurice Trintignant	France	Cooper, Maserati	12
9	Stuart Lewis-Evans	Great Britain	Vanwall	11
10	Phil Hill	USA	Maserati, Ferrari, Ferrari	9
	Taffi von Trips	Germany	Ferrari, Porsche	9
	Jean Behra	France	Maserati	9

1959

1	Jack Brabham	Australia	Cooper	31
2	Tony Brooks	Great Britain	Ferrari Dino, Vanwall	27
3	Stirling Moss	Great Britain	Cooper, BRM	25.5
4	Phil Hill	USA	Ferrari Dino	20
5	Maurice Trintignant	France	Cooper	19
6	Bruce McLaren	New Zealand	Cooper	16.5
7	Dan Gurney	USA	Ferrari Dino	13
8	Jo Bonnier	Sweden	BRM	10
	Masten Gregory	USA	Cooper	10
10	Rodger Ward	USA	Watson Offenhauser	8

1960

1	Jack Brabham	Australia	Cooper	43
2	Bruce McLaren	New Zealand	Cooper	34
3	Stirling Moss	Great Britain	Cooper, Lotus	19
4	Innes Ireland	Great Britain	Lotus	18
5	Phil Hill	USA	Ferrari Dino	16
6	Olivier Gendebien	Belgium	Cooper	10
	Taffi von Trips	Germany	Ferrari Dino, Cooper	10
8	Jimmy Clark	Great Britain	Lotus	8
	Richie Ginther	USA	Ferrari Dino, Scarab	8
	Jim Rathmann	USA	Watson Offenhauser	8

Juan Manuel Fangio

1961

1	Phil Hill	USA	Ferrari Dino	34
2	Taffi von Trips	Germany	Ferrari Dino	33
3	Stirling Moss	Great Britain	Lotus, Ferguson	21
	Dan Gurney	USA	Porsche	21
5	Richie Ginther	USA	Ferrari Dino	16
6	Innes Ireland	Great Britain	Lotus	12
7	Jimmy Clark	Great Britain	Lotus	11
	Bruce McLaren	New Zealand	Cooper	11
9	Giancarlo Baghetti	Italy	Ferrari Dino	9
10	Tony Brooks	Great Britain	BRM	6

1962

1	Graham Hill	Great Britain	BRM	42
2	Jimmy Clark	Great Britain	Lotus	30
3	Bruce McLaren	New Zealand	Cooper	27
4	John Surtees	Great Britain	Lotus	19
5	Dan Gurney	USA	Porsche	15
6	Phil Hill	USA	Ferrari, Porsche	14
7	Tony Maggs	South Africa	Cooper	13
8	Richie Ginther	USA	BRM	10
9	Jack Brabham	Australia	Lotus, Brabham	9
10	Trevor Taylor	Great Britain	Lotus	6

1963

1	Jimmy Clark	Great Britain	Lotus	54
2	Graham Hill	Great Britain	BRM	33
3	Richie Ginther	USA	BRM	29
4	John Surtees	Great Britain	Ferrari	22
5	Dan Gurney	USA	Brabham	19
6	Bruce McLaren	New Zealand	Cooper	17
7	Jack Brabham	Australia	Brabham	14
8	Tony Maggs	South Africa	Cooper	9
9	Innes Ireland	Great Britain	Lotus, RP	6
	Lorenzo Bandini	Italy	BRM, Ferrari -Aero	6
	Jo Bonnier	Sweden	Cooper	6

1964

1	John Surtees	Great Britain	Ferrari	40
2	Graham Hill	Great Britain	BRM	39
3	Jimmy Clark	Great Britain	Lotus	32
4	Lorenzo Bandini	Italy	Ferrari - Aero	23
	Richie Ginther	USA	BRM	23
6	Dan Gurney	USA	Brabham	19
7	Bruce McLaren	New Zealand	Cooper	13
8	Jack Brabham	Australia	Brabham	11
	Peter Arundell	Great Britain	Lotus	11
10	Jo Siffert	Switzerland	Lotus, Brabham	7

1965

1	Jimmy Clark	Great Britain	Lotus	54
2	Graham Hill	Great Britain	BRM	40
3	Jackie Stewart	Great Britain	BRM	33
4	Dan Gurney	USA	Brabham	25
5	John Surtees	Great Britain	Ferrari	17
6	Lorenzo Bandini	Italy	Ferrari	13
7	Richie Ginther	USA	Honda	11
8	Bruce McLaren	New Zealand	Cooper	10
	Mike Spence	Great Britain	Lotus	10
10	Jack Brabham	Australia	Brabham	9

1966

1	Jack Brabham	Australia	Brabham	42
2	John Surtees	Great Britain	Ferrari, Cooper	28
3	Jochen Rindt	Austria	Cooper	22
4	Denny Hulme	New Zealand	Brabham	18
5	Graham Hill	Great Britain	BRM	17
6	Jimmy Clark	Great Britain	Lotus	16
7	Jackie Stewart	Great Britain	BRM	14
8	Lorenzo Bandini	Italy	Ferrari Dino	12
	Mike Parkes	Great Britain	Ferrari	12
10	Lodovico Scarfiotti	Italy	Ferrari	9

1967

1	Denny Hulme	New Zealand	Brabham	51
2	Jack Brabham	Australia	Brabham	46
3	Jimmy Clark	Great Britain	Lotus	41
4	John Surtees	Great Britain	Honda	20
	Chris Amon	New Zealand	Ferrari	20
6	Pedro Rodriguez	Mexico	Cooper	15
	Graham Hill	Great Britain	Lotus	15
8	Dan Gurney	USA	Eagle - Climax	13
9	Jackie Stewart	Great Britain	BRM	10
10	Mike Spence	Great Britain	BRM	9

1968

1	Graham Hill	Great Britain	Lotus	48
2	Jackie Stewart	Great Britain	Matra	36
3	Denny Hulme	New Zealand	McLaren	33
4	Jacky Ickx	Belgium	Ferrari	27
5	Bruce McLaren	New Zealand	McLaren	22
6	Pedro Rodriguez	Mexico	BRM	18
7	Jo Siffert	Switzerland	Cooper, Lotus	12
	John Surtees	Great Britain	Honda	12
9	John-Pierre Beltoise	France	Matra	11
10	Chris Amon	New Zealand	Ferrari	10

1969

1	Jackie Stewart	Great Britain	Matra	63
2	Jacky Ickx	Belgium	Brabham	37
3	Bruce McLaren	New Zealand	McLaren	26
4	Jochen Rindt	Austria	Lotus	22
5	Jean- Pierre Beltoise	France	Matra	21
6	Denny Hulme	New Zealand	McLaren	20
7	Graham Hill	Great Britain	Lotus	19
8	Piers Courage	Great Britain	Brabham	16
9	Jo Siffert	Switzerland	Lotus	15
10	Jack Brabham	Australia	Brabham	14

1970

1	Jochen Rindt	Austria	Lotus	45
2	Jacky Ickx	Belgium	Ferrari	40
3	Clay Regazzoni	Switzerland	Ferrari	33
4	Denny Hulme	New Zealand	McLaren	27
5	Jack Brabham	Australia	Brabham	25
	Jackie Stewart	Great Britain	March, Tyrell	25
7	Chris Amon	New Zealand	March	23
	Pedro Rodriguez	Mexico	BRM	23
9	Jean-Pierre Beltoise	France	Matra Simca	16
10	Emerson Fittipaldi	Brazil	Lotus	12

Jackie Stewart

1971

1	Jackie Stewart	Great Britain	Tyrrell	62
2	Ronnie Peterson	Sweden	March	33
3	Francois Cevert	France	Tyrell	26
4	Jacky Ickx	Belgium	Ferrari	19
5	Jo Siffert	Switzerland	BRM	19
6	Emerson Fittipaldi	Brazil	Lotus – Turbine	16
7	Clay Regazzoni	Switzerland	Ferrari	13
8	Mario Andretti	USA	Ferrari	12
9	Chris Amon	New Zealand	Matra-Simca	9
	Peter Gethin	Great Britain	McLaren	9
	Denny Hulme	New Zealand	McLaren	9
	Pedro Rodriguez	Mexico	BRM	9
	Reine Wisell	Sweden	Lotus – Turbine	9

1972

1	Emerson Fittipaldi	Brazil	Lotus	61
2	Jackie Stewart	Great Britain	Tyrrell	45
3	Denny Hulme	New Zealand	McLaren	39
4	Jacky Ickx	Belgium	Ferrari	27
5	Peter Revson	USA	McLaren	23
6	Francois Cevert	France	Tyrell	15
	Clay Regazzoni	Switzerland	Ferrari	15
8	Mike Hailwood	Great Britain	Surtees	13
9	Chris Amon	New Zealand	Matra-Simca	12
	Ronnie Peterson	Sweden	March	12

1973

1	Jackie Stewart	Great Britain	Tyrrell	71
2	Emerson Fittipaldi	Brazil	JPS/Lotus	55
3	Ronnie Peterson	Sweden	JPS/Lotus	52
4	Francois Cevert	France	Tyrell	47
5	Peter Revson	USA	McLaren	38
6	Denny Hulme	New Zealand	McLaren	26
7	Carlos Reutemann	Argentina	Brabham	16
8	James Hunt	Great Britain	March	14
9	Jacky Ickx	Belgium	Ferrari, McLaren Iso Williams/Marlboro	12
10	Jean-Pierre Beltoise	France	BRM	9

1974

1	Emerson Fittipaldi	Brazil	McLaren	55
2	Clay Regazzoni	Switzerland	Ferrari	52
3	Jody Scheckter	South Africa	Tyrell	45
4	Niki Lauda	Austria	Ferrari	38
5	Ronnie Peterson	Sweden	Lotus	35
6	Carlos Reutemann	Argentina	Brabham	32
7	Denny Hulme	New Zealand	McLaren	20
8	James Hunt	Great Britain	March – Hesketh	15
9	Patrick Depailler	France	Tyrell	14
10	Mike Hailwood	Great Britain	McLaren	12
	Jacky Ickx	Belgium	Lotus	12

1975

1	Niki Lauda	Austria	Ferrari	64.5
2	Emerson Fittipaldi	Brazil	MacLaren	45
3	Carlos Reutemann	Argentina	Brabham	37
4	James Hunt	Great Britain	Hesketh	33
5	Clay Regazzoni	Switzerland	Ferrari	25
6	Carlos Pace	Brazil	Brabham	24
7	Jochen Mass	Germany	McLaren	20
	Jody Scheckter	South Africa	Tyrell	20
9	Patrick Depailler	France	Tyrell	12
10	Tom Pryce	Great Britain	Shadow	8

1976

1	James Hunt	Great Britain	McLaren	69
2	Niki Lauda	Austria	Ferrari	68
3	Jody Scheckter	South Africa	Tyrell	49
4	Patrick Depailler	France	Tyrell	39
5	Clay Regazzoni	Switzerland	Ferrari	31
6	Mario Andretti	USA	Lotus, Parnell	22
7	Jacques Laffite	France	Ligier	20
	John Watson	Great Britain	Penske	20
9	Jochen Mass	Germany	McLaren	19
10	Gunnar Nilsson	Sweden	Lotus	11

1977

1	Niki Lauda	Austria	Ferrari	72
2	Jody Scheckter	South Africa	Wolf	55
3	Mario Andretti	USA	Lotus	47
4	Carlos Reutemann	Argentina	Ferrari	42
5	James Hunt	Great Britain	McLaren	40
6	Jochen Mass	Germany	McLaren	25
7	Alan Jones	Australia	Shadow	22
8	Gunnar Nilsson	Sweden	Lotus	20
	Patrick Depailler	France	Tyrell	20
10	Jacques Laffite	France	Ligier	18

1978

1	Mario Andretti	USA	Lotus	64
2	Ronnie Peterson	Sweden	Lotus	51
3	Carlos Reutemann	Argentina	Ferrari	48
4	Niki Lauda	Austria	Brabham	44
5	Patrick Depailler	France	Tyrell	34
6	John Watson	Great Britain	Brabham	25
7	Jody Scheckter	South Africa	Wolf	24
8	Jacques Laffite	France	Ligier	19
9	Gilles Villeneuve	Canada	Ferrari	17
	Emerson Fittipaldi	Brazil	Copersucar	17

1979

1	Jody Scheckter	South Africa	Ferrari	51
2	Gilles Villeneuve	Canada	Ferrari	47
3	Alan Jones	Australia	Williams	40
4	Jacques Laffite	France	Ligier	36
5	Clay Regazzoni	Switzerland	Williams	29
6	Carlos Reutemann	Argentina	Lotus	20
	Patrick Depailler	France	Ligier	20
8	Rene Arnoux	France	Renault	17
9	John Watson	Great Britain	McLaren	15
10	Mario Andretti	USA	Lotus	14

1980

1	Alan Jones	Australia	Williams	67
2	Nelson Piquet	Brazil	Brabham	54
3	Carlos Reutemann	Argentina	Williams	42
4	Jacques Laffite	France	Ligier	34
5	Didier Pironi	France	Ligier	32
6	Rene Arnoux	France	Renault	29
7	Elio De Angelis	Italy	Lotus	13
8	Jean- Pierre Jabouille	France	Renault	9
9	Riccardo Patrese	Italy	Arrows	7
10	Derek Daly	Ireland	Tyrell	6

1981

1	Nelson Piquet	Brazil	Brabham	50
2	Carlos Reutemann	Argentina	Williams	49
3	Alan Jones	Australia	Williams	46
4	Jacques Laffite	France	Talbot-Ligier	44
5	Alain Prost	France	Renault	43
6	John Watson	Great Britain	McLaren	27
7	Gilles Villeneuve	Canada	Ferrari, Arrows	25
8	Elio De Angelis	Italy	Lotus	14
9	Rene Arnoux	France	Renault	11
	Hector Rebaque	Mexico	Brabham BT49C	11

1982

1	Keke Rosberg	Finland	Williams	44
2	Didier Pironi	France	Ferrari	39
	John Watson	Great Britain	McLaren	39
4	Alain Prost	France	Renault	34
5	Niki Lauda	Austria	McLaren	30
6	Rene Arnoux	France	Renault	28
7	Patrick Tambay	France	Arrows, Ferrari	25
	Michele Alboreto	Italy	Tyrell	25
9	Elio De Angelis	Italy	Lotus	23
10	Riccardo Patrese	Italy	Brabham	21

1983

1	Nelson Piquet	Brazil	Brabham	59
2	Alain Prost	France	Renault	57
3	Rene Arnoux	France	Ferrari	49
4	Patrick Tambay	France	Ferrari	40
5	Keke Rosberg	Finland	Williams	27
6	John Watson	Great Britain	McLaren	22
	Eddie Cheever	USA	Renault	22
8	Andrea De Cesaris	Italy	Alfa Romeo	15
9	Riccardo Patrese	Italy	Brabham	13
10	Niki Lauda	Austria	McLaren Austria	12

1984

1	Niki Lauda	Austria	McLaren	72
2	Alain Prost	France	McLaren	71.5
3	Elio De Angelis	Italy	Lotus	34
4	Michele Alboreto	Italy	Ferrari	30.5
5	Nelson Piquet	Brazil	Brabham	29
6	Rene Arnoux	France	Ferrari	27
7	Derek Warwick	Great Britain	Renault	23
8	Keke Rosberg	Finland	Williams	20.5
9	Nigel Mansell	Great Britain	Lotus	13
	Ayrton Senna	Brazil	Toleman	13

1985

1	Alain Prost	France	McLaren	73
2	Michele Alboreto	Italy	Ferrari	53
3	Keke Rosberg	Finland	Williams	40
4	Ayrton Senna	Brazil	Lotus	38
5	Elio De Angelis	Italy	Lotus, Brabham	33
6	Nigel Mansell	Great Britain	Williams	31
7	Stefan Johansson	Sweden	Tyrell, Ferrari	26
8	Nelson Piquet	Brazil	Brabham	21
9	Jacques Laffite	France	Ligier	16
10	Niki Lauda	Austria	McLaren	14

1986

1	Alain Prost	France	McLaren	72
2	Nigel Mansell	Great Britain	Williams	70
3	Nelson Piquet	Brazil	Williams	69
4	Ayrton Senna	Brazil	JPS/Lotus	55
5	Stefan Johansson	Sweden	Ferrari	23
6	Keke Rosberg	Finland	McLaren	22
7	Gerhard Berger	Austria	Benetton	17
8	Jacques Laffite	France	Ligier	14
	Rene Arnoux	France	Ligier	14
	Michele Alboreto	Italy	Ferrari	14

1987

1	Nelson Piquet	Brazil	Williams	73
2	Nigel Mansell	Great Britain	Williams	61
3	Ayrton Senna	Brazil	JPS/Lotus	57
4	Alain Prost	France	McLaren	46
5	Gerhard Berger	Austria	Ferrari	36
6	Stefan Johansson	Sweden	McLaren	30
7	Michele Alboreto	Italy	Ferrari	17
8	Thierry Boutsen	Belgium	Benetton	16
9	Teo Fabi	Italy	Benetton	12
10	Eddie Cheever	USA	Arrows	8

1988

1	Ayrton Senna	Brazil	McLaren	90
2	Alain Prost	France	McLaren	87
3	Gerhard Berger	Austria	Ferrari	41
4	Thierry Boutsen	Belgium	Benetton	27
5	Michele Alboreto	Italy	Ferrari	24
6	Nelson Piquet	Brazil	Lotus	22
7	Ivan Capelli	Italy	March	17
	Derek Warwick	Great Britain	Arrows	17
9	Alessandro Nannini	Italy	Benetton	12
	Nigel Mansell	Great Britain	Williams	12

Graham Hill

1989

1	Alain Prost	France	McLaren	76
2	Ayrton Senna	Brazil	McLaren	60
3	Riccardo Patrese	Italy	Williams	40
4	Nigel Mansell	Great Britain	Ferrari	38
5	Thierry Boutsen	Belgium	Williams	37
6	Alessandro Nannini	Italy	Benetton	32
7	Gerhard Berger	Austria	Ferrari	21
8	Nelson Piquet	Brabham	Lotus	12
9	Jean Alesi	France	Tyrell	8
10	Derek Warwick	Great Britain	Arrows	7

1990

1	Ayrton Senna	Brazil	McLaren	78
2	Alain Prost	France	Ferrari	71
3	Nelson Piquet	Brazil	Benetton	43
	Gerhard Berger	Austria	McLaren	43
5	Nigel Mansell	Great Britain	Ferrari	37
6	Thierry Boutsen	Belgium	Williams	34
7	Riccardo Patrese	Italy	Williams	23
8	Alessandro Nannini	Italy	Benetton	21
9	Jean Alesi	France	Tyrell	13
10	Roberto Moreno	Brazil	EuroBrun, Benetton	6
	Ivan Capelli	Italy	March	6
	Aguri Suzuki	Japan	Lola/Larrousse	6

1991

1	Ayrton Senna	Brazil	McLaren	96
2	Nigel Mansell	Great Britain	Williams	72
3	Riccardo Patrese	Italy	Williams	53
4	Gerhard Berger	Austria	McLaren	43
5	Alain Prost	France	Ferrari	34
6	Nelson Piquet	Brazil	Benetton	26.5
7	Jean Alesi	France	Ferrari	21
8	Stefano Modena	Italy	Tyrell	10
9	Andrea De Cesaris	Italy	Jordan	9
10	Roberto Moreno	Brazil	Benetton, Jordan	8

1992

1	Nigel Mansell	Great Britain	Williams	108
2	Riccardo Patrese	Italy	Williams	56
3	Michael Schumacher	Germany	Benetton	53
4	Ayrton Senna	Brazil	McLaren	50
5	Gerhard Berger	Austria	McLaren	49
6	Martin Brundle	Great Britain	Benetton	38
7	Jean Alesi	France	Ferrari	18
8	Mika Häkkinen	Finland	Lotus	11
9	Andrea De Cesaris	Italy	Tyrell	8
10	Michele Alboreto	Italy	Footwork	6

1993

1	Alain Prost	France	Williams	99
2	Ayrton Senna	Brazil	McLaren	73
3	Damon Hill	Great Britain	Williams	69
4	Michael Schumacher	Germany	Benetton	52
5	Riccardo Patrese	Italy	Benetton	20
6	Jean Alesi	France	Ferrari	16
7	Martin Brundle	Great Britain	Ligier	13
8	Gerhard Berger	Austria	Ferrari	12
9	Johnny Herbert	Great Britain	Lotus	11
10	Mark Blundell	Great Britain	Ligier	10

1994

1	Michael Schumacher	Germany	Benetton	92
2	Damon Hill	Great Britain	Williams	91
3	Gerhard Berger	Austria	Ferrari	41
4	Mika Häkkinen	Finland	McLaren	26
5	Jean Alesi	France	Ferrari	24
6	Rubens Barrichello	Brazil	Jordan	19
7	Martin Brundle	Great Britain	McLaren	16
8	David Coulthard	Great Britain	Williams	14
9	Nigel Mansell	Great Britain	Williams	13
10	Jos Verstappen	Netherlands	Benetton	10

1995

1	Michael Schumacher	Germany	Benetton	102
2	Damon Hill	Great Britain	Williams	69
3	David Coulthard	Great Britain	Williams	49
4	Johnny Herbert	Great Britain	Benetton	45
5	Jean Alesi	France	Ferrari	42
6	Gerhard Berger	Austria	Ferrari	31
7	Mika Häkkinen	Finland	McLaren	17
8	Olivier Panis	France	Ligier	16
9	Heinz-Harald Frentzen	Germany	Sauber	15
10	Mark Blundell	Great Britain	McLaren	13

1996

1	Damon Hill	Great Britain	Williams	97
2	Jacques Villeneuve	Canada	Williams	78
3	Michael Schumacher	Germany	Ferrari	59
4	Jean Alesi	France	Benetton	47
5	Mika Häkkinen	Finland	McLaren	31
6	Gerhard Berger	Austria	Benetton	21
7	David Coulthard	Great Britain	McLaren	18
8	Rubens Barrichello	Brazil	Jordan	14
9	Olivier Panis	France	Ligier	13
10	Eddie Irvine	Ireland	Ferrari	1

1997

1	Jacques Villeneuve	Canada	Williams	81
2	Heinz-Harald Frentzen	Germany	Williams	42
3	David Coulthard	Great Britain	McLaren	36
	Jean Alesi	France	Benetton	36
5	Gerhard Berger	Austria	Benetton	27
	Mika Häkkinen	Finland	McLaren	27
7	Eddie Irvine	Ireland	Ferrari	24
8	Giancarlo Fisichella	Italy	Jordan	20
9	Olivier Panis	France	Prost	16
10	Johnny Herbert	Great Britain	Sauber	15

1998

1	Mika Häkkinen	Finland	McLaren-Mercedes	100
2	Michael Schumacher	Germany	Ferrari	86
3	David Coulthard	Great Britain	McLaren-Mercedes	56
4	Eddie Irvine	Ireland	Ferrari	47
5	Jacques Villeneuve	Canada	Williams-Mecachrome	21
6	Damon Hill	Great Britain	Jordan-Mugen Honda	20
7	Heinz-Harald Frentzen	Austria	Williams-Mecachrome	17
	Alexander Wurz	Austria	Benetton-Playlife	17
9	Giancarlo Fisichella	Italy	Benetton-Playlife	16
10	Ralf Schumacher	Germany	Jordan-Mugen Honda	14

1999

1	Mika Häkkinen	Finland	McLaren-Mercedes	76
2	Eddie Irvine	Great Britain	Ferrari	74
3	Heinz-Harald Frentzen	Germany	Jordan-Mugen Honda	55
4	David Coulthard	Great Britain	McLaren-Mercedes	48
5	Michael Schumacher	Germany	Ferrari	44
6	Ralf Schumacher	Germany	Williams-Supertec	35
7	Rubens Barrichello	Brazil	Stewart-Ford	21
8	Johnny Herbert	Great Britain	Stewart-Ford	15
9	Giancarlo Fisichella	Italy	Benetton-Playlife	13
10	Mika Salo	Finland	Ferrari	10

2000

1	Michael Schumacher	Germany	Ferrari	108
2	Mika Häkkinen	Finland	McLaren-Mercedes	89
3	David Coulthard	Great Britain	McLaren-Mercedes	73
4	Rubens Barrichello	Brazil	Ferrari	62
5	Ralf Schumacher	Germany	Williams - BMW	24
6	Giancarlo Fisichella	Italy	Benetton-Playlife	18
7	Jacques Villeneuve	Canada	BAR-Honda	17
8	Jenson Button	Great Britain	Williams-BMW	12
9	Heinz-Harald Frentzen	Germany	Jordan-Mugen Honda	11
10	Jarno Trulli	Italy	Jordan-Mugen Honda	6

2001

1	Michael Schumacher	Germany	Ferrari	123
2	David Coulthard	Great Britain	McLaren - Mercedes	65
3	Rubens Barrichello	Brazil	Ferrari	56
4	Ralf Schumacher	Germany	Williams - BMW	49
5	Mika Häkkinen	Finland	McLaren - Mercedes	37
6	Juan-Pablo Montoya	Colombia	Williams - BMW	31
7	Jacques Villeneuve	Canada	BAR - Honda	12
	Nick Heidfeld	Germany	Sauber - Petronas	12
	Jarno Trulli	Italy	Jordan - Honda	12
10	Kimi Räikkönen	Finland	Sauber - Petronas	9

2002

1	Michael Schumacher	Germany	Ferrari	144
2	Rubens Barrichello	Brazil	Ferrari	77
3	Juan-Pablo Montoya	Colombia	Williams - BMW	50
4	Ralf Schumacher	Germany	Williams - BMW	42
5	David Coulthard	Great Britain	McLaren - Mercedes	41
6	Kimi Räikkönen	Finland	McLaren - Mercedes	24
7	Jenson Button	Great Britain	Renault	14
8	Jarno Trulli	Italy	Renault	9
9	Eddie Irvine	Great Britain	Jaguar - Ford	8
10	Nick Heidfeld	Germany	Sauber Petronas	7
	Giancarlo Fisichella	Italy	Jordan – Honda	7

2003

1	Michael Schumacher	Germany	Ferrari	93
2	Kimi Räikkönen	Finland	McLaren - Mercedes	91
3	Juan-Pablo Montoya	Colombia	Williams - BMW	82
4	Rubens Barrichello	Brazil	Ferrari	65
5	Ralf Schumacher	Germany	Williams - BMW	58
6	Fernando Alonso	Spain	Renault	55
7	David Coulthard	Great Britain	McLaren - Mercedes	51
8	Jarno Trulli	Italy	Renault	33
9	Jenson Button	Great Britain	BAR - Honda	17
	Mark Webber	Australia	Jaguar - Ford	17

2004

1	Michael Schumacher	Germany	Ferrari	148
2	Rubens Barrichello	Brazil	Ferrari	114
3	Jenson Button	Great Britain	BAR - Honda	85
4	Fernando Alonso	Spain	Renault	59
5	Juan-Pablo Montoya	Colombia	Williams - BMW	58
6	Jarno Trulli	Italy	Renault, Toyota	46
7	Kimi Räikkönen	Finland	McLaren - Mercedes	45
8	Takuma Sato	Japan	BAR - Honda	34
9	Ralf Schumacher	Germany	Williams - BMW	24
	David Coulthard	Great Britain	McLaren - Mercedes	24

2005

1	Fernando Alonso	Spain	Renault	133
2	Kimi Räikkönen	Finland	McLaren - Mercedes	112
3	Michael Schumacher	Germany	Ferrari	62
4	Juan-Pablo Montoya	Colombia	McLaren - Mercedes	60
5	Giancarlo Fisichella	Italy	Renault	58
6	Ralf Schumacher	Germany	Toyota	45
7	Jarno Trulli	Italy	Toyota	43
8	Rubens Barrichello	Brazil	Ferrari	38
9	Jenson Button	Great Britain	BAR - Honda	37
10	Mark Webber	Australia	Williams - BMW	36

2006

1	Fernando Alonso	Spain	Renault	134
2	Michael Schumacher	Germany	Ferrari	121
3	Felipe Massa	Brazil	Ferrari	80
4	Giancarlo Fisichella	Italy	Renault	72
5	Kimi Räikkönen	Finland	McLaren - Mercedes	65
6	Jenson Button	Great Britain	Honda	56
7	Rubens Barrichello	Brazil	Honda	30
8	Juan-Pablo Montoya	Colombia	McLaren - Mercedes	26
9	Nick Heidfeld	Germany	BMW Sauber	23
10	Ralf Schumacher	Germany	Toyota	20

2007

1	Kimi Räikkönen	Finland	Ferrari	110
2	Lewis Hamilton	Great Britain	McLaren - Mercedes	109
	Fernando Alonso	Spain	McLaren - Mercedes	109
4	Felipe Massa	Brazil	Ferrari	94
5	Nick Heidfeld	Germany	BMW Sauber	61
6	Robert Kubica	Poland	BMW Sauber	39
7	Heikki Kovalainen	Finland	Renault	30
8	Giancarlo Fisichella	Italy	Renault	21
9	Nico Rosberg	Germany	Williams	20
10	David Coulthard	Great Britain	Red Bull	14

2008

1	Lewis Hamilton	Great Britain	McLaren - Mercedes	98
2	Felipe Massa	Brazil	Ferrari	97
3	Kimi Raikkonen	Finland	Ferrari	75
	Robert Kubica	Poland	BMW Sauber	75
5	Fernando Alonso	Spain	Renault	61
6	Nick Heidfeld	Germany	BMW Sauber	60
7	Heikki Kovalainen	Finland	McLaren - Mercedes	53
8	Sebastian Vettel	Germany	Toro Rosso	35
9	Jarno Trulli	Italy	Toyota	31
10	Timo Glock	Germany	Toyota	25

Nigel Mansell

Constructors' Title 1958–2008

1958

Car	Country	Points
1 Vanwall	Great Britain	48
2 Ferrari Dino	Italy	40
3 Cooper	Great Britain	31

1959

1 Cooper	Great Britain	40
2 Ferrari Dino	Italy	32
3 BRM	Great Britain	19

1960

1 Cooper	Great Britain	40
2 Lotus	Great Britain	32
3 Ferrari Dino	Italy	24

1961

1 Ferrari Dino	Italy	40
2 Lotus	Great Britain	32
3 Porsche	Germany	22

1962

1 BRM	Great Britain	42
2 Lotus	Great Britain	36
3 Cooper	Great Britain	29

1963

1 Lotus	Great Britain	54
2 BRM	Great Britain	36
3 Brabham	Australia	28

1964

1 Ferrari	Italy	45
2 BRM	Great Britain	42
3 Lotus	Great Britain	37

1965

1 Lotus	Great Britain	54
2 BRM	Great Britain	45
3 Brabham	Australia	27

1966

1 Brabham	Australia	42
2 Ferrari	Italy	31
3 Cooper	Great Britain	30

1967

1 Brabham	Australia	67
2 Lotus	Great Britain	50
3 Cooper	Great Britain	28

1968

1 Lotus	Great Britain	62
2 McLaren	New Zealand	51
3 Matra Ford	France	45

1969

1 Matra	France	66
2 Brabham	Australia	51
3 Lotus	Great Britain	47

1970

1 Lotus	Great Britain	59
2 Ferrari	Italy	55
3 March	Great Britain	48

1971

1 Tyrrell	Great Britain	73
2 BRM	Great Britain	36
3 March	Great Britain	34

1972

1 Lotus	Great Britain	61
2 Tyrrell	Great Britain	51
3 McLaren	New Zealand	47

1973

1 JPS/Lotus	Great Britain	92
2 Tyrrell	Great Britain	82
3 McLaren	New Zealand	58

1974

1	McLaren	New Zealand	73
2	Ferrari	Italy	65
3	Tyrrell	Great Britain	52

1975

1	Ferrari	Italy	72.5
2	Brabham	Australia	54
3	McLaren	New Zealand	53

1976

1	Ferrari	Italy	83
2	McLaren	New Zealand	74
3	Tyrrell	Great Britain	71

1977

1	Ferrari	Italy	95
2	Lotus	Great Britain	62
3	McLaren	New Zealand	60

1978

1	Lotus	Great Britain	86
2	Ferrari	Italy	58
3	Brabham	Australia	53

1979

1	Ferrari	Italy	113
2	Williams	Great Britain	75
3	Ligier	France	61

1980

1	Williams	Great Britain	120
2	Ligier	France	66
3	Brabham	Australia	55

1981

1	Williams	Great Britain	95
2	Brabham	Australia	61
3	Renault	France	54

1982

1	Ferrari	Italy	74
2	McLaren	New Zealand	69
3	Renault	France	62

1983

1	Ferrari	Italy	89
2	Renault	France	79
3	Brabham	Australia	72

1984

1	McLaren	New Zealand	143.5
2	Ferrari	Italy	57.5
3	Lotus	Great Britain	47

1985

1	McLaren	New Zealand	90
2	Ferrari	Italy	82
3	Williams	Great Britain	71

1986

1	Williams	Great Britain	141
2	McLaren	New Zealand	96
3	JPS/Lotus	Great Britain	58

1987

1	Williams	Great Britain	137
2	McLaren	New Zealand	76
3	Lotus	Lotus	64

1988

1	McLaren	New Zealand	199
2	Ferrari	Italy	65
3	Benetton	Italy	46

1989

1	McLaren	New Zealand	141
2	Williams	Great Britain	77
3	Ferrari	Italy	59

1990

1	McLaren	New Zealand	121
2	Ferrari	Italy	110
3	Benetton	Italy	71

1991

1	McLaren-Honda	New Zealand	139
2	Williams-Renault	Great Britain	125
3	Ferrari	Italy	55.5

1992

1	Williams-Renault	Great Britain	164
2	McLaren-Honda	New Zealand	99
3	Benetton-Ford	Italy	31

1993

1	Williams-Renault	Great Britain	168
2	McLaren-Ford	New Zealand	84
3	Benetton-Ford	Italy	72

Ayrton Senna

1999

1	Ferrari	Italy	128
2	McLaren-Mercedes	Great Britain	124
3	Jordan-Mugen Honda	Great Britain	61

2000

1	Ferrari	Italy	170
2	McLaren-Mercedes	Great Britain	152
3	Williams	Great Britain	36

2001

1	Ferrari	Italy	179
2	McLaren-Mercedes	Great Britain	102
3	Williams	Great Britain	80

2002

1	Ferrari	Italy	221
2	Williams	Great Britain	92
3	McLaren-Mercedes	Great Britain	65

2003

1	Ferrari	Italy	158
2	Williams	Great Britain	144
3	McLaren-Mercedes	Great Britain	142

2004

1	Ferrari	Italy	262
2	BAR	Great Britain	119
3	Renault	France	105

1994

1	Williams-Renault	Great Britain	118
2	Benetton-Ford	Italy	103
3	Ferrari	Italy	71

2005

1	Renault	France	191
2	McLaren-Mercedes	Great Britain	182
3	Ferrari	Italy	100

1995

1	Benetton-Renault	Italy	137
2	Williams-Renault	Great Britain	112
3	Ferrari	Italy	73

2006

1	Renault	France	206
2	Ferrari	Italy	201
3	McLaren-Mercedes	Great Britain	110

1996

1	Williams-Renault	Great Britain	175
2	Ferrari	Italy	70
3	Benetton-Renault	Italy	68

2007

1	Ferrari	Italy	204
2	BMW Sauber	Germany	101
3	Renault	France	51

1997

1	Williams-Renault	Great Britain	123
2	Ferrari	Italy	102
3	Benetton-Renault	Italy	67

2008

1	Ferrari	Italy	172
2	McLaren-Mercedes	Great Britain	151
3	BMW Sauber	Germany	135

1998

1	McLaren-Mercedes	Great Britain	156
2	Ferrari	Italy	133
3	Williams-Mecachrome	Great Britain	38

Acknowledgements

Thanks to everyone at LAT especially Peter Higham, Tim Wright,
Kevin Wood, Zoë Mayho and the digital team John Tingle,
Tim Clarke and Alastair Staley.

Thanks also to Oliver Higgs, Kate Truman, Cliff Salter and John Dunne.

BEAR GRYLLS

SURVIVAL CAMP

BEAR GRYLLS
SURVIVAL
CAMP

THE ULTIMATE ALL-TERRAIN TRAINING MANUAL

CONTENTS

Oceans & Rivers 86

Navigation 110

SURVIVAL CAMP

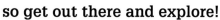

INTRODUCTION

I've been so lucky in my life to have been on some truly incredible adventures around the world. From the icy cold of the Arctic to the scorching heat of the desert, from the thin air and icy faces of Everest to the humid, snake, and mosquito-filled jungles of the Tropics. I've battled the elements and survived the extremes and through it all I have learnt two things.

Firstly, that the human spirit is incredible and we are all capable of much more than we might think. Our persistence, courage, positivity, and determination are always our greatest weapon.

Secondly, I have learnt that knowledge is power. If you want to survive efficiently then you have to learn as much as you can about the techniques and the skills needed for the wild.

So whether you find yourself lost in a jungle, dehydrated in a desert, facing off with a bear in a forest, or lost at sea, this book is here to help empower you with the skills and knowledge to survive. I have packed this book full of tips and tricks I have learnt to help you survive almost any extreme situation.

Our planet is an incredible place and life is all about adventure, so get out there and explore!

ESSENTIAL KIT

Packing for an explorer's adventure isn't like packing for the seaside, although in both cases you should take a hat. Unless you are the Duke of Abruzzi, grandson of the king of Italy, who travelled to Alaska in 1897 with dozens of servants and porters, and four cast-iron beds, you will probably have to plan carefully so that you can carry all the gear you need in a single rucksack.

Boot up

Unless you are planning to fly or sail for the entire expedition, you will need to rely on your own two feet at some point, making the right boots possibly your most important piece of equipment. Your boots need to be a perfect mixture: light and flexible but sturdy and waterproof, warm but not too sweaty. The exact boot will depend on where you are going.

Basic hiking boot

- For walking and exploring in forest, mountains, rough ground, or grassland anywhere in the temperate zone (places that are not too hot and not too cold), this boot is best.

- It is tough but flexible and relatively lightweight, and will let your foot breathe.

Jungle boot

- Made from canvas and rubber to cope with wet ground and constant rainfall, waterproof below and quick-drying above.

- This boot is tough enough to resist thorns, insect bites, and snake fangs, but light enough not to overheat your feet.

Mountain boot

- Much more rigid than hiking boots, these boots are stiff and heavy but keep your feet warm and dry in snow and ice, and won't slip or buckle when jammed against a rock.

Desert boot

- Usually made of suede, which keeps out hot sand, but is very light and lets your feet breathe to stay relatively cool.

Bear necessities

Pack a few warm but light and quick-drying clothes, a sleeping bag suited to your destination (don't take a heavy, super-warm one to a jungle), waterproof jacket, fire-lighting equipment, first-aid kit, maps and compass, and a survival kit.
This should be in a tough container like a tin, and should be kept on you at all times. It should have: a button compass, fishing line and hook, lighter, wire saw, and a needle and thread.

Camping stove

Backpack

Jacket

First-aid kit

Clothes

Sleeping bag

Lighter

Fishing line and hook

Map

Survival tin

Wire saw

DOUBLE UP

The best gear is stuff that is multi-use. For instance, when Norwegian polar explorer Fridtjof Nansen made the first crossing of Greenland in 1888, he used the groundsheet from his tent as both a sail for his sledge and the bottom of a makeshift boat.

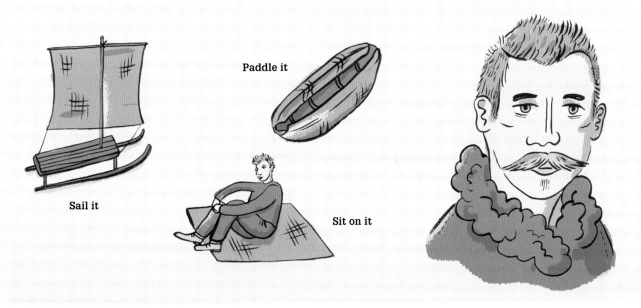

Paddle it

Sail it

Sit on it

JUNGLE & SAVANNAH

You're hacking your way through the jungle with your machete, when suddenly the ground gives way and you slide down a muddy ravine, tumbling through a giant spider's web and into a pool of deadly quicksand. The crumbling ruins of an ancient temple loom on either side. Should you call for help or grab a vine and haul yourself out?

EXPLORER'S QUEST

The tropical regions of the world, with their thick jungles and wide, grassy savannahs, are rich in exotic animals and unsolved mysteries – in other words, they are perfect for explorers. Will you track down the lost treasure city of the Inca or find the source of the Nile?

Finding the source

Victorian explorers were obsessed with tracing the course of the world's longest river – the Nile – and discovering its source deep in the African interior. Can you retrace their footsteps and make the journey across the "Mountains of the Moon"?

Monster snakes

The biggest snakes in the world are found in the rainforests of South America, Africa and Indonesia; some are over 10 m (33 ft) long. But there have been rumours of much bigger snakes, so enormous that they could swallow whole canoes. Can these legendary snakes really exist, and can you stun the world of science by finding one?

BEAR SAYS

We have everything to learn from traditional tribes: tracking, hunting, and survival skills. But we must be careful not to pass on to them our own diseases and bad habits!

Welcome to the world

Thousands of tribes make the thick jungles of the world their home. Some tribes are so remote that they have never been contacted by the modern world. Can you be the first to introduce yourself to an uncontacted tribe?

BIG GAME

For the big-game hunters who visited Africa looking for animal heads to stick on their walls, nothing compared to the "Big Five" – the animals considered most dangerous and difficult to hunt: lion, elephant, leopard, rhino, and buffalo. Can you track down these fierce beasts and shoot them in a less bloodthirsty way – with your camera?

| Lion | Elephant | Leopard | Rhino | Buffalo |

Lost city of the Inca

In the early 1500s, the Spanish conquistador Francisco Pizarro conquered the Inca empire, but some Inca escaped over the mountains into the Amazon rainforest, taking with them a vast fortune in gold. Adventurers and explorers have long believed that they founded a secret city in the jungle, which might yet contain a fabulous treasure beyond belief. Could you be the one to discover the lost city when so many others have died trying?

BEAR SAYS

Before setting out, plan your expedition: what kit, maps, and training do you need?

IT'S A JUNGLE OUT THERE

Jungle terrain is difficult to move through, and the combination of heat and constant rain makes it very uncomfortable – as do the swarms of insects.

Emergent layer

Canopy layer

Jungle anatomy

This illustration shows how the jungle is divided into vertical levels, with giant trees forming a thick canopy that blocks out most of the light. Down at ground level, the plants are crowded together, making it hard to move around. Your machete is the most important piece of kit you have! (But always use with adult supervision.)

Understorey layer

BEAR SAYS

There's plenty of rain in the rainforest, but little fresh drinking water. Learn to recognize water vines – they hold fresh water in their hollow stems. Use your machete to hack them open.

Shrub layer

Herb layer

JUNGLE KIT

You need clothes and kit that will cope with heat, constant rain, and insects. Clothes need to be light and loose to keep you cool, tough so that they don't get shredded by thorns and spikes, and quick-drying so that you're not constantly damp.

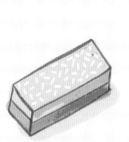

Whetstone for sharpening your machete

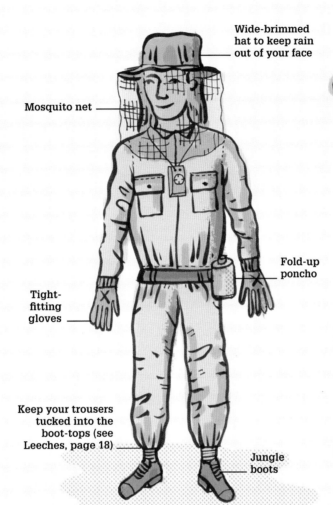

Wide-brimmed hat to keep rain out of your face

Mosquito net

Tight-fitting gloves

Fold-up poncho

Keep your trousers tucked into the boot-tops (see Leeches, page 18)

Jungle boots

Insect repellent

Plastic map case

Waterproof bags

HOW TO USE A MACHETE

A machete is a long-bladed knife for slashing a path through leaves and vines. Get your technique right or you will waste precious energy and take too long to get through the jungle. Always cut at an angle, and keep your wrist parallel to the cut. Chop down to cut through stems and vines, and up to cut through leaves. Follow a three-step cut:

1 Let your shoulder drop.

2 Lead with your elbow.

3 Flick your wrist at the last second.

RIVER MONSTERS

The best way to get about in the jungle is to travel by river, but you won't be the only one in the water! Crocodiles and alligators infest the waterways of the tropical world, and they're not even the worst things.

Piranha safety

Rivers in the Amazon are infested with deadly piranhas – small fish with razor-sharp teeth. They attack in shoals of 20 or more, and can strip all the flesh off an animal in minutes, leaving just bones. Here's how to swim with piranhas and survive:

1 Swim at night – piranhas are active during the day.

2 Avoid low rivers and pools left behind during the dry season – piranhas attack in large numbers only when they are hungry and desperate. In the wet season, a river at its normal level should be safe, but in the dry season, when water and food levels are low, piranhas become more dangerous.

3 Chuck in some meat – throw an animal carcass into the river downstream and cross while the piranhas are busy eating it.

HOW TO WRESTLE A CROCODILE

Crocodiles and alligators were swimming in rivers when dinosaurs walked the Earth. Their mouths are packed with teeth and they're horribly strong, but they do have weaknesses. If you're attacked by an alligator or a (smallish) crocodile you can fight back!

1 Distract the croc. You need to get on the croc's back, but you could end up jumping in its mouth if it's not distracted – get someone else to wave and shout at it. If you're on your own, throw your T-shirt over its eyes.

2 Jump on its back. Aim for its neck, just in front of its front legs. When you land on it, push its head down – it can't do much while its head is on the ground.

River crossings

If you're trekking in the jungle, sooner or later you'll have to cross a river. The best way is to fix a rope line and climb over the water, but someone has to go over first to set it up.

Float aids

You can quickly make a flotation aid by tying the legs of your trousers into knots at the ankles. Swing the trousers through the air to fill them up, like a balloon, then thrust them into the water.

Rope or nail some logs together

You can whip up a quick raft by lashing a few short logs together with rope.

BEAR SAYS

When I build a raft, I use five or six thick logs as a base, with two slimmer branches as cross-braces. Lash together with vines. Get an adult to check your raft before taking it on the water.

Make a raft

To cross a really big river it might be worth taking a day or two to build a proper raft.

The only tools you'll need

3 Lift up its back legs. Use your back legs to pin the croc's back legs to its sides while keeping its feet off the ground. This will stop it from rolling over on you.

4 Blind the croc. Slide one hand down the middle of its head until you're covering the eyes; it will pull them back into its head. Press down.

5 Hold its mouth closed. Slide one hand around its bottom jaw line and clamp its mouth shut. Now bring your other hand down to hold the other side shut.

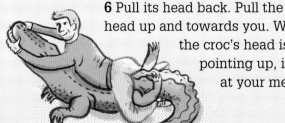

6 Pull its head back. Pull the head up and towards you. When the croc's head is pointing up, it is at your mercy.

SUCKERS AND STINGERS

The jungle might be full of adventure and mystery, but unfortunately it's also full of horrible things that want to bite, sting, and eat you.

Leeches

In the jungle, leeches are everywhere. They can smell you – stand still long enough and you'll see some dropping off leaves and squirming towards you. Leeches fix onto any exposed skin and suck your blood. You have to be careful about removing them so the bites don't collect germs.

TO REMOVE A LEECH...

1 Look for the small end – this is its head. Use your fingernail to loosen it, then flick it away.

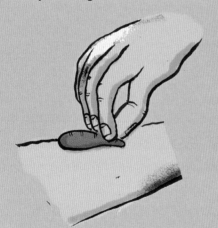

2 You can force a leech to let go with salt, alcohol, vinegar, or a flame, but this might make it vomit blood and germs into the bite wound. It's probably better to keep flicking or wait until the leech is full, when it will drop off.

3 Immediately clean the wound with antiseptic – in the jungle even tiny bites can quickly become nasty infections.

Creepy crawlies

The jungle is home to the greatest variety of insects anywhere on the planet. A lot of these insects see you as a meal, home, or target practice. This is especially bad news in the jungle because every bite, wound, or scratch is a horrible infection waiting to happen. Check yourself frequently, keep any bites clean and covered, and treat them with disinfectant.

Ticks
These nasty little blood-suckers clamp onto you. Some carry deadly diseases but don't try to rip them out in case their head parts break off in your skin. Choke them with tree sap or oil.

Bees
In the jungle, bees are bigger and nastier than the ones you are used to. If you disturb a hive or swarm, try not to panic. Protect your eyes and mouth and walk quickly away, through a bush if possible. If you have a clear path you might even outrun them.
If you get stung, take out the bee stingers carefully with a blunt knife edge or fingernail.

STINGING TREES

As if the animals weren't bad enough, in the jungle even the trees are vicious. Stinging trees are covered in tiny "hairs", like minute shards of glass, which are full of poison. They are so fine that they get into your skin, even through clothing, and can drive you mad with pain. If you can't avoid them, you can get them out using hair-removal wax or sticky tape.

Botflies
Botfly babies bore into your skin and wriggle about in your flesh. Learn how to remove them on page 23.

Poisonous caterpillars
Hairy, brightly coloured caterpillars may be dangerous. If one lands on you, brush it off with your machete blade, brushing in the direction of its head.

LOST CITIES OF GOLD

Explorers dream of filling in the great blank spaces on the map, and two of the biggest and blankest spaces in western history were the great jungles of Africa and South America. Add the possibility of finding vast treasure, and it's easy to see why explorers were drawn to the rainforest.

El Dorado

Early European explorers in South America dreamed of discovering the legendary El Dorado (Spanish for "the Golden One"), a city of gold hidden in the Amazon jungle. Hundreds of men died trying to find this place, which probably never existed. The famous English explorer Sir Walter Raleigh tried to find El Dorado in what is now Guyana and Venezuela in 1617, but his trip was not a great success. His son was killed, his best friend shot himself when things went wrong, and his head was cut off when he got home.

BEAR SAYS

Raleigh's mistake was that he lost his head – literally! In the wild, it is essential to stay level headed. Accidents happen when you start to panic, or set yourself unrealistic goals.

20

Dr Livingstone, I presume

David Livingstone was a Scottish doctor and missionary who crossed the Kalahari desert and explored central Africa, where he spread Christianity and fought the slave trade. Then he went missing on an expedition to find the source of the Nile, deep in the jungle. In 1871 the English-American journalist and adventurer Henry Morton Stanley was sent to find him. After seven months, Stanley found Livingstone on the shores of Lake Tanganyika. The Scottish explorer was probably the only other white man for a thousand miles, but Stanley famously greeted him with the polite question, "Dr Livingstone, I presume?" Livingstone later died while still hunting the source of the Nile, and Stanley went on to explore the Congo, the greatest jungle river in Africa.

The lost city of Z

Another man who believed in a mysterious city of gold in the Amazon was the British explorer Colonel Percy Fawcett. He called the lost city "Z", and believed it was a place of magical power. He had many adventures in the deep jungle, during which he claimed to have shot a 20-m (65-ft) long anaconda and discovered a two-nosed dog. In 1925, Fawcett disappeared while exploring the dangerous Matto Grosso region of the Amazon rainforest. Nearly 50 explorers have died while searching for some trace of Fawcett, but his body has never been discovered.

JUNGLE SURVIVORS

The jungle is dangerous and difficult, but it can also provide everything you need to stay alive, if you know how to find it. The stories of the Gremlin Special crash and Juliane Koepcke offer valuable survival tips for jungle explorers.

BEAR SAYS

You can't survive in the jungle without listening to the advice of local people. They know what plants are safe to eat, where to find water, and how to keep clear of predators.

Cannibal crash landing

During World War II, United States Air Force pilots discovered a hidden jungle valley in the centre of New Guinea. The people who lived there had never made contact with the outside world. It was impossible for Aeroplanes to land there and the overland route was blocked by Japanese soldiers and native headhunters. This didn't stop military people from flying over the valley for thrill rides, and in 1945 an aeroplane called the Gremlin Special crashed into a mountainside. Twenty-one people died but three people survived. Thanks to the help of local tribespeople, they survived until a daring rescue was arranged, involving a glider and an aeroplane with a big hook.

The woman who fell out of a plane

Seventeen-year-old Juliane Koepcke was flying over the Amazon jungle in 1971 when her plane was hit by lightning and broke into pieces in midair. Amazingly, she survived falling from 3 km (2 miles) up, crashing through the trees and landing with little more than a black eye. Everyone else on the plane, including her mother, was killed. Lost in the middle of thick jungle and with nothing to eat except a few sweets, Koepcke remembered some advice from her father: find a stream and follow it downhill. Streams lead to rivers, and rivers will eventually lead to people. Koepcke walked for days along a stream until she found a lumberjack's cabin. By now her skin was infested with baby botflies, so to get rid of them she poured petrol over her wounds and pulled out 50 larvae. Soon after, some lumberjacks turned up and she was rescued.

REMOVING A BOTLFY LARVA

1 The larva needs to breathe. Suffocate it with duct tape or petroleum jelly.

2 Apply pressure around the wound, then pinch the larva tail when it emerges.

3 Pull steadily until the larva is completely out. Clean and bandage the wound.

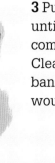

ESCAPING QUICKSAND

Quicksand is a mixture of fine sand, clay, and water. In the movies when someone steps in quicksand they get sucked in, and the more they struggle the more they sink, until they drown. Thankfully, in real life you won't sink deeper than your chest. But quicksand is very hard to get out of, so you could die if you are stuck too long!

Sticky situation

Quicksand is strange stuff: it can change from being as solid as concrete to being oozy like porridge, depending on whether it is being stirred about. When you tread on quicksand, you start mixing it up, so it goes porridgy and you start to sink in. But it is impossible for a person to completely sink into quicksand because the human body is less dense than quicksand, so you will always end up floating in it – probably no deeper than your waist. Quicksand can kill you in other ways, though! Once you stop moving, the quicksand sets into its hard form, and it becomes incredibly hard to pull yourself out. This means you could easily get stuck until you starve, or until you're drowned in a flood.

Swimming in porridge

To get out of quicksand, you first need to stop yourself from sinking in too deep.

1 As soon as you realize you are in trouble, take off your pack and throw it to one side.

2 Lie down on your back to spread your weight. You should now stop sinking.

3 To get the quicksand to let go, you need to wriggle your stuck parts until they are free.

4 Once you are unstuck, you need to get back to solid ground. If you have a friend, get them to pull you out – but make them do it very slowly at first or they'll pull your arms out of their sockets!

5 If you are alone, use swimming or snakelike motions. It may take hours to move a few metres, but you can take a rest break at any time.

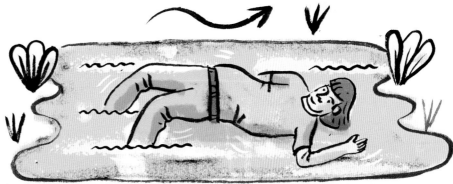

BEAR SAYS

Swamps, bogs, and marshes are even deadlier than quicksand! Stay clear of them. If you do fall in, do not panic or flail around. Call for help. You need to float yourself free.

JUNGLE JUMBOS

Elephants are found in jungles and savannah grasslands of Africa and Asia. They can be fierce and dangerous, but their intelligence and great strength also mean they can be a great help to an explorer.

How to survive an elephant attack

- Keep downwind of elephants and give them lots of space to start with.

- If one starts charging, stand still – running may encourage it.

- If the elephant has its ears out, it's probably a mock charge. Wait until it's stopped and then move slowly away.

- If the elephant's ears are back, it's probably not kidding. Find a large tree and climb it as quickly as possible.

- If there are no trees, throw a decoy, like a hat or rucksack. The elephant may start attacking it, giving you time to escape.

- If all else fails, squeeze into a hiding place or curl up into as small a ball as possible.

Ears out – mock attack, stand your ground.

Ears back – uh-oh, this elephant is really angry!

TUSK RIDER

When explorer Mike Fay was charged by an elephant in Gabon, Africa, in 2002, he grabbed hold of its tusks and rode them. It was a clever plan, because the elephant couldn't stab him with them.

How to ride an elephant

You can only ride a tame elephant (try riding a wild one and you will end up dead), and only Indian elephants can be tamed, so if you're in Africa, forget about it.

1 Get on board. Give the elephant the command for "lift" – it should raise its foot to form a natural ladder. Grab hold of an ear and put your foot on the leg, then grab a rope or part of the saddle and pull yourself on.

2 Practise giving the commands for "forward", "left", "right", etc. Use your knees to give nudges behind the ears.

3 Tap the elephant's back. This is the signal for the elephant to sit down so you can get off.

If you're faced with a rushing river, hitching a lift on a tame elephant can be a safe way to cross.

27

BITE BACK

Most snakes are shy and want to avoid you, but some can be aggressive and may attack without warning.

Snakes to avoid

Fer-de-lance

Tiger snake

King cobra

Tropical rattlesnake

Brown snake

Bushmaster

Black mamba

Coastal taipan

SNAKE SNACK

Many snake species are endangered, but if you have to kill a snake because you are starving, your best bet is to break its back with a heavy stick or club. Aim for just below its head. Use a forked stick to hold its head still and then cut off the head with your machete. But be careful – dead snakes can still bite you!

WHAT TO DO IF YOU ARE BITTEN

If you are bitten by a snake, do not panic. Do not wash the bite, as venom left on the skin could identify the snake. Those are the don'ts. Here's what you **should** do:

- Remember what bit you – you need to describe the snake so you get the right antivenom.

- Apply a wide pressure bandage over the entire limb.

- Lower the limb – keep the bite below the rest of your body to slow the spread of venom.

- Stay still – if you're with someone, send them to get help, while you stay as motionless as possible. This will help keep your circulation slow and slow down the spread of venom.

- Drink lots of water.

What snake is that?

Send for help.

Drink water.

MIND YOUR STEP!

Snakes can feel vibrations, so one of the best ways to avoid getting bitten is to stomp. But mind where you're stomping! When walking in the jungle or savannah, look at the ground to make sure you're not treading on a snake. When you come to a log, don't step over it without looking on the other side.

BEAR
SAYS

In an emergency, grill snake over a campfire. It's sinewy and bony, but full of protein.

BIG GAME

The savannah of Africa is famous for its big, dangerous beasts. Lions and leopards are pretty lethal, but not the most deadly of all. So what is the animal that's polished off the most explorers? Believe it or not, it's the hippo.

Buffalo bash

As a modern explorer, you are more interested in shooting animals with a camera than a gun, but the Cape buffalo doesn't know that. This animal is the ultimate enemy for the big-game hunter – if you bother one, it gets angrier and angrier. Cape buffalo can weigh up to 1 tonne (2,200 lb), and can run at 55 km/h (35 mph). In Africa, they are nicknamed the "Black Death" because they are so mean.

Hungry birds provide a buffalo bug-cleaning service.

Lethal lions

Lions generally don't attack humans, although sometimes they go bad and become terrifying man-eaters (see page 32). If a lion is coming for you and you are stuck in the open, do not run! Stand your ground and wave your arms to make yourself look bigger. Hopefully the lion is only mock charging you, but if it is for real you have two options. You can play dead by lying down on your front, and hope the lion loses interest. Or if the lion is definitely trying to eat you, thrash and yell – it might put the lion off.

Horrible hippos

Hippos are bad-tempered and unpredictable, and have huge chomping teeth. They can run faster than you and climb steep riverbanks, but they are most dangerous in the water. As an explorer you depend on rivers and lakes to get around, but as far as the hippo is concerned this just makes you a target. Hippos like to come up underneath boats, overturn them, and then chomp people. Another charming habit of the hippo is to spray poo out of its bottom while twirling its tail like a propeller, spraying muck in all directions.

The leopard's spots camouflage it so it can move stealthily through the shadows.

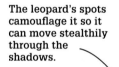

Leaping leopards

Leopards are the least likely of all these animals to attack you – they generally avoid humans. Only if they are wounded or ill are they likely to become dangerous. Keep safe by staying away from leopard cubs, and if a leopard charges you, shout, clap your hands, and wave your arms to deter it.

BEAR
SAYS

When I came across a herd of hippos in Kenya, I remembered two important rules. One: never get between a hippo and the water. Two: don't get too close to a hippo's young.

31

AFRICAN ADVENTURERS

The Nile is the world's longest river, and one of the most mysterious. The hunt for the source of the Nile was one of the great prizes in the history of exploration. Many Europeans set off to Africa to investigate with big plans but little knowledge. Many did not return.

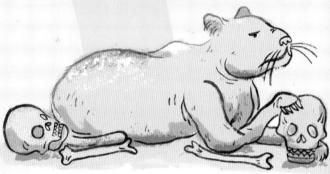

Man-eaters of Tsavo

Colonel John Henry Patterson was a surveyor in charge of a British scheme to build a railway bridge across the Tsavo River in Kenya. The project was stopped in March 1898 when man-eating lions started attacking and killing the railway workers. According to Patterson, two large male lions killed 135 people. Their ability to get through fences and sneak past guards led the terrified workers to call them the "Ghost" and the "Darkness".

Patterson spent months trying to shoot the lions, finally managing to kill the first one in December and the second one a few weeks later. The first lion was 3 m (almost 10 ft) long, and eight men were needed to carry the body. It turned out that at least one of the lions had dental problems, which meant it could not hunt its normal meals and turned to hunting humans instead.

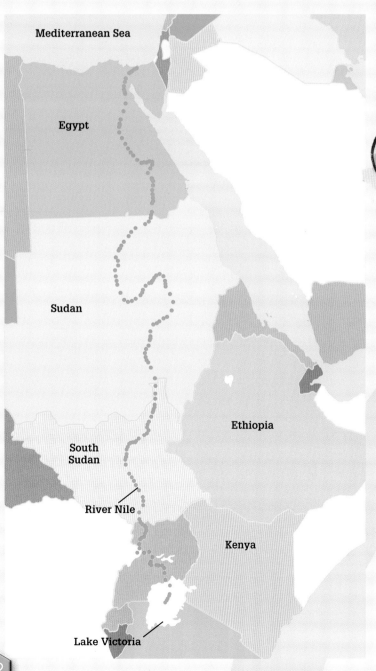

Mediterranean Sea

Egypt

Sudan

Ethiopia

South Sudan

River Nile

Kenya

Lake Victoria

Tragic trek

In 1857 the English explorers Richard Burton and John Hanning Speke set off from the East African coast towards a series of lakes they had heard rumours about. After struggling for months with terrible illness and unfriendly locals, they reached Lake Tanganyika in 1858. Burton was too ill to go much farther, but Speke went north and discovered Lake Victoria, which he believed to be the source of the Nile.

The two men argued about whether the lake really was the Nile's source, so Speke returned there in 1862, trying to prove it once and for all.

Although Speke found the place where the Nile flows out of Lake Victoria, he was not able to follow the river all the way down because of the hostility of local people. (Today, we are still not entirely sure, but we think the Nile probably starts a little farther south than Lake Victoria.)

In 1864, a day before Burton and Speke were supposed to meet in London to discuss their argument, Speke shot himself while out hunting. Was it a terrible accident, or was Speke so upset about falling out with his former friend that he ended his own life on purpose?

Burton and Speke didn't go exploring alone. This is who and what they took with them:

- 36 African porters

- 30 pack donkeys (with 4 donkey drivers)

- 13 Pakistani soldiers

- 10 slaves to carry the soldiers' guns

- 1 ironclad boat

DESERT

An enormous sand dune as high as a three-storey building blocks your way. Soon it will be hot enough to fry an egg on your water bottle, and the sand will start to burn your feet through your boots. Can you uncover the hidden mysteries of the desert, armed with little more than a bad-tempered camel, a plastic bag, and a headscarf soaked with wee?

EXPLORER'S QUEST

The desert sands conceal incredible secrets and undiscovered mysteries, from lost armies of the ancient world to the most extreme animals on Earth. What will you discover?

BEAR SAYS

Study the animals of the desert for a crash course in vital survival skills. They teach us how to find and conserve water, and they show us how to protect ourselves from the burning sun.

The lost army of Cambyses

Cambyses was a Persian emperor and conqueror of Egypt. In the year 252 BCE he sent a massive army of 50,000 heavily armed warriors to invade the mysterious oasis kingdom of Siwa, where the great temple of the Egyptian god Amun-Ra was located. The story goes that a huge sandstorm swallowed up the army as they struggled across the desert, and they vanished without a trace – every single one of them. The last resting place of Cambyses' army remains one of history's great mysteries. Located deep within Egypt's forbidding Western Desert, where boiling winds of over 40°C (100°F) blow for days on end, this warrior's graveyard would be a priceless treasure trove of ancient weapons and other relics, winning fortune and glory for the explorer who discovers its whereabouts. Of course, that's if the story is true...

ROCK ART OF THE DEEP DESERT

On a rocky plateau hidden deep within the Sahara is remarkable evidence that the world's most enormous desert was once a lush, watery paradise. Prehistoric rock art shows animals that lived here over 6,500 years ago, including giraffes, crocodiles, and hippos. Once there must have been rivers and lakes here, but now there is only sand and rock. Can you track down these ancient and sacred artworks?

Extreme animals of the desert

In the hellish desert environment, it seems impossible that anything could survive, but there are animals who can take the heat. These special species have unique adaptations that allow them to resist the heat and survive with little water. Can you discover which animal is the ultimate desert survivor?

Kangaroo rat

Tok tokkie beetle

- Camels can lose up to 40 per cent of the water from their blood and still survive.

- Kangaroo rats of North America's hottest deserts, such as the Mojave and Sonoran, build air-conditioned burrows and never need to drink.

- Tok tokkie, or fog-basking, beetles stick their bums in the air during the frosty desert mornings, so that dew will collect on their butts and run down to their mouths.

UNEXPECTED DESERT

The popular image of a desert is of sand dunes as far as the eye can see, but there is more to deserts than just sand. The deserts of the world include an amazing variety of landscapes and even temperatures – remember, what makes a desert isn't heat, but lack of water.

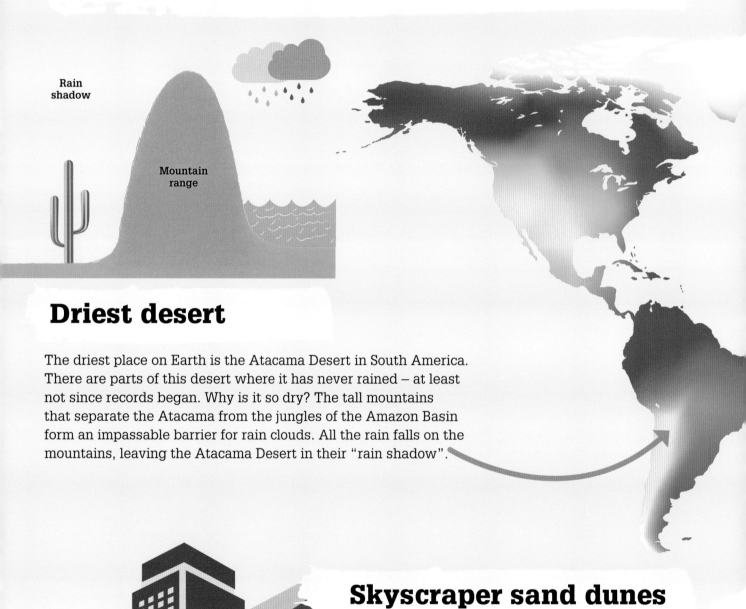

Rain shadow

Mountain range

Driest desert

The driest place on Earth is the Atacama Desert in South America. There are parts of this desert where it has never rained – at least not since records began. Why is it so dry? The tall mountains that separate the Atacama from the jungles of the Amazon Basin form an impassable barrier for rain clouds. All the rain falls on the mountains, leaving the Atacama Desert in their "rain shadow".

Skyscraper sand dunes

Sand dunes form where the wind piles up sand. If you've only ever seen a dune at the beach, it can be a shock to realize that tiny grains of loose sand can pile up into giant mountains over 300 m (almost 1,000 ft) high, as tall as a skyscraper.

The empty quarter

The immense desert known in Arabic as the Rub al Khali ("the quarter of emptiness") is what you think of when you close your eyes and imagine a desert – a vast stretch of sand known as a sand sea. In fact, the Rub al Khali is the largest sand sea on Earth. Crossing this sandy wasteland is seen as the ultimate challenge for the desert explorer.

BEAR SAYS

It is easy to become disorientated among the shifting sand dunes and featureless landscapes of the desert. Practise your navigation skills using a compass and always trust it.

Cold deserts

Deserts like the Gobi Desert of Central Asia get extremely cold because they are high up. In the Gobi it is common to see frost on sand dunes. The coldest desert in the world is actually made of water – in the form of ice! In the middle of Antarctica it never rains and hardly ever snows.

FINDING WATER

You can lose up to a litre of water an hour in the desert. Since deserts by definition are very dry places, you're not likely to find this much water helpfully lying around, so your number one priority is to preserve water – stay in the shade and try not to do too much unless you have a plan. If your own supplies are running low, you need to find a plentiful source of clean water. If you know where – and how – to look, you can find these even in a desert.

Follow the clues...

Spot green
Although valleys, gullies, and riverbeds may look dry, there will often be water beneath the surface, especially at the outsides of dry river bends and wherever you see green plants growing. Dig a hole and wait for it to fill with water. Empty out the first, dirtiest holeful of water and let it refill. Try lining the hole with stones to keep the water clean.

Track animals
Desert animals will be regular visitors to reliable sources of water, so look out for fresh animal droppings and animal trails (especially ones coming together or all leading in the same direction).

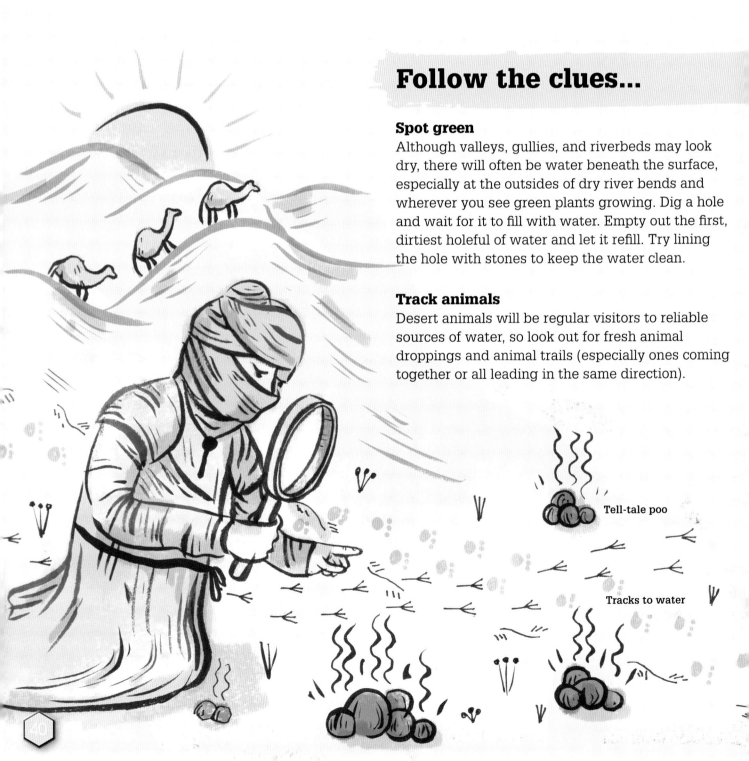

Tell-tale poo

Tracks to water

Watch birds

Desert birds drink early in the morning or late in the day. If you see some flying past they may be on their way towards water, or if they are flying low they might be on their way back with heavy bellies full of water.

BEAR
SAYS

No one can survive without water for longer than 3–4 days in the desert. Signs of serious dehydration are irritability, confusion, and sunken eyes. Stay calm, find water, and survive!

Detect critters

These creatures don't stray far from water. If you see a fly, you are probably within half an hour's walk of water. If you see a mosquito, you must be very close. Ants climbing up a tree may be heading towards a small pool of water that has collected in the branches.

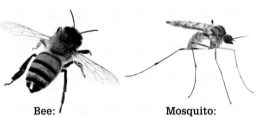

Bee: Usually within 4 km (2.5 miles)

Mosquito: Usually within 500 m (1,600 ft)

Frog: Usually in the immediate vicinity

DRINK WITH CARE

Remember that desert water will often be dirty and even poisonous, so you need to filter and purify it. In the desert, a simple method of purifying water is to leave a clear plastic bottle of water in direct sunlight for several hours.

It will take two days to purify the water during very cloudy conditions.

If there's no puddle, get digging!

Find cliffs

When rain falls, some of it will soak into the ground. Some of this water may reappear as a spring, often at the base of a cliff. In very sheltered spots, you may even find puddles left over from the last time it rained.

KNOW YOUR NATURE

Explorers know how to get the most out of nature, and even in the desert there are lots of natural resources. Here's a guide to finding fuel and even a recipe for making drinking water, using plants, a few simple tools, and a sprinkling of knowledge.

Make a solar still

A solar still is a way to use the heat of the sun to get moisture out of the ground. It also gets water out of any plants you can find, and from salty water such as your wee. Dig a hole and place a bucket in the middle. Fix a clear plastic sheet over the hole and weigh it with a rock so the sheet droops down over the bucket. The sun heats the air under the sheet, evaporating water from the ground and whatever else you put in, which then condenses on the underside of the sheet and drips into the bucket.

Copy the Tuareg of the Sahara

The Tuareg are nomadic people who live in the Sahara. They are known as "the people of the veil", because of the traditional face-covering tagelmust, or headscarf, worn by all men over 25; or as "the blue people", because the indigo dye from the tagelmust stains their skin. Keeping your head and skin covered by loose cotton is a perfect way to stay cool and reduce the amount of water you lose through sweat.

The Tuareg travel across vast areas of desert to find enough food and water. They are brilliant at navigating between oases, and are master camel herders. They use every part of the camel, including its dung, which is vital as fuel for fires because there is very little wood in the desert.

Be careful with that cactus

Everyone thinks that cacti are the drink dispensers of the desert, but cacti are only found in the Americas, and in reality most species are poisonous or too bitter to drink. Exceptions include the fishhook barrel cactus and the cactus fruit known as prickly pear, which you can mash up into a wet pulp.

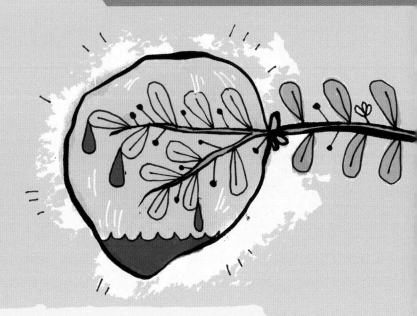

Bag it up

All green plants produce water vapour from their leaves in a process called transpiration. Collect this water by tying a clear plastic bag around a branch or whole plant. Make sure air can't get out but sunlight can get in. After a couple of hours, some water should have collected at the bottom of the bag.

BEAR SAYS

To reduce the amount of water you lose from your body, breathe through your nose rather than your mouth. Travel once the sun has gone down. Try not to waste energy climbing up dunes.

WET, WET, WET

To survive the intense heat of the desert you need to drink up to four times as much water as normal – perhaps a litre an hour during the day, which is equivalent to guzzling three cans of soda every hour for eight hours! The rule of thumb is: if you're sweating, drink. If you're sweating lots, drink lots!

DESERT DANGERS

The desert is beautiful but deadly, and an explorer needs more than a big bottle of water to survive and discover. Danger lurks over every dune, from the stinging scorpion to the mysteries of the mirage.

Sandstorms: death from above

A sandstorm is a cloud of dust and sand picked up by a strong wind, which blows across the desert like a giant scouring pad. Sandstorms can kill by suffocating you, and the fast-moving grains of sand can hurt or blind you. If you see one approaching, take shelter in a building or vehicle if possible. Close all the doors and windows. If there is no shelter, put on goggles and tie a scarf or wet cloth over your face. Try to find a rock to shelter behind, curl up into a ball, and cover your head. Camels simply close their eyes and nostrils and wait out the storm – if you know a friendly camel, get it to "koosh" (see page 47) and use it as a windbreak.

BEAR SAYS

A surprising desert danger is flash floods. When it rains in the desert, it rains hard. Do not pitch camp in a dry riverbed or creek. If there's a storm, it could become a raging torrent.

44

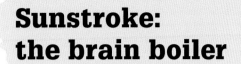
Sunstroke: the brain boiler

Heatstroke or sunstroke is what happens when your body absorbs heat faster than it can get rid of it. In the fierce sunlight and heat of the desert, sunstroke is the greatest danger facing the explorer. Try to avoid sunstroke by keeping your head covered at all times (see pages 48–9). Wear loose clothing and do not take your clothes off. Stay in the shade, and don't do anything during the heat of the day; exploring is for the early morning, evening, and – if the Moon is full – the night time. If you get dizzy or have a headache, stop whatever you are doing and lie down in the shade. Soak your head covering in water and sip water slowly but continuously.

Scorpions: small but deadly

Related to spiders, scorpions are fearsome-looking with their poisonous stinger, but are mostly harmless. However, there are some scorpions that can be deadly, especially to children. How can you tell which ones are dangerous? Look out for small, straw-coloured scorpions with long, thin tails – these are the worst. Scorpions generally want to stay away from you, so if you see one give it some room to escape. In the cold desert night, they might crawl into boots, hats, rucksacks, or even sleeping bags looking for warmth, so make sure you shake everything out carefully in the morning.

Mirages: tricks of the eye

A mirage is an optical illusion, caused by hot air near the desert surface bending light from the sky. When you see what looks like water in the distance, what you are really seeing is the sky. Don't be fooled!

45

CAPABLE CAMELS

Camels are amazing creatures: they can go without water for more than ten times longer than you can, and when they fill up they drink up to 150 litres (40 gallons) at once (enough to kill you several times over). A camel is essential for any desert explorer. It can lug your water and tent; provide shade from the sun, shelter from sandstorms, and warmth at night; and carry you places even a 4WD vehicle could never reach.

BEAR SAYS

In the Sahara desert, I once sheltered inside the body of a dead camel. It can keep you warm during the surprisingly cold desert nights or safe during sand storms. This is a survival tip you must not try at home!

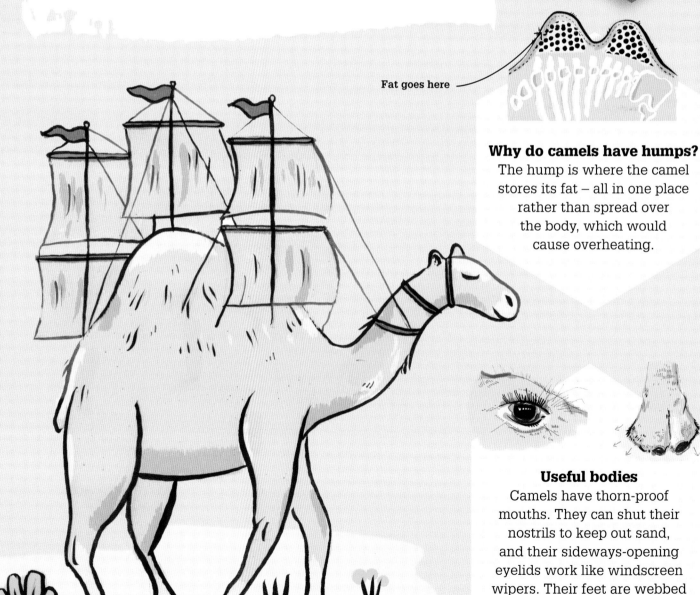

Fat goes here

Why do camels have humps?
The hump is where the camel stores its fat – all in one place rather than spread over the body, which would cause overheating.

Useful bodies
Camels have thorn-proof mouths. They can shut their nostrils to keep out sand, and their sideways-opening eyelids work like windscreen wipers. Their feet are webbed to stop them sinking into sand.

Harry the Horrible

Harry was the first ever camel in Australia, brought over from the Canary Islands in 1840. Six years later he was recruited by explorer John Ainsworth Horrocks for an expedition into the Outback, but it didn't work out for either of them. While exploring a dried-up lake, Horrocks stopped to shoot a bird. As Horrocks was loading his gun, Harry lurched sideways and his saddle caught on the trigger. The gun went off, blasting Horrocks in the jaw. The unfortunate explorer died of infection three weeks later, but got his revenge by giving orders for Harry to be shot! Bad-tempered Harry managed to bite his executioner on the hand before the deed was done.

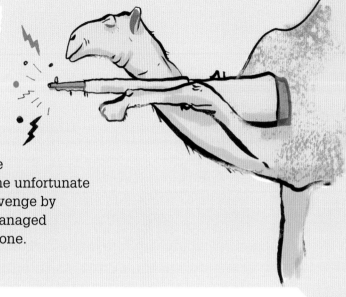

HOW TO TAME A WILD CAMEL

1 Round up some wild camels and put them together in a fenced yard. Pick your camel with care. A two- to three-year-old female is best. Avoid angry-looking males.

2 Use a "coach" camel to help. Having a coach camel that is already tame and trained will reassure and calm the wild camel.

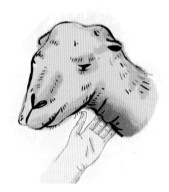

3 Let your camel get used to you. Eventually she will be comfortable with your presence and touch, especially if you bribe her with food and salt-licks.

4 A halter is what you use to guide the camel around and eventually to ride it. Start by getting the camel used to having a rope over and then around her neck. Then train her to move her head and then her whole body in response to pressure on the halter ropes.

5 Koosh train your camel. "Koosh" is the command you give to a camel to make her kneel down so you can get on.

6 It's time to ride your camel! When you get on the kooshing camel, wrap your legs around the saddle horn or hump. Get ready to be tipped at an alarming angle when she gets up on her hind legs and then front legs.

WHERE DID YOU GET THAT HAT?

Dressing up is half the fun of being an explorer! Wearing the right thing on your head will save your life – but what is the right thing? It depends who you want to copy. Do you see yourself as a member of the French Foreign Legion, or would you prefer to be a desert tribesman, like the Tuareg?

BEAR SAYS

Here's a way to stop you overheating if you need to save your valuable drinking water. Pee on a T-shirt and wrap it round your forehead. It will cool you right down. I've done it many times!

Indigo dye is made from soaked and fermented leaves

Tagelmust

A tagelmust is a scarf that winds round the head and covers the face, so that a single piece of cloth can protect you from the sun and keep out sand and dust. The Tuareg (see page 42) wear a blue tagelmust, while Bedouin often wear a black one. Dark colours screen out harmful sunlight, like sunglasses for your head, but they also soak up the heat more. The best combination is probably a dark cloth covered with a light, white cloth.

SAND DUNES

Desert dunes are created by windblown sand. The shape a dune takes depends on the prevailing wind direction and the amount of sand there is to blow about.

Star: Where winds come from three or more different directions, star dunes form.

Parabolic: The horns of these U-shaped dunes point upwind.

Safari hat

This favourite item of African exploration is made from cork or pith, a spongy plant material that can be pressed into almost any shape. The safari hat lets air through, which helps to keep your head cool.

French kepi

Foreign Legionnaires wear hats called kepis. The brim shades the eyes (and adds a touch of military style), while the high boxy bit captures an insulating pocket of air. A cloth down the back shades the neck and ears.

Cap and cloth

If you have to improvise, tuck a cloth into the headband of an ordinary cap to create a DIY kepi. You can even soak the neck cloth in water, so that it cools you as the water evaporates in the desert heat.

Cork hat

In the Australian Outback, thirsty flies try to get into your mouth, nose, and eyes to get a drink. The solution to this problem is the cork hat. The corks swing around as you move to stop the flies from landing.

Linear: These dunes form parallel to the average wind direction where sand is plentiful.

Barchan: Crescent-shaped dunes with horns pointing downwind form where wind direction is constant but sand is limited.

DRASTIC MEASURES

The desert is a harsh and potentially dangerous environment.
For safety's sake it's best to travel in a group, tell someone where you
are going, and always get a responsible adult to carry out first aid!
Aron Ralston broke all these rules. When he got stuck in the desert,
he came up with an escape plan – but it was rather a painful one.

Extreme first aid

It's an explorer's worst nightmare. You have
an accident but there's no one around to help.
All of the first-aid procedures described here have
been done at some time by somebody stuck in the
wilderness. While it's important to learn basic first
aid, definitely leave these medical procedures to
someone who knows what they are doing.

Globe luxation

This is the fancy medical term
for when your eyeball pops out
of your head. Happily this will
almost certainly never happen
to you, but it can occur if you
are poked in the eye in exactly
the right (or wrong) way.
To return the eyeball to
its proper place, push
gently on the white bits of
the eye with clean fingers.

Suture

These stitches hold
the sides of a wound
together to help it
heal. They sting
going in and they
sting coming out.

Tooth extraction

Almost nothing hurts as
much as a toothache –
just ask one of the many
explorers who have
decided to tear out a tooth
rather than put up with
an aching one for a minute
longer. It helps to have a pair
of pliers and a strong arm.

Appendectomy

One morning in April 1961 at a remote Antarctic
scientific base, Leonid Rogozov began to feel very
ill. All his symptoms indicated that his appendix
had burst – he had to be operated on
or he would surely die. One problem
though: he was the only doctor at
the base and he would have
to operate on himself!
Fortunately he
had some local
anaesthetic available
and some friends
to assist (although
they almost
fainted).

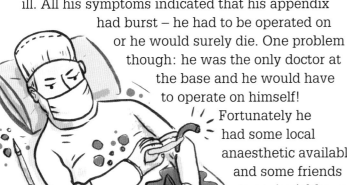

Tracheotomy

A tracheotomy is
a little hole cut in
the throat that allows
a person to breathe
when their airway isn't
working. It can be the only
way to save a person's life if
they have a serious throat
injury or an obstruction
that can't be removed.
The hole needs to be kept
open. The body of a pen or
a drinking straw can help.

Give the man a hand: the Aron Ralston story

In April 2003, Aron Ralston was exploring Bluejohn Canyon, in the Utah desert, when he slipped and fell down a crevasse. The fall dislodged a boulder, which pinned his hand to the wall. It was impossible to free his hand or move the rock, and Ralston hadn't told anyone where he was going, so he knew there would be no one to help him. After six days, suffering from dehydration and low body temperature, he decided to amputate his own hand, using a blunt multi-tool he had with him. After cutting off his hand, he lowered himself to the floor of the canyon and walked to safety.

POLAR

According to your GPS tracker you are just a two-day hike from the Pole, but things aren't going well. The food for the dogs ran out two days ago; you could butcher one of them to feed to the others, or maybe try producing one of their favourite delicacies – human poo. Now a blizzard is closing in – when the short day ends the temperature will drop to 60 below. Should you press on, turn back, or try to build a shelter using nothing but snow and a shovel?

EXPLORER'S QUEST

The ultimate ends of Earth are the absolute limit of human exploration, and true explorers are always looking to push themselves to the limit. Icy deserts, frozen seas, impenetrable mountains, savage bears, and less savage penguins protect the secrets of the polar regions. What will you discover at the top or bottom of the planet?

Race to the Poles

Unfortunately you've missed your chance to become the first person to reach either the North or South Pole. Although you may be joining this race a little late, the contest to see who can reach the North and South Poles in the most challenging ways possible continues. Perhaps you could be the first person to walk to the South Pole backwards, or the first person to kayak to the North Pole if the ice cap keeps melting?

Mountains at the end of the world

The most remote and unexplored mountains on Earth are the Transantarctic Mountains, a range 3,200 km (2,000 miles) long and 4,500 m (14,800 ft) high that cuts across the polar continent. All the great Antarctic adventurers explored these mountains, but they still hold many secrets – perhaps you could scuba dive in a lake that has been frozen over for millions of years, or look for water in the Dry Valleys, one of the driest environments on Earth?

THE LOST EXPEDITION

In 1845 Sir John Franklin set off into the icy waters of the Canadian Arctic Archipelago to search for the Northwest Passage (see below), but he vanished, along with his two ships and all 127 people aboard. A few bodies and artefacts have been found but the whereabouts of his ships, and most importantly his expedition logs (notes telling the story of the expedition), are still unknown – can you find them?

The Northwest Passage

A way for ships to sail from the Atlantic to the Pacific, across the top of North America, was the Holy Grail for Arctic explorers for centuries. In fact there is a sea passage through the islands of the Canadian Arctic Archipelago, but much of it is choked with ice for most of the year. Today less ice forms every year, so there is a greater chance than ever that you could open up a Northwest Passage for the ships of the world.

BEAR SAYS

In 2008, a trip I took to the Antarctic was cut short when I broke my shoulder kite-skiing on the ice shelf. High winds meant I had to wait two days to be flown out for medical treatment!

HOME SWEET DOME

After a hard day's walking or sledding across the ice, you need somewhere to rest and stay warm. And when a polar storm or blizzard arrives, you'd better take shelter or you will soon freeze to death. The Inuit came up with one of the best and simplest ideas – use snow to make a little house that keeps heat inside and won't blow away in the wind: an igloo.

HOW TO BUILD AN IGLOO

1 Mark a circle on the ground, about 2 m (6.5 ft) across. Stamp down the snow inside the circle until is hard.

3 Lay the first row of blocks in a circle. Use your saw to cut a ramp in them.

2 Use your saw to cut blocks of hard snow (you may have to dig down to find it). First cut two parallel horizontal lines, then make two vertical cuts.

4 Now lay blocks in a spiral around the ramp. Trim the sides of the blocks so that as you go up they slant inward. The last block should sit in the hole at the top, and should be wider at its top so it is held in place.

BEAR SAYS

You must find shelter before night falls, and with it the temperature. In an emergency, dig a cave in the snow using whatever tools you have. Dig into a slope that faces away from the wind.

Exploring mistakes

Learn from the mistakes of past explorers. When the Duke of Abruzzi went to Alaska in 1897 he took several iron beds with him, as he was too posh to sleep on the floor. In fact, air circulates under a raised bed, so it is warmer to sleep on the floor. Also, remember to bring stuff inside your shelter! When a storm buried his tent in snow, British polar explorer Augustine Courthauld was unable to dig himself out for six weeks because he had left his shovel outside.

5 On the side facing away from the wind, dig down to make an entrance. Use two slabs of hard snow to make a roof for it.

6 A proper igloo has a raised platform around one side, to make a seat and sleeping area.

THE POLAR EXPRESS

Walking on snow and ice in the freezing cold burns up so much energy that you can effectively starve to death in a few days even though you are eating what seem like normal meals. The Inuit long ago learned to use man's best friend to give themselves an easier ride.

Dog driving

Driving a team of dogs while riding a sled is not easy. The traces (the ropes that hold the dogs together and attach them to the sled) get easily tangled, and the dogs fight and may become lazy if not properly commanded. Your sled should have a handlebar, skis or runners, and a brake.

1 Keep your foot hard on the brake until you are ready.

2 Ease off on the brake and give the "go" command (such as "Mush!").

3 Brace yourself for a jerk when you start off.

4 You may need to push with one foot as though you were on a scooter to get the dogs going.

5 Keep some pressure on the brake until the dogs have pulled the lines taut.

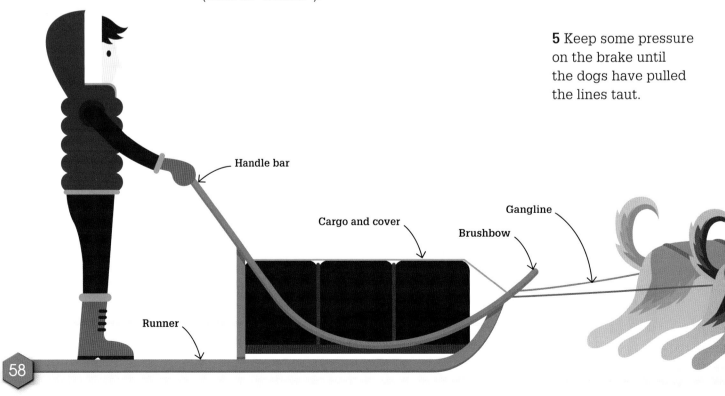

Handle bar

Cargo and cover

Gangline

Brushbow

Runner

DOG'S DINNER

In 1911 Amundsen and Scott raced to reach the South Pole (see pages 62–3). Amundsen beat Scott and made it back alive. One reason was that he used dogs, whereas Scott hated using dog-sleds so travelled on foot. Sled dogs, or huskies, are strong and light, making them perfect for travelling on snow and ice. They eat meat, so you can hunt for their food as you travel instead of having to bring it with you. It's pretty horrible, but Amundsen also shot some of his dogs and fed them to each other, and to his men. Dogs also like to eat human poo!

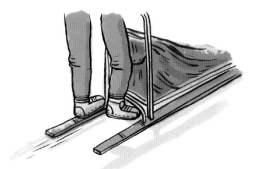

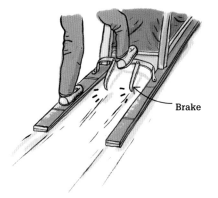

Brake

6 Turn by leaning on one ski or the other (for example, put weight on left ski to turn left).

9 Push with your feet when going uphill, to help the dogs. You may need to run alongside, but don't let go of the handlebars.

7 Use your knees to absorb bumps and shakes, as you would in skiing or mountain-biking.

Don't let go!

8 Use the brakes when going downhill to make sure you don't overrun the dogs or slip sideways.

10 Always watch your dogs to make sure they aren't falling over or getting tangled in the lines.

BEARS AND BITES

Arctic explorers have to worry about two kinds of bites: bear bites and frostbite. At least in the Antarctic there are no bears!

Survive a polar bear attack

Bears are huge and dangerous, but at least most species of bear will avoid you given the chance. Polar bears – the biggest land carnivores on Earth – are different: they will hunt humans, especially if they are hungry.

- If you see a polar bear in the distance, move in the opposite direction. Don't run: back away slowly.

- If one comes towards you, put your hands up in the air and shout and stamp. Sound an air horn if you have one. This will make you seem bigger and scarier, and could make the bear change its mind.

- The best defence against an attacking polar bear is a big gun, but you could try pepper spray.

BEAR SAYS

Only a handful of people have come face to face with a polar bear and lived to tell the tale. Set up a trip-wire alarm system around your camp. Take it in turns to keep watch.

HAMMER TOE

Danish explorer Peter Freuchen got frostbitten toes when he was trapped in a blizzard in 1923. An Inuit medicine man offered to bite the toes off, but Freuchen decided to smash them off with a hammer! He ended up losing his whole foot.

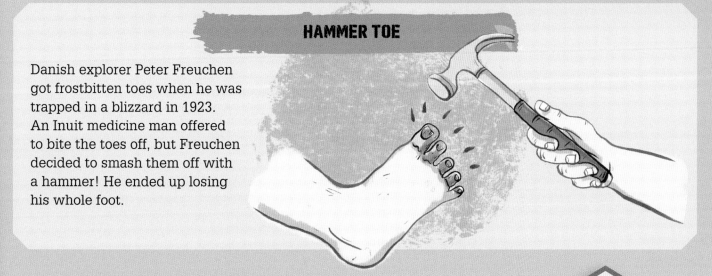

Frostbite

Frostbite is when the blood stops flowing to a part of the body and it freezes. If one of your toes freezes and then thaws out, it won't come back to life: it is dead, and will start rotting. It will also be incredibly painful. The parts of the body most at risk of frostbite are the toes and feet, fingers and hands, and the nose. If you don't want to lose some or all of these, be careful!

- Keep everything covered with the right sort of gloves and boots: warm and not too tight.

- Watch out for frost-nip. This is the first stage of frostbite, which you can recover from: your skin goes pale and loses feeling. It is a warning that you need to take extra care.

- Keep dry. The biggest danger is when your socks or gloves get wet and then freeze. Change your socks often if you need to. Dry out wet socks by putting them inside your pants (while wearing them!).

- If your feet get badly frostbitten, you are probably better off leaving them frozen. If they thaw out, they will become incredibly painful, but if they stay cold you can still walk on the frozen stumps.

BEAR SAYS

I've had frostnip in my fingers and toes from climbing on Everest, so they don't work as well as they used to.

Outer gloves

Inner gloves

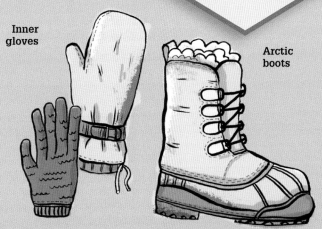

Arctic boots

RACE TO THE POLE

The three greatest names in Antarctic exploration are probably Robert Falcon Scott, Ernest Shackleton, and Roald Amundsen. Their successes and disasters offer valuable lessons for trainee explorers.

Shackleton's endurance

In 1914 Ernest Shackleton set out to reach Antarctica, intending to cross from coast to coast, but disaster struck when his ship, the *Endurance*, was trapped in the ice. Eventually the ship was crushed and Shackleton had to lead his crew onto the ice, and then to a small island. The only hope of rescue was to reach the whaling station on South Georgia Island, 1,500 km (800 miles) away, in a small lifeboat. Shackleton made it and eventually every one of his men was rescued.

Amundsen the airman

Roald Amundsen was the first to reach the South Pole, in December 1911, and managed to get there and back without losing any men. His success was down to his ruthlessness, careful planning, and attention to detail. Amundsen later became interested in flying, and made the first trans-Arctic flight, but he died in 1928 when his aeroplane crashed while he was helping search for survivors of an airship disaster. It was probably the only time he hadn't prepared properly.

Bubble burst

The most modern equipment is no good without a decent plan. In 1897 explorer Salomon Andrée set off for the North Pole using all the latest technology, including a hydrogen balloon and remote-controlled cooker. But the balloon didn't work properly in the freezing air. Andrée and his crew crashed not far from where they started, and were eaten by bears!

Scott of the Antarctic

Scott was heroically brave but he made many terrible mistakes. He refused to use sled dogs, and tried instead to use ponies. He and his men mostly hauled their own sleds. His attempt to reach the Pole involved a complicated plan, and he was not as thorough or professional in his preparations as his rival Amundsen. Although Scott made it to the Pole, in January 1912, he was beaten there by Amundsen, and he and his companions died on the way back to base.

BEAR SAYS

Scott and his team stuck together, right to the bitter end. Teamwork is essential in the wild. It's important that everyone in the team discusses the plan and then commits to it. Together we are stronger.

FOREST & MOUNTAIN

The mountain peak is hidden by clouds. If you wait for it to clear before trying to reach the summit, the hot sun will set loose a rain of killer boulders and deadly avalanches, but since you spent the night in a bivy bag hanging off a vertical cliff face, above a 300-metre drop to a forest filled with hungry wolves and fierce bears, it would help to see where you are going. On top of all this, you need to go to the toilet and your zip is stuck. Should you take off your gloves to fiddle with it, or rub a pencil on the zipper?

EXPLORER'S QUEST

With forests covering their lower slopes and peaks jutting into the sky, mountain ranges attract a very special type of explorer. The type willing to dodge bears and wolves, and brave the terrors of the death zone, to be the first person to stand on top of a mountain. But claiming the first ascent is not the only challenge for explorers in the forest and mountain zone.

Find the Yeti

The people of the Himalayas speak of an ape-like beast who lurks among the snowy peaks. Many visiting explorers have seen footprints or claim to have spotted the creature. Can you find proof that the Yeti or Abominable Snowman is real?

BEAR SAYS

In 1998, aged 23, I became one of the youngest Britons to climb Everest. The oldest person to reach the summit was Japanese climber Yuichiro Miura in 2013. He was 80 years old – an incredible man!

Find Mallory and Irvine's camera

George Mallory and Sandy Irvine died in 1924 trying to make the first ascent of Everest (see page 83). No one knows whether they made it to the top before they perished, but the mystery could be solved if Irvine's body is found, and with it the camera he was carrying, which might contain images of the men at the summit. Can you solve the greatest mystery of mountain exploration by tracking down a body lost for nearly a century and recovering an antique camera?

Circumnavigate the taiga belt

The taiga is the immense forest that runs in a belt around the top of the Earth. Pick the right route and you could circumnavigate (travel all the way around) the globe almost without leaving the forest, but would you be able to cope with bears, wolves, and intense cold without losing your way?

Climb an unclimbed monster

Believe it or not, there are lots of mountains in the world that no one has ever climbed. Some of them are almost as high as Mount Everest! You could write your name in the history books by being the first person to get to the top of one of these unclimbed monsters, but you will need to travel somewhere remote.

Track down a living fossil

Hidden away in the mountain ranges of the world are some very special places – isolated valleys where ancient forests still grow. In these unique spots, trees have survived the passing of ice ages, and even the passing of the dinosaurs. Trees like the 80,000-year-old grove of quaking aspens found in Utah, or the Wollemi Pines of Australia's Blue Mountains that until their discovery in 1994 were known only through fossils. Can you penetrate the deep mountains snd discover the living remnants of a prehistoric forest?

BIG BAD BEASTS

Since the first humans left Africa and started to move through the endless forests of the north, explorers have battled with terrifying beasts among the trees. Today, there are far fewer big predators of all kinds, including bears and wolves, but if you get lost in the wilderness you still run the risk of becoming food for a hungry animal.

Brown bear

Black bear

Bear necessities

Bears come in different varieties. Polar bears are the most dangerous (see page 60), but in the forest or mountains you could meet brown or black bears. Black bears are smaller and less dangerous. Brown bears, especially the type known as grizzly bears, are big and very dangerous, but even they generally prefer not to attack humans. The greatest danger comes from bumping into one, so that it feels cornered, or from a bear being attracted by the smell of your food. To avoid a bear attack, make a lot of noise as you walk and keep your food "bear safe" (see below). Never get between a mother and her cubs. If you see a baby bear, start backing away the way you came.

Front track

Back track

Front track

Back track

BEAR ATTACK!

If you come face to face with a bear...

1 Don't look it in the eye – turn slightly sideways.

2 Do not run! Bears can run faster than you.

3 If the bear is coming for you, stand up straight and wave your hands over your head, yelling and screeching.

4 If the bear still attacks, fall face down on the ground with your fingers locked around your neck and play dead. If the bear starts biting you, stab it in the eyes or mouth with a knife, or squirt pepper spray in its eyes.

When wolf packs attack

Wolves live and hunt in packs, and they are cunning and dangerous predators. They very rarely attack humans, but if you are alone in a remote place, especially in winter when food is scarce and the wolves are hungry, they may start to hunt you. Here's how to survive a wolf attack:

BEAR SAYS

Wolf packs show us just how formidable a team can be. The pack works together to bring down prey much larger than themselves. Then the wolves take turns to devour the meat.

1 Do not look a wolf in the eye or show your teeth. This looks aggressive and might prompt it to attack.

2 Don't run: the wolf will chase you, and a wolf can run much faster than you.

3 Get on top of a rock or climb a tree if possible.

4 Stand up tall and make yourself look as big as possible. Hold your backpack up or wave your arms above your head.

5 If a wolf attacks, fight back! Aim for the nose. Protect your throat and face with your forearm. If all else fails, ram your hand down its throat – hard.

FRUITS OF THE FOREST

The forest can be frightening, but it is also one of the friendliest places to go exploring, because you can find a fantastic range of things to eat, if you know how and where to look. Explorers like to travel light so living off the land is an essential skill to learn.

Forest feast

What's on the menu? There are 120,000 types of plant in the world that you can eat, and many of them can be found in the forest. Look for the fruits, nuts, seeds, and roots of plants. But beware – there are lots of poisonous plants, so foraging for food is a very dangerous business. Never ever eat anything unless a knowledgeable adult has checked it.

BEAR SAYS

Every year, a handful of people die from eating poisonous mushrooms or berries. The worst offender is the death cap mushroom. It looks like other, harmless mushrooms!

AVOID

- Mushrooms and toadstools unless you are an expert and know which ones are safe.

- Anything from a plant with milky white sap.

- Anything from a red or white plant or a plant covered with fine hairs or spines.

- White or yellow berries. Blue, black, and red berries are often poisonous, too!

Mushrooms and toadstools

Trees with milky sap

POSSIBLY SAFE

- Plants growing in wet soil or in the water.

- Roots, bulbs, and tubers (but always cook them first to destroy any poison).

- Some ferns.

- Blue and black berries, checked by an adult. Berries that have little bits joined together (like a raspberry or blackberry).

- Grass seeds (but don't eat them if there are little black bits growing out of them).

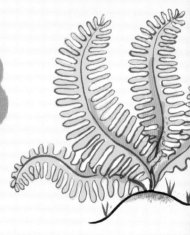
Some ferns

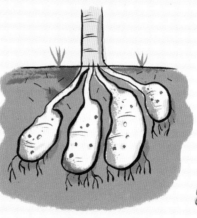
Roots, bulbs, and tubers

Fishy business: DIY fish trap

Mountains and forests are usually wet, which means lots of rivers and streams. Freshwater fish make for brilliant eating. A good way to catch them is to make a fish trap. You could make one at home, then try catching a fish in your nearest stream, as long as fishing is allowed there.

1 Cut the top off a large plastic bottle, about two-thirds of the way up.

2 Put some bait in the bottom part – you could use a worm or insect.

3 Turn the top half round and stick it into the bottom half. Make sure the cap is off!

4 When a fish swims through the narrow neck of the bottle to get the bait, it won't be able to find its way out again.

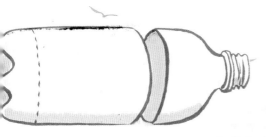

Red or white plants

White berries – or any unknown berry

5 Put the bottle in a stream, at the outside of a bend, in the shade of the overhanging bank. Keep it in place with rocks and sticks.

Plants growing in water

Berries checked by an adult

Grass seeds

AXE AWAY!

One of the most important and useful things for climbing a snowy mountain is an ice axe. Knowing how to use it can get you to the top of a mountain no one has ever been up before, and could save your life if you start coming down faster than you want to.

Ice axe to the rescue

An ice axe is more like a pick or hammer – the head of the axe has both a blunt and a spiky end, and the bottom of the shaft is also pointy. All these bits can be used to stick the axe into the snow or ice, giving you something to hold onto. The ice axe is also used for chipping out footholds in the ice, and for carving a snow cave if you need to take shelter.

When you are walking up a snowy slope, with every step, push the shaft of the axe into the snow up the slope from where you are standing. If you start to slip you can put one hand on the head and push down, and hold the bottom of the shaft with the other hand. This is called a self-belay.

Adze – mainly used for chopping ice

Pick – for jamming into ice

Leash

Ferrule – for jamming into snow

BEAR SAYS

When I climbed Everest, we used our ice axes to secure the tent so it didn't get blown away in a storm. But don't forget to retrieve your ice axe in the morning – you will need it at 8,000 m (26,000 ft)!

Self-arrest

The ice axe can save your life if you start to slide down a slope, using a technique called self-arrest. You need to practise this before trying to climb Everest. The aim is to end up on your stomach with your feet pointing downhill and the head of your ice axe buried in the snow.

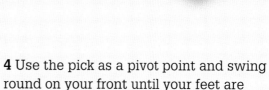

BEAR SAYS

I once used my ice-axe to self-arrest when I was hurtling down an icy face in the Canadian Rockies!

1 Stay calm – hurtling down a slope towards a cliff or sharp rocks is pretty terrifying, but if you stay calm you can survive.

4 Use the pick as a pivot point and swing round on your front until your feet are pointing downhill.

2 Hold onto the ice axe with both hands.

5 Arch your body slightly so that your knees and toes are digging in, and so that your weight is pressing the axe into the snow. Now you should come to a halt!

3 Stick the pick part of the ice axe into the snow on one side of your body.

GET KNOTTED

If you are going mountain climbing, you will need plenty of rope, and you will need to practise your knots. Knots are amazingly useful for the explorer. You also need them for everything from building a raft to fixing a rope bridge across a bottomless chasm. Here are three useful knots you can practise at home, but it's worth getting a special book showing you all kinds of different knots!

DOUBLE FISHERMAN'S

Use this knot to tie two ropes together (for instance, when repairing a rope bridge across a gorge).

1 Lie the ends of the two ropes together.

2 With each rope, make two turns around both ropes, back in the direction of the rest of the rope.

3 Pass the end through the loops and pull each end tight. You should end up with two "X" shapes.

PRUSIK

A prusik knot slides up and down a rope when unweighted but doesn't slip under a downward force. Use two prusik knots (one for your feet and another clipped to a harness) to ascend a rope.

1 Create a loop of cord. Wrap it around the rope, and back through itself.

2 Repeat this process twice more so there is a triple loop top and bottom.

3 Push the knot together. It will slide up but will hold when pulled downwards.

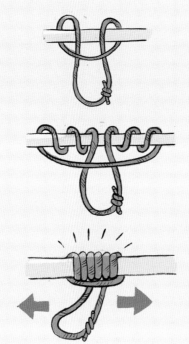

Prusik cord must have a smaller diameter than the main rope

FIGURE OF EIGHT LOOP

This knot provides a good way to make a loop at one end of a rope, which won't get jammed tight.

1 Loop the rope and bend the looped end (called a "bight") around the double "tail". This creates an eye.

2 Push the bight around the tail and up through the eye.

3 Now you have a strong loop you can put over a branch or into a carabiner (a metal clip used by climbers).

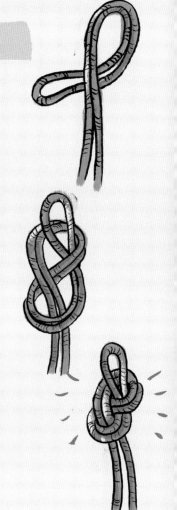

Help from your friends

Climbing is best done with at least two people: one reason why you need a companion is so that you can belay your way up a mountain. Belaying is a method of climbing where there is always one person holding a rope tied to the other person – to catch the climber if he or she falls.

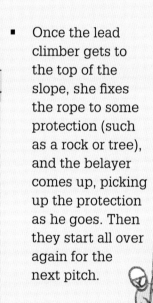

> ## BEAR SAYS
>
> I could not have climbed Everest without help from my kind and brave Sherpa friends.

- The first or lead climber goes up first, with a rope tied round her waist, and she fixes "protection" (places where the rope can be fixed to the rock) along the way. If she slips and falls, the second climber, or belayer, is holding the rope taut so the lead climber will only fall as far as the first protection.

- Once the lead climber gets to the top of the slope, she fixes the rope to some protection (such as a rock or tree), and the belayer comes up, picking up the protection as he goes. Then they start all over again for the next pitch.

AVALANCHE!

An avalanche is a massive flood of snow travelling at up to 360 km/h (225 mph), pushing hurricane force winds ahead of it. As a mountain explorer you need to know how to avoid getting hit by an avalanche, and what to do if you can't.

Avalanche danger signs

The most dangerous avalanches are dry snow avalanches where a whole slab of snow slips off the mountainside. These generally travel at around 130 km/h (80 mph), breaking up into chunks and powder as they go. Most people who get killed by an avalanche are walking on the snow slab when it starts sliding, rather than hit by one from above.

Avalanches are most likely to happen when a lot of snow builds up very quickly on a steep slope. So you need to watch out after a heavy storm or snowfall, and especially where the wind has blown snow onto a slope.

Windblown snow
equals danger

Avalanches are more likely to occur on slopes that are being warmed by the sun. In avalanche danger areas, move early in the day or wait until the slopes are in the shade. The other big danger is that your weight will make a slab of snow slip. If you step on snow and cracks go out from your foot, you are in danger. Back away from the slope and look for a better route.

Avoid sunlit slopes

How to survive an avalanche

1 If you see an avalanche coming, try to move out of its way. Shelter behind a rock or tree if possible.

2 If you are caught in the start of an avalanche, try to get to the edge of the slide.

3 Cover your mouth so you don't choke on powder snow.

4 While the avalanche is flowing, it behaves like water. Once it stops, it will start to get hard and solid. If you get caught in one, try to get to the edge using swimming motions, and aim to stay afloat.

5 If you come to a stop underneath the snow, clear a breathing space in front of your face. Do this quickly before the snow sets hard.

6 You will probably be disorientated. Spit or pee to see which way is up – you can tell from the direction the spit or pee is dribbling.

7 You will have to wait for your companions to dig you out. The good news is that the snow is about 70 per cent air, but the bad news is that you only have about 20 minutes before the stale air you exhale suffocates you.

ARMED AND DANGEROUS

The 1953 Hunt expedition to Everest was equipped with a mortar (a kind of cannon), so that they could clear away dangerous snow by blasting the slopes with explosives and triggering avalanches. In the end, they only used the mortar as a firework launcher.

BEAR SAYS

I'm not a fan of avalanches at all! I was inches away from death when a colossal avalanche missed me by a whisker in the Himalayas. I just felt grateful that luck was on my side.

THE DEATH ZONE

The mountains are full of dangers for explorers, from mountain sickness to crevasses. Worst of all is the "Death Zone", above 8,000 m (26,000 ft) in altitude, where the human body cannot survive without help. Every minute you spend in this zone, your body is dying.

Cracks of doom

A glacier is a frozen river of ice. High mountains often have glaciers filling their valleys, and you might have to cross one. The ice bends and stretches, causing cracks known as crevasses to open up. They can be very narrow but very deep, and what makes them so dangerous is that they can get covered in snow, so you can fall in easily. If you fall into a crevasse, you probably won't ever come out. It is always best to walk around them unless you are part of an experienced team all roped together. That way, if you fall in, your friends can help pull you out again.

MISSION IMPOSSIBLE

To conquer Everest or other mountains over 8,000 m (26,000 ft), you need to carry oxygen cylinders and breathing equipment, unless you can climb quickly enough to get to the top and back down before you die. The first people to climb Everest without oxygen were Reinhold Messner and Peter Habeler in 1978. Early British explorers thought taking oxygen to help you climb was unsporting, and one of the organizers of the 1922 Everest expedition called anyone who used oxygen a "rotter".

Sick as a dog

Altitude sickness – technically known as acute mountain sickness (AMS) – is what happens when the human body climbs to heights it is not used to. We need oxygen to live, but the higher up you go, the less oxygen there is. In the thin air, you get tired very quickly, you lack energy, you can't think clearly, and you can start seeing and hearing things. You even run the risk of getting a swollen brain, which can easily kill you. To cope with AMS, you need to spend time getting used to high altitudes, moving to higher ground one day at a time.

The best cure for AMS is to head downhill

HOW TO ABSEIL INTO A VOLCANO

A volcano is a crack in Earth's crust, where hot liquid rock (lava), ash, and gas escape from underground. A volcano is an exciting place for an explorer. There aren't many people who've climbed into a volcano (and even fewer who've climbed out!).

Crazy craters

A typical volcano has a cone made of ash and lava that has cooled into solid rock. At the top of the cone is a crater, which is where most of the lava, ash, and gas come from. Some craters have molten lava at the bottom; others have cracks, with boiling steam and poisonous gas blasting out; and some have cooled enough to become solid and fill up with water, creating a crater lake. Under the lake the pressure could be building, waiting to explode.

Watch where you step!

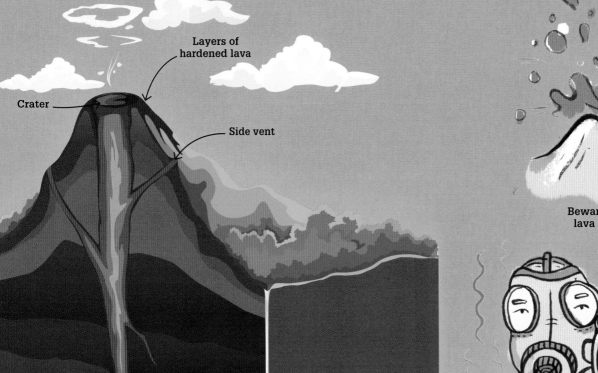

Layers of hardened lava

Crater

Side vent

Beware flying lava bombs

Gas mask may be required

THE MOUTH OF HELL

Mount Erebus in Antarctica is a mysterious volcano. The explorer Ernest Shackleton visited in 1908. When he looked into the crater, it was full of steam. In 1955 there was only solid rock in the crater. When New Zealand scientists visited in 1974, it was full of lava. They tried abseiling into the crater to collect molten lava, but the lava lake burped, throwing lava bombs at them. They got out as quickly as they could.

Abseiling basics

1 You can abseil with nothing more than a long piece of rope – it must be at least twice as long as the cliff you want to go down.

2 Loop the rope in half and put the loop over something very strong (e.g. a big rock) – this is your anchor point.

3 Face the anchor point and pass the doubled-up rope between your legs and around the back of your right thigh.

4 Pull the rope up across your chest and over your left shoulder, then back down across your back so you can hold it in front of you with your right hand.

5 Carefully walk backward to the edge of the cliff and lean back. Use your right hand to very slowly release the rope. Make sure you are leaning right out from the slope as you move down.

6 If you are going too fast, bring your right arm around in front of you.

VOLCANO ABSEILING PLAN

You will need a harness, rope, a metal descender to control your speed, heat-proof clothes and boots, and oxygen masks. Before descending, test for poisonous gas, and listen to expert advice on whether the volcano is about to blow.

EVEREST EXPLORERS

Everest is a mountain that inspires legends. Two of the greatest are the expeditions of Mallory and Irvine in 1924, and Norgay and Hillary in 1953. The first of them was a heroic failure, resulting in the deaths of both men. The second was a glorious success.

BEAR SAYS

Why was one of these expeditions a success and the other a failure? As explorers, we can learn a lot from them about the importance of knowledge, skill, kit, and planning.

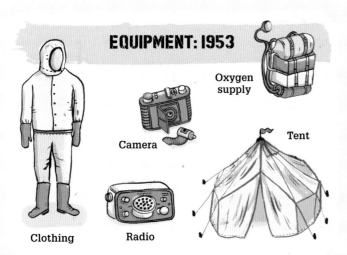

EQUIPMENT: 1953

Oxygen supply

Camera

Tent

Clothing

Radio

EQUIPMENT: TODAY

Oxygen supply

Camera

Tent

Clothing

Satellite phone

Top of the world

The 1953 British expedition to Everest was very well organized and prepared. It had a great leader – John Hunt – who made sure everyone did what they needed to. They had the best equipment, including specially developed boots, tents, and oxygen cylinders, and had scientists working out the best way to use their oxygen. They used clever tricks, like bringing builder's ladders to get across crevasses (a trick still used today). Above all they had teamwork, with some members doing lots of hard climbing and carrying, so that Edmund Hillary and Sherpa Tenzing Norgay had the best possible chance to get to the top.

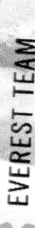

EVEREST TEAM

Death on Everest

Mallory and Irvine were last seen when some clouds briefly parted. They were two moving specks not far from the summit.

George Mallory was one of the best mountaineers of his time, and Sandy Irvine was an expert in using oxygen cylinders, the new technology that made it possible to climb into the Death Zone. But several things were against the two men. The cylinders available were heavy and leaky, so they may have run out of oxygen. The weather that year was very bad, and Mallory rushed his attempt to reach the top to try to beat snow that was due to arrive. Most importantly, Mallory and Irvine probably chose the wrong route to the top, which is why most experts believe they never made it.

BEAR SAYS

One day you might be on an expedition that starts to go wrong. Perhaps someone will get hurt, a storm will blow up, or you will lose your way. Stop to consider calmly the safest course of action.

ALIVE!

Mountain explorers go into the mountains with lots of equipment and supplies. What happens to people who end up on a mountain without any of these? Could you survive if you were stranded on a mountain?

BEAR SAYS

If disaster strikes, it is not physical strength that will keep you going, it is mental strength. Being brave does not mean you are not afraid. It means you can find a way through your fear.

The miracle of the Andes

In 1972 a Uruguayan plane carrying 45 people crashed in the high Andes Mountains. Some of the passengers died in the crash and others in an avalanche that hit the crashed plane, but 16 of them survived for 72 days. With no other options, the survivors made the difficult decision to eat the only food available – the frozen bodies of their dead friends. Eventually two survivors climbed several mountains and trekked down out of the Andes to get help, using insulation from the aeroplane they had stitched into a sleeping bag to survive the freezing nights.

DIY SIGNALLING FOR RESCUE

If you need rescuing, you should make rescue symbols on the ground so that they can be seen from the air. Try this in your back garden.

- Three of anything is the basic international rescue symbol. For instance, arrange three piles of white stones to form a triangle.

- Use light-coloured cloth or white stones, or even branches, to make ground-to-air symbols. "V" means "need help"; an "X" means "need medical help".

- Make the symbols at least 2 m (6.5 ft) wide and 6 m (20 ft) high.

Touching the void

In 1985, British climbers Joe Simpson and Simon Yates climbed the West Face of Siula Grande in the Peruvian Andes, a previously unclimbed route. Disaster struck on the way down when Simpson slipped and broke his leg. To get down a cliff, Yates had to lower Simpson on a rope, but Simpson ended up stuck in mid-air, unable to go up or down. Eventually Yates had to cut the rope. Simpson fell into a deep crevasse in a glacier but survived. He knew that Yates would think he was dead, so he had to ignore the pain, climb up onto the glacier, and hop and crawl back to camp. Without food or water, it took him three days. Somehow, he made it.

OCEANS & RIVERS

Twisting the cloth tight, you squeeze the last drops of water out of the chopped-up fish bones and into your mouth. A frigate bird gets caught in one of your traps. Should you rip out its throat with your teeth and drink its blood, or let it go and follow it to the remote island you are searching for, the one inhabited by a tribe who know the location of buried pirate treasure?

EXPLORER'S QUEST

Exploring the watery world is the closest you can get to exploring outer space without leaving Planet Earth. The oceans are completely alien to humans, and even travelling by river can be strange and dangerous. But water is also the explorer's friend – it is easier to travel great distances by boat than on foot, and only by crossing water can you explore truly unknown lands. Which challenge will you go for?

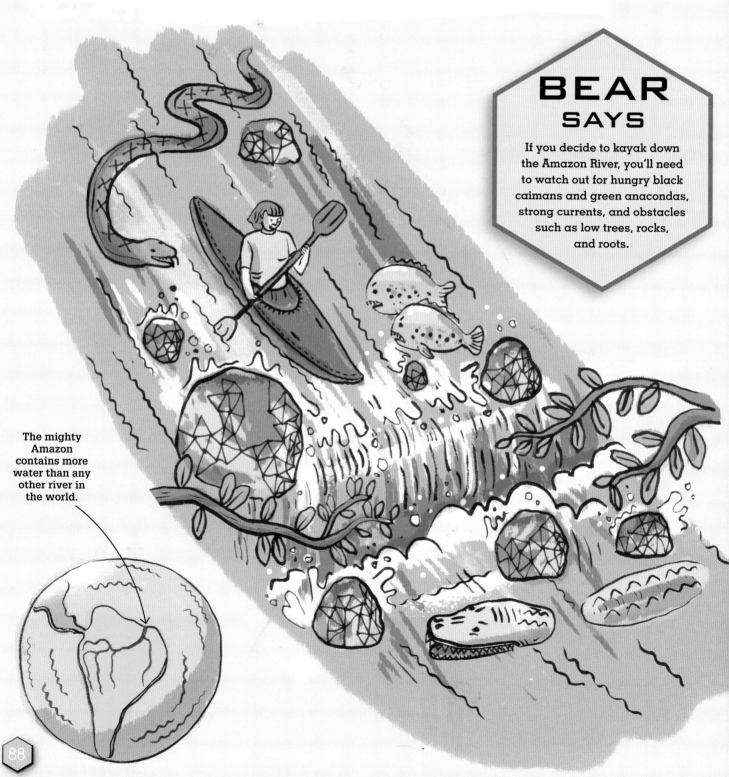

BEAR SAYS

If you decide to kayak down the Amazon River, you'll need to watch out for hungry black caimans and green anacondas, strong currents, and obstacles such as low trees, rocks, and roots.

The mighty Amazon contains more water than any other river in the world.

TREASURE HUNTERS

Treasure hunting is a specialized branch of exploring, combining the excitement of pirates, shipwrecks, and lost gold with the scientific and historical interest of uncovering old coins and ships of bygone eras. There are more than 3 million shipwrecks in the oceans and seas of the world, and some of these contain so much treasure they are worth over a billion dollars each. To give just one example, a Spanish treasure fleet of 11 ships was lost in 1715 off the coast of Florida. Four of the ships, and the fleet's most valuable treasure, the dowry for the Queen of Spain, have never been found. Can you brave storms, strong currents, and sharks to find the priceless jewels of a lost queen?

Fisherman's fiend

There are some very big fish in the sea but you don't expect to be eaten while exploring by river. Meet the Mekong giant catfish and think again. This freshwater monster can be up to 2.7 m (9 ft) long and weigh nearly 300 kg (660 lb). It is as big as a grizzly bear. Could you catch one while exploring Southeast Asia's mighty Mekong?

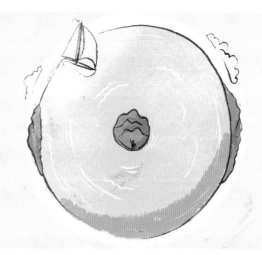

The middle of nowhere

Explorers like to get away from the hustle and bustle, and you can't get any further away than by visiting one of the world's most remote islands. The speck of land that is officially furthest away from any other speck of land is Bouvet Island in the South Atlantic, 1,750 km (1,090 miles) off the coast of Antarctica, and 2,200 km (1,400 miles) away from the nearest humans. The most remote inhabited island is Tristan de Cunha, in the South Atlantic about halfway between South Africa and South America. Could you sail there and land safely?

VESSELS OF DISCOVERY

Heading over the horizon without knowing where you are going – or even if there is somewhere to go – is brave, especially when you may have to deal with terrifying storms, giant waves, sea monsters, and scurvy. You need a trustworthy vessel.

Explorers' boats

If you are a billionaire explorer, you might want to equip your luxury super-yacht with a mini submarine, helicopter pad (and helicopter), and a seaplane slingshot launcher. On the other hand, if you are more into classic, solo exploration, you are likely to be interested in one of these three vessels.

1 Yacht
Consider a small sailing yacht with a cosy cabin and equipment that lets you steer and work the sails on your own. This is the sort of boat that single-handed round-the-world sailors use. The modern explorer can take advantage of technology such as satellite tracking systems, so you always know exactly where you are (although this seems like cheating); satellite phones; and sonar and radar to help you avoid obstacles.

TIMELINE OF EXPLORERS' BOATS

Thousands of years ago, the earliest sea explorers were the brave peoples who travelled by canoe to populate places such as Australia and Polynesia. Since those times, sea-going technology has advanced a long way.

Prehistory: Dugout canoe – hollowed-out logs used to paddle close to shore or to reach offshore islands.

400s: Currach – a simple boat made from a wooden frame covered with oak or hides, with a single mast. Irish monks may have reached Iceland as early as CE 790 using these boats.

800s: Outrigger canoe – used by the Polynesians to settle islands spread across thousands of kilometres of ocean in the Pacific.

800s: Viking longship – a long wooden boat with high pointed ends, equipped with a sail and oars. These had a shallow enough draft to travel rivers but were also capable of crossing oceans.

900s: Junk – Chinese sailing ship. Some versions were enormous, such as the fleet used by 15th-century explorer Admiral Zheng He, who travelled to Africa.

2 Trans-oceanic rowboat

Perhaps you could break the record for the youngest person to row across an ocean? You will need a specialized rowboat, which has an enclosed, waterproof cabin for sleeping and riding out storms, and sliding seats for long hours of rowing.

BEAR SAYS

Anyone can brave the world's oceans in a cruise liner – sometimes the challenge is in the choice of vessel. I've crossed the Atlantic in a small inflatable boat, and rowed the Thames in a bathtub!

3 Life raft

If things don't go well, you could find yourself adrift in one of these. Modern life rafts have shelters, special pumps for making drinking water out of seawater, and radio beacons to help rescuers find you. But you will still need to know how to survive on the ocean (see pages 94–5).

1450: Caravel – a small but very tough ship with a round belly, high back end, and two lateen (triangular) sails, developed by the Portuguese to explore the coast of Africa and eventually reach Asia and the Americas.

1691: Diving bell – a bell-shaped metal vessel for exploring underwater. The basic technology had existed for 2,000 years, but in 1691 astronomer Edmund Halley designed one for exploring.

1768: Collier – a ship for carrying coal. The sturdy design of the 18th-century collier made it the perfect ship for Captain Cook's first voyage of exploration. His *Endeavour* explored Australia.

1947: Balsa log raft – explorer Thor Heyerdahl built a raft called the *Kon-Tiki* and sailed it from South America to Polynesia.

1960: Bathyscape – a submersible designed to withstand pressure. The *Trieste* was the first vessel to reach the deepest point on Earth: Challenger Deep.

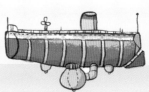

1968: Bermudan ketch – a small two-masted sailing yacht. Robin Knox-Johnston's ketch *Suhaili* was the first boat to be sailed single-handed non-stop around the world.

2012: Deep-sea submarine – film director James Cameron piloted his specially developed solo submarine *Deepsea Challenger* to the bottom of Challenger Deep, at 10,916 m (35,814 ft) below the Pacific Ocean, in 2012.

OCEAN DANGERS

Water is not your natural environment – you can't breathe under it, you can't swim as well as any of the creatures that live in it, and in most parts of the world you will lose heat so quickly that you will be dead from the cold within a few hours at most.

Storms

Don't be a fair-weather sailor. Learn how to cope with storms, or you will never sail round Cape Horn at the bottom of South America, or even make it through the Bay of Biscay to exotic France. Watch for storm warnings, such as growing swells (heaving of the ocean) and changes in the colour of the sky. Reef (roll up) your sails, so they don't get ripped to shreds by the wind, and put out a sea anchor. This will keep your boat facing the oncoming waves, so you won't capsize.

BEAR SAYS

When you're on a boat in stormy seas, there's one thing you should not forget: your life jacket. Even on a passenger ship, make sure you know the location of the life jackets and rafts.

Holed below the waterline

The greatest threat to your ship is having a hole gashed in it by rocks, reefs, or ice. Use the best charts available to steer clear of rocks and reefs. Don't sail in waters filled with icebergs, and if you have to, remember that they are bigger below the water than above, so give them plenty of space.

BATTLE A SHARK

Although sharks are terrifying, you are much more likely to be struck by lightning or fall down a manhole than get eaten by one. However, in shark-infested waters don't go swimming, especially when it gets dark, and don't trail your hands or feet over the edge of the boat. A shark can smell a drop of blood in an Olympic-size swimming pool, so be careful if you have a cut. If you are attacked by a shark, here's what to do.

1 Don't splash about or panic. The shark will think you are a wounded fish and is more likely to attack.

3 If you're with someone else, get back to back in the water so it can't sneak up on you. If near a rock or reef, back up against it.

2 Move slowly towards your boat or the shore.

4 If a shark attacks you, fight back! Aim for the eyes and gills, the most sensitive spots, with any weapon you can use or make up. Use a fast stabbing motion.

Expect the unexpected

Danger can come from the most unlikely places. Ask Toby, the pig taken to the Antarctic Ocean in 1904 by French explorer Jean-Baptiste Charcot. Toby ate a bucket of fish without waiting for anyone to take the hooks out of them, and died a painful death.

LOST AT SEA

Disaster! A passing whale has carelessly smashed a hole in your hull. Freezing water crashes into your cabin, waking you to a living nightmare. You have less than a minute to grab what you need and get off your sinking ship!

BEAR SAYS

The hardest decision you will ever make is to abandon ship. But if your vessel is sinking or on fire, you must calmly board your life raft. Once on board, throw out the life ring for other survivors.

Abandon ship

Ocean explorers should always pack a "grab bag" – a large bag containing the essentials for survival. This should include a torch, dry clothes, foil blanket, emergency rations, fishing gear, signalling mirror, and flares. In an emergency, activate your inflatable life raft, grab the bag, and go.

Life raft

Paddles

Entertainment

Flares

Survival bag

Fishing kit

Canned food

Whistle

Knife

Locator beacon

Bailing bucket

Water purifier

First-aid kit

SEA SURVIVAL TIPS

- Never drink seawater. It is too salty and will just make you more thirsty. Eventually it will drive you mad and kill you.

- Don't eat unless you have enough to drink. Digesting food uses up water.

- Don't drink on the first day, so that your body goes into water preservation mode.

- Protect your skin from the sun by smearing oil from fish livers onto it. Dry the livers in the sun first.

- Fish eyes, bones, and flesh are sources of water. Eat the eyes and flesh raw and squeeze the bones in a cloth.

- If you are overheating, soak a cloth in seawater and put it round your neck.

- Water that is not good for drinking can still be used – by putting it up your bottom! This is called a rehydration enema.

DIY compass

To make your compass, you will need a magnet, a needle, a cork, pliers, a thimble, and a bowl of water.

1 Rub the magnet along the needle several times, always in the same direction.

2 Using the pliers and the thimble, push the needle through the middle of the cork, long ways. Warning! This can be difficult and dangerous. Try using a flat piece of cork with a needle-shaped groove across the top, and lay the needle in the groove.

3 Float the cork in a bowl of water on top of a table. The needle should swing around to line up with north and south. You have made your own compass!

BEAR SAYS

Use a mirror, or anything with a shiny surface, to signal for help. Reflect the sun's rays in the direction of a passing ship or plane, flashing the signal on and off. The light can be seen for a long way.

DESERT ISLAND SURVIVAL

Robinson Crusoe is a character from a book by Daniel Defoe: he was shipwrecked on an island and survived. Crusoe was based on a real-life survivor, but don't be fooled into thinking that desert island survival is easy!

Desert island menu

Your priorities are the same as in any survival situation: find shelter, find water, find food, in that order. On a desert island you need to be careful of sunstroke (see page 45), sunburn, and getting soaked by rain storms. If the island is big enough, there should be streams for fresh water, but otherwise look for coconuts, bamboo, vines, and banana trees, which can all be useful sources of drinking water. Don't eat fish from the reef, as they may be poisonous, but do eat crabs, lobsters, sea urchins, sea cucumbers, mussels, barnacles, and sea slugs. Rinse seaweed in fresh water and then boil it.

Open a coconut

Coconut water is delicious and good for you. If you find a green coconut, cut off the top. A hard, brown one is more difficult to break into. Stick a thick branch into the ground and sharpen the end to a point. Use it to split the hairy outer husk and then to make a hole in the top of the shell.

ALEXANDER SELKIRK

Robinson Crusoe was based on real-life Scottish sailor Alexander Selkirk. He was working on a pirate ship in 1704, but he was so sure that the poorly-captained ship would sink that he demanded to be abandoned on a tiny uninhabited island called Más a Tierra (now known as Robinson Crusoe Island), 675 km (420 miles) off the coast of Chile. He sat down and read his Bible, waiting to be rescued, but soon realized that no one was coming. Over four years later, Selkirk was picked up by a passing ship. They discovered a "wildman" dressed in goat skins. Being left behind had saved Selkirk's life because his original ship had indeed sunk and its crew were either drowned or rotting in jail.

Selkirk made friends with some wild cats. They kept rats from attacking him at night.

Message in a bottle

Your best hope of rescue is by building a triangle of signal fires or using a mirror to signal passing aircraft, but you could put a message in a bottle and throw it in the sea. Just don't expect an answer any time soon. Although glass is resistant to seawater, the cork could rot and the bottle could get smashed on rocks. If it catches the right current, it could end up anywhere. One message in a bottle took 92 years (from 1914 to 2006) to travel from the middle of the North Sea to the Shetland Islands – hopefully it wasn't from someone asking to be rescued!

TO BOLDLY GO...

The greatest names in exploration are ocean-going explorers who made incredible voyages of discovery. They were brave men because setting off in a sailing ship across the ocean, when no one knew what was on the other side, was history's equivalent of going into space.

Calamity Columbus

Christopher Columbus is famous as the man who discovered America, although it had already been discovered around 13,000 years ago by prehistoric settlers known today as Native Americans. And the Vikings got there in around CE 1000. And possibly the Polynesians a bit earlier. But Columbus was still a great explorer. An Italian who got backing from the King and Queen of Spain, Columbus thought he could find a new route to Asia by sailing west. Setting off in 1492, he landed on what is now called the Bahamas and went on to explore Cuba and other islands. He returned in three later voyages of discovery. For the Native Americans and Caribbeans, his journeys were disastrous, because he brought disease and death.

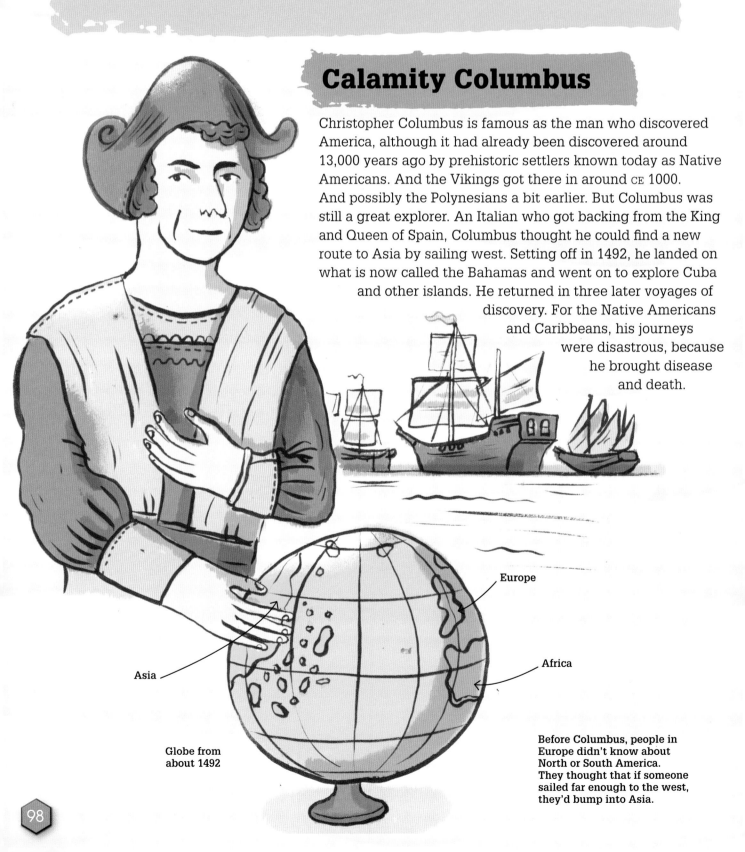

Europe

Africa

Asia

Globe from about 1492

Before Columbus, people in Europe didn't know about North or South America. They thought that if someone sailed far enough to the west, they'd bump into Asia.

A load of junk

Zheng He is possibly the greatest explorer no one has ever heard of. He was prime minister of the Ming dynasty empire of China, and was put in charge of a series of massive expeditions of discovery, trade, and tribute between 1405 and 1433, which travelled through Southeast Asia to India and Africa. He sailed in fleets of junks, Chinese sailing ships. On his fourth voyage he had 63 huge ships, some of which were 80 m (260 ft) long.

BEAR SAYS

Thor Heyerdahl was told that his plan was foolish and wouldn't work. Don't ever let anyone tell you that your dreams are silly. If you believe in yourself, you will accomplish all your goals.

The Kon-Tiki expedition

In 1947 Norwegian explorer Thor Heyerdahl set out to prove that Polynesia could have been settled by explorers from South America, after hearing Polynesian legends about a mythological god called Tiki who came to Polynesia from the East. In Peru he built a 14-m (45-ft) long raft out of nine balsa tree trunks, with a cabin and a mast for sails. He called it *Kon-Tiki*, after an old name for the Inca sun god. Heyerdahl and his crewmates sailed and drifted nearly 6,500 km (4,000 miles) until they reached islands near Tahiti.

Balsa wood is very light and strong

99

UNDER THE SEA

Technology has made it possible for ocean explorers to go beneath the waves, at first for short periods and only to shallow depths, but now for long periods to the ocean floor. The ocean deeps are the last great frontier for exploration on Earth. It is often said that we know more about the surface of the Moon than the bottom of the sea, yet the oceans cover more than 70 per cent of our planet.

GOING DOWN

If you want to explore underwater you have a number of options, depending on how deep you want to go.

Snorkelling

This lets you swim at the surface, looking down while breathing through a tube called a snorkel. Put some fins on your feet and you can move along quite fast.

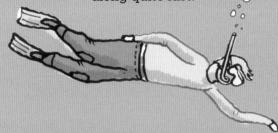

Scuba diving

Scuba (Self-Contained Underwater Breathing Apparatus) diving uses tanks of compressed air to allow people to breathe underwater. This is the nearest you can get to being a fish.

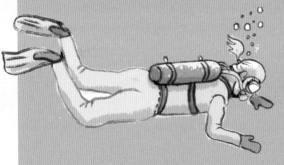

Diving suit

This functions in a similar way to a diving bell – it is basically a diving bell that covers your head, leaving your legs free to walk around on the bottom.

Submarine

A submarine is a vehicle that travels underwater. The most advanced exploration submarine is *Deepsea Challenger*, which in 2012 descended 11 km (6.8 miles) to the lowest point on Earth's surface.

Diving bell

If you turn a bucket over in the bath and push it down, the air inside is trapped. The water pressure may squash it very slightly but it won't disappear. If you were inside you could breathe the air and look at the bottom of the bath. A diving bell works on the same principle. Hoses supply fresh air to replace the air you've used up, and you can look out of the bottom of the bell at the seabed.

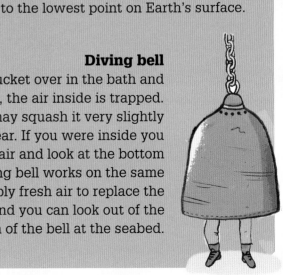

Under pressure

Freediving is simply swimming underwater while holding your breath. If you know how to equalize the pressure of the air inside your ears with the water pushing into them, there is no limit to how deep you can go, except for how long you can hold your breath. The record is 214 m (702 ft), but be warned: freediving is very dangerous. Never, ever dive without an adult dive buddy (someone to keep an eye on you).

When you freedive your blood gets thicker and your heart slows right down

BEAR SAYS

Freediving makes you feel like you've entered the world of the fishes. It's a highly dangerous and often deadly sport. The biggest risk is fainting from lack of oxygen to the brain. Always have a buddy nearby.

Greatest sunken treasures of all time

Three of the most valuable sunken treasure shipwrecks of all time are...

- **SS Republic:** A United States Civil War-era steamship loaded with gold and silver that sunk off the coast of Georgia in 1865. It was found in 2003. Salvors have recovered about a quarter of its estimated $300 million worth of coins.

- **Titanic:** The world's most famous shipwreck sank in 1912 after hitting an iceberg in the North Atlantic. Passengers included dozens of the world's richest people, who would have carried their jewels with them, and one treasure hunter believes that $300 million worth of diamonds were on board. The interest in the wreck means anything recovered from it automatically has immense value, but many people argue that salvaging objects from the *Titanic* is grave robbing.

- **Nuestra Señora de Atocha:** The richest wreck ever salvaged, the Atocha was a Spanish treasure galleon that sank off the Florida Keys in 1622. It was carrying treasure from Spanish colonies in the New World to Spain. Treasure hunter Mel Fisher found it in 1985 and over $450 million of treasure has since been recovered.

RIVER DANGERS

What do you think of when you imagine canoeing down a river? Probably clear water running slowly and smoothly between grassy banks, while you paddle lazily along. Wrong! Think again. Rivers can be murky, violent places, hiding deadly dangers that want to kill you (it's probably not personal).

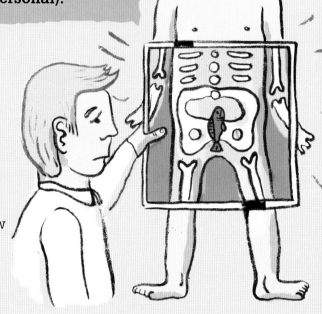

Penis-piercing fish

Perhaps the most terrifying danger in the world for explorers is the candiru, a tiny catfish with a horrible habit. It lives in the Amazon, where it burrows into the gills of bigger fish and uses its spines to stick there while feeding off their blood. It can squirm into all sorts of narrow passages, including the urethra – that's the tube that you pee out of! Once in there it gets stuck fast and will burrow into your flesh to drink your blood. Explorers should stay covered up while in the Amazon, and keep a safe distance from the water while having a wee.

Electric eels

Lurking in muddy pools around the rivers of South America are huge fish with amazing superpowers. Known as electric eels, they are actually relatives of the catfish. They can grow to 2.5 m (8 ft) long (about twice the height of an eight-year-old boy). These eels have hundreds of tiny natural batteries in their bodies, and they can give an electric shock five times stronger than you would get from sticking your fingers in a plug at home – powerful enough to knock a horse off its feet.

BEAR SAYS

As well as being shocking, electric eels are pretty clever – that can be a nasty combination. Watch out for them jumping out of the water to administer shocks with an extra punch.

Bull sharks

This shark species survives happily in the open ocean and hundreds of kilometres up rivers. Because of their wide distribution and aggression, many experts consider them the most dangerous sharks in the world.

Whirlpools

Whirlpools are circular currents spiralling down into the water. They are formed where streams collide or where the water is blocked by things like big rocks or sharp bends. If the whirlpool is big and strong enough, it can suck down a whole boat – and you with it. This could be deadly news for an open canoe, which will fill with water and sink, but if you're in a kayak you should be fine because most whirlpools die out quickly as they move along the river, allowing you to bob up to the surface. Either way, the best way to handle a whirlpool is to avoid it or, if you can get a good look at it, work out on which side the current is going downstream. Paddle into that part and you can get an acceleration boost that will slingshot you out the other side.

BOATS AND RAFTS

Your boat is not just for carrying you up or down river – it is also your pack mule, shelter, safety capsule, and, probably, heaviest piece of gear. So you need to make sure you choose the right vessel for your needs. Consider its weight, speed, how easy it is to handle, and how many people it can carry. Hardcore explorers don't believe in cheats like motors or engines, so for a small expedition you have three main choices of self-powered river craft: canoe, kayak, or raft.

Canoe

Based on old Native American boats, canoes are small, narrow, open boats, with seats for two or more people, each using a paddle with a single blade (although you can also use oars, sails, or poles). Canoes are the first choice for most river explorers: good for carrying people and supplies, they can even be carried from one watercourse to another.

BEAR SAYS

A scary moment was when I was floating through jungle rapids after a storm. The water threw me to the edge and pinned me under a rock ledge. Luckily, my camera crew hauled me out!

Kayak

Modelled on old Inuit boats, kayaks look a bit like small canoes, except they usually have covered decks. There are one or two cockpits, depending on how many pilots the kayak has, and each of these is fitted with a spray "skirt" (cover), so that when the pilot is seated there are no gaps to allow water to get into the boat. Kayak pilots use a paddle with a blade at each end. Kayaks are best for explorers who want to go off on their own, or expect to go over rapids, where a river flows over rocks and down steep slopes.

LEWIS AND CLARK'S IRONBOAT

Perhaps the greatest river exploration expedition in history was the United States' Lewis and Clark Expedition of 1804–06. A small party of explorers known as the Corps of Discovery travelled up the Missouri and down the Columbia rivers to reach the Pacific. The Corps used 25 boats of five different types during their epic journey, including an unusual contraption called the Ironboat. It had a collapsible iron frame so that it could be carried around and set up when needed. Unfortunately, the boat leaked and was abandoned.

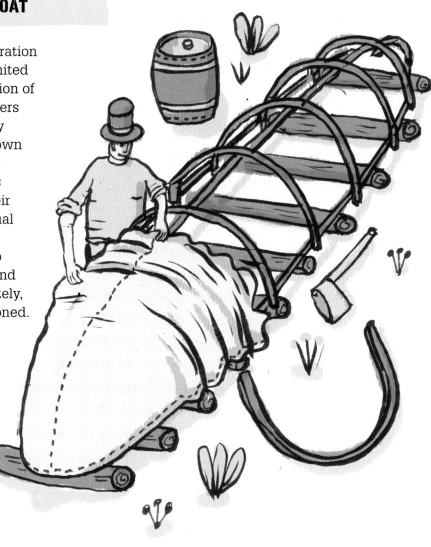

BEAR SAYS

The Ironboat is a reminder that even the most careful plans can need a rethink!

Raft

A raft is a simple platform that floats on the water, although you can build cabins and other structures on top. Rafts are hard to move and even harder to steer – you can try using sails or poles, but rafts are best for travelling downriver with the current. A raft cannot go over rapids, and is too heavy to pick up and carry, so it is not generally the best choice for an explorer. Even so, some amazing feats of exploration have been carried out by raft, such as the voyage of the Kon-Tiki (see page 99). For advice on building your own raft using logs and vines, turn to page 17).

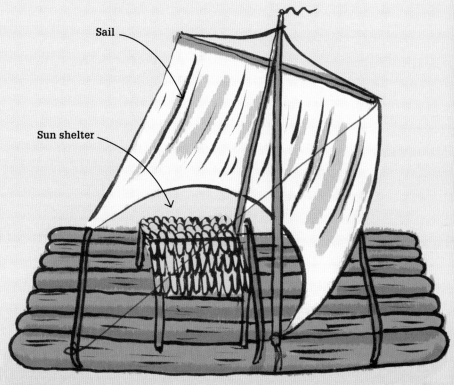

Sail

Sun shelter

ROLLING ON THE RIVER

The river explorer's greatest foes are not crocodiles or piranhas, although these are pretty nasty, but rapids and waterfalls. You could try to canoe or kayak over these, in which case you have to be prepared for your boat to capsize (see opposite); or you could go around them by land, in which case you need to know how to pick up your boat.

Portage

Sometimes you will have to pick up your boat and carry it around an obstacle or to another river on foot – this is called portage. Even though river boats are designed to weigh as little as possible for their size, they are still heavy. In fact, portage can be the most difficult and tiring part of river exploration. Kayaks are light enough to carry like a suitcase or hoist onto your shoulder, but picking up a canoe is a special skill that you will need to practise.

3 Move your forward hand along the yoke bar to grip the far gunwale. Move your other hand along the bar until it reaches the near gunwale. Keep the canoe balanced on your thighs.

1 Face the canoe and grab the near gunwale (rim) in the middle. Lift the side of the canoe and take a step forward.

4 Roll and swing the canoe onto your head.

2 Lean into the canoe and grab the bar across the middle – this is called the carrying yoke. Keep your back straight and lean backward, bending your knees so the canoe lifts onto your thighs.

5 Lower the canoe onto your shoulders so that the yoke bar sits across them. You are now ready to portage your canoe.

Screw roll

Before you set off exploring in your kayak, make sure you know how to roll out of a capsize. One technique is the screw roll.

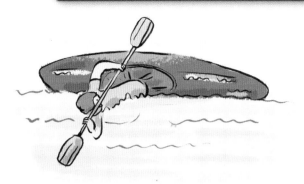

1 If you roll over, wait until you're upside down, then twist your body, lean forward, reach up, and put your paddle out of the water.

4 When the paddle is pointing straight down, snap up your right hip.

2 Roll your right wrist to make sure the right paddle blade is facing the water. Bring it down into the water in a sweep away from the front of the kayak towards the back.

5 Keep your head and body in the water until the last moment. When the boat rolls level they will come out of the water.

BEAR SAYS

If all else fails and you are still underwater, release your spray skirt, put your hands on the rim of the cockpit, and push the kayak up and forward to get your legs clear so you can float free.

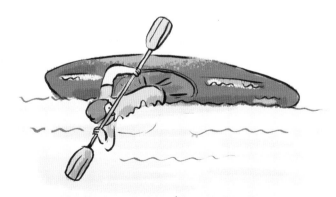

3 The kayak will start to twist. Untwist your body so that you face forward, while still sweeping the paddle back.

GETTING WET FEET

Many great explorers travelled by river for some or all of their voyages of exploration. Rivers are brilliant ways to cover large distances while carrying plenty of equipment and food, but most importantly they will almost always lead you to safety, because if you follow them downstream far enough you will eventually find other people.

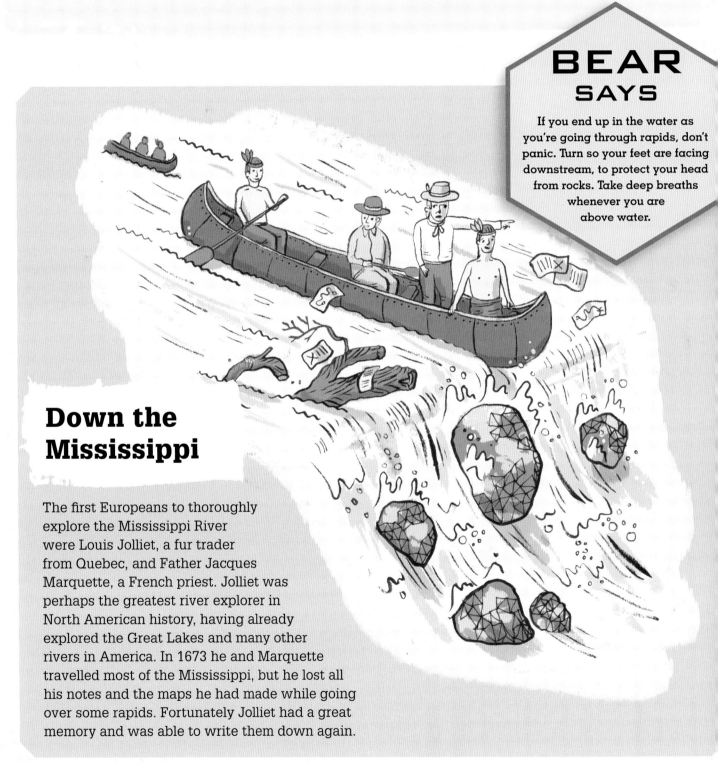

BEAR SAYS

If you end up in the water as you're going through rapids, don't panic. Turn so your feet are facing downstream, to protect your head from rocks. Take deep breaths whenever you are above water.

Down the Mississippi

The first Europeans to thoroughly explore the Mississippi River were Louis Jolliet, a fur trader from Quebec, and Father Jacques Marquette, a French priest. Jolliet was perhaps the greatest river explorer in North American history, having already explored the Great Lakes and many other rivers in America. In 1673 he and Marquette travelled most of the Mississippi, but he lost all his notes and the maps he had made while going over some rapids. Fortunately Jolliet had a great memory and was able to write them down again.

The Amazon by accident

One of the great voyages of river exploration was made by accident in 1538. Spaniard Francisco de Orellana was part of an expedition looking for El Dorado, the fabled city of gold in South America (see page 20). He and his men became separated from the rest of the expedition and decided to build some boats, as he was sure that El Dorado was just around the bend. Eventually he followed the river all the way to the sea, travelling almost the entire length of the Amazon River. He returned to South America in 1546, but the expedition was a disaster and he died.

Maddening mosquitoes

Mina Hubbard's husband, Leonidas, died while exploring the rivers of Labrador, eastern Canada, in 1903. She decided to finish what he had started, so in 1905 she set off down the North West River with the help of four guides. Although they braved fierce rapids, Hubbard's biggest problems were the swarms of mosquitoes and flies that constantly tried to eat her. She wore home-made masks with netting covering her face, but she could feel the blood running down her neck from all the bites!

DIY DRY BAG

You need a dry bag to hold valuable things so they don't get wet. Use a plastic bag with no holes (e.g. a large freezer bag).

1 Put your stuff (e.g. maps, pictures) inside the bag and squeeze out the air.

2 Roll up the top, from one side to the other.

3 Twist the rolled-up section.

4 Fold it over and put a tight rubber band around the fold.

5 Test it out by putting it underwater in a sink or bath.

NAVIGATION

It's dark and you are lost. If only you hadn't shredded your map when you were trying to fold it, and then lost your compass crossing that river! Luckily it's a clear night, with a crescent moon and a good view of the stars – you should have no trouble working out which way is north. The only question is, should you head off in the dark, or wait until morning and find a hill so you can get a good look around you?

MAP READING

Exploring isn't just about having adventures, fighting off sharks, and abseiling into volcanoes (although these are the best bits). Explorers like to visit places where few, if any, people have ever been, but to get there they need to be able to navigate (find their way) using a map, compass, and – sometimes – the Sun, Moon, and stars.

The joy of maps

In the old days the explorer started off with a big blank sheet of paper decorated with some drawings of sea monsters, and it was his or her job to fill it in and make a map. Today there aren't many blank spots left on the map, and as a result, your map is probably your most valuable piece of equipment (after your comfortable walking boots). Before you head off into the wilderness, make sure you know how to use your map. You need to know how to read and fold your map, and how to use it with a compass.

A person who makes maps is called a cartographer.

BEAR SAYS

Never depend on your GPS alone. Make sure your map-reading skills are first class. That way, when your GPS is on the blink, you won't find yourself heading the wrong way off a cliff.

DIY MAP

A map doesn't have to be covered in contours and symbols, but it should show where things are compared to each other. Explorers should be good at making maps, so practise by drawing a map of your house and garden, or maybe your street and neighbourhood. Start off by drawing a grid, and try to keep the same scale throughout the map.

Folding a map

This sounds like a simple task but actually it's all too easy to get wrong. Maps are usually big, with lots of folds, so if you do muck it up you will end up with a big bundle of paper that won't fit in your map case, and the map will tear at the folds and fall apart.

1 Open up your map until it is fully spread open.

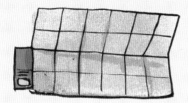

2 Check the creases and folds. If they are fresh, they will indicate where to fold.

3 Fold the map in half, so that the cover is still sticking out of the side.

4 Squeeze the map together like an accordion, but make sure the cover stays on top.

5 Fold over the cover so that it is on the outside.

Walk the line

If you look at your map you will notice two sorts of lines (not counting roads, rivers, railways, etc). The straight lines that form a grid on your map are lines of longitude and latitude. These are imaginary lines that map-makers and explorers use as reference points when describing where they are. Lines of longitude run from Pole to Pole. They show where you are from east to west. Lines of latitude circle round Earth parallel to the equator. They show where you are from north to south.

The other sort of lines on your map are contour lines. A contour line joins up places that are the same height, and they are used to represent hills, mountains, cliffs, and valleys on a flat piece of paper. Contour lines close together mean a steep hill while ones that are spread apart indicate a gentle slope. This is important when planning your route.

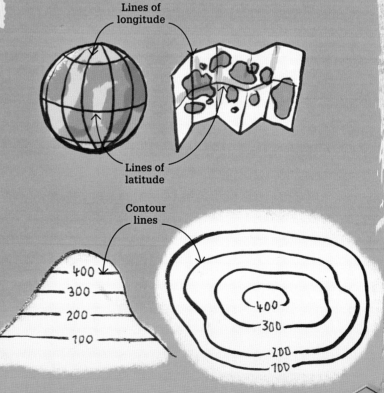

Lines of longitude

Lines of latitude

Contour lines

400
300
200
100

400
300
200
100

TRUE NORTH

North doesn't just mean "up" on your map. If you understand what north and south mean, and how to find them, you will never get truly lost.

Earth is a giant magnet

Earth is a sphere or globe, and when we say "north" what we really mean is the top of this globe. Earth spins around, and if you imagine it is spinning round a very big stick running through the planet from top to bottom, the North Pole is where the stick comes out of the top of the planet, and the South Pole is where it comes out of the bottom. These places are known as "true north" and "true south". Earth doesn't really have a big stick, but it does have liquid iron in the middle (like a soft-boiled egg with a runny yolk). This iron core makes Earth into a giant magnet.

A compass works because the ends of a metal needle are attracted to the north and south magnetic poles of Earth, so that the compass needle will point to magnetic north.

But Earth's magnetic poles don't line up exactly with "true" north and south. In most of the world you have to make adjustments because of this. If you're exploring near the Poles your compass may not be much use, and you'll have to use a different way of working out north and south.

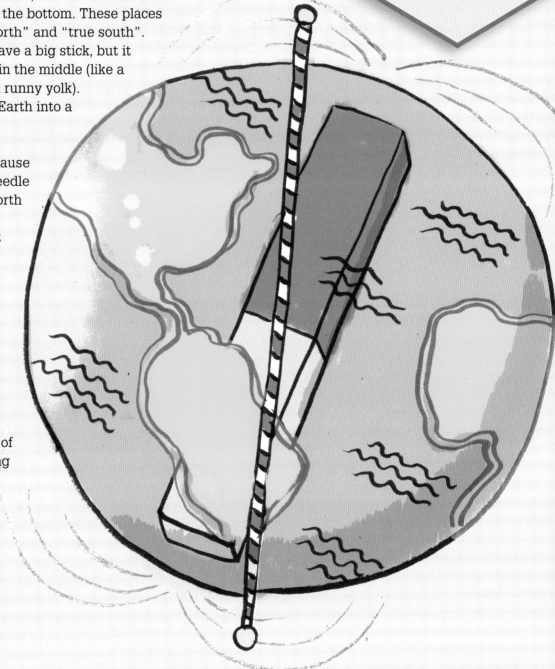

Finding north

There are lots of ways you can find north without a compass – probably the simplest use the movement of the Sun and Moon across the sky. Try out these methods in your back garden.

1 Using a watch If you have a wristwatch with hands, put the watch in the palm of your hand and point the hour (little) hand at the Sun. A line pointing halfway between the 12 o'clock marker and the hour hand points south. Before noon, you'll have to measure clockwise from your hour hand to the 12 o'clock marker. In the afternoon, measure anticlockwise. If you are in the southern hemisphere, point the 12 o'clock marker at the Sun and the line between it and the hour hand will be pointing north. If you have a digital watch, draw a clock face on the ground.

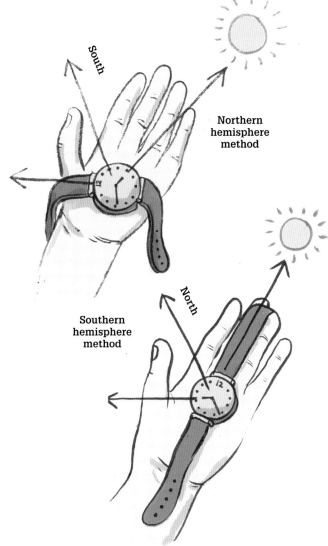

South

Northern hemisphere method

North

Southern hemisphere method

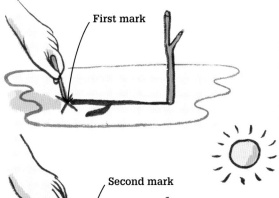

First mark

Second mark

2 Sun stick Put a straight stick upright in the ground in a flat place. Mark the tip of its shadow with a rock. Wait 15 minutes and then mark the shadow's tip again. Stand with your left foot at the first marker and your right foot at the second marker. In the northern hemisphere, you are now facing north. You can do the same thing at night if the Moon is bright enough.

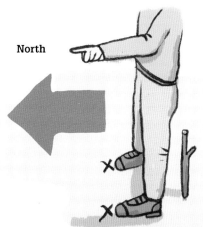

North

COMPASS CLASS

A compass has a needle that points towards the magnetic north pole. Compasses come in many different shapes and sizes, from tiny button ones (keep one of these in your emergency pack) to complicated electronic ones. The most common one for explorers is an orienteering compass.

Natural north

Because the Sun shines from the south, if you are in the northern hemisphere, you can tell which way is north by looking carefully at the trees. In the southern hemisphere, reverse all these signs, because the Sun shines from the north.

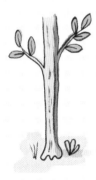   

- Young trees will be lighter on the south side and darker on the north side.

- Branches grow out sideways to the south, but to the north, they stick up.

- A tree on its own will usually have more moss on the north (shady side).

- Trees growing on a south-facing slope will be thicker and taller.

COMPASS TYPES

 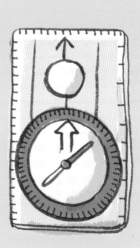 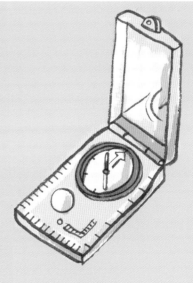

Ancient Chinese   Orienteering   Mirrored sighting

Orienteering with a compass

An orienteering compass is made to use with a map. It is fixed into a see-through plastic card with lines on it, and has a dial you can turn, with an arrow. You can use these to make sure your map is the right way round, to decide which direction to go in and to make sure you keep going in the right direction.

To orient your map (i.e. make sure it is lined up with north), follow these steps:

BEAR SAYS

Using your compass and the grid lines on a map, practise giving an exact grid reference for where you are. This is essential for naming a meeting point – or if you need rescue. Horizontals first then verticals!

1 Line up the sides of the compass with the north–south lines on your map.

2 Turn the big arrow until is pointing to map north.

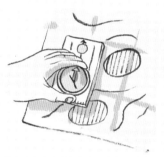

3 Hold the map and compass together as you turn round, until the red end of the compass needle lines up with the big arrow.

4 Your map is now oriented, and if you draw a line from your position on the map to a landmark (e.g. the top of a hill), you should find that this line points to the landmark in real life.

Lensatic   Button   Direct sighting

NAVIGATING BY THE STARS

BEAR SAYS

If darkness falls as you are trudging the last kilometres to camp, knowing how to navigate by the stars could save your life! Don't get spooked by the dark – hold your nerve.

Try not to get lost in the Antarctic mountains in winter: not only will it be cold enough to kill you in seconds with raging winds that knock you off your feet, but it will be hard to navigate back to base. The Sun never rises and your compass will go haywire because you are too near the southern magnetic pole. Your only hope is to use the stars – the same navigational tools that people have been using since earliest prehistoric times.

Sextant

You can use a sextant to measure the angle between a star (including our nearest star – the Sun) and the horizon. With this information you can calculate your latitude – your position north or south of the Equator. Navy navigators are still taught how to use the sextant in case their electronic systems get blown up in battle.

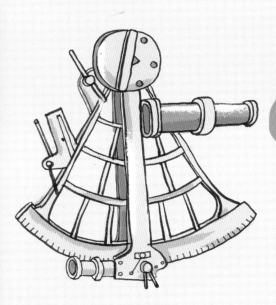

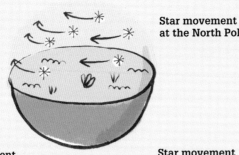

Star movement
at the North Pole

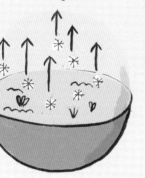

Star movement
at the Equator

Star movement
in between

The sky at night

Look up on a cloudless night and you will see thousands of stars scattered across the sky. With just your eyes you can see around 2,000 stars at a time (if you have binoculars you can see around 50,000). These stars seem to move very slowly across the night sky, but in fact they are not moving – you are, or at least Earth is moving and taking you with it. As Earth rotates towards the east, the stars above seem to move from east to west, like the Sun and Moon. You can use this simple fact to work out north, south, east, and west.

Star tracking

Stars move very slowly so working out which way a star is moving just by looking at it is impossible. You need to watch the star against something close to hand. You can use two sticks stuck in the ground close together and upright, and track how a star moves between them. If you are in the northern hemisphere and the star moves left, it is to the north, if it moves right it is to the south, if it moves up the star is in the east, down and it is in the west.

Star shadow

Another method is to hang a string from a stick set in the ground at an angle. Lie on your back with the string by your eye and line it up with a star. Mark the point where the string touches the ground. Follow the star for ten minutes and then do it again. This is the same as the Sun stick method, with the string in place of the shadow the first mark is in the west and the second is in the east.

FINDING NORTH AND SOUTH BY THE STARS

The North or Pole Star, Polaris, is above the North Pole, so all the other stars seem to rotate around it. If you can find it you know which way is north. There is no bright star above the South Pole, but you can find south with the help of the constellation called the Southern Cross.

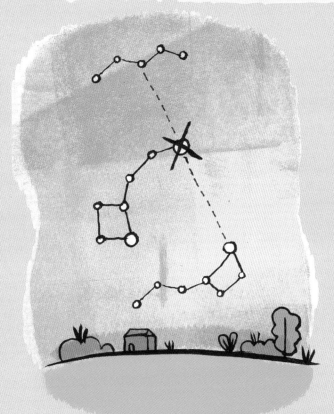

Find the Southern celestial pole

- Find the Milky Way (a milky band across the sky).

- Follow it until you find a dark patch called the Coal Sack.

- Look for a cross of four stars, two of which are very bright. This is the Southern Cross.

- Near the Southern Cross are two bright stars – the pointer stars (Rigil Kent and Hadar). Draw an imaginary line between these stars. The point where this line intersects with a line extended from the long axis of the Southern Cross is the celestial south pole.

Find the North Star

- Find the Plough (also known as the Big Dipper or Ursa Major). The two stars in the outer edge of the "saucepan" point at the North Star, which is one of the brightest stars in the sky.

- Find Cassiopeia, a constellation that looks like a big "M" or "W". A line pointing straight through the inner angle of the "W" points to the North Star.

- The North Star is the last star in the "handle" of the "Little Dipper", also known as Ursa Minor.

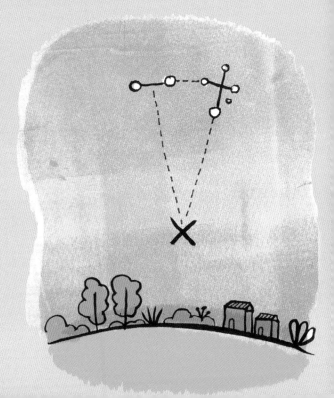

By the horns of the Moon!

The Moon goes round Earth once every 28 days. We can only see it when the Sun shines on the side that is facing us. When the Sun shines on the whole of the facing side, we see a full Moon, and when it shines entirely on the opposite side, we can't see the Moon at all (this is called a "new Moon"). In between, the Sun only lights up part of the Moon, so that we see a "crescent Moon".

You can use the crescent Moon as a quick way to find north or south, depending on your hemisphere. The tips of the crescent are known as the "horns". Imagine a straight line between the horns, extending down to the horizon. In the northern hemisphere this line points roughly south, and in the southern hemisphere it points roughly north.

Sastrugi signs

If you are exploring in Antarctica, you don't want to get off course because the landscape is featureless, so there are few landmarks to help you get back on track. A good tip is to use the sastrugi – wavy ridges in the snow, like sand dunes, formed by the wind, which run for great distances in parallel lines. Are you heading straight across them, along them, or at an angle to them? Memorize this information and use it to set your course.

BEAR SAYS

If you get lost, then head down hill until you find a stream. Follow the stream until it becomes a river and then follow this until you find people.

INDEX

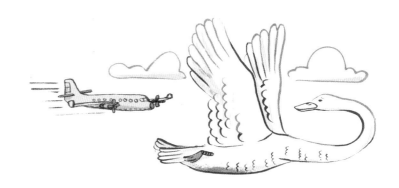

BEAR GRYLLS
SURVIVAL CAMP

THE ULTIMATE ALL-TERRAIN TRAINING MANUAL

1st Edition
Published September 2016

Conceived by Weldon Owen
in partnership with Bear Grylls Ventures

Produced by Weldon Owen Ltd
Suite 3.08 The Plaza, 535 King's Road,
London SW10 0SZ, UK

Copyright © 2016 Weldon Owen Publishing

WELDON OWEN LTD
Publisher Donna Gregory
Designer Shahid Mahmood
Editors Jo Casey, Hazel Eriksson, Fay Evans
Editorial Assistant Sarah Ross-Smith

Printed in Latvia
10 9 8 7 6 5 4 3 2 1

A WELDON OWEN PRODUCTION.
PART OF THE BONNIER PUBLISHING GROUP.

PICTURE CREDITS
While every effort has been made to credit all contributors, Weldon Owen would like to apologize should there have been any omissions or errors, and would be pleased to make any appropriate corrections for future editions of this book.

All images below from Shutterstock.com
©ActiveLines; ©2630ben; ©3drenderings; ©Albo; ©Aleksandrs Bondars; ©Aleksey Vanin; ©Alex Staroseltsev; ©Alexander Raths; ©Alexyz3d; ©Ana Vasileva; ©Andrei Nekrassov; ©Andrey_Kuzmin; ©Anna Kulikova; ©Anton Balazh; ©Art House; ©Ase; ©Ati design; ©Benoit Daoust; ©Betabaqe; ©Brandon Bourdages; ©Byelikova Oksana; ©Cameramannz; ©Catmando; ©cellistka; ©Chekky; ©Christian Weber; ©Colin Edwards Wildside; ©corbac40; ©Cortyn; ©Cosmin Manci; ©Crystal Eye Studio; ©CS Stock; ©Dario Lo Presti; ©defpicture; ©Dejan Stanisavljevic; ©derter; ©Digital Storm; ©DigitalHand Studio; ©Dirk Ercken; ©Dr. Morley Read; ©DVARG; ©Eduard Radu; ©Elenamiv; ©Elenarts; ©Elesey; ©Eric Isselee; ©Evlakhov Valeriy; ©eye-blink; ©fivespots; ©goldnetz; ©Guan jiangchi; ©Hellen Grig; ©Iconic Bestiary; ©iFerol; ©Igor Kovalchuk; ©IhorZigor; ©Imaake; ©imnoom; ©Incredible Arctic; ©James BO Insogna; ©Jan Cejka; ©Jan Martin Will; ©Jaromir Chalabala; ©Jin Yong; ©Jorg Hackemann; Jos Beltman; Joseph Sohm; ©Jurik ©Peter; ©Kevin Key; ©KittyVector; ©Kletr; ©Krisztian; ©Lena Lir; ©Lena Serditova; ©leungchopan; ©luckypic; ©Magnia; ©mapichai; ©Mario Hagen; ©Martin Maun; ©Miceking; ©Migel; ©mistral9; ©Murat Cokeker; ©Nagib; ©NatalieJean; ©NEILRAS; ©nikolae; ©notkoo; ©Olga Reznik; ©Osokin Aleksandr; ©ostill; ©Pakhnyushchy; ©Pan Xunbin; ©pandapaw; ©Pavel Burchenko; ©PavloArt Studio; ©Phant; ©Piotr Snigorski; ©R Gombarik; ©R. Formidable; ©RCPPHOTO; ©RedKoala; ©Reinke Fox; ©Rich Carey; ©Ridkous Mykhailo; ©S-F; ©Sanit Fuangnakhon; ©Scott Rothstein; ©Sergey Kohl; ©Sergey Uryadnikov; ©skelos; ©Skunkeye; ©Somprasong Khrueaphan; ©srbh karthik; ©Stanislav Fosenbauer; ©Stefano Garau; ©Super Prin; ©Sviluppo; ©tanatat; ©tashechka; ©Tawee wongdee; ©Theeradech Sanin; ©tovovan; ©Triduza Studio; ©Ursa Major; ©Valentyna Chukhlyebova; ©Vector Goddess; ©Vertyr; ©violetkaipa; ©Vladimir Melnik; ©Weenee; ©weltreisendertj; ©yunus85; ©Zaichenko Olga

ILLUSTRATIONS
All illustrations by James Gulliver Hancock/The Jacky Winter Group. All illustrations copyright Weldon Owen Publishing

Discover more amazing books in the Bear Grylls series:

Fantastic colouring and activity books packed with fun activities and cool facts. Learn survival tips and tricks for almost any extreme situation in *Survival Camp*, and explore the most extreme stuff on Earth in *Extreme Planet*.